CANADA

1939-1957

DONALD CREIGHTON

The Forked Road

CANADA 1939-1957

The Canadian Centenary Series

McClelland and Stewart

McClelland and Stewart Limited
The Canadian Publishers
481 University Avenue
Toronto, Ontario
M5G 2E9

Canadian Cataloguing in Publication Data
Creighton, Donald, 1902-1979.
The forked road: Canada 1939-1957

(The Canadian centenary series; 18)
Includes bibliographical references and index.
ISBN 0-7710-2360-X (bound). - ISBN 0-7710-2361-8 (pbk.)
1. Canada—History—1939-1945.   2. Canada—History—1945-
I. Title.   II. Title: Canada 1939-1957.   III. Series.
FC609.C73 1976   971.06'3   C77-006026-9
F1034.C73 1976

Printed and bound in Canada

THE
CANADIAN
CENTENARY
SERIES

A History of Canada

W.L. Morton, EXECUTIVE EDITOR

D.G. Creighton, ADVISORY EDITOR

Ramsay Cook, EXECUTIVE EDITOR, 1983

*1. *Tryggvi J. Oleson* Early Voyages and Northern Approaches, 1000-1632

*2. *Marcel Trudel* The Beginnings of New France, 1524-1663

*†3. *W.J. Eccles* Canada Under Louis XIV, 1669-1701

*4. *Dale Miquelon* Canada from 1701 to 1744

*5. *G.F.G. Stanley* New France, 1744-1760

*†6. *Hilda Neatby* Quebec, 1760-1791

*†7. *Gerald M. Craig* Upper Canada, 1784-1841

*†8. *Fernand Ouellet* Lower Canada, 1792-1840

*†9. *W.S. MacNutt* The Atlantic Provinces, 1712-1857

*†10. *J.M.S. Careless* The Union of the Canadas, 1841-1857

*†11. *E.E. Rich* The Fur Trade and the Northwest to 1857

*†12. *W.L. Morton* The Critical Years, 1857-1873

*†13. *P.B. Waite* Canada, 1874-1896

*†14. *R. Craig Brown and G.R. Cook* Canada, 1896-1921

*†15. *John Herd Thompson with Allen Seager* Canada, 1922-1939

*†16. *Morris Zaslow* The Opening of the Canadian North, 1870-1914

17. *Morris Zaslow* The North, 1914-1967

*†18. *D.G. Creighton* Canada, 1939-1957

*†19. *J.L. Granatstein* Canada, 1957-1967

VOLUMES STARRED ARE PUBLISHED

†ALSO AVAILABLE IN PAPERBACK

Volumes I, III, VII, and XII of The Canadian Centenary Series were published with the help of grants from the Humanities Research Council of Canada.

CONTENTS

The Forked Road

The Canadian Centenary Series

Half a century has elapsed since *Canada and Its Provinces,* the first large-scale co-operative history of Canada, was published. During that time, new historical materials have been made available in archives and libraries; new research has been carried out, and its results published; new interpretations have been advanced and tested. In these same years Canada itself has greatly grown and changed. These facts, together with the centenary of Confederation, justify the publication of a new co-operative history of Canada.

The form chosen for this enterprise was that of a series of volumes. The series was planned by the editors, but each volume will be designed and executed by a single author. The general theme of work is the development of those regional communities which have for the past century made up the Canadian nation; and the series will be composed of a number of volumes sufficiently large to permit adequate treatment of all the phases of the theme in the light of modern knowledge.

The Centenary History, then, was planned as a series to have a certain common character and to follow a common method but to be written by individual authors, specialists in their fields. As a whole, it will be a work of specialized knowledge, the great advantage of scholarly co-operation, and at the same time each volume will have the unity and distinctive character of individual authorship. It was agreed that a general narrative treatment was necessary and that each author should deal in a balanced way with economic, political, and social history. The result, it is hoped, will be an interpretative, varied, and comprehensive account, at once useful to the student and interesting to the general reader.

The difficulties of organizing and executing such a series are apparent: the overlapping of separate narratives, the risk of omissions, the imposition of divisions which are relevant to some themes but not to others. Not so apparent, but quite as troublesome, are the problems of scale, perspective, and scope, problems which perplex the writer of a one-volume history and are magnified in a series. It is by deliberate choice that certain parts of the history are told twice, in different volumes from different points of view, in the belief that the benefits gained outweigh the unavoidable disadvantages.

The following volume, by the Advisory Editor, has had the onerous task of giving historic form to the yet new events of 1939-1957. It attempts to carry into the years through which many of its readers will have lived the same scholarship and detachment exemplified by its predecessors in the Series. The author and the Executive Editor hope that it will be received for what it is meant to be, an effort on a major scale to discern historical orientations and to evaluate historical perspectives.

W.L. MORTON,
Executive Editor

D.G. CREIGHTON,
Advisory Editor

The Forked Road

The time limits of the period covered in this book require a few words of explanation. It was originally intended that the final volume in the Canadian Centenary Series would begin with the opening of the Second World War and end with the centenary of Confederation in 1967. Apparently nobody noticed the fact that this span of time—nearly twenty-eight years—was unusually long. It was, to be sure, shorter than that alloted to each of the two volumes on the Canadian North, but it was longer than the period given to any of the four authors writing on the general development of Canada from 1857 to 1939. This greater length may not have seemed to present much difficulty when the Series was first planned, and when the Centenary itself was a decade away in the future; but, in fact, the twenty-eight years from 1939 to 1967 turned out to be a particularly crowded and complex period in Canadian history. It was a formidable assignment for an historian, and not simply because of its length. An equally serious difficulty was that it lacked the essentials of unity. September, 1939, was certainly a valid punctuation point in time; but July, 1967, brought none of the themes of the turbulent 1960's to a conclusion. Yet to add more years to an already overly long span would simply make the subject still more unmanageable.

I was thus driven reluctantly to the conclusion that the period as a whole would have to be divided and that the general election of 1957 was the obvious point of division. I hope to write another book on the period from 1957 to the present; but, in the meantime, this volume justifiably stands alone, for it has its own distinctive themes, and a character and significance of its own. I have called it "The Forked Road", by which I mean the forked road to the future, the future as it was to Canadians in the 1940's and early 1950's, and the present as it is to Canadians of today. It seems to me that in the eighteen years from 1939 to 1957, Canada made a number of crucial decisions about its direction. It chose one fork of the road to the future; and the Canada we inhabit today is, for both good and ill, very largely the result of that decisive choice.

PREFACE

It remains for me to thank Dr. W.L. Morton, the Executive Editor of the Canadian Centenary Series, and its publisher, Mr. J.G. McClelland for the encouragement and assistance they have given me. I am grateful also to my editor, Mr. John A. Roberts, who has been helpful and considerate throughout the exacting process of publication. I owe much to Massey College, where I have been a Fellow for a number of years now; and a considerable part of the research for this book was carried out in the quiet retreat of its library. I should like to thank the Master of the College, Dr. Robertson Davies, and the College librarians, for many kindnesses.

Finally, I should like to acknowledge my obligation to the Humanities Research Council of Canada which has defrayed part of the expense of typing the manuscript of this book.

Donald Creighton

CHAPTER 1

Ambiguous Prelude

On the morning of September 10, 1939, Vincent Massey, Canada's High Commissioner to the United Kingdom, drove to the Royal Lodge, King George VI's country house in Windsor Great Park. It was Sunday, a beautiful day in early September; but the Sabbath calm which normally brooded over England on Sundays was strangely disturbed for the second time that fateful September. Only a week before, at 11 o'clock in the morning, England had declared war on the German Reich; and at once a vast range of organized and purposeful activities began to change the familiar tenor of English life. Huge barrage balloons floated in the blue sky; at night, motorists turned off their headlights and the blackout darkened streets and roads. Soldiers in khaki uniforms took over guard duty; civilians went about carrying little boxes containing gas masks; and packed trains carried hundreds of thousands of primary school children away from the supposed danger zones to the security of the countryside. In London, the nervous tension was acute. Once, the sirens shrieked a warning by mistake, and people watched and listened apprehensively for air raids. Twenty miles west of London, in the Windsor region, the pace of events was not so agitated; but there was no peace that morning in the country house in which the Canadian High Commissioner, his wife, and their son Hart were living.

L.B. ("Mike") Pearson had telephoned from Canada House, London, to say that an important communication had arrived from Ottawa which must be presented to the King for his approval as soon as possible; and Canada House had ascertained that His Majesty and Queen Elizabeth were even then on their way from Buckingham Palace to the Royal Lodge at Windsor. Windsor was only a few miles away from the Massey residence. The matter was urgent, and there was no reason for delay and no occasion for ceremony. The High Commissioner got into his son's small sports car, and Hart found his way through the bewildering expanse of Windsor Great Park to the small but charming Lodge which owed its origin to the building mania of George IV. The royal couple had only recently arrived, the furniture in the dining

1

room was still sheeted in dust covers; but the King appeared in a few minutes and Massey, having apologized for his unseemly Sunday morning intrusion, handed him the slip of paper on which the telephone message from Canada House had been copied out in longhand. "It is expedient," the portentous document read, "that a proclamation should be issued in the name of His Majesty, in Canada, declaring that a state of war with the German Reich has existed in Canada as of and from September tenth."

The King wrote "Approved" and below his signature, "George R.I." It was a few minutes past one o'clock.[1]

I

Canada had declared war on what, at that time, was undoubtedly the greatest military power in world history; but there was a huge disparity between the heroic terms of the Canadian declaration and the half-hearted "state of war" actually existing in Canada. In Parliament, Mackenzie King, the Prime Minister, had certainly talked as if his government was planning a war effort without stint or limitation. He had never doubted, he told the members, that "the free spirit of the Canadian people would assert itself in the preservation and defence of freedom," and he urged his listeners to reflect on the origin of their liberties before they uttered "a word against full participation by this country in the great conflict which is now raging in Europe."[2] King had always had a great talent for verbal flatulence; and now, sixty-four years of age, with nearly fifteen years' experience as Prime Minister, he was a master of rotund but empty generalities. Actually he had not the slightest intention of asking Canada to make a real contribution to "the great conflict now raging in Europe." He did not in the least mean the all-out effort needed to defeat Germany. What he intended was a modest effort which would keep Canada politically quiet and the Liberal Party in power.

It followed naturally, as the first and most important requirement, that the war should be waged with the greatest possible economy of men and money. A limited-liability war, it was defined, as was indeed appropriate, chiefly by negatives. Home defence and internal security enjoyed unquestioned priority. The protection of its own coasts, of the Gulf of St. Lawrence, Labrador and Newfoundland, was declared to be Canada's first obligation; but what military tasks, if any, it might undertake beyond North America were not even vaguely suggested.[3] The navy was to be increased, the Royal Canadian Air Force rapidly expanded; but the role the Canadian Army might play was left in total obscurity. In the First World War, the army had been Canada's greatest wartime achievement; but its reinforcement had also brought on the conscription controversy of 1917, the greatest of Canada's wartime crises; and it was the political troubles of the First World War, and not the military necessities of the Second, which were uppermost in King's mind. An army in Europe would inevitably suffer casualties, and casualties would mean the need of reinforcements and the problem of reinforcements might end in the demand for conscription, the opposition of Quebec, and conflict in Canada. Conscription was, of course, a political decision, which could be prudently rejected in advance; and on September 8, King formally repeated the promise, made earlier in March, that his government would not introduce conscription for overseas service.

This portentous announcement was full of danger for the future; but at the moment, before war had yet been declared, it seemed to King an easy and politically very useful commitment to make. The problem of a voluntary expeditionary force was much more difficult and uncertain. Before the international crisis broke, King had indulged the hope that the dispatch of a Canadian force to Europe was "now wholly out of the question."[4] As late as September 5, the Cabinet Defence Committee, over which the Prime Minister presided, had summarily rejected, as premature, a proposal by the Chiefs of Staff for an overseas army corps of two divisions.[5] In his speech to Parliament on the 8th, King had reminded the members that the aims and methods of 1914 might not be applicable in 1939, and he had insisted that the government would have to make the fullest examination of all available information before it could come to any decision regarding Canadian "action in other theatres of war."

At this point, the attitude of the Cabinet began to alter. Up until September it had had no communication whatever with the British government about the part Canada might play in the impending war. Canadian troops abroad would almost certainly fight in close co-operation with British formations and there was a high degree of uniformity in the organization, training and equipment of the two armed services; but joint planning for the common defence of the two countries had ceased to exist. In King's suspiciously evasive mind, a co-operative Commonwealth policy in foreign affairs and defence might involve Canada in undesirable external commitments which could prove fatal to Canadian unity. He had systematically destroyed the earlier institutions of Commonwealth solidarity, the Imperial War Cabinet of the First World War, and its successor, the Prime Minister's Conference. Canada had remained severely and ostentatiously aloof from all discussions of foreign policy as late as the Commonwealth Conference of 1937; and the Canadian High Commissioner in London was never authorized to attend meetings of the Committee of Imperial Defence.[6]

Thus on the very eve of war, neither the habit nor the machinery of joint planning between the two countries existed; and it was left to the Prime Minister to inquire, in a direct, rather simple-minded fashion, what kind of military co-operation would be acceptable to Great Britain. The reply, which reached Ottawa on September 6, seemed pleasantly reassuring to King; all, apparently, that the British wanted was "a small Canadian unit which would take its place alongside the United Kingdom troops."[7] This modest request, King confided complacently to his diary, would avert "the necessity of our thinking of an expeditionary force."[8] He felt highly gratified that day; but next morning, when the Cabinet met before the opening of Parliament, he was surprised and disconcerted to note how many of his colleagues seemed to favour a considerable overseas force.[9] He was still more discomfited to discover how accurately his ministers had anticipated public opinion. During the following week, the growing popular clamour for the dispatch of troops proved politically irresistible; and on September 16, though still restating its early position that "no large expeditionary force" was intended, the Cabinet decided that one division would be sent overseas.

Ten days after this decision was taken, King was suddenly assailed by regret that he had made it. An alternative Canadian contribution to the war effort, which promised fewer casualties and much less political danger, became unexpectedly available. On September 26, the British Prime Minister, Neville Chamberlain, informed King that the British government was now planning a vastly enlarged air force, which would require the addition of approximately 50,000 air crew annually, a total beyond the capacity of the British training facilities and manpower to produce. In this desperate necessity, Chamberlain proposed the establishment of about fifty overseas training schools in the senior British Dominions of Canada, Australia and New Zealand, with advanced training concentrated in Canada. Obviously, this scheme held an immediate and powerful appeal for King. It was, above all, a training scheme, which was certain to keep a large number of Canadian airmen peacefully instructing in Canada instead of carrying out dangerous operations in Europe. Two days later, the Cabinet heartily approved the plan, with only one qualification. "There was general regret," King recorded, "that it had not been made at the outset so that our war effort could have been framed on these lines instead of having to head so strongly into expeditionary forces at the start."[10]

In October, a British delegation, headed by Lord Riverdale, together with delegations from Australia and New Zealand, arrived in Ottawa to settle the details of the plan. Riverdale was a Sheffield businessman, with a good deal of experience in public affairs, an offhand yet commanding manner, and a Colonel Blimp moustache which enhanced the extremely British aspect of his countenance. King took an instant dislike to Riverdale, to his large, easy assumptions, and his apparently total disregard of costs; and the first of the formal discussions between the British delegation and the Canadian Cabinet nearly ended in total disaster. Riverdale, in his outline of the project, incautiously referred to the British contribution, which was to consist chiefly of the necessary aircraft, as "a free gift to you" – a casual remark which intensely irritated King who naturally assumed that the whole plan was really a huge

Canadian gift to the United Kingdom. His reply to Riverdale was long, argumentative, and rambling; but one of his phrases – "This is not our war" – stuck like a burr to his British auditors. King subsequently and rather laboriously tried to explain that he had used these words simply to remind the British that their contribution was a gift, not to Canada alone, but to the whole Commonwealth at war. On their part, the startled British interpreted the words literally, to mean that this was a war for which Canada disclaimed all major responsibility and obligation. And the suspicion remains that, at the moment at least, this was exactly the meaning King intended. The news that his fatal sentence had been reported to London infuriated him. He saw himself once again as the victim of others' misrepresentation; and, in his vindictive fashion, he sought to retaliate. He went so far as to request the Governor-General, Lord Tweedsmuir, to rebuke the British High Commissioner, Sir Gerald Campbell, for permitting such an invidious report to be sent through his office.[11]

The negotiations had got off to a very bad start indeed. But they continued, though very laboriously, for neither side could abandon them. The British desperately needed the vastly enlarged air force which only the British Commonwealth Training Plan could give them; the Canadians saw in the British Commonwealth Air Training Plan the most satisfactory vehicle for their principal war effort. The Canadian government, in fact, actually insisted on stipulating that the British should formally acknowledge the priority of the air training scheme as the most effective form of assistance Canada could give. The Chamberlain government, oppressed by its promise to provide an army of thirty-two divisions for the war in Europe, shied away from the unqualified acknowledgement which the Canadians demanded. Chamberlain altered the Canadian draft announcement by adding a second significant sentence which asserted that his government "would welcome no less heartily the presence of Canadian land forces in the theatre of war." This statement, as King saw instantly, virtually denied the priority of the air training plan; and, with all his devious ingenuity, he laboured to change the emphasis of the Chamberlain sentence. He proposed the addition of a final phrase, "at the earliest possible moment." This, he reflected complacently, would imply that the early arrival of Canadian land forces was more important than their ultimate presence in strength![12]

This elaborate verbal fencing was one illustration of the Canadian government's attitude to the war; another, far more serious for the future, was its cost accounting methods in finance. The British had devised an air training plan which would fit their crucial necessities on the assumption that the money for it must and would be found. The Canadians just as naturally took it for granted that any air training scheme they could possibly accept must be reduced and modified so as to come within their already established budgetary limits. The outcome of this conflict of views was, of course, a compromise, a compromise which was to have much more serious effects for the Royal Canadian Air Force than it did for the plan itself. The number of advanced training schools in Canada was cut, and the Canadian government's financial obligations somewhat reduced; but these trifling economies were insignificant in comparison with the serious losses which the Royal Canadian Air Force was to suffer as a result of the plan and the huge benefits which it was to confer on the British R.A.F. The R.A.F. was, in fact, the plan's first and principal beneficiary; and its huge advantage was guaranteed from the start by the vital clause in the agreement which provided that all pupils under the plan, on the completion of their training, were to be "placed at the disposal of the government of the United Kingdom".[13]

This clause which, as King himself acidly observed, gave the whole plan the look of "a recruiting scheme for the R.A.F." was, of course, slightly modified. The next article in the agreement provided that the Canadian, as well as the Australian and New Zealand graduates of the plan, would be "identified with their respective Dominions," either by organizing Dominion air formations, or "in some other way," to be decided later.[14] The settlement of a definite method was left to the future for the simple and sufficient reason that the two parties had failed to come to an agreement in Ottawa. The crux of the difficulty lay in the fact that the training plan was designed to produce aircrew – pilots, gunners, observers – but not ground crew, and ground crew were obviously essential to the operation of independent Canadian squadrons. If, in 1939, the Canadian government had been willing to supply its own ground crew, and to pay the full cost of its integrated squadrons abroad, it could have used the air training plan, as the British did, to build up a great national air force in England and Europe. But the Canadian government was shackled by its obsession for economy; it was determined that the cost of the air training plan in Canada would be its principal expenditure for the air division of the Canadian armed forces; and, as a result, the British government assumed the whole burden of the pay and maintenance of the Canadian airmen once they had left Canada. This arrangement gave the British authorities all the power of the purse; it put the Canadian government into the position of a suppliant, who could ask for more Canadian squadrons only as a concession which, even if granted, would be carried out by others, not by its own officials. Later on, when Canada was spending money for the war as freely as any other nation, the King Cabinet tried to repair the damage of this act of tragically mistaken stinginess; but it never really recovered the ground that had been lost, and the Royal Canadian Air Force never overcame its initial handicap.

On December 17, after weeks of bickering, a good deal of it over petty details, the British Commonwealth Air Training Agreement was signed; but long before this, the main lines of the King government's war policy had become evident. It was a safe, cautious, niggardly, middle-of-the-road policy, which would likely satisfy the great central mass of the Canadian people, and was obviously open to attack by critical extremists on either side.

II

The first challenge came from the left, from those who argued that King's war policies had gone too far, and it was delivered by Maurice Duplessis, who, for the past three years, had been Premier of the Province of Quebec. Duplessis was a short, spare French Canadian, with black hair, a neat black moustache, and a wary, neutral expression. He had gained power by what was essentially a blatant electoral fraud; and he was to keep it, through most of the remainder of his life, by an elaborate system of organized electoral corruption. The leader of a small Conservative minority in the provincial legislature, with almost no hope of overthrowing the long-established Liberal government, he had joined forces with a dissident group inside the Liberal Party, which was highly impatient of the "Old Guard" and wished to end its rule. This unlikely coalition took the name of Union Nationale; and it fought and won the general election of 1936 on the basis of what was, for French Canada, a radical programme of social and economic reform.

This progressive platform was, of course, the work of the ex-Liberal members of the coalition; Duplessis's special contributions were his debating skill, his considerable parliamentary experience, and his masterful command of all the devices of machine party politics. An obscurantist Conservative himself, with a set of primitive economic assumptions, he had not the smallest intention of acting the part of a social reformer; and, once the general election of 1936 had been safely won, he lost no time in getting rid of most of his radical associates, ruthlessly monopolizing the control of the party, and discarding its radical programme.[15] By the time the war broke out in 1939, all that remained of Union Nationale's original character was its French-Canadian nationalism; and it was to this that Duplessis appealed in his attack on King's war policies. The war, Duplessis claimed, and its hideous offspring, the War Measures Act, had accelerated the campaign of "assimilation and centralization," which the federal government had already carried so far and which was certain to destroy Quebec's provincial autonomy, the only real rampart of French Canada's distinctive culture, if it were not immediately checked. On the basis of this appeal, the Quebec provincial legislature was dissolved and a general election set for October 25.[16]

The federal Liberals regarded this unexpected assault with the greatest gravity. "It is a diabolical act on his [Duplessis's] part," King reflected angrily, "to have made the issue Provincial Autonomy versus Dominion Government."[17] In effect Duplessis had ensured that a victory for Union Nationale would be a provincial vote of want-of-confidence in the war policies of the federal government; and this, only a fortnight after the declaration of war, was something the King government could never accept. The three Quebec members in King's Cabinet – C.G. ("Chubby") Power, P.J.A. Cardin, and Ernest Lapointe – decided to take up Duplessis's challenge and openly enter the provincial election.[18] Power was a party politician in the most literal sense of the word, Cardin a fine speaker and a good parliamentarian. The best known and most distinguished member of the trio was Ernest Lapointe, a tall, heavy, spectacled French Canadian, given to occasional outbursts of emotional eloquence, who for two decades had been King's most devoted and influential associate from French Canada. Power persuaded the other two to join with him in publicly announcing that, if Quebec did not reject Duplessis and thus declare its support for King's war policies, they would resign their portfolios and as a result, leave King's Cabinet a wholly English-speaking government – a government which might conceivably impose conscription.[19] This was playing politics for very high stakes indeed; but the very recklessness of the Quebec ministers was impressive, and the picture of the bulky Lapointe standing like a bastion against conscription was more effective than the image of Duplessis manning the ramparts of provincial rights. If Duplessis had had time to consolidate his power in Quebec, the result might have been different; but he had not yet grasped complete control of Union Nationale and his betrayal of its reforming programme had injured his popularity. On October 25, the Liberals, under Adelard Godbout, won seventy seats against Union Nationale's 15 and thus almost exactly reversed the results of the previous election.[20]

The resistance of the powerful community which might have condemned King's war policies as too extreme had thus been met and overcome; but its defeat was followed almost immediately by the growing opposition of a potentially still larger body of Canadians who were beginning to feel that King had not gone far enough. The base of the first protest movement had been the powerful Province of Quebec; the base of the second was the equally powerful Province of Ontario and its mouthpiece was Ontario's new Premier, the defiantly cocky Mitchell Hepburn, who, like Duplessis, was a characteristic product of the impatient and angry politics of the Depression. For nearly a decade Hepburn's plump, round countenance, his impish grin, his offhand, swaggering manner, and slangy and abusive eloquence had had a curious fascination for the people of Ontario. He had won power in 1934 as an advocate of radical reform; but his innate rural conservatism, though it was perhaps less reactionary than Duplessis's, emerged very quickly when a serious labour dispute erupted at the General Motors plant in Oshawa.

At the bottom of Hepburn's character there was a reserve of honesty, directness, and good intentions; he hated sham and pomposity and complacent inertia. But he was capricious, arrogant, and quarrelsome in temperament, and he took readily to both vindictive intrigue and vulgar demagoguery. In very many ways – though with certain significant exceptions – he was the direct opposite of Mackenzie King; and their mutual antagonism, which broke out in open warfare in the autumn of 1939, had its origin back four years earlier, in an unfortunate sequel to the federal election of 1935. Hepburn had campaigned actively for King in that contest. He expected political reward – the appointment of at least one of his Ontario friends to the new federal Cabinet – and reward was denied him. He felt slighted and humiliated. He never forgot or forgave King's polite but perfunctory rejection of his request. Subsequently, of course, he found concrete issues – the St. Lawrence waterway and the appointment of a Royal Commission to review the workings of the Canadian federal system – which gave an air of political significance to his quarrel with King; but at bottom it remained an emotional antagonism, an irrepressible clash of temperaments. "I am a Reformer. But I am not a Mackenzie King Liberal any longer," he declared in 1937, with an air of bravado. "I will tell the world that, and I hope he hears me."[21]

Strangely enough, it was the war that brought the dispute to its angry climax, though on the record there was not a great deal to suggest that it would. During his early years as party leader and Premier, Hepburn had shown extremely little interest in Great Britain, the Empire-Commonwealth, and world affairs in general. The Crown as a symbol of domestic law and order and Empire solidarity conspicuously failed to move him; and his contemptuous disregard for the formalities of constitutional monarchy was obvious from the beginning. During the election campaign of 1934, he referred to Chorley Park, the handsome but expensive residence which the Conservative government had built for the Lieutenant-Governor of Ontario, as "a haven for broken-down English aristocrats who should be paying for their rooms at the hotels."[22] He ended the state dinner, held annually at Chorley Park on the opening day of the legislative session, by the simple expedient of refusing to attend it. A few years later he stopped all activities, domestic and official, at Chorley Park by the equally decisive method of closing it down. In 1937 he disappointed the Lieutenant-Governor's earnest hopes by declining to attend the coronation of King George VI.

Yet, despite these ostentatious displays of rude democratic simplicity, a significant change in Hepburn's character had already begun. The General Motors strike in Oshawa aroused his fears of Communism and brought out his basically conservative convictions. The rapidly worsening political situation in Europe forced him to look beyond the extremely narrow limits of his early interests and gave him a strangely new and anxious concern for the future of England and the Empire-Commonwealth. The progress of this novel sympathy was so characteristically swift that by the early spring of 1938, at the time of the Czechoslovakian crisis, he was eager to join with George Drew, the Leader of the Opposition, in sponsoring a special resolution which, he hoped, would be "a demonstration of loyalty to the Empire and of our affection to the Crown."[23] A year later, when Hepburn welcomed King George VI, the visible symbol of monarchy and empire to Toronto, his political conversion reached its rapturous climax: "I am so enthusiastic I don't know what to say . . . ," he declared – and a more eloquent testimony to his transport could hardly have been imagined.[24]

The outbreak of the war in Europe gave Hepburn an exceptional opportunity for testifying publicly to his fervent new faith. He grasped it eagerly. He quickly became a prominent and vociferous patriot. A special session of the provincial legislature was called, and the official Ontario War Resources Committee established. Unfortunately there was not a great deal that a single province could do alone to speed the war effort; but these limitations did not greatly bother Hepburn. He could always urge the nation as a whole to greater endeavours – a course which was doubly advantageous since it might possibly electrify the federal government to faster action and at the same time was certain to annoy Mackenzie King. As far back as the spring of 1938, at the time of the Czechoslovakian affair, Hepburn had used the moderate tone of King's statement in Parliament to justify his own far more sweeping declaration of purpose; and once war had been declared, interference in the federal sphere became a congenial habit. He rapidly reached the conclusion that conscription for overseas service was vitally necessary and that it could be imposed only by a union government. He bombarded Ottawa with helpful wartime suggestions, and journeyed down to the capital, with his Ontario War Resources Committee, to urge stronger measures. All apparently in vain. "The situation at Ottawa," he told a correspondent, "would break your heart."[25] It certainly didn't stop his own tongue. He decided that the time had finally come for an open denunciation of the federal government's criminal apathy; and on December 18 he moved a resolution in the provincial legislature "regretting that the federal government at Ottawa has made so little effort to prosecute Canada's duty in the war in the vigorous manner the people of Canada desire to see."[26] The resolution passed by forty-four votes to ten. Ten members of Hepburn's Liberal majority bolted the party.

III

All that autumn, King had watched Hepburn's antics with mingled embarrassment and annoyance. He had kept his polite composure, as he had always managed to do in his relations with the excitable Premier of Ontario, and he now suddenly realized that his patience had been rewarded. Hepburn had overreached himself; he had forced the passage of an official Ontario censure on the national war effort. This open attack on the war policies of the King government was a direct invasion of federal affairs; and King saw at once that the truth of Hepburn's accusation was a national issue which justified federal action just as it had done in the case of Duplessis. Duplessis had appealed to the people of his own province for support and the federal ministers from Quebec had vigorously campaigned in the provincial election. Hepburn, confirmed in power two years earlier, was very unlikely to call an election in Ontario; but fortunately, with King's astonishing good luck, a far more comprehensive test of public opinion, a federal general election, was now available. The Eighteenth Parliament was well into its fourth year, and according to custom an election would be due sometime in the summer of 1940. In what he himself called "a moment of weakness" King had given an undertaking at the special session in September, that another regular session would be called before the nation went to the polls. A pre-election session, he knew, was certain to be "contentious"; with his war policies up for debate, it would be doubly so. He dreaded the prospect; but he now realized that Hepburn's extraordinary want-of-confidence motion might cut short his ordeal by justifying an early election. The Legislature of Ontario had impudently asserted that his government was not prosecuting the war in "the vigorous manner the people of Canada desire to see." Very well then, he would appeal to the whole people of Canada for their verdict!

At first King planned no more than a short session; but, on the morning of January 25, the day of the opening of Parliament, as he sat at his desk, putting the final smooth touches on the Speech from the Throne, he was suddenly visited by the most outrageous political inspiration of his entire career. He would dissolve Parliament immediately and go to the country at once![27] Hurriedly he consulted Ernest Lapointe. Lapointe doubtfully agreed to a dissolution and they both decided that for the moment the Cabinet was not to be consulted. King carefully stayed away from the Cabinet meeting that morning, and it was not until after midday that Lapointe was authorized to inform the ministers. Not a hint of what was coming was given to the other M.P.'s, and the copy of the Speech from the Throne, traditionally offered in advance to the Leader of the Opposition, was carefully withheld from Dr. R.J. Manion, the Conservative leader. The Governor-General, Lord Tweedsmuir, was "immensely pleased," King reported, that the secret had been kept so successfully; and he agreeably performed his own comic turn in King's parliamentary farce by invoking the guidance of Divine Providence in the "responsible duties" of the session! As Eugene Forsey said later: "Divine Providence never had an easier job. There were no 'responsible duties'."[28] The Governor-General ended his speech by informing the members that his ministers had decided that they must make immediately "a direct and unquestioned appeal to the people." King then explained briefly that he had hoped to hold a final session, but that Hepburn's charges had raised a public issue which must be settled quickly. He ended by moving the adjournment and sat down.

Manion was on his feet in a second. "Mr. Speaker – " he began excitedly. "The motion is not before the House. The motion is not debatable," King interjected smoothly. Then he hesitated, inhibited perhaps by the enormity of an immediate closure of debate. "If my honourable friend wishes to speak," he continued with patronizing condescension, "I should be quite pleased to have him do so."[29]

Poor Manion did his best. He had only recently been elected Leader of the Conservative Party; and to the baffled Tories, who were always vainly hoping to acquire a little popularity in Quebec, one of his chief qualifications seemed to lie in the fact that he had married a French-Canadian wife! He was a genial, outgoing, attractive man, with a talent for both Irish wit and vituperation, and an unschooled but vigorous platform manner. His prede- cessor Arthur Meighen, intellectually the Conservative Party's ablest leader, had thought Manion deficient in disciplined argument and logical thought; but, in the monstrous situation which confronted him on January 25, his angry Irish volubility was an asset. He briefly reminded the House that he had just as much right as the Prime Minister to speak to a motion that was not debatable, and he briefly complained that he had not received the customary advance copy of the Speech from the Throne. He then launched into an indignant denunciation of King. His main point, which cut to the quick of the political immorality of the Prime Minister's indefensible deed, was that King had violated his democratic responsibility to Parliament. "I say," he declared, "that it is the duty of the Prime Minister and his govern- ment to come before Parliament and give an account of their stewardship."[30] He reminded the members that for years King had been travelling about the country exalting the supremacy of Parliament; and Woodsworth, the C.C.F. leader, pointed out that no words had been more frequently on the Prime Minister's lips than the pious assurance, "Parliament will decide."[31] The contradiction between profession and practice was obvious and glaring, but it did not embarrass King in the slightest. He kept repeating that his only democratic duty was to go before the people of Canada. "Democracy does mean ... ," he insisted "that I am answerable to the people of this country ... by direct approach to the people themselves, face to face with the problem."[32] He did not feel in the least guilty of violating his democratic principle, because he held not one democratic principle, but two. He professed parliamentary democracy when it suited his political convenience, and plebiscitary democracy when it was politically advantageous to do so. The one constant element in his political philosophy was the unctuous complacency with which it was invariably expressed.

The general election, which was held on March 26, was an easy victory for the Liberals. King's war policies had already produced what, at the time, seemed satisfactory results. The Canadian navy had promptly taken up its chief wartime duty of convoying men and military equipment across the North Atlantic. The First Division had arrived in England at the end of December, and the dispatch of a second had been announced. The British Commonwealth Air Training Plan was now in operation, and despite its monopolizing demands for personnel, one complete R.C.A.F. squadron had flown to England to provide air support for the First Division. In the tranquil and undemanding climate of the "phoney" war, all this seemed to constitute a sensible, moderate programme; and Manion's election demand for that extreme wartime emergency, a union government, appeared hysterically inappropriate. King, in fact, occupied an almost impregnable position; but not for a minute did he neglect the slightest defensive details. He stayed in Ottawa, hoping to convey the impression that he was constantly occupied with the war effort, and he did his public speaking by radio, preferring expensive national broadcasts "especially in view of the other parties having no money."[33] Very few Canadians were surprised, and the great majority were satisfied when King won the general election with 178 Liberals, six Independent Liberals and Liberal-Progressives, to thirty-nine Conservatives.[34]

A fortnight later on April 8, the first great crisis of the war began with the bungled British attempt to close the Norwegian coast to German shipping and the successful German occupation of Denmark and Norway. After two months of incredible reverses and capitulations, the crisis reached its final disastrous conclusion in the downfall of France. Canadians played only a very small part in the military operations of these fatal weeks. They got no further than Dunfermline, Scotland, in the abortive attack on Norway; and although they joined the second British Expeditionary Force in its misconceived invasion of Brittany and Normandy, the final collapse of the French armies brought a quick end to this inglorious enterprise. The Canadian government was informed in advance of the second of these two operations, but not of the first; and it had no voice whatever in the huge strategical miscalculations which led directly to the catastrophe. Great Britain and France placed the general direction of their joint effort in the hands of a Supreme War Council, on which they were equally represented, with the French General Gamelin as supreme commander in the field. Subsequently, representatives of the defeated and exiled governments of Poland, Norway, the Netherlands, and Belgium were added to the Supreme Council; but Canada had no separate representation on this body and no independent access to it; and Canadian liaison with the Anglo-French alliance and the high command was entirely through the civil and military authorities of Great Britain.[35]

This subordination did not trouble Mackenzie King in the least. He had always believed that consultation and joint planning with the British would lead to dangerous commitments in the future; and even though the greatest of all possible commitments, war, had now been irrevocably made, he was still locked immovably in his pre-war mental fixations. The permanent officials of the Department of External Affairs, even including the head, O.D. Skelton, one of the principal authors of the doctrines of isolationism, were much more concerned at Canada's exclusion from all control of its own forces. In Ottawa, Skelton argued in vain that the vast expenditures on the air training plan would justify Canada in demanding "consultation on objectives and policy"; and over in London, in the Canadian High Commissioner's office, L.B. Pearson reflected angrily on the humiliating fact that, while exiled and powerless governments were given representation on the War Council, Canada, with its great potential, was denied admittance.[36]

Pearson conceded that the Canadian government, by its suspicious avoidance of all peacetime consultation on foreign policy and defence, was largely to blame for this infuriating state of affairs. But he seemed to feel nevertheless that Canada ought to be able to shift from a system suitable for peace to another, quite different system appropriate for war, and that the British and everybody else concerned ought to recognize the need for this change and act on it immediately. This was a naive assumption; it was impossible to escape from the burden of the past so quickly. The truth was that the Canadian Department of External Affairs was now face to face with the inevitable consequences of a policy which its Deputy Minister had largely helped to inspire, and which its career diplomatists, Robertson, Wrong and Pearson, had been faithfully carrying out ever since the Imperial Conference of 1926. The habit of consultation and the routine of confidential communication had been dropped and forgotten; the machinery of imperial co-operation had been left neglected and unused for all but constitutional issues and ceremonial occasions. Earlier, it might have been possible to revive these old customs and rebuild this shattered mechanism; but now it was too late. By the declaration of war, Canada had proved that she still felt herself a member of the British Commonwealth; but by her persistent refusal to accept the responsibilities of membership, she had forfeited all claim to a share in the direction of Commonwealth policies. King's obstinate adherence to his essentially isolationist and colonial attitudes was one, but only one, of the obstacles to the return of the old Commonwealth relationship. As time would very soon show, the increasing weakness of the Commonwealth in world politics made its revival for ever impossible. The return which Canada was most likely to experience was a return to an older and more primitive status – colonialism, with a new imperial suzerain, the United States.

CHAPTER 2

The Canadians Before The Battle

I

The sudden end of the "phoney" war in the spring of 1940 and the dramatic start of the real war marked a turning point in Canadian history. It saw the beginning of a new and astonishing period, a period all the more astonishing to Canadians because of their unpreparedness for it and their nearly total failure to anticipate its coming. It was not, of course, that they had missed the ups and downs of experience during the nearly seventy-five years since Confederation. They had endured long stretches of frustration and adversity and enjoyed much briefer periods of expansion and success; and the nearly sixty thousand casualties they had suffered in Europe in 1914-1918 had forced them to realize the tragic losses of war. They had come to know a good deal about themselves and their country – its qualities and defects, its strengths and weaknesses; but in only one previous period – the first quarter of the twentieth century – had they ever felt a strong surge of self-confidence and and a real awareness of self-realization and achievement. During those twenty-five creative and expansive years, Canada had settled a half-continent, fought a great war, changed an empire into a commonwealth, and helped, in a small way, to found the world's first international organization. It was a long and crowded record of accomplishment, and it got under way so swiftly and with such explosive force at the beginning of the century that the pace of progress seemed likely to continue undiminished until its end. When Stephen Leacock confidently predicted that Canada would have a population of a hundred million by the year 2000, he was being soberly realistic and not intentionally funny.

Forty years of the twentieth century had now elapsed, and obviously the extravagant prophecies of Canada's future were very far away from fulfilment. The nation's rapid forward movement in the first decades of the century had not simply slowed down; it had nearly been reversed. Evasion had replaced positive commitment, withdrawal had succeeded participation in world affairs, and depression had followed boom at home. Canada had turned inward upon itself, had retreated to the security of fortress North America.

The urge towards isolation in an increasingly dangerous world, the defensive instinct for non-involvement in other peoples' troubles, was certainly strongest in French Canada, which had long since learnt to preserve its cultural identity by collective detachment; but a good many English Canadians also believed firmly that safety was to be found by avoiding foreign entanglements, and this was the principle on which the Canadian government had increasingly acted for nearly two decades. Canada had dismantled the machinery of imperial co-operation and turned its back on the new Commonwealth it had helped to create. Canada had done its little bit in reducing the League of Nations to the ineffectual level of a debating society. Many Canadians silently approved. They thought the world well lost abroad, but there was no gain at home in which they could take equal comfort.

The retreat from the world outside had been followed by a sharp defeat on native ground. For ten years the Depression had plunged the country into distress and gloom; but it had also dealt a more particular injury to Canadian pride and confidence. It called into question the validity of the great expectations which successive generations of Canadians had nursed for the future of the West. The settlement of the West had been one of the great objects of Confederation, and its successful realization under Sir Wilfrid Laurier and Sir Robert Borden was one of the most spectacular achievements of that wonderful first quarter of the twentieth century. Canadians had always believed that the West would make the nation; the first quarter of the century seemed to prove the truth of their belief. For decades the steadily expanding wheat economy of the three western provinces was the main basis of the national prosperity. Wheat was a monarch whose reign seemed likely to last for ever; but, in fact, his rule was tottering even before the coming of the Depression, and the Depression completed his downfall. In a few years, the West seemed almost destroyed. Drought, sand storms, ruined harvests and tragically low prices had beggared its people and depopulated its settlements.

The repulse of western expansion was a major catastrophe in Canadian history; and, together with the retreat from world affairs, it exercised a serious negative effect on Canadian confidence and sense of purpose. Canada's onward march towards maturity and recognition had been arrested, very near the point of completion, by the anxious inhibitions of its government and people, and by the force of adverse circumstances. It was true, of course, that the long struggle for the reorganization of the Empire had ended at last in the creation of the British Commonwealth. But there was an acrid irony in the fact that the Statute of Westminster, which completed this constitutional process, had been passed late in 1931, near the nadir of the Depression, and an even more derisive inappropriateness in the grant of "Dominion Status," which signified national standing in a world community, to a nation which had deliberately and systematically cut itself off from world affairs. Isolation had robbed "Dominion Status" of most of its meaning and the collapse of the West had turned the claim of transcontinental Dominion into an empty boast. Canada was a colony which had hesitated on the edge of nationhood, a young country which had failed to complete the tasks and to accept the responsibilities of maturity, and had stopped growing just before it came of age.

II

The Canadians were certainly small in numbers. The census of 1941 recorded a population of 11,506,655, less than a quarter of the population of the United Kingdom and only about a twelfth of that of the United States.[1] It was a discouraging total for a people who had been promised that they were going to inherit the twentieth century, but even more discouraging than the total itself was the slow rate by which it had grown. The amazing expansion of the first quarter of the century had convinced Canadians that a high growth rate was to be a characteristic and permanent feature of their future. The population had very nearly doubled in the period 1901-1931; but a decade later, at the beginning of the Second World War, it was obvious that this rapid advance had slowed down to a crawl. During the 1930's, the population grew so slowly that only the decade of the depressed 1890's showed an equally low rate of increase. The birth rate declined steadily until in 1937 it reached a low point of 20.1; and immigration fell away to disappointing levels which had not been seen since the 1860's, three-quarters of a century earlier.[2] Canada was gaining people very slowly, and it was losing them, almost as fast as it had ever done, to the United States. Mass emigration continued, although the Depression had ended the Republic's open-door immigration policy; and during the 1930's there was an estimated net loss by migration of 90,000 immigrants and native Canadians.[3] All this was vaguely depressing to Canadians, and Canadian demographers predicted pessimistically that this decline in population growth rate might persist for another twenty or thirty years.[4]

This continual renewal, displacement and alteration of its components had left an indelible stamp upon the Canadian population. It had long been evident that Canada was to be heterogeneous rather than homogeneous, plural rather than singular in character. The migrants who settled in the northern half of the continent in the seventeenth and eighteenth centuries were diverse in ethnic stock and culture; and Canada had not been strong enough, or culturally united enough, to impose a rapid assimilation on the great migrations of the nineteenth and twentieth centuries. Everybody agreed, either proudly or regretfully, that Canada, unlike the United States, had not become a "melting pot". On the contrary, it was described, in a phrase which later became fashionable, as a "cultural mosaic".[5] A mosaic normally embodies a picture or an agreeable design, but there was little national significance in the large blotches, and the smaller blots and dabs of contrasted colour that made up the crazy pavement of Canadian society. Its major cultural divisions, on the eve of the Second World War, were popularly supposed to be only three. British stocks made up something under 50% of the population, French about 30%. The third division, usually referred to by the comprehensive designation of the "New Canadians" but in fact composed of about twenty different national groups, of whom the Germans, Ukrainians, Dutch, Poles, Jews, and Norwegians were the most numerous, amounted to nearly 18%. Asiatics numbered fewer than 150,000 and native Indians and Eskimos, the prehistoric migrants from East Asia, totalled about 125,000, a number which had altered little since the beginning of the century.[6] Since 1900, the most conspicuous changes in the composition of the Canadian people had been the slow decline of the British and the gradual rise of European groups other than French. The French, whose birthrate during the Depression had been markedly higher than the national average, had slightly improved their relative position. Was it possible that the "revanche des berceaux," the revenge of the cradles – the French-Canadians' reconquest of Canada through its higher birthrate – would be realized and the French become the nation's dominant ethnic community?

Ethnic origin certainly implied an increasing subordination for the British; but ethnic origin was no longer a wholly reliable criterion. It did not necessarily indicate mother tongue, the language learnt first in childhood and normally used thereafter; and, classified by this standard, the composition of the Canadian people had a rather different appearance. In 1941, Canadians who usually spoke English in daily life numbered more than 56% of the whole.[7] About 375,000 of the New Canadians had abandoned their mother tongue, and the vast majority of these had adopted English, rather than French, as their main language. It was natural that these newcomers, who had probably been attracted more to North America in general than to Canada in particular, should wish to learn the dominant language of the continent; but the adoption of English was also growing in the second of the two original ethnic communities, the French, though at a slower rate, and chiefly beyond the boundaries of Quebec. In 1941, a little less than 130,000 French Canadians, or about 3.5% of the population of French ethnic origin, had changed to English.[8] English, the folk language of the continent north of Mexico, was inexorably spreading.

Its advance had its main impetus in the growth of industrialization and urbanization. In 1941, 54.4% of the population lived in cities and towns and 45.6% in the countryside.[9] Montreal was a city of well over a million; Toronto counted about 900,000 citizens and Vancouver 350,000. The urban and rural proportions of the people had not changed greatly during the

1930's, for the Depression had drastically thinned the trek from the farms to the factory and office. Urbanization, and the growing industrialization upon which it was based, had been arrested, at least temporarily; but this recovery of farm lands and villages was likely to be only a brief interruption in what were now well-established economic and social trends. The old primary occupations – farming, fishing, and lumbering – which at the time of Confederation had provided a livelihood for half of the Canadian labour force, now gave employment to only a third.[10] Workers in secondary industry – manufacturing and construction – had declined, after a decade of low production during the Depression, to about 28% of the gainfully occupied; but this drop was more than made up by the rapid rise of the so-called service industries – transportation, communications, trade, finance, the professions and clerical occupations – which now accounted for nearly 39% of the wage earners and salaried employees.[11] Most of the women workers occupied positions as librarians, secretaries, typists, stenographers, clerks, saleswomen, and domestic servants within this broad division. In 1939 they numbered about 20% of the labour force, and the great majority of them were unmarried, since the scarcity of jobs during the Depression had effectively discouraged the employment of wives.[12]

The economic upswing which began in 1933 was gradually gaining strength; but the country had not yet dragged itself clear of the thick mire of the Depression and in 1939 about 530,000 people, or over 11% of the labour force, were still unemployed.[13] A large number of Canadians lived a stinted, harassed existence with a good many on a bare subsistence level; but there was no doubt that some improvement had definitely set in. Farm income in cash was up in every province. Wages, particularly in the skilled trades and protected industries, had also begun a very gradual upward climb. On a national average, plumbers, electricians, and carpenters earned rather less than a dollar an hour, and employees in manufacturing and trade something below 50¢.[14] An average weekly wage of between $20.00 and $30.00 was common to a good many employments in transportation, public utilities, finance, insurance, real estate and manufacturing.[15] On a national average, managerial salaries were about $2000.00 a year, and professional incomes which, particularly where they were dependent on fees, as in law, medicine, and dentistry, had sunk badly during the Depression, did not average much more than $1500.00 a year.[16] The slump had considerably reduced the inequalities of income of the different social groups and it had made the business of living a lot less expensive for everybody. Prices for shelter, clothing and food were sharply lower; in the late summer of 1939, one could buy prime ribs of beef for 20¢ a pound and legs of lamb for 27¢ a pound in Toronto.[17] The cost-of-living index had dropped from 121.6 in 1929 to 101.5 in 1939 – a decline of twenty points.[18]

The Canadian society which faced the Second World War was a relatively simple society, hard-working and plain-living in character. There were, as there had always been, a very large number of people with low incomes and a very small group of the truly rich.[19] Canadians had never enjoyed either the inherited wealth which was still so widely distributed in England or the quick, spectacular riches which had been so frequently gained in the United States. In Canada, there were very few broad estates and stately houses, rich in furniture, pictures, plate, china and jewellery; and the short list of highly successful Canadian self-made men was dwarfed by the apparently endless succession of magnates in industry, finance, transport and merchandising which in every generation in American history had been famous or notorious for their fabulous fortunes. Free enterprise and private initiative had never found so many opportunities or accumulated so much wealth in Canada as they had in the United States; and Canada, and the British North America out of which it had grown, had never been willing, or able, to elevate the rights of the individual man to the level of categorical imperatives. While the makers of the American Revolution had declared that governments were instituted to protect the liberty and happiness of the individual, the aims of government in Canada and British North America, as set out in all their constitutions, including the British North America Act of 1867, were defined as the "peace, welfare and good government," or the "peace, order and good government" of the community. Canadian history and political theory implied a belief in the health and tranquillity of society as a whole; and the harsh necessities faced by a small people in building a nation in the northern half of the continent had compelled a repeated reliance on collective action directed by the state. The reorganization of New France under Colbert and Talon was an impressive historical precedent; and the coming of the Loyalists, the settlement of the western prairies, the opening of the mining frontier, the building of railways and the provision of public utilities were all collective enterprises which had been carried through largely at the charge and under the supervision of government.

Canada had depressed the importance of the individual and enforced a general simplicity and a rough social equality upon its citizens. Yet Canadians cherished a lingering sense of the fitness of social hierarchy, a sense which was undeniably weaker than that of the British, but equally stronger than that of the Americans. It was a legacy of the unbroken continuity of Canada's development, of its refusal to break with the past; and it had been carried from the Old to the New World as a part of the transfer of the entire British legal and political system and the hierarchical order of the Roman Catholic Church. In theory, and still largely in practice, offices, dignities, and honours were not in Canada the rewards of popularity with the electorate, but the gifts of the Crown or the papacy, bestowed on merit. The American constitution declared that no title of nobility could be granted by the United States; but throughout Canadian history most of the senior government officials, whether French or British administrators or Canadian politicians, had been either peers or knights. The higher dignities of the peerage were conspicuously absent among the native Canadians; but, by the end of the First World War, they had been granted a few baronies and baronetcies and a much larger number of knighthoods. In 1919, as a result of some popular criticism of a few of the wartime awards, the House of Commons passed a resolution requesting the Crown to grant no more honours; but, as Prime Minister R.B. Bennett pointed out later, the majority vote of only one of the two houses of a single Parliament could not be regarded as a permanent limitation on the royal prerogative, exercised on the advice of the government of Canada.[20] During the early 1930's, Canadian names reappeared in the Honours List; and the new knights, among whom were a musician, an author, a scholar, and a scientist, effectively invalidated the charge of political patronage.

III

A million people had been added to the Canadian population in the 1930's; but although building construction had declined sharply during the Depression, most Canadians were still fairly comfortably housed. The slump had not forced a great deal of doubling up; most dwellings – single houses, apartments or flats – were occupied by a single household, and on an average across the nation, the members of a household numbered from four to five. New apartment blocks, seldom more than five storeys high, were now beginning to appear in city streets; but although in 1940 the number of new apartment units actually exceeded the number of new separate dwellings, most Canadians were still living in single houses, detached, semi-detached, or in what were now regarded as old-fashioned terraces.[21] Normally houses were heated, as they had been for generations, by furnaces or stoves fuelled with coal, coke, or wood. Central heating was usual in cities and towns, and increasingly frequent in the countryside; and the only important new device which had improved this old equipment – and that only in a relatively small number of houses – was a thermostatically-controlled forced draft. Only a few rich householders owned oil-fired furnaces, and only a few communities, near the newly discovered fields in Alberta, were heated with natural gas.

The revolution in marketing, which was to change the economy of the typical Canadian household in the next quarter-century, had gone only a short distance along its triumphant, ever-broadening avenue into the future. The chain stores had already appropriated a good deal of the retail business which once belonged to the independent merchants; but the ingenious merchandising devices which were to free the shopkeeper of many of his expenses and responsibilities and force the customer to make his own choices, do his own fetching and carrying, and provide his own transport, were still in the early stages of their development. T.P. Loblaw and his partner J. Milton Cork, who had founded the Loblaw Groceterias in 1919, were not, of course, the founders of the self-service shop; but their enterprise was a conspicuous Canadian success, and its example was catching. The established independent merchants, as well as the dairies and bakeries, still continued to make home deliveries; and most shops, including the chain stores, many of which had formerly belonged to independent merchants, were still relatively small. The really spacious store, with its carefully organized divisions and long rows of shelving, had made only a few tentative appearances by the beginning of the Second World War. Its spread had been held back by the Depression, by the lack of new building construction, the slow growth of the suburbs, and by the relative decline in the number of passenger cars, that indispensable adjunct of the community supermarkets and shopping centres of the future. In 1939, with a million plus more people than in 1929, Canadians owned fewer than 1,200,000 cars, an average of only one car for every eleven citizens, and not quite 200,000 more than they had owned ten years earlier.[22]

The Canadian brides of the late 1930's must have found that the business of housekeeping differed, but did not differ greatly from what they remembered it to have been during their mothers' time. Hydro-electric power had been lighting Canadian houses for more than a generation; but domestic uses of this cheap new source of energy had grown steadily in number and popularity during the last two decades. Electric refrigerators were still something of a novelty and relatively expensive; but electric washers had become increasingly common and electric ranges were replacing gas and coal stoves. Many household operations could be performed more easily and swiftly; but the time-saving "convenience" foods of the future were still in an embryonic form which gave only the slightest indication of their enormous possibilities. Charles Birdseye had already invented his practical process for the fast freezing of fresh fruits and vegetables; but the expansion of this new method of preserving and storing food was, of course, dependent on the development of household electric refrigeration, which was still in its infancy. Most Canadian cooks used fresh meat and vegetables prepared in traditional ways. Housewives in a hurry were content to buy the cans of tomatoes, peas, and corn, and the packages of prepared breakfast cereals which had been just as familiar to their mothers in the first decades of the century. Or, if they were prepared to spend time on quality, they often went back to the elaborate process of preserving fruits and making jams and jellies at home, just as their grandmothers and great-grandmothers had been doing throughout the nineteenth century. Apart from citrus fruits and grapes from Florida and California, few exotic fruits or vegetables varied the familiar products of Canadian orchards and market gardens. Truffles and artichokes, and even zucchini, egg-plant and Brussels sprouts appeared infrequently on Canadian dinner tables. Few herbs and spices were used in the preparation of food and only the simplest sauces dressed it. The day of gourmet cookery, of highly specialized and sophisticated cook books, was still far in the future.

Prohibition, that brief, misguided experiment in post-war puritanism, had certainly not elevated the art of good eating in Canadian homes and restaurants. It was true that prohibition in the real sense lasted a few years only, and that during the 1920's most of the provinces adopted a system of government control of the sale of beer, wine, and spirits. This mistaken application of the fond Canadian belief that public ownership or control invariably meant greater public welfare, produced, in fact, as many disadvantages as benefits. It effectively closed the noisome barrooms and saloons of the past. It gave the provincial government a powerful new monopoly and a lucrative new source of revenue. But, on the other hand, it did little or nothing to improve the good taste or the good manners of Canadian drinkers.[23] The wine and spirits merchants of pre-prohibition days had possessed knowledge of their trade and could offer their customers useful advice. The salesmen in the new government liquor stores knew little and cared less about their imported wines and adopted a pose of discreet neutrality concerning their domestic beers and whiskeys. It was long years before bars and lounges were legalized and wine permitted with meals in hotels and restaurants. In the meantime, beer only could be sold by the glass, and in bare, sparsely furnished rooms, quaintly called "beer parlours," and even more sordid than the vanished saloons. Except in Montreal and Quebec City, where good food and drink was a durable tradition, the fine restaurants of Edwardian days gradually languished and by the 1930's most of them had disappeared.

During the lean years of the Depression, the great majority of Canadians had lived a plain, hard, drab existence. Yet, on the whole, they were fairly well housed and fed, for there was a cheap abundance of the necessities of life, and their collective health had been gradually improving. Stillbirths and infant deaths had declined steadily, though the maternal mortality rate was not a great deal lower than it had been twenty years earlier.[24] Deaths from heart disease and cancer had already started their rapid upward climb. Tuberculosis, the great killer of the nineteenth and early twentieth century, was slowly losing its fatal power, as were influenza, bronchitis and pneumonia, while the ravages of typhoid, diphtheria, measles, and other communicable diseases, had lessened by more than two-thirds.[25] A man aged twenty at the beginning of the Second World War had a longer life expectancy than he would have had in 1871, when Canada was still a predominantly agricultural country. A man of forty, born at the start of the century, in the early stages of industrialism and the still primitive sanitation of early urban growth, had a shorter life expectancy than he would have had either earlier or later. Public health had made great advances during the early decades of the century and most of the improvement was the result of the efforts of municipal governments, voluntary associations, public-spirited individuals and popular subscriptions.[26] Governments, federal and provincial – with the provinces bearing by far the greater part of the burden – built and maintained the asylums or mental institutions and assumed most of the cost of the sanitoria. In 1939, their combined expenditures for health amounted to about $32 million, the federal government contributing only a little over $1 million; and this sum came to barely 3% of their total outlay for all functions.[27] There were no government medical or hospital insurance plans and no government health service. Provision in advance for illness and hospitalization could be made only through voluntary schemes; and enrolment in these, though it nearly doubled in the year 1939-40, was still extremely small.[28]

The idea of collective insurance, or government provision for the main calamities of life – illness, injury, old age, and unemployment – had its beginning in the early years of the century; but it gained popular support very slowly and for a long time had few practical results. Some provincial governments launched insurance schemes for injured workmen and their dependents, and began to pay monthly grants to widowed or deserted mothers and their children. The first federal venture into the neglected social service field was the original Old Age Pension Act of 1927, which offered 50% of the cost of pensions for the needy over seventy years of age. During the next decade, most of the provinces accepted this shared-cost programme, and in 1939 there were about 186,000 old-age pensioners, and rather more than 5000 blind pensioners.[29] The faltering progress of the welfare state might very well have stopped here, if it had not been for the Depression. The Depression, which halted political growth and heightened the sense of alienation from the outside world and its interminable political tensions, forced Canadian governments of all levels to concern themselves with the welfare of their citizens. During the 1930's, nearly a billion dollars – an enormous sum for the time – had been expended on direct relief for the unemployed and destitute; but these were temporary expedients, hastily granted to cope with an appalling emergency, and they emphasized the fact that only more permanent and organized methods could meet the needs of an industrialized and urbanized society. The Co-operative Commonwealth Federation, founded in 1932, had from its inception advocated a broad range of social services; and in 1935, under Prime Minister R.B. Bennett, the Conservative Party accepted wider government responsibilities for welfare, and proposed unemployment and health insurance.

Yet the Bennett government was defeated. English Canadians were not yet convinced of the necessity or wisdom of the Conservative proposals and French Canadians still regarded state intervention in family affairs, whether advocated by Tories or C.C.F.ers, as dangerously socialist in tendency. Also, it was by no means clear how the Conservative projects were to be carried out. The British North America Act seemed to give responsibility for health and welfare to the provinces. Yet, during the Depression, the federal government had been obliged to pay about 40% of the cost of relief. Before social services could be introduced, it must obviously be decided how they were to be paid for and administered; and the future of social welfare was thus a constitutional problem as well as a political issue. In the summer of 1937, a Royal Commission on Dominion-Provincial Relations was appointed to investigate these questions; and its public hearings revealed both the growing popular interest in the welfare state and the strength and variety of the opposition to it. When the war began, the Commission had not yet reported. Here again, in another crucial phase of its existence, Canada had not made up its mind.

IV

Canada was overwhelmingly a Christian country, and the Christian churches had played an active and influential part in its growth. They had provided sanction for the public order and private restraint which had come to characterize nineteenth century Canada and still distinguished it in the twentieth. They had helped to sustain the Canadians in their colonial seclusion and their rural simplicity; and, at the same time, they had largely inspired some of the nation's most repellent qualities, its bigotry, sectarian quarrelsomeness and repressive puritanical morality. Down to the end of the First World War, the churches had certainly been a major power in the land, and, at the start of the Second, they still exercised a considerable influence on Canadian life. In French Canada, their power had hardly declined at all; but their position in English Canada had changed considerably in the twenty years that separated 1939 from 1919. Like most other social organizations, the churches had been deeply affected by the successes and failures, the advances and retreats which had marked the nation's history during the first decades of the century. They had had to come to terms with the settlement of the West, the direct impact of war, the social evils of the new industrialism, the secular values of affluent urban society, and the widespread distress of the Depression.

The spiritual needs of the newly settled West, which could be met only by some co-operation among the different denominations, had helped materially to push the oecumenical movement forward to its greatest triumph. In 1925, after anxious debates and long postponements, the Methodist, Presbyterian and Congregational communions came together to form the United Church of Canada. It was a characteristic achievement of the first creative quarter of the new century, but a partial and imperfect achievement nevertheless. The Anglicans declined to join the new organization, and what

was worse, more than a third of the Presbyterians stayed outside and formed
a new church of their own. After twenty-five years of earnest oecumenical
effort the Christians of Canada were almost as badly divided as they had been
before. The United Church, with a little less than 20%, and the Church of
England, with a little more than 15% of the Christian population as a whole,
were the two largest Protestant communions at the opening of the Second
World War.[30] After them came the "Continuing Presbyterians," still a
considerable though declining body, the Lutherans, and the Baptists. The
Roman Catholics, who numbered nearly 42% of all Canadian Christians, were
divided almost as seriously by ethnic and cultural differences as the Protestants were by their denominational disagreements. While the Irish and Scots
Roman Catholics were emphatically English-speaking and Pan-Canadian in
outlook, the French-Canadian Roman Catholics devoted themselves to the
defence of their own language and separate cultural identity.

By the beginning of the twentieth century Canadian Protestants were
rapidly growing less evangelical in spirit as well as more oecumenical in
outlook. The factories and the degraded slums of the new towns and cities
inspired a different thinking about the nature of the Christian mission. Many
Protestant clergymen came to realize that the social evils of the new age were
not so much the results of original sin as they were the consequence of
poverty and squalor, and that poverty had its ultimate source far too often
in acquisitive free enterprise and ruthless economic individualism. They
began to emphasize social welfare more than individual salvation. They urged
brotherhood and co-operation more than personal piety and self-help. They
tried to reorganize the institutions of the churches and to redirect its energies
along social lines.[31] This radical new version of the old evangel, which came
to be called the "Social Gospel," found its strongest advocates among the
Methodists and Anglicans; it awakened very little response at first from
English-speaking Roman Catholics and virtually none at all from their fellow
churchmen in French Canada. It was true that French-Canadian clergy and
laymen were becoming increasingly critical of the operations of financial and
industrial capitalism in Quebec; but their protest, which was directed largely
against English-Canadian and American economic control, was basically
nationalistic rather than economic and social in character.

Influential clerics and laymen in French Canada were still convinced, as
they had been for generations, that the only real escape from the evils of
industrialization and urbanization was in a movement back to the land and
a return to the simplicity and sobriety of rural life. The manifest urban
miseries of the Depression revealed the glaring inadequacy of this traditional
solution and the urgent need of some more realistic approach. By this time
the C.C.F. had appeared in Ontario and the West; but to clerical nostrils
in Quebec, the C.C.F. reeked of materialism and socialism and its policies
were duly denounced as unworthy of the support of Roman Catholics. It

was not until after Pope Pius XI, in his encyclical *Quadragesimo Anno* had expanded and clarified the teaching of the church on social and economic questions, that the leaders in Quebec felt free to move towards a specifically Roman Catholic plan of social reform. At the suggestion and the encouragement of the Jesuit order, a group of prominent French-Canadian laymen set out to apply the principles of the Pope's new pronouncements to the actual conditions of French-Canadian society and the result was *Le Programme de Restauration Sociale* which appeared late in 1933.[32] The new radical Liberal party in Quebec, L'Action Liberale Nationale, and its leader, Paul Gouin, drew much of their inspiration from the *Programme*, just as much as the enthusiasm generated by the "Social Gospel" in English Canada quickly found its way into the C.C.F.

Along with this growing concern for social welfare there went an increasing preoccupation with the state of international affairs. Before the First World War, Canadian churchmen, in the main, had been naive, professed pacifists, with limited colonial horizons, whose only external interest lay in foreign missions. When war came in 1914 and brutally forced their gaze abroad, they interpreted the unexpected conflict in terms of simple, Christian idealism. They regarded the war and strongly supported it as a righteous crusade, a holy war which would end war and begin a new era of democratic government, international harmony, and social justice. The peace and the inter-war years, with their increasing racial persecution and threats of renewed violence, brought bitter disillusionment. Some clergymen confessed their tragic mistake and reconfirmed their pacifism. Others, together with a good many laymen, placed their hopes for the future in the League of Nations. It was a long drawn-out and painful experience which ensured that English-Canadian churchmen would look at the Second World War in a fashion very different from that in which they had viewed the First. It was also an experience which passed by the clergy of French Canada almost completely. They had accepted the war coolly and with many reservations. The furious struggle over conscription virtually destroyed whatever concern they felt for the Allied cause, and strengthened the instinctive French-Canadian urge for withdrawal from the terrifying complications of world affairs. Apart from Ernest Lapointe and Raoul Dandurand, almost nobody of any importance in French Canada showed the slightest interest in the League of Nations, and the Canadian League of Nations Society utterly failed to win members in Quebec.[33]

From the beginning the churches had provided the strongest support for the public order and private restraint which still characterized Canadian life. They had successfully preached belief in marriage, the family, the home and the Church as the main bases of a stable society; and a good deal of the rural simplicity and colonial innocence which distinguished Canada at the opening of the First World War still survived at the start of the Second. The clergy

of French Canada had tried longest and fought hardest to preserve these old
Christian and rural values. They had dared to hope that industrialization and
urbanization could be stopped by a movement back to the land, even by
highly questionable settlements on the hardscrabble frontiers of the province.
They had defended the historic family hierarchy so zealously that the women
of Quebec were not given the right to vote in provincial elections until 1940,
a generation or more after their sisters in other provinces possessed it.[34] These
exposed conservative positions had long ago been abandoned by the Protestant churchmen; but, on the other hand, some Protestant communions, the
Baptists, the Methodists, and the evangelical and fundamentalist sects, only
gradually gave up their narrow nineteenth-century puritanical causes, including the most determined of all those campaigns, the fight for prohibition.
The brief possession and swift loss of this long-sought goal forced the ascetics
to recognize that there were limits beyond which they could not hope to
pass. It was this moment of truth which marked the beginning of the gradual
decline of the repressive morality of Victorian Canada.

Canadians had lost, or were losing, some of their moral extremism as well
as their evangelical zeal; but Canada, on the eve of the Second World War,
despite its increasing industrialization, was still a very orderly and peaceable
country, with a people whose conduct was still governed by an effective code.
At night, citizens walked the streets of the new industrial cities with as much
security as the pioneers had enjoyed on the western plains or the adventurers
in the frontier mining towns. The incidence of violent crime was still low.
Thirty-seven people, or a rate of .33 per 100,000 of the population, were
charged with murder in 1939, and of these twenty were acquitted; the total
of homicidal deaths of all kinds in the same year was 124, or a rate of 1.1
for 100,000 of population.[35] Convictions under the Opium and Narcotics
Drug Act, which had been declining fairly steadily since the early 1920's,
numbered 150, and the death rate from alcoholism, which had been falling
also, was 1.8 per 100,000 of the population, or nearly as low as it had ever
been since the beginning of the century.[36] There was, however, at least one
conspicuous exception to the rule of fairly steady conformity to an older
code. The average annual number of divorces in the five years from 1936
to 1940 was 2013, or a rate of 18.0 per 100,000 population, which was nearly
twice as high as it had been for even the previous five years.[37]

For a very large number of Canadians, the inculcation of this moral code
had begun very early, in school as well as at home. The British North
America Act gave the provinces virtually exclusive control over education;
but this legislative monopoly, which had been jealously and fiercely defended
ever since, was qualified by an important provision which permitted Protestant or Roman Catholic minorities in several provinces to establish and oper-
ate separate schools, outside the general public school system, according to
their religious beliefs.[38] In 1939, Roman Catholic separate schools existed

by law in three provinces, Ontario, Saskatchewan and Alberta. In Alberta
and Saskatchewan, they were comparatively few in number; in Ontario, they
were distinctly more frequent, and their proportion of the school population
of the province had been steadily rising. In all three provinces a provincial
department of education, headed by a responsible minister, presided over the
entire school system, both public and separate; and thus, in English Canada,
secular control over education was firmly established. In Quebec, the
accepted clerical principle that religion and education were inseparable had
led the province to delegate its administrative authority to two separate
superintending bodies, according to religious persuasion, one for the Roman
Catholic majority, the other for the Protestant minority. By the time the
Second World War broke out, the so-called Protestant school system had,
in fact, become non-sectarian, if not secular; but schools of the religious
majority were controlled and largely taught by the Roman Catholic Church.
This division of Canadian education among provinces and its further
fragmentation among churches had resulted in obvious differences in its
character and quality. Throughout the nation, but particularly in the Province of Quebec, there existed an incipient conflict between the growing
demand for equality of opportunity and advancement and the actual inequalities of training and skills.

Attendance was compulsory in both the public and separate schools at the
primary level and a very large majority, 94.3% of all Canadian children
between the ages of six and fourteen, were going to school at the beginning
of the Second World War.[39] Once primary education was finished, the
number of pupils began to decline considerably, although, in most provinces,
secondary education was free; and in 1941, only 35.4%, or somewhat better
than a third of the Canadian population between ages 15-19, was still carrying
on its formal education.[40] In most of the secondary school institutions, the
curriculum was still made up of the familiar nineteenth century subjects –
English and French, other modern and ancient languages, history and geography, mathematics and the basic sciences. School children gained some
understanding of the world, its peoples, their languages, their history, and
their main systems of scientific inquiry. It was a liberal education in the
traditional sense, an education directed to general mental enlargement; and
undoubtedly the pupils of the first decades of the century were much more
literate than their post-war successors were to be. They had been prepared
in some measure for civilized life, but they had not necessarily been trained
to make a living. The system was entirely appropriate for those who were
going on to the universities and the professions; but it was less than satisfactory for those whose education would end with high school or collegiate
institute and who would then have to find jobs in an increasingly industrialized world. The old apprenticeship system had largely broken down early
in the twentieth century, and in English Canada the provincial governments

had tried to provide a substitute by establishing technical and occupational secondary schools, although these did not carry the pupil very far in the increasingly complicated technology of industrialism. In French Canada, where secondary education was dominated by the classical colleges with their mainly humanistic curriculum, there were few comparable changes.[41] Although the legal-clerical governing class of Quebec bitterly resented English-Canadian dominance in industry and finance, it still did extraordinarily little to prepare its young people for the tasks and opportunities of industrial society.

There were approximately thirty universities and colleges in Canada at the opening of the Second World War, with about 35,000 undergraduates, of whom considerably less than a quarter were women, in full-time attendance.[42] It was a relatively small proportion, only 3.7% of the age group between twenty and twenty-four years, and drawn mainly from the middle class.[43] The provincial governments, as well as the universities themselves, offered a limited number of highly competitive scholarships, together with a few bursaries, but student aid on any large scale simply did not exist. As in Great Britain, the universities regarded undergraduate teaching as by far their most important task; and, in the older institutions, the pride of the professoriate lay in the so-called "honour courses," with their carefully integrated programmes of specialized knowledge, akin to the Oxford "schools" and the Cambridge tripos. Post-graduate studies got far less attention, and took up much less time, and in 1939 there were only 1550 full-time and part-time graduate students enrolled in Canadian universities, and only eighty doctorates were conferred.[44] Research, for both students and university teachers, was an independent and rather solitary activity, and, except in the sciences, usually carried on at the scholar's own expense. The National Research Council, established in 1917, and the Research Councils of Ontario and Alberta provided financial support for research in the physical and biological sciences; but no aid from any public body was available for scholarship in the humanities and social sciences. Canadian scholars were quite literally on their own financially. They were also often very much alone in their isolation from their fellows with similar interests in institutions scattered across a vast country. They came together occasionally, but usually only once a year, at the meetings of the Royal Society of Canada, which was a late nineteenth century institution, and of the Canadian Historical Association and the Canadian Political Science Association, both of which had been founded after the First World War.

The appearance of these two new post-war learned societies offered fresh encouragement to students of Canadian anthropology, Canadian political and economic history, and Canadian political institutions. The publication of two post-war learned quarterlies, the *Canadian Historical Review*, and the *Canadian Journal of Economics and Political Science,* the first issue of which came out in 1934, made space available on a scale previously unknown for articles, documents, discussions, and reviews. In the two decades between the First and the Second World Wars, the systematic, professional study of Canadian history and politics made a sudden, unprecedented advance. Books like Chester Martin's *Empire and Commonwealth*, Harold Innis's *The Fur Trade in Canada* and W.A. Mackintosh's *Prairie Settlement: the Geographical Setting* amply revealed the new methods and the new themes; and the volumes of that giant series, the *Relations of Canada and the United States*, which began to appear in the late 1930's, offered fresh evidence of the range and variety of the new scholarly interest in Canada. Even in university curricula, where hitherto British and European courses had monopolized the humanities and social sciences, Canadian studies were beginning to win a significant place; but here, at the level of the student and the general reader, the growing popularity of the new subject was held up by the sheer lack of books and teaching aids. Harold Innis complained that he could not get suitable maps for his course on Canadian economic geography. There was as yet no good general economic history of Canada, and no good general study of Canadian political institutions. George M. Wrong's popular history of Canada, published in 1938, did not get beyond the completion of the Canadian Pacific Railway; and the only available survey of the subject which dealt with modern times was written by an American!

V

Distance and language, which had divided and weakened Canadian education and isolated Canadian scholarship, had somewhat similar effects on journalism and creative writing. The twenty years since the close of the First World War had greatly altered Canadian newspapers; but Canadian journalism had not yet won complete self-sufficiency and independence. The new cities provided a hitherto unknown mass readership and the new industrialism supplied both the technology and the commercial advertising which enabled the metropolitan dailies to reach it. The stresses and losses of this rapid change were serious. Efficiency, conformity, and standardization tended to crowd out originality, variety, and unsystematic journalistic flair. Rising costs and fierce competition drove many newspapers either into failure or amalgamation; and the economies of size encouraged the growth of groups or chains of newspapers, such as the Sifton and the Southam group, or the Roy Thomson chain, which started its meteoric rise in the 1930's. The survivors of this savage struggle for readers, especially the big metropolitan dailies, could now afford a wider news coverage and broader interests; but, although they tried to interpret the news from an independent Canadian point-of-view, they were dependent upon sources outside Canada for most of their information about world affairs. The Canadian Press had been founded in 1917, in part as a defence against the slanted war news of the American agencies; but its scope was relatively small and individual Canadian newspapers were normally able to send their own correspondents abroad only on special occasions and for brief periods. More regrettably still, they made no great effort to survey the Canadian scene as a whole, and no Canadian daily could justly claim the proud title of national newspaper. The Montreal *Gazette* and the Toronto *Globe and Mail* fought for the readership of Ottawa and the upper St. Lawrence valley; the *Winnipeg Free Press* held sway over most of the prairies; *La Presse* dominated French Canada. Without exception, they were limited and parochial in their outlook. A Winnipegger visiting Montreal, or a Torontonian spending a few days in Vancouver, could often find no evidence in the local morning paper that his native city so much as existed.

The largely Canadian subject matter of Canadian newspapers gave them a natural protection against the press of other countries, even that of the United States; but Canadian books and magazines, the contents of which were much less topical and more general, were extremely vulnerable to the literary invasion from abroad. In 1939, Canada was still very much a colony of the British and American – and, to a lesser extent, the French – literary empires, empires which had been built up by well-known authors, publishers of international repute, and an influential periodical press.[45] This foreign dominance was maintained by the direct import of British, American and French books, and mainly American magazines, and by the establishment of subsidiaries or branch plants of the major British and American publishing houses. It was true that most of these subsidiaries were managed by Canadians, of whom Hugh Eayrs of Macmillan was perhaps the most notable, and that they carried on a certain amount of independent Canadian publishing; but there were very few houses owned and controlled by Canadians, and mainly concerned with issuing Canadian books and even these normally sought to increase their turnover by acting as agents for British or American firms that lacked branches in Canada. The two most important autonomous Canadian publishers on the eve of the Second World War were McClelland and Stewart and the Ryerson Press, the latter of which was the very liberal and catholic descendant of the old Methodist Book and Publishing House, whose chief editor, Lorne Pierce, was a man of strongly independent views and wide sympathies. Maclean-Hunter was another successful Canadian firm which specialized in periodical publication, and its magazines, *Maclean's* and *Chatelaine*, were among the most popular in Canada. Most Canadian publishers drew a substantial part of their revenue from semi-protected markets – school books or, in the case of Maclean-Hunter, trade journals.

A writer who wished to write out of his own experience as a Canadian, or about a specifically Canadian subject, faced a cruel dilemma. If he sought publication by a British, French, or American firm, and hoped for the wider market of the English-speaking or French-speaking world, he soon ran up against the hard fact that these kindred but distant peoples knew very little about Canada and were interested, if at all, only in its remote areas and specialized activities, subjects which lay quite outside the range of normal Canadian experience. If the writer was prepared to deal with a Canadian publisher and to base his expectations chiefly on Canadian sales, he very quickly became aware of the unpleasant truth that the English-speaking book market in Canada was less than 60% – and the French-speaking less than 30% of a total of only 11,500,000 people. Publishers' catalogues usually contained only one or two, or, at most, a handful of Canadian books and on many magazine stands it was difficult to find more than a token Canadian periodical. The death of the *Canadian Magazine* in 1939 proved once again how difficult it was to establish a serious Canadian monthly in the style of the American *Harpers* or the *Atlantic Monthly*. *Saturday Night*, ably edited by the witty and urbane B.K. Sandwell, was the only English-Canadian weekly of any standing.

Earning a living by the pen was a precarious business in Canada in the 1930's, and very few succeeded. Frederick Philip Grove, who had certainly tried hard enough, continued to write, and two of his novels, *Fruits of the Earth* and *Two Generations: A Story of Present Day Ontario*, were published during the decade. The failure in 1931 of the Graphic Press, a small Canadian publishing house in which he had acted as editor, brought an end to his hopes of a full-time literary life, and he retreated to a farm in southwestern Ontario. Two writers who devoted themselves entirely to literature and Canadian themes were Morley Callaghan and Mazo de la Roche, the latter of whom was now about half-way along the long cavalcade of the *Jalna* novels. Both acquired international reputations, and de la Roche, though her novels seemed curiously exotic to some Canadians, achieved a substantial commercial success. For most Canadian authors, however, writing as a livelihood was quite out of the question; they were compelled to regard it as secondary to their main, and different, avocation. Jean-Charles Harvey, the author of "Les Demi-Civilisés", combined novel writing with journalism. E.J. Pratt, whose *Titanic* came out in 1935, was Professor of English at Victoria College, University of Toronto; and Philippe Panneton ("Ringuet"), the author of *Trente Arpents*, published in 1938, was Professor of Medicine at the University of Montreal. Writing was still a marginal activity in a country which valued other skills more highly and was disposed to look with prudish alarm at the realism of serious authors. Some of Callaghan's novels of the 1930's were banned from the Toronto Public Library, just as Grove's *Settlers of the Marsh* had been banned in Winnipeg in the 1920's. No Canadian author – except perhaps Stephen Leacock in his earlier books – had succeeded in convincing the Canadians that they could find a revealing and absorbing image of themselves in literature.

While the writers mainly failed to capture the imagination of their fellow citizens, the painters triumphantly, though briefly, succeeded. The quarter century from the start of the First World War to the beginning of the Second was an uniquely creative and expansive period in the history of Canadian art. Emily Carr, T.J. ("Tom") Thomson, David Milne, and the members of the Group of Seven, particularly, A.Y. Jackson, J.E.H. Macdonald, Lawren Harris, Arthur Lismer and Frederick Varley were a highly gifted generation of painters who, for the first time, made Canadians aware of the vast range and endless variety of the extraordinary country they inhabited. Milne drew his inspiration from the quiet scenes of central and southern Ontario, Emily Carr from the rain forests of British Columbia, and Tom Thomson from the tangled woods and streams of Algonquin Park. The members of the Group of Seven sought their subjects in regions as diverse and as far apart as the Rocky Mountains, the Atlantic Coast and the Arctic; but it was their earlier pictures, the bold canvases of the wild country around Georgian Bay and the North Shore of Lake Superior which first startled, annoyed, and yet compulsively attracted the attention of Canadians. The Group of Seven had, in fact, created a new conception, a new image of Canada. They had left the old settled country of the St. Lawrence and the Lower Lakes behind and moved into the harsh and rugged north, where mines, lumber camps, paper mills and huge hydro-electric installations were making the riches of the prosperous 1920's. The landscape of these last frontiers was austere, heroic, and yet lovely; and, in the pictures of the Group of Seven, its characteristic forms and patterns – the immense, clumsy masses, sweeping lines, and hectic and solemn colours – came home to the spectator almost with the force of a blow. At first, Thomson and the members of the Group were denounced and derided; but derision soon gave way to an acclaim more general and unqualified than any generation of Canadian painters had ever won before. The strong colour and decorative design which were so characteristic of the movement became a dominant influence which at first awakened the initiative of others and gradually degenerated into a fashion which a host of younger and lesser painters proceeded to imitate, exaggerate, and cheapen. "Canadian art," G. Campbell McInnes wrote in *Saturday Night* in 1935, "is at present passing through the doldrums that have always tended to beset a national art when the force of an early movement has been spent and the new one has yet gathered way."[46]

The success of Thomson and the Group of Seven was one of the most astonishing achievements of the period. Yet their popularity was hardly more remunerative than the comparative neglect and disapproval in which the writers languished.[47] Thomson earned a living by working as a bushranger in Algonquin Park. Milne, who waited long for recognition, lived a solitary and austerely simple existence. Emily Carr's work was so completely ignored for so long that for years she gave up painting entirely and resumed it only in the late 1920's, with the encouragement of Marius Barbeau and the members of the Group of Seven.[48] Galleries and other institutions patronized the new movement and rich and discriminating citizens such as J.S. McLean and Vincent Massey built up handsome collections; but the Depression closed the purses of even the relatively wealthy, and the picture-loan societies, which were founded for the benefit of those who could not buy, were not, of course, a real substitute. The painters, like the writers, found that they could not live on creative art alone, and, like the writers also, they fell back on teaching. Macdonald, Varley and Carmichael all taught in the numerous art schools which had been founded or reorganized in the early decades of the century and Lismer made teaching his main profession.

No other art produced as much conspicuous talent and acquired as much prestige in the interwar years as painting. Music had no immediate and evident connection with the Canadian scene and drew little support from the surge of Canadian nationalism. The best Canadian singers and musicians became members of the international musical world, and Edward Johnson and Kathleen Parlow returned to Canada only after their careers were virtually over. Ernest MacMillan gained his reputation as a conductor in Canada, Wilfrid Pelletier won his mainly in the United States. Healey Willan and Claude Champagne were composers of real talent and Champagne had made a serious attempt to use Canadian themes; but to the great majority of Canadians their works were utterly unknown. The symphony orchestras of Montreal, Toronto, Winnipeg, and Vancouver were established institutions which had their origin in the early twentieth century; but as yet there was no sign of that most ambitious and costly of all musical enterprises, opera. Ballet had at least succeeded, but only on the very eve of the Second World War, in making a start. In 1938, Boris Volkoff founded the Canadian Ballet in Toronto, and a year later, a western ballet directed by Gweneth Lloyd had its inception in Winnipeg; both, of course, were amateur in status.

The fact was that in the performing arts, as in literature, Canada remained a cultural colony of the United States and Great Britain throughout the interwar period. The most striking illustration of this dependence had always been the theatre; but never had it produced such stereotyped and commonplace entertainment as in the last decade before the Second World War. In the past, the chief Canadian cities had been served, and fairly well served, by travelling companies from England and the United States; but in the 1930's the long procession of tragedies, comedies, musicals, and revues – known affectionately as "the Road" – came finally to an end. It was halted and slowly stopped in part by increasing costs and the squeeze of the Depression, and in large measure by the rapid rise and astounding popularity of the cinema, which not only half-emptied the theatres of their former patrons, but also in the end appropriated the very theatres themselves. In a tragically short time, professional theatre almost literally disappeared, leaving a huge gap in the entertainment of Canadians which they themselves were as yet quite incapable of filling. What they had to be content with during most of the 1930's was a steady diet of inferior motion pictures and radio dramas, most of them American, varied occasionally, for an interested minority, by a good film or amateur performances put on by local dramatic societies. In the week the war began in September, 1939, Mickey Rooney in "Andy Hardy Gets Spring Fever" was one of the big cinema attractions in Toronto!

Yet, despite their long tradition of cultural dependence, the triviality and the obviously foreign origin of their entertainment in the 1930's drove the Canadians to take three important steps in defence of their own identity. The first and most significant of these was the founding in 1932 of the Canadian Radio Broadcasting Corporation. In 1933 came the inauguration of the Dominion Drama Festival and six years later, in the year the war opened, the National Film Board had its beginning. The contribution of the Film Board lay in the future but the value of the Drama Festival and the Canadian Broadcasting Corporation became obvious long before the decade of the 1930's ended. The Festival kept alive an interest, which had nearly died for lack of nourishment, in the legitimate theatre and gave a few Canadian play-wrights and a good many amateur actors a chance of learning something of their trade.[49] It inspired vigorous competition, quickly acquired popularity, and in short order became something of a national institution. Potentially, the Canadian Broadcasting Corporation was certain to attract a far larger following than the Festival could ever hope to do; but it was not destined to become so wholly and exclusively a native Canadian enterprise. It was, in fact, an uncertain compromise between the British and American methods of developing the new medium of mass communication.

In the United States, radio was a private commercial undertaking; in England it was a public service, directed and operated by an independent corporation. Canada might have gone – was, in fact, already going – the American way. Canadian broadcasting might have become a submissive dependency of a continental commercial radio system controlled in the United States. It was saved from this extreme fate by the prestige of the British example and the force of Canadian national feeling; but it did not escape completely from the clutch of the dominant North American commercialism. The Aird Commission Report of 1929 had recommended complete and exclusive public ownership; but a national system could have achieved national coverage only by the expropriation of all existing private commercial radio systems, and this, in the early years of the Depression, was simply too heroic a course to pursue. The private stations continued and kept themselves alive by advertising. Soon the C.B.C. itself began to derive a substantial revenue from commercially-sponsored programmes, American as well as Canadian. Early in 1938, about 12% of its network offerings were commercially-sponsored and about 25% American in origin, sponsored or unsponsored. "The Happy Gang," a Canadian variety programme, had to struggle against the overwhelming popularity of such continental favourites as "Charlie McCarthy," "Fibber McGee and Molly," the "Jack Benny" show and "Kraft Music Hall," with Bing Crosby.[50] It was all very far away from the great national service envisaged by the Aird Report; but, when the Second World War opened, the C.B.C. was offering Canadian performers more varied opportunities than they had ever had before.

VI

The Second World War was to have immense and prolonged effects on the Canadian people. In some respects, the First World War had been a more grievous ordeal, for its far heavier human losses were borne by a much smaller population; but, although it killed and injured more Canadians, and drastically affected the fortunes of more Canadian individuals and families, the First World War had not affected Canada as a whole so profoundly as the Second was to do. In many important ways, the nation which faced the Depression in 1929 did not differ greatly from the nation which had entered the war fifteen years earlier. It was the Depression that brought to an end the great period of expansion which had begun with the settlement of the West; and there followed a long pause of ten bitter years. The Second World War marked a fresh beginning in the Canadian experience. The nation changed its direction and its pace. The next eighteen years brought an equally important alteration in its character.

CHAPTER 3

The Unco-Operative Commonwealth

I

The Canadian Parliament met on May 16, less than a week after Churchill's War Cabinet had been formed, and inevitably the dramatic events in London affected Canada's political thinking. In England, the leader associated with appeasement and the "phoney" war had yielded place to a new and far more dynamic Prime Minister, backed by the united support of Conservatives and Labour. Didn't the British action provide a good example which Canada would do well to follow? Premier Hepburn, the federal Conservatives, and a number of others, including at least one member of King's own Cabinet, thought so; but a wartime coalition, on the British model, never had a chance of becoming a reality in Canada. With his usual effective mixture of threats and blandishments, King overawed the doubtful and re-established his ascendancy over his party. The Liberals realized that he was their indispensable wartime leader; they had been taught to regard Union government as a Tory political monstrosity, and they knew that their huge majority made the very thought of it unnecessary. All King had to do, in order to satisfy the vague hopes raised by the new British united front, was to make a few gracious gestures towards broadening the base of his government. He suggested a committee, composed of prominent Canadians outside politics, which, under J.L. Ralston's chairmanship, would be associated in some undefined and vague way with the War Committee of the government.[1] He even went so far as to offer a Cabinet position to a few people not in Parliament, including, incredibly enough, a Conservative![2] The proposed committee came to nothing, and, one by one, the few outsiders declined King's invitation. Only one, a veteran Liberal, Angus L. Macdonald, Premier of Nova Scotia, accepted office.

King considered that his patriotic, non-partisan effort to get the services of the "best brains" of the country, irrespective of party, had been ungratefully frustrated, and he turned back in relief to the task of reconstructing his Cabinet with trusty Liberals. Colonel J.L. Ralston, he was convinced, enjoyed the confidence of the country more fully than any of his other

ministers and he determined to make him the foundation of the new government.[3] Ralston, a Nova Scotian who had been a fighting battalion
commander in the First World War, was a slight, distinguished looking man,
with good features and thoughtful eyes. As Minister of Finance, he had been
a very tenacious watchdog of the treasury during the whole of the "phoney"
war; but he was now persuaded, with some difficulty, to leave his old department and to take on the crucial office of Minister of National Defence, with
special responsibility for the army. With him were to be associated the
newcomer from Nova Scotia, Angus L. Macdonald, as Minister for Naval
Services, and C.G. Power, of Quebec, as Minister for Air. Power was a good,
routine party politician, a man after King's own heart in many ways, though
at times he seemed a little inclined to recklessness. Macdonald, despite his
bland, affable manner, turned out most unfortunately to have a mind of his
own, an infirmity which, in his Cabinet colleagues, King always regarded
with disquiet and suspicion.[4] Still a third Nova Scotian, J.L. Ilsley, moved
up from the Department of National Revenue to take Ralston's place as
Minister of Finance. Ilsley was a tall, red-haired, spectacled man, with unas-
suming, offhand ways, and a rugged strength of character. The simplicity
and directness of his approach to any problem differed so completely from
the elaborate involutions of King's habit of mind that the two men might
have been foreigners speaking two mutually unintelligible languages.[5] As
Ilsley's prestige in the country grew, King learnt to give him a grudging
respect. He was more ready to admire his new Minister of Munitions and
Supply, C.D. Howe, though Howe, who showed an impolitic urge to get
things done in a hurry and an unseemly disrespect for the slow procedures
of parliamentary government, often seemed an even odder politician than
Ilsley.

Mackenzie King had shuffled the pack and dealt himself a new hand,
although most of the old cards were still there. The names and faces were
the same, but it was a strangely different company nevertheless. The crisis
of May and June, 1940, had altered its outlook almost beyond recognition.
The isolationist bias and the obsession with economy, which for nine months
had limited and weakened Canadian military policy, were now suddenly
forgotten. King, who only a year before had been gratefully reflecting that
the days of great army expeditionary forces were over, now proudly
announced the formation of a Canadian Corps of three divisions overseas.
The man who had recoiled in horror from conscription, as from one of the
Seven Deadly Sins, now hustled a bill through Parliament, the National
Resources Mobilization Act, which conscripted Canadian manpower for
home defence, though not, as he and Lapointe repeatedly and emphatically
explained, for overseas service.[6] Four destroyers, the entire disposable force
of the tiny Canadian navy, sailed for England. The Royal Canadian Air Force
had, of course, put most of its effort into the Commonwealth Air Training

Plan, not into its own expansion; but its two available fully-equipped squadrons flew to England in June. Moreover, since the planes which were intended to be Great Britain's chief contribution to the Training Plan could obviously no longer be provided, the R.C.A.F. undertook to produce them itself, with air frames made in Canada and engines from the United States.

The spring crisis of 1940 had radically changed the Canadian war effort; but Canada's position as a belligerent and its relations with Great Britain remained completely unaffected. The capitulation of France left the United Kingdom and the Commonwealth as the one surviving antagonist of Hitler's Germany; and for an entire year, from June, 1940 to June, 1941, when Hitler invaded Russia, Canada was England's most important ally. It was a special and perilous situation which might conceivably have led to a reorganization of the Commonwealth, comparable in significance to that which had taken place in 1917 when the Imperial War Cabinet was formed; but in fact it exerted no influence and had no consequences whatever. King was as unlike Sir Robert Borden as Churchill was unlike Lloyd George; and neither felt any need, or any desire, to exploit the circumstances which had left them alone together. In complete contrast with Borden, King never conceived of Canada as a distinct and separate principal in the war. His own phrase "Canada at Britain's side" was a perfect summary of his view. Twenty years after Laurier's death, he still cherished the Laurier belief that Canada was an irresponsible colonial subordinate which had taken no part in the diplomacy leading up to the war, wanted no share in its planning and conduct, and would not be bound by any commitment arising out of it.

This conception suited Churchill perfectly. His situation, as well as his character and training, differed markedly from those of Lloyd George. George had felt obliged to propitiate the Dominions because he was dependent on Commonwealth manpower. Churchill wanted Commonwealth manpower also, as much of it as he could get; but he did not really believe that Britain and the Commonwealth could win the war alone and unaided. From the very first, his hopes were set on the material aid and, if possible, the armed might of the United States. On May 15, only five days after he became Prime Minister, he sent the first of a long series of informal, confidential communications to Franklin D. Roosevelt.[7] He looked forward eagerly to the day when he would share the grand strategy of the war with the President of the United States – and with him alone. George had thought he needed the Dominion Prime Ministers as civilian support in his struggle with obstinate generals; but Churchill was, or considered himself to be, a military and naval expert in his own right. Increasingly, he ran the war himself, with the Service Chiefs as his instruments. The War Cabinet, supposedly the supreme authority, was a pious parliamentary sham. Churchill dominated it. "All I wanted," he declared with naive candour, "was compliance with my wishes after reasonable discussion."[8] Compliance was what he invariably got. C.R. Attlee's usual contribution at Cabinet meetings was apparently the brief comment, "I agree."[9] On this basis, Churchill was ready to expound and get formal approval for his plans; but he had no intention of enlarging this small group of pliant intimates by admitting Commonwealth Prime Ministers.

II

The crisis did not create a new Commonwealth organization; but it profoundly affected the relations of both Great Britain and Canada with the United States. Churchill had already appealed to Roosevelt for American aid, and King always believed that one of the most important objects of his political life was to win and keep the friendship of the United States for Canada and the British Empire. England and Canada had the best of reasons for wanting new and closer connections with the Republic; but also – what was less immediately obvious – the Republic had its own peculiar need for a new and more intimate relationship with England and Canada. The fall of France had aroused in the American administration a sudden, fearful apprehension that the security of North America, as well as the fate of Europe, was now at stake. In the summer of 1940 most Canadians, like most Britons, assumed that the expected Nazi invasion of the British Isles would be repelled. Roosevelt and his advisers thought otherwise. They were convinced that England, like France, would go down to defeat, and it was this fear that prompted Roosevelt's first approach to Mackenzie King. He sought to use King as his agent in an attempt to prevent the British government from making "a soft peace." King was to urge – as if it was his own idea, not Roosevelt's – that England should fight on to the end, even if it meant the abandonment of the British Isles, the flight of King George VI and the transference of the Royal Navy to the United States![10]

King's stomach was certainly strong enough for most political enormities, but the cool effrontery of this modest proposal was too much even for him. "For a moment it seemed to me," he wrote in pained astonishment, "that the United States was seeking to save itself at the expense of Britain."[11] His first impulse was to decline to act as Roosevelt's stooge; but the President had cunningly appealed to his vain conception of himself as the linch-pin between Great Britain and the United States, the interpreter of America to England. He set out to expound Roosevelt's views for the benefit of Churchill and in the process largely convinced himself of their wisdom. American policy virtually became Canadian policy; and when, in his famous speech of June 4, Churchill prophesied that, even if England were subjugated, the overseas Empire, "armed and guarded by the British fleet," would continue the struggle until the New World came to the liberation of the

Old, King jumped at once to the complacent conclusion that his message had been the direct inspiration of Churchill's speech![12] He and Skelton were jubilant; but their jubilation was considerably deflated when Churchill refused to amplify his statement and soon began to explain it away.[13] "We must be careful," he wrote with blunt caution to King, "not to let the Americans view too complacently the prospect of a British collapse, out of which they would get the British fleet and the guardianship of the British Empire, minus Great Britain."[14]

No, there was to be no quick American takeover of the Royal Navy. There were, however, other British assets – territorial assets in Newfoundland, Bermuda, and the British West Indies – which might be plundered before the British ship of state went down and could be profitably used in the defence of the United States. Churchill had asked Roosevelt for fifty over-age destroyers. Could these be handed over in an extremely profitable exchange for strategic "facilities" in the British Atlantic islands? It was military bases Roosevelt wanted, not colonies. "See here, Philip," he bluntly informed Lord Lothian, the British ambassador to Washington. "You may as well get this straight once and for all; I'm not purchasing any headaches for the United States. We don't want your colonies."[15] Imperial suzerainty in the British Empire had always meant political responsibility and social obligation. Roosevelt didn't want to be bothered with either. What he wanted was absolute and irresponsible military power; and empire without "headaches" in the North Atlantic would certainly be a "steal" for the United States. In fact, the destroyers-bases exchange so grotesquely favoured the Republic that Churchill would have preferred to think of it as a double, not a single, trans-action, an exchange of gifts between two kindred and friendly peoples.[16] This comradely notion seemed simply puerile to the Americans. They insisted that they must have a *quid pro quo* for their ships, and they wanted everybody to know that they had got very much the best of the bargain. To the Roose-velt administration and to the American nation as a whole the destroyers-bases exchange was a shrewd "deal," a typical "Yankee swap," in which once again the United States had outsmarted Great Britain.[17]

Newfoundland was included in the list of islands on which Washington wished to secure bases; and its inclusion ought to have been a matter of grave concern – or even serious alarm – to the Canadian government. Ever since 1864, when Newfoundland had sent delegates to the Quebec Conference, called to devise a scheme for British-American federal union, Canadians had always assumed that ultimately the island would join Confederation. The connections between Canada and Newfoundland were old and close, and the crisis of June, 1940, brought the quick dispatch of Canadian ground and air forces to the island's aid. Canada was thus on the spot, helping to organize defence with the local government, some time before the destroyers-bases deal was announced. King had a strong case for insisting that no ninety-nine year leaseholds should be granted to the United States in Newfoundland. He could very well have argued that Canada's historic interest in the island, her existing commitment to its defence, and her confident expectation of its eventual entrance into Confederation all justified the Canadian government in resisting any territorial concession in Newfoundland to a foreign power. He did nothing of the kind. Both he and Ralston – who did not even trouble to consult the Canadian Chiefs of Staff – gave the scheme their hearty approval. On July 16, the Canadian government informed London, without any qualification, that it was "highly desirable" to grant the American request.[18]

Roosevelt had now made good his military control of the Atlantic approaches to the United States. What still lay open, and unprotected by any special defensive arrangements, was the Republic's northern frontier, its boundary with Canada, and the huge, sparsley populated country beyond it. Roosevelt now moved to close this enormous gap in the direct impulsive way so characteristic of him. He had already warned King of his abrupt, informal diplomatic methods during the Prime Minister's visit to Washington in the previous April. "Well, Mackenzie," he had said, "if there is more trouble you will not mind if I ring you up."[19] Less than four months later, early on Friday afternoon, August 16, he made his first telephone call.

"Hello, is that you, Mackenzie?" he asked.
"Yes," King replied.[20]

This sparkling dialogue did not continue long. The President informed King that he was coming up on the following day, Saturday, to Ogdensburg, to review American troops, that he hoped King would come down in the evening to spend the night in his private railway car, and that they could discuss the common problems of North American defence together. King instantly agreed. He was electrified with eager enthusiasm. He behaved like a puppet which could be animated only by the President of the United States. He made no attempt to call a meeting of the Canadian War Committee. He told none of his ministers about his portentous telephone call, and Ralston, the Minister of Defence, learnt of the proposed meeting only from the Saturday morning papers.[21] No Canadian, either M.P. or civil servant, accompanied the Prime Minister on his journey down to Ogdensburg. The only other occupant of the car was J. Pierrepont Moffat, the American Minister to Canada, who came at the President's own suggestion.

The conference in the railway carriage that Saturday night was brisk, cordial, and conclusive. Roosevelt evidently regarded it as a continuation of his negotiations with the British for the lease of the Atlantic bases. He proposed a joint United States-Canada commission for the study of common problems of defence; but his chief concern was obviously the security of the northeastern coast of Canada, and he made it plain that he would like to

acquire an air and naval base somewhere in Nova Scotia, presumably on the
same terms as those already in Newfoundland and the West Indies. King
indicated that his government "would not wish to sell or lease any sites in
Canada but would be ready to work out matters of facilities"; and this vague
but generously accommodating word "facilities" – which, in fact, was the
very word King usually employed to describe the leased Atlantic bases –
was all and more that Roosevelt could have desired.[22] He suggested that the
proposed new body should be designated as "permanent" and King agreed.
Next morning, when the President drafted a brief statement for the press,
the Prime Minister merely proposed that the word "board," as being less
official, should be substituted for "commission".[23] This was done and the
"Ogdensburg Declaration," a press release of only half a dozen short
sentences, was immediately issued to the assembled newsmen.

In the past, Mackenzie King had repeatedly and solemnly assured the
Canadian people that he would make no external commitments – above all,
no permanent external commitments – without the concurrence of the
Canadian Parliament. He had invariably rejected all proposals for a
Commonwealth secretariat or continuing committee on the ground that such
a body might entangle Canada in sinister diplomatic or military engage-
ments. Yet now, without consulting Parliament, or his colleagues, or even
his own Minister of Defence, he had accepted a compact with a foreign
country for wholly unspecified objects and for an indefinite length of time.
The Ogdensburg Declaration was not a treaty; it was an executive agreement
disguised in the disarming form of a press release. Yet it effectively bound
Canada to a continental system dominated by the United States and largely
determined Canadian foreign and defence policy for the next thirty years.

III

In the First World War, Canada had put its greatest effort into the Canadian
Army Corps. The Corps had left a proud record, but a record which, in the
eyes of Liberal politicians, was marred by the violent controversy over
conscription. Accordingly, during the late 1930's, the King government had
tried to qualify the preponderance of the army by giving priority to the other
services. Once the Second World War began, the pressure of public opinion
forced King reluctantly to abandon much of this tentative reorganization.
The army regained its former pre-eminence in government calculations and
national prestige; but the other services, although they did not play the stellar
role that King had fondly designed for them, certainly took on a new importance. During the First World War, the Canadian navy had been merely a
patrol of small vessels on the East Coast, and the Royal Canadian Air Force
had barely begun a separate existence when the war ended. The new struggle

and, in particular, the events of the spring and summer of 1940, brought a fresh incentive to the growth of the junior Canadian services. The capitulation of France and the evacuation of Dunkirk put a stop, for a time at least, to land operations. It was the hour of the air force and the navy.

The navy had already undertaken the task – the convoy of the men and materials across the North Atlantic to the United Kingdom – which was to be its principal contribution to the winning of the war. But now the nature of this escort duty began to alter rapidly. During the first nine months of the war, Canadian ships had been based on Canadian ports and had confined their operations mainly to coastal waters. The crisis of May, 1940, radically changed this minor role. The four Canadian destroyers sailed at once for England, and, a few months later, Canada's share in the fifty over-age American destroyers brought the Canadian squadron operating out of British ports to a total of ten vessels. For a year, the Canadian ships remained in British waters; but, by the spring of 1941, the nature of the war at sea, and the tasks of convoy duty, had again begun to alter. German submarines were pushing their raids further and further westward across the Atlantic; and the original convoy system, which provided a strong escort in European waters, and weaker protection on the North American side, was obviously insufficient. The British Admirality decided that a continuous convoy, which would be organized in three stages – England to Iceland, Iceland to Newfoundland, and Newfoundland to continental North America – would alone meet the now widespread dangers of the German submarine campaign; and the Canadian navy undertook responsibility for the third leg of the voyage. Once again, the Canadian destroyers crossed the Atlantic, and, early in June, 1941, three corvettes, the first products of Canada's wartime shipbuilding industry, joined them at their new naval base, St. John's, Newfoundland.[24]

The Royal Canadian Air Force had grown rapidly during the last pre-war years; and, if it had not been for the British Commonwealth Air Training Plan, its expansion after the summer crisis of 1940 might have been much more impressive than that of the navy. The training plan did, of course, provide that the Canadian pupils, after the completion of their training, were to be "identified" with Canada, either by the formation of separate Canadian squadrons, or by "some other way" to be decided later. Nine months went by, months in which the defeat of the Anglo-French armies and the Battle of Britain had enormously enhanced the importance of air power, but the Canadian government made no serious attempt to settle the method of "identifying" Canadian airmen with Canada. It was not until the autumn of 1940, when the first graduates of the plan had received their wings at Camp Borden, that the Canadian government and its advisers finally got around to the intractable problem of indentification. The Canadian Air Staff apparently assumed at first that the Canadian graduates would simply be absorbed in the R.A.F. The Cabinet thought differently.[25] It wanted to see the Canadians organized in Canadian squadrons, but it still failed to devise a plan which would produce the desired results. In December, 1940, when Ralston, the Minister of Defence, at last sat down in London to discuss the problem with the British Air Minister, Sir Archibald Sinclair, he found himself in the embarrassing position of a diplomat whose government had given him no instructions. The result of this unequal negotiation was the Sinclair-Ralston agreement of January, 1941, which provided for the staged formation of twenty-five R.C.A.F. squadrons, to be completed in the spring of 1942 and for the gradual exchange of R.A.F. ground crew for the R.C.A.F. ground crew now employed in Canada on the B.C.A.T.P.[26] Obviously a very large number of the oncoming Canadian graduates of the plan could not possibly find a place in these twenty-five squadrons, and it was virtually certain that they would serve with the R.A.F.

This result, the future source of much resentment and contention, might easily have been avoided. The Canadian government might have cancelled the clause in the original agreement of December, 1939, which provided that all Canadian graduates of the plan, once they had arrived in England, were to be paid and maintained by the United Kingdom. It might, in keeping with its new realistic disregard for economy, have met the whole cost of its graduates abroad, and thus created a great, national Canadian air force. But apparently this thought never crossed Ralston's or King's mind. The air training plan had been, and remained, a colonial agreement; and the real trouble lay in the fact that its character was an only too accurate reflection of the nature and outlook of King and his ministers. For nearly twenty years, the Canadian government had existed in a state of unco-operative seclusion. The Canadian ministers were colonial, provincial politicians, largely ignorant of the personalities and ways of world politics, and, once outside their own limited local experience, easily intimidated and imposed upon. The wartime visit to England was, for most of King's colleagues, the first occasion on which they had met the more knowledgeable and sophisticated English ministers and civil servants. All too often, these encounters found them diffident, ill-at-ease, and inarticulate. Vincent Massey, the Canadian High Commissioner, a man of the world in his own right and deeply suspected by King for that very reason, noticed with surprise and regret that the Canadians frequently behaved like awkward and tongue-tied country cousins.[27] In the light of the burden of the British Commonwealth Air Training Plan which Canada now carried alone, Ralston might well have insisted on the more rapid formation of a much larger number of Canadian squadrons in England. He made no attempt to do so. The confident frankness with which Borden and Meighen had talked in London had vanished along with the easy Commonwealth relationship of which it was the natural expression.

In organization and direction, the Canadian Army was the most Canadian of all the armed services. Appropriately enough, it acquired a new and more impressive name during the course of that crucial year, 1940. In the past, Canada's military forces had always been known collectively as the "militia," a term which, in the old imperial military parlance, meant auxiliary troops, either home or colonial. General H.D.G. Crerar, who became the new Canadian Chief of General Staff during the summer of 1940, proposed that the Canadian militia should henceforth be called "the Canadian Army," and the Cabinet accepted this new title without a murmur.[28] Crerar may have been already hoping and planning for an overseas army of two corps; but the formation of even the first of these was held up for some months as a result of the temporary detachment of some of the units of the Second Division for the defence of Iceland. It was not until the end of 1940 that the last battalions of the Second Division reached England and the First Canadian Corps was officially constituted. It was reinforced during the summer of 1941 by the arrival of the Third Division, an infantry division like its two predecessors. Crerar was convinced that further additions should be armoured, and he planned the formation of an armoured brigade group; but, at the earnest request of the British authorities the Canadian government agreed to convert the brigade into an armoured division. It moved overseas in the autumn of 1941, and by the end of the year the Canadian Army Overseas numbered approximately 125,000 of all ranks.[29]

Apart from their brief, futile foray into northwestern France in June, 1940, the Canadians had had no battle experience, and for a while it looked as if there was very small prospect of their getting any. The Battle of Britain had been fought and won; the German invasion of England had been either cancelled or postponed. A major attempt by British and Commonwealth forces against northwest Europe was utterly impossible for the present. Hitler seemed invulnerable on the continent; but fortunately his ally Mussolini was obviously susceptible to attack on the Mediterranean and in North Africa, and in the autumn of 1940, the British quickly won some striking victories against the Italian fleet and army. Hitler never intended to make North Africa a major theatre of the war; but he realized that he must come to the rescue of his humiliated ally and the broken and demoralized Italian army. In mid-winter of 1941, Erwin Rommel arrived in Libya with the Afrika Korps, and from then to the end of the year, the history of the war on the Mediterranean and in North Africa was a nearly unbroken tale of British failures and losses.

Was this the opportunity for which the Canadians in England had been waiting? The British military authorities made no move to send all or part of the Canadian Corps to the Middle East, but the Canadian government anxiously and doubtfully considered the project on several occasions. As early as November, 1940, Power, the Minister for Air, was arguing that the morale of the Canadian troops had suffered regrettably through inaction; and, six months later, when Rommel had swept the fleeing British back as far as Tobruk, he repeated his criticism and this time went so far as to propose that a Canadian brigade should be offered for service in Egypt.[30] The other members of the Cabinet were not much impressed by this daring idea, and King himself was simply horrified. His first duty, he felt strongly, was not to invent ways of getting the Canadians into action, but "to seek to protect their lives."[31] Active service would inevitably mean casualties, and casualties would raise the question of conscription, and that would bring dissension and agitation to Canada. The war in the Middle East was a sideshow in which Australians might, but Canadians need not, interest themselves. If a Canadian brigade were to join the British army in Egypt, its presence there, King firmly believed, would be for "spectacular purposes" only, not real military advantage.[32] The Canadians were in England. Very well, let them stay in England until they were called upon to fight in its defence or to join the invasion of Europe. The argument seemed irrefutable to King; but it did not entirely satisfy his colleagues and, in the end, the Cabinet decided not to recommend any particular employment for the Canadian Corps, but to consider favourably any new suggestions that the British might make.

IV

By the end of 1941 there were nearly 300,000 Canadians in the armed services, and the business of supplying them, and their British and Commonwealth comrades-in-arms, with weapons and equipment of almost all kinds had become the main industry of Canada. It was this vast expansion of manufacturing that started Canada on a career of economic prosperity which was to last, with only brief and not very serious interruptions, for over thirty years. From 1939 to 1941 the gross national product rose by 47%.[33] In 1939, there had been more than half a million unemployed Canadians, and two years later the number had dropped to less than 200,000.[34] Production in iron and steel had more than doubled, and in transport equipment had tripled.[35] The upward movement was rapidly gathering strength in 1941; but it had had a very slow start, partly because neither the British nor the Canadian government had placed many orders in Canada before the fall of France, and partly because Canadian industry had had almost no experience in the manufacture of arms and was totally unequipped to make a quick beginning in the summer of 1940. The Canadian armed services had always used standard British equipment, and if the Commonwealth had developed a co-operative foreign and defence policy, this would probably have led to a decentralization of its arms industries throughout the senior Dominions. King's "nationalism" had prevented such a development; but his innate colonialism, which his "nationalist" disguise so imperfectly concealed, had also prevented, almost completely, the growth of a separate arms industry in Canada.

As in the past, the Canadian armed services, right up to the war, continued to rely on British manufacturers for the bulk of their military requirements. The Canadian Service Chiefs knew very well that this total dependence on overseas supply meant delays and frustrations which would likely grow steadily worse as the British government plunged into its own rearmament programme in the middle 1930's. They tried to persuade the King Cabinet to enlarge the arsenal at Quebec and to equip it for the manufacture of small arms; but this modest proposal never fought its way through the barriers of government delays and economies.[36] The only important step towards arming the Canadian land forces with modern weapons produced in Canada was taken in the spring of 1938 when the Department of National Defence signed a contract with the John Inglis Company for the production of 7000 of the light machine gun known as the Bren gun.[37] The Royal Canadian Air Force, which was favoured at the expense of the army, did a little better. It had to start from scratch, of course, for until 1934 there was no aircraft industry in Canada; but in the last prewar years, a few inexperienced Canadian firms began the slow construction of some service-type airframes — though not, of course, of the engines which would make them aircraft. The British Air Ministry, encouraged by these developments, ventured in 1938 to order a fairly substantial number of airframes for both Hampden bombers and Hurricane fighters.[38]

The coming of the war might have revolutionized this state of affairs, but in fact it brought almost no change at all. The British government placed very few orders in Canada during the first nine months of the war; and — what was a good deal more surprising — the Canadian government was in no hurry to provide its own soldiers, sailors and airmen with Canadian-made equipment. Oddly enough, this suspended animation in wartime caused it no embarrassment whatever; and, by a characteristic exercise of the colonial mind, it charged the British government and British manufacturers with the whole blame for the lack of production in Canada. Without British orders, Canadian emissaries to London kept insisting, arms manufacture in Canada was impractical. If Canadian industry was required to tool up and produce for the Canadian services alone, the high unit cost of production would make the enterprise doubtfully profitable for Canadian manufacturers and highly expensive for the Canadian government. The Canadian manufacturers hoped to make a very good thing out of the war, and the King Cabinet was equally anxious to spare expense. It therefore did nothing but wait for British initiative and British orders and to complain when they didn't come. It got so accustomed to complaining and doing nothing that it even failed to match the one important early British order placed in Canada for field guns and gun carriages.[39]

The summer crisis of 1940 abruptly ended this complacent inertia. With startling suddenness, Canada was called upon to produce war materials not only for itself but also for a motherland which faced the possibility of a German invasion, had lost much of its army equipment in the Dunkirk evacuation, and needed all the help it could get. Now the results of Canada's inexperience, procrastination, and colonial irresponsibility became manifest. There was astonishingly little that Canada could produce immediately and in volume. The only strong industry capable of moving fairly quickly into full-scale production for the war effort was the automotive industry, an industry which was, of course, wholly owned and controlled in the United States. Even here some delay was inevitable since the specifications for military vehicles differed considerably from those of passenger cars and commercial trucks. In other departments of supply, where Canadian factories had to be largely, if not wholly, reorganized and re-tooled to manufacture for the services, progress was a great deal slower, and it was well into 1941 before production in most lines got into full swing.

Its range and variety were vastly greater than they had been in the First World War when Canada had concentrated on the making of shells; but there were, nevertheless, some obvious and serious limitations. In the construction of elaborate types of equipment, where the costs of domestic manufacture were likely to be higher than its possible benefits, Canada fell back inevitably on the United States. A number of types of small arms and guns were produced; but aircraft engines and tank engines had to be imported. Canada took over the British obligation of providing light trainers for the British Commonwealth Air Training Plan; but the production of the Ansons, as well as of the Hurricane fighters and Hampden bombers which the British Air Ministry had ordered in 1938, went forward very slowly at first. Canadian shipyards built corvettes, frigates and mine-sweepers; but the four destroyers which were added to the Canadian navy during the war were all constructed in England. The Ram Tank, C.D. Howe's special pride and joy, could hardly be regarded as a Canadian production, or, indeed, as a very useful contribution to the British Commonwealth cause. All its principal components came from the United States. It was never used by the Canadian armoured divisions in actual operations, and, in fact, never saw active service at all.[40]

V

The rapid growth of the Canadian armed services and the build-up of Canadian war industry had an immense impact on Canadian government and the Canadian federal system. The federal government quickly realized that it had the constitutional power, as well as the political and military need, to take on a wide range of novel governmental functions. Its authority to legislate for the peace, order, and good government of Canada had become virtually an emergency power; but there was no doubt – for the precedent of 1914-18 was conclusive – that war qualified as an emergency. At one stroke, the federal government acquired a legislative and executive paramountcy which was vast but also transitory, for, if events followed the course of 1914-1918, the close of the Second World War would bring it to an end. A more permanent increase of federal power was conceivable, of course, although highly unlikely in Canadian experience; but by a curious and completely fortuitous coincidence, an opportunity for radical constitutional reform presented itself at the very moment when the crisis of the war had brought a huge enlargement of the federal government's responsibilities. The Report of the Royal Commission on Dominion-Provincial Relations, which was published in the spring of 1940, recommended that the federal government should be granted exclusive right to personal income, corporation and inheritance taxes, in return for which it was to assume all existing provincial debt, take over certain costly social responsibilities such as unemployment insurance and unemployment relief, and to pay needy provinces a so-called National Adjustment Grant which would enable them to maintain their provincial services at the average Canadian level. If the King Cabinet could have persuaded the provincial governments to accept these substantial amendments to the British North America Act, much of the enlarged federal authority of wartime would have become permanent. Ottawa could then have taken on the leadership of both the war effort and the post-war reconstruction.

On January 14, 1941, when the Dominion-Provincial Conference assembled in the Commons Chamber in Ottawa with bitter sub-zero temperature outside, an exceptional, and, as it turned out, unique opportunity lay waiting to be seized. It was an historic moment which would almost certainly never be repeated; but the crowd of delegates which nearly filled the huge room seemed completely oblivious to its significance. King and his ministers were gloomily convinced that the Report would be rejected and the meeting would be over in a few days, if not a few hours. It was true that one of the Commission's most inveterate enemies, Maurice Duplessis, had been removed by the Quebec election of 1939 and that the much less intransigent Adelard Godbout had taken his place. But all the other declared opponents of the new federal scheme – Hepburn of Ontario, Aberhart of Alberta, and Pattullo of British Columbia – were present, grim and irreconcilable. Mackenzie King opened the proceedings with a characteristically laboured address, delivered without enthusiasm or conviction. Hepburn, who was the first provincial premier to speak, mingled abuse of the authors of the Report – "three professors and a Winnipeg newspaperman" – with scandalized denunciations of the inexpediency of any formal discussion of such a contentious document at a time when all loyal Canadians ought to be concerned solely with the successful prosecution of the war.[41] Most of the other premiers agreed that calling a conference to consider constitutional changes in wartime was ill-timed and injudicious; and only three provinces – Manitoba, Saskatchewan and Prince Edward Island – declared their general acceptance of the Report. A nominating committee which met next morning to plan the detailed consideration of the Commission's proposals broke up because the premiers of Ontario, Alberta and British Columbia refused to discuss the details of a Report which they rejected in principle. Early in the afternoon session which followed, T.B. McQuesten got up to announce with truculent rudeness that Ontario's "association with this so-called conference is over."[42] Hepburn self-righteously explained that he and his colleagues had no alternative but to withdraw "and leave these wreckers of Confederation . . . to carry on their nefarious work."[43] At six o'clock King rose to deliver a soothing valedictory, and the futile two-day conference was over.

Its most cogent and forceful speech had been given by J.L. Ilsley, the Minister of Finance. Ilsley strongly supported the Rowell-Sirois recommendations because he saw in them the certainty of an improved and simplified tax system which would win the war and ensure the post-war future. Bluntly, with the candour for which he became famous, he warned the delegates that if the plan of the Report was not adopted "the Dominion will be reluctantly forced to take measures which will adversely affect provincial revenues."[44] Late in April, three months after the Conference had broken up, he disclosed the stark reality of these warnings. The federal government, he announced, would raise its personal and corporation income taxes as if the provinces had no claim whatever to these taxation fields. [45] It would act as tax-gatherer for the entire country, just as the Rowell-Sirois Report had proposed that it should. In return for this wartime sacrifice of provincial fiscal rights, Ilsley offered the provinces a choice between two kinds of compensation. They would be given either the amount of revenue they had actually collected from personal and corporation taxes during the previous fiscal year, or they would be paid the net cost of the service of their debt, plus a special subsidy for proved fiscal need. All the provinces signed the taxation rental agreements for one year beyond the duration of the war; and the federal government, having thus obtained a monopoly of the most lucrative modern taxes, attacked the problem of war finance with a new boldness and efficiency. It was determined to avoid the inflationary methods by which the First World War had been largely financed, and, in Ilsley's words, to follow a "pay-as-you-go" policy as far as possible.[46] It raised taxation rates to heights which would have been terrifying even if imaginable only a few years before. The revenue from individual income tax, $296 million in 1941, was more than six times greater than it had been as recently as 1939.[47] The government actually succeeded, during 1939-41, in paying 70% of wartime expenditure out of current revenue; and at the same time it substantially reduced private purchasing power and prevented the private competition which could have diverted labour and materials from the war effort.[48]

Taxation was a powerful weapon in the nation's arsenal of economic controls; but by degrees it became evident that other forms of regulation would have to supplement it. The Wartime Prices and Trade Board, which was established early in September, 1939, was at first mainly concerned with the supply and distribution of commodities, and its regulation of prices extended only so far as a few "necessaries of life" such as wool, sugar, and butter. So long as labour, materials, and machinery were available to satisfy domestic demand, this system of supervised procurement and allocation, together with a modest amount of price-fixing, proved amply sufficient. Prices jumped up during the first three months of the war, but thereafter they remained fairly stable. Unemployment was dropping, but there were still large numbers of people out of work and on relief. The crisis that followed the collapse of France ensured that this state of affairs was coming close to its end; but there was still a good deal of slack to be taken up in the economy and it was not until the summer and early autumn of 1941 that total war began to produce its inevitable effects.

By that time the country was very close to full employment, and since the early spring the cost-of-living index had been moving up at the rate of 1.1% a month. It was this swift ascent of the inflationary spiral that convinced the government that it must now move forward from its previous system of selective price controls to a general or overall ceiling on the prices of all goods and services. Early in November, the Wartime Prices and Trade Board announced that the overall ceiling would take effect on December 1, and that it would be based on the highest level of prices current during the period from September 15 to October 11, 1941.[49]

The competitive price system ceased to exist within Canada; it had also been suspended, in all Canada's external monetary transactions, since the very beginning of the war. The Foreign Exchange Control Board was set up on September 16, 1939, less than a fortnight after the establishment of the Wartime Prices and Trade Board. Its openly avowed purpose was to conserve Canada's supply of United States dollars, and it immediately devalued the Canadian dollar by 10% and imposed a variety of restrictions on the purchase of American funds for any but essential war purposes. During the 1930's Canada's external trade had come to result in an annually recurring surplus, on current account, with the United Kingdom, and an annually recurring deficit with the United States. It had been easy, as long as peace lasted, to convert sterling into dollars, and thus to cover the deficit; but, with the coming of war, this multilateral exchange system ended. Great Britain needed American dollars for its rapidly mounting purchases in the United States even more urgently than Canada did, and it had promptly instituted exchange control with the outbreak of the war. Sterling was no longer freely convertible and Canada found itself compelled to work out its own separate and independent financial relationship with both the United States and the United Kingdom.[50] The problem of British-American exchange was solved, at least for the future, by the passage of Lend-Lease in March, 1941: but Canada was not included in the ambit of Lend-Lease, and Lend-Lease increased rather than lessened Canada's difficulties. It did nothing to reduce its chronic shortfall on American account, and it threatened to divert large British armament orders to the United States and thus to stultify the network of war industries which Canada was creating. This appalling prospect was more than the Canadian government could face, and, before March ended, it had agreed to finance British purchases in Canada itself, provided they were not curtailed.[51]

Slowly, the unusable sterling balances began to pile up in London. Inexorably the drain of American dollars gathered speed. By April, only a month after the passage of Lend-Lease, the shortage had become so acute that Mackenzie King made a special visit to Washington and New York, proposed "a sort of barter" of war materials between the two countries, and won Roosevelt's approval in a friendly meeting at Hyde Park, the President's country house on the Hudson River. The Hyde Park Declaration, the economic corollary of the Ogdensburg Declaration, was based on the principle that "each country should provide the other with the defence articles which it is best able to produce." It also provided that parts or components obtained from the United States and used in equipment which Canada was producing for Great Britain could be charged to Lend-Lease. "Certain kinds of munitions, strategic materials, aluminium, and ships" were listed as probable Canadian contributions to the exchange; and the Declaration estimated that within the next twelve months, Canada might supply the United States with between $200 million and $300 million of these and other defence articles.[52] A Crown company established by the Department of Munitions and Supply began energetically to promote the sale of Canadian-made equipment in the United States, and the American purchasing agents proved ready to make good the terms of their President's promise.[53] The drain of American dollars gradually slowed down and ceased. A two-way flow of dollars and equipment rapidly came into being.

By the end of the year the Canadian balance of payments was in a far healthier state than it had been since the beginning of the war. It was, in fact, so prosperous that the Canadian government was able to continue and extend the long line of credit it had granted the United Kingdom. King announced that the sterling balances accumulated in London up to the end of 1941 would be converted into an interest-free loan to Great Britain, to the amount of $700 million for the duration of the war, and that, in addition, all future British war purchases in Canada, including food, would form part of an outright gift to the amount of $1 billion. Churchill described Lend-

Lease as "the most unsordid act in the history of any nation." In fact, Lend-Lease was fettered by a number of self-interested conditions, present and future, while the Canadian "billion dollar gift" was made without reservation or qualification. King regarded it as an enormously important contribution to the common war effort, but in fact Canada had done little more than make a virtue of a necessity.[54] By this time Great Britain had been very systematically stripped of its financial assets, a process in which Canada had been almost as active as the United States. Canada had received large shipments of British gold, and had repatriated a considerable amount of Canadian securities owned in Great Britain.

On one occasion the Canadian government gave a still harder, quite unexpected turn to the financial screw. It deliberately prevented the British from using a convenient source of gold and United States dollars which even the American government regarded as legitimately theirs. The story was an extraordinary one which went back to the days of the close Anglo-French alliance of 1939-40. The French government and the Bank of France had deposited gold to the amount of $400 million in the Bank of Canada as an aid to Great Britain in case it ran short of funds for its war purchases in the United States. The French had also agreed that the planes they themselves had ordered in the United States might be transferred to Great Britain provided the British deposited the required amount of United States dollars in the Bank of Canada to the credit of the Government of France. The British government had made the necessary deposit and not unnaturally regarded it as "our dollars." King emphatically disagreed. He refused to sanction the transfer of either dollars or gold to Great Britain. Both Roosevelt and Henry Morgenthau, the Secretary of the United States Treasury, evidently expected that the funds would be used to finance British purchases in North America and King's own personal advisers, W.C. Clark, the Deputy Minister of Finance, and Graham Towers, Governor of the Bank of Canada, evidently made the same assumption. But King was adamant. "I told him (Sir Frederick Phillips of the British Treasury) that I thought the money was there on trust; that we were trustees. . . . "[55]

King's self-righteous firmness was a very imperfect disguise for different and obvious political motives. What moved him was not so much his moral responsibility to France as his political dependence on the Province of Quebec, the province whose sixty-five constituencies had returned sixty-four Liberals in the general election of 1940. He was always hypersensitively alert to the moods of his faithful Quebec, and he was well aware now that French Canada differed radically from English Canada in its attitude to the new Pétain government in France. The governing class in Quebec was inclined to believe that the collapse of France was a just retribution for the profligacy and irreligion of the Third Republic and that Pétain's semi-fascist regime would restore order, stability, and discipline to France.[56] It was for this reason that Ottawa had ambiguously retained a tenuous relation with Vichy, and that René Ristelhueber, the recently arrived French Minister, was allowed to remain in Ottawa with diplomatic privileges.[57] Exactly the same reason now kept the French gold and dollars securely inside the Bank of Canada. Everyone of any consequence knew that King's excuse was a hypocritical evasion, and that his refusal was really dictated by his sedulous concern for public opinion in Quebec.[58]

VI

In the twelve months from April, 1940, to April, 1941, King had had three fairly extended and confidential conferences with President Roosevelt. He had met and talked with Henry L. Stimson, Secretary for War, Cordell Hull, Secretary of State, and Henry Morgenthau, Secretary of the Treasury, three prominent members of the Roosevelt Cabinet. He was, in fact, far better acquainted with the politicians of the neutral United States than he was with those of his wartime ally, Great Britain. It was four years since he had visited England, and in the meantime the British political scene and its principal actors had changed almost completely. King regretted Chamberlain's fall in the spring of 1940 and his acquaintance with Churchill and the other new British ministers was slight. Besides, he had never really got to know British politicians very intimately, for he had always distrusted their intentions and disliked their methods. His visits to Washington were always easy and relaxed, untroubled by anxieties or apprehensions; but his journeys to London were invariably fraught with deepest fears and suspicions. He saw not the slightest danger to Canadian independence in the Canada-United States Joint Board on Defence; but, for him, the association of the Commonwealth bristled with snares and entanglements. In war, even more than in peace, he regarded a Commonwealth Conference or Council as the easy instrument of the incurable centralizing tendencies of British imperialism.

In April, 1940, just after the German occupation of Denmark and Norway, Chamberlain had proposed an Empire council in London; but King declined the invitation firmly and without delay.[59] He made no protest in the following December when Churchill announced in the British House of Commons that he "did not contemplate adding representatives of the Dominions to the War Cabinet at the present time."[60] Two months later, in response to questions and criticisms, King made his own position abundantly clear in a lengthy statement in the Canadian House of Commons. A Commonwealth Council or Conference, he argued, was quite unnecessary since the existing rapid methods of telegraphic communication, amply sufficient in themselves, were now supplemented by frequent visits of Canadian

Cabinet ministers to London. Moreover – and this King regarded solemnly as the clinching argument – the presence of the Canadian Prime Minister in Canada was essential and his personal contacts with the American President were a far more important contribution to the war effort than any service he could render at an Empire council in London.[61] Instinctively King thought of himself not as a Commonwealth, but as a North American statesman.

In the end, King's – and Churchill's – belief in the supreme importance of North America triumphed, but only after one last battle with the older allegiance to the Commonwealth. Robert Menzies, Prime Minister of Australia and Peter Fraser, Prime Minister of New Zealand, did not share the British and Canadian obsession with the aid, present and potential, that the United States might give. Despite Lend-Lease and some naval assistance in the western Atlantic, the United States was still neutral; the war was actually being fought by the Commonwealth alone, and, in Fraser's and Menzies's view, every senior member of the Commonwealth ought to have a say in its conduct and direction. Menzies pressed this argument on King when he visited Ottawa on his way home from England in the spring of 1941. In London, he had quickly reached the dismaying conclusion that "there was no British Cabinet, no War Cabinet – that Churchill was the whole show and that those who were around him were 'yes men' and nothing else."[62] If this was news to King, it did not cause him the slightest concern. He did not for a minute believe that the Dominions should have a share in the conduct of the war; and, in his view, occasional Commonwealth meetings in London simply meant responsibility without real participation or power. He had little knowledge of Europe and no strategic ideas of his own. With his instinctive colonial outlook, it never occurred to him that any of his advisers in Canada, either civil or military, could have anything of the smallest importance to say about the way the war was being waged. Proffering advice on grand strategy, he felt sure, was a risk no Canadian should run. His true role, he informed Menzies impressively, was to stay in Canada and cultivate his friendly relations with the leaders of the United States.[63] Menzies, he thought, went away convinced of the wisdom of his reasoning.

Yet the apparent capitulation of Menzies did not quite end the possibility of a Commonwealth Council. Peter Fraser of New Zealand followed Menzies to London and his presence there coincided with the second great crisis in the war the Commonwealth was trying to fight alone. The spring and early summer of 1941 was a period of accumulating and apparently endless disasters. Rommel's advances in North Africa, the British evacuation of Greece, the German parachute occupation of Crete and the terrifying bombing attacks on Birmingham and London all helped to build up a sense of impending crisis comparable to that of the early September days of 1940. Great Britain seemed to stand at bay, and Fraser's London visit was a reminder that in the past at least the Motherland's survival had seemed to be bound up with the solidarity of the Empire-Commonwealth. Churchill, more vulnerable to criticism than at any period since he had gained power a year ago, was pressed in the House of Commons to take advantage of the New Zealand Prime Minister's presence in London, and on June 12, he telegraphed King proposing a conference of Commonwealth leaders in July. King was annoyed by the very thought of such a meeting: "Its practical value would, I think, be absolutely nil," he commented acidly.[64] He bluntly refused to go, and, luckily for him, Smuts of South Africa also declined the invitation. Armed with these refusals from the two senior Commonwealth leaders, Churchill, much to King's annoyance, was able to cancel the conference and to escape all responsibility for the failure of his proposal.

Menzies and Fraser had tried and failed and the whole idea of a Commonwealth Prime Ministers' Conference had been killed beyond hope of resuscitation. Yet the discussion had awakened King's interest in making an early personal visit to London himself. The war was still going badly. Hitler seemed to be carrying everything before him in a whirlwind of success, and on June 22, his armies attacked Soviet Russia. This, as it turned out, was the decisive event of the war, the event which, above all others, ensured the defeat of Germany. But in June, 1941, there were very few people who were able to draw any comfort from the fact that Napoleon's advance guard had also reached the banks of the River Nieman on June 22, and fewer still who were confident enought to predict that Hitler's forces would suffer the same fate as France's Grand Army. Most people expected another quick German victory, and the prospect of Nazi domination over the whole of Eurasia was a terrifying one. Fear mounted everywhere in the summer of 1941, and Mackenzie King began to realize that Canadians, as a natural result, were becoming increasingly critical of his government's apparent isolation from Europe and his own failure to visit England. On June 24, two days after the German invasion of the Soviet Union, he left Ottawa for a speaking tour of the West. At Calgary, Vancouver, and again at Winnipeg on his way home, he encountered some ominous support for conscription and several signs of dissatisfaction with his apparent retirement in Ottawa. He was immensely pleased with the way he handled these criticisms and won over his audiences; but he returned to Ottawa in a thoughtful frame of mind, and from then on he began to make preparations for a journey to England. Characteristically, it was the signs of political unrest in Canada, and not the mounting evidence of danger in Europe, which finally brought him to a decision.

VII

What followed was an anticlimax of the highest order of comedy! On August 6, only a few hours after C.D. Howe had informed him that a bomber plane was being fitted out to carry him to England, Malcolm MacDonald, the British High Commissioner to Canada, brought the startling news that Churchill was even then on his way for a meeting with President Roosevelt in Placentia Bay, Newfoundland. For a while King was almost beside himself with rage and mortification! His most important function in the war, as he conceived it, had suddenly become otiose! The invaluable linch-pin, the vital connection between England and the United States had turned out to be quite easily dispensable after all! He had been used by the two great leaders of the English-speaking world, while they found it convenient to do so, and then abruptly and unceremoniously dropped when he no longer suited their purpose. He felt humiliated by his exclusion from the meeting at Placentia Bay, and, at the same time, alarmed and exasperated by the risks Churchill and Roosevelt ran in attending it. It was, he ruminated angrily, "a gambler's risk . . . the apotheosis of the craze for publicity . . . a matter of vanity."[65] If the President and the Prime Minister had met together privately, it would have been hazardous enough; but they had enormously increased the danger of the meeting by bringing with them some of their ministers and advisers as well as their principal Chiefs of Staff. In effect, it was "a conference on war plans," King expostulated to Malcolm Macdonald, a conference from which Canada had been deliberately excluded! Only two months before he had been insisting that conferences on war aims were totally unnecessary. Yet now he felt irrationally but deeply aggrieved at being left out of the famous meeting in Placentia Bay. Its grandiose press release, the so-called Atlantic Charter, which Robert Sherwood later called a "cosmic and historic document," but which differed little from an ordinary publicity handout, increased King's already acute sense of injury. The commonplace rhetoric of the Charter was exactly the kind in which he liked to indulge himself and he would have been highly gratified to have had a hand in it.

He waited only long enough to ensure Churchill's safe arrival home, and flew to England on August 19. His visit simply confirmed the now well-established trends in the conduct of the war. It put an end to all hopes of a Commonwealth Council and thus assured Canada's exclusion from any effective part in the strategy of the future. King expressed himself as completely satisfied with the existing methods of consultation. He attended four meetings of Churchill's War Cabinet; but at these, apart from some rather futile talk about getting the United States into the war, nothing of any real substance was discussed. Military operations, either present or future, were never mentioned at these sessions or in King's lengthy private discussions with Churchill. He had brought none of his service chiefs with him and he himself was not interested in or concerned about strategy. He had no questions to ask and no suggestions to make.[66] A visit to the Canadian forces in England was, of course, an obligatory part of his visit; but he could not help feeling ill at ease in the presence of soldiers. He was booed by the troops on one occasion and later "felt what was like a dart pass through my bowels," when asked to say a few words to them.[67] Facing the Canadian Army was a terrifying ordeal; but the other occasions of his visit, formal and informal, were an almost unalloyed delight. He was the guest of honour at a luncheon at the Savoy Hotel, spent a weekend at Chequers, visited the King and Queen at Balmoral Castle, and spoke at the Mansion House. On September 7, he was back in Canada again.

The next three months were a period of curiously uneasy calm. The immediate surroundings of the Canadians seemed quiet enough; but far away, at the horizon, east and west, there were low mutterings of thunder and faint flashes of lightning. At home in Canada, the general price ceiling, which Mackenzie King announced on October 18, was the most conspicuous domestic sign of the coming of total war; but abroad its reverses, dangers and uncertainties were evident everywhere. Rommel still had the better of the fighting in Libya; and although the ragged Russian line still held, the German armies had plunged deep into the Soviet Union and captured masses of prisoners. In the Far East, the relations between the United States and Great Britain and Japan had gone from bad to worse during the past three months, and in October a new and much more militant government gained power in Tokyo. It was this distant and still ambiguous threat which was to bring the war home to Canadians in a far more direct and tragic fashion than anything else had done so far. The Canadian government had, of course, not been informed, but for some time the British had been concerned about the defence of Malaya and Hong Kong. These anxieties they kept to themselves. The security of the British possessions in the Far East might have come up at a Commonwealth Council, as indeed it had done at the Prime Ministers' Conference in 1921; but Churchill and King had combined to prevent such a meeting. The possibility of Canadians being asked to reinforce the garrison at Hong Kong might have been discussed during King's visit to England in August and September; but somehow it never got mentioned. Yet less than a fortnight after King's return to Canada, the Dominions Office dispatched a formal request for one or two Canadian battalions as a reinforcement for Hong Kong.[68]

Churchill's candid and realistic opinion of the criminal futility of reinforcing Hong Kong had been given as far back as January, 1941. "If Japan goes to war with us," he wrote, "there is not the faintest chance of holding Hong Kong or relieving it. It is most unwise to increase the loss we shall suffer there."[69] This blunt judgement was not, of course, communicated to the

Canadians; they were not even given a hint of the general military considerations on which it was based. Since Canada had no intelligence service of
its own, it was dependent on British sources. It ought to have been given
the arguments for and against such a questionable project as the reinforcement of Hong Kong; but the British uncertainties were carefully
concealed. All that the Dominions Office sent was the request for one or
two Canadian battalions, preceded by a brief description, mainly political in
character, of the current situation in the Orient. Since the Canadian government had already indicated that it would consider favourably any British
suggestion for the employment of Canadian troops, the "request" of the
Dominions Office was virtually an order. Two battalions, the Royal Rifles
of Canada and the Winnipeg Grenadiers, were selected, though both had
been previously described as "not recommended for operational consideration
at present."[70] The fact was that the only highly trained Canadian troops were
in England; and the Dominions Office had specifically asked for battalions
"from Canada." Late in October, the Royal Rifles and the Winnipeg Grenadiers sailed from Vancouver.

If Mackenzie King had any qualms about the departure of this forlorn
hope, he did not record them at any great length. As the autumn wore on,
he had other, far more important things to think about – the selection of
Arthur Meighen, his dreaded antagonist of the 1920's, as the new leader of
the Conservative Party, the death of his faithful French-Canadian associate,
Ernest Lapointe, and the choice of Louis St. Laurent, the Quebec corporation
lawyer, as Lapointe's successor. In the meantime, the political uncertainties
of the Far East grew more frightening every day. Japan seemed determined
on imperialist expansion, but would she attack both Great Britain and the
United States, or Great Britain alone, or the United States alone? And if only
the United States, would the Republic put its whole military strength into
the war in the Pacific and leave Great Britain to face Germany alone? The
dropping of the Japanese bombs on the American fleet in Pearl Harbor and
Hitler's declaration of war against the United States answered all these
questions in what, for Canada as well as Great Britain, was the only possible
way. The Anglo-American alliance, which would fight the war in both west
and east, came instantly into being.

CHAPTER 4

The Excluded Middle Power

I

Brigadier J.K. Lawson sat at his desk at Brigade headquarters at Wong Nei Chong Gap. It was early morning and he had passed a harassed and anxious night. Less than a week ago he had been given the command of the western sector of the Island of Hong Kong; and early on the previous night, December 18, the Japanese had crossed the narrow strait which separated the island from the Chinese mainland and had occupied Hong Kong's whole northeastern coast in force. All through the night and the early hours of morning, they had been pressing swiftly and expertly southward through the rugged, scrub-covered, mountainous terrain. Wong Nei Chong Gap and West Brigade headquarters were situated almost at the island's centre. It was a strategic point of great importance. Yet, incredibly enough, the Japanese seemed to be drawing close to it already. The flying columns of Winnipeg Grenadiers that Lawson had sent north against them had been repulsed. A whole company seemed alarmingly to have disappeared! Lawson began preparations to move Brigade headquarters to a safer, pre-arranged site.

From the beginning the demoralizing feature of the fight for Hong Kong had been the deadly efficiency of the Japanese planning and the astonishing speed of their movements. In these two vital respects, the attack on Hong Kong was simply a characteristic episode in a vast, comprehensive, and skilfully co-ordinated onslaught on the Pacific empires of Great Britain, the United States, and the Netherlands. The assault began early in the morning of December 7, with bombs raining on the American fleet in Pearl Harbor, and it spread westward, with the advancing light of dawn, to the Philippines, Northern Malaya, Guam, Wake Island, and Hong Kong. At 8:00 a.m. on December 8, Japanese aircraft began to bomb the British positions in Hong Kong, and Japanese ground forces advanced into the mainland territories of the colony, towards a line of fortified entrenchments designed to defend the city of Kowloon and the peninsula on which it stood. It had been fondly hoped that these defences might delay an enemy advance for as much as a week; but within two days the Japanese broke the line in a frontal assault. During the night of December 11, the British withdrew to Hong Kong Island. And only one week later, on the evening of December 18, landing craft and collapsible assault boats began to carry the Japanese forces across the narrow strait to the island.

The British had complacently dismissed their enemies as ineffectual night fighters. Yet in a few hours the Japanese had pushed their string of beach-heads nearly half-way across the island. The removal of the West Brigade headquarters was only half finished, when suddenly they were upon it! In a minute, they were firing at point-blank range into the shelters. Lawson picked up the telephone and called General Maltby, the Com-mander-in-Chief. Hurriedly he told him the appalling news, "I'm going outside to fight it out," he said.[1] He died just outside his shelter, and the Japanese honourably buried him. His death disorganized the West Brigade command for a day, but it did not end the defence of Wong Nei Chong Gap. For three more days, the Winnipeg Grenadiers stubbornly held the enemy at bay. It was an heroic, but a vain resistance. By this time the Japanese had cut a path between the two British brigades; and the Royal Rifles of Canada, now the only substantial force in the eastern sector, were driven southward and isolated in the Stanley Peninsula. In the meantime, the Japa-nese, having at last secured Wong Nei Chong, were driving the West Brigade steadily backward towards the capital, Victoria, and fortress headquarters.

After nearly a week of continuous and savage fighting, the British troops were hungry, sleepless and exhausted. Winston Churchill, the strategist who had declared so firmly that Hong Kong was indefensible, now urged its governor, in a special message, to maintain "vigorous fighting in the inner defences, and, if need be, from house to house."[2] In fact, the defenders of Hong Kong were nearly at the end of their tether; and three days later, on Christmas Day of all ironic occasions, the bloody struggle ended. That morning the governor, Sir Mark Young, assured London that all were "in a very good heart" and added Christmas greetings.[3] It was a last gesture of defiance. By mid-afternoon the Japanese were inside Victoria and close to fortress headquarters. Young and Maltby did what had to be done. The white flag climbed the staff and firing died out over Hong Kong Island.

The Canadians suffered grievously in their first battle in the war. Twenty-three officers and 267 other ranks – a total shared almost equally by the Winnipeg Grenadiers and the Royal Rifles – were killed or died of wounds. These fatal numbers, although they included some butchered and mutilated prisoners of war, were by no means the sum of the Canadian calamities. Twenty-eight officers and 465 other ranks were wounded; and these, together with the supposedly lucky who had escaped death or injury, were forced to endure the horrors of Japanese prison camps for the rest of the war. One hundred and twenty-eight died in Hong Kong, where they were imprisoned until 1943; another one hundred and thirty-six succumbed under the brutal burden of forced labour in Japanese mines and industries on the mainland. Of the 1975 Canadian soldiers who sailed from Vancouver on October 27, 1941, 557 never saw Canada again.[4]

II

"Hello, Mackenzie," said the voice over the telephone.

Nobody, not even one of his few close friends, ever called King "Mackenzie"; and Roosevelt's continued use of this familiar salutation casts a revealing light on the nature of their friendship. King, though he was eight years older than Roosevelt, found great difficulty in calling him "Franklin". This was partly because he rarely called his political associates by their first names, but partly also because his relationship with Roosevelt was not that of two equals, but of master and pupil, with the younger man as the acknowledged senior.[5]

It was December 22, the day on which the Winnipeg Grenadiers were finally driven out of Wong Nei Chong Gap; but King's mind was on higher things than the fate of the Canadians in Hong Kong. For some time there had been persistent rumours of Churchill's imminent arrival in Washington; and now, without preamble, Roosevelt announced that "a certain person" would be arriving in two hours time. "I will want you here while he is here," the President commanded.[6] Two days later, Moffat, the American Minister to Canada, informed King that he was expected to appear by midday on December 26 and that the three Canadian defence ministers might accompany him. Nobody else was invited or expected. The President, Moffat reported, "did not wish to have military advisers." Obviously this meant exclusion from the strategic planning which was certain to be the main business of the conference at Washington, and Ralston was perturbed. King tried to soothe him. The Canadian ministers, he said earnestly, would "just have to seek to assist in every way we can, keeping as true a sense of proportion in all things as possible . . . ."[7]

In Washington, the Canadians quickly realized that "a true sense of proportion" was just about all they would be permitted to contribute to the conference. King, in fact, spent most of his first day in the capital in soothing the highly excitable Cordell Hull, the American Secretary of State, who was beside himself with rage over an essentially minor incident, the Free French occupation of St. Pierre and Miquelon. It was not until the afternoon of December 27 that King was permitted to present his defence ministers to Churchill and Roosevelt. The Canadians sat around the two leaders in a respectful semi-circle. Obviously the meeting was a pure formality, nothing of the smallest importance was discussed; and while the awkward, self-conscious little group exchanged banal generalities, the real decisions were being reached elsewhere. Roosevelt and Churchill, King commented resentfully, "were both just filling in time while behind the scenes the Chiefs of the two Staffs were working together."[8] What the Chiefs of Staff and the British and American politicians were actually planning remained a secret of which nothing was revealed to the Canadians in Washington. And although Churchill accompanied King back to Ottawa and spent two days in the Canadian capital, he divulged nothing of any importance. All the information that King could present to the Canadian War Committee was contained in a public document called "the Declaration of the United Nations." Churchill assured the members of the War Committee solemnly that King had taken an active part in its composition. All that had happened, in fact, was that the British Ambassador in Washington had briefly shown him the document, with the earnest plea that he change nothing in it, not even the bad grammar![9]

Although the Canadian government was firmly excluded from the "Arcadia" Conference of December-January, 1941-42, it affected Canada deeply. The conference created the machinery by which the British Empire-Commonwealth and the United States were to fight the Second World War. It established the Combined Chiefs of Staff Committee, to which was entrusted the grand strategy and general conduct of the war, and three additional but subordinate boards charged with such important economic questions as munitions, shipping and raw materials. Finally, as an impressive ideological front for the war effort, the conference published the United Nations Declaration, embodying the principles of the Atlantic Charter, to which all respectable nations in the Western Europe and the Americas world were expected to subscribe. The Combined Chiefs of Staff Committee and the three economic boards were composed exclusively of British and American service men and civilians; and Canada, despite prolonged efforts, never gained direct admission to any of them. She was not even admitted to equal status with the great powers in the list of signatories of the United Nations Declaration, where a common ideological commitment might have seemed to justify equality. Roosevelt was convinced that the post-war peace could be maintained only by the dominance of the superpowers; and the twenty-eight states that signed the Declaration were listed accordingly, not in alphabetical order, but in two divisions.[10] The first of these contained the great powers, the United States, the United Kingdom, Soviet Russia, and China, at Roosevelt's special insistence; all the other signatories, including Canada, were listed alphabetically in a second, subordinate division. "The Americans," Pearson reported to Massey from Ottawa, "insisted on breaking them up into a major league and a minor league. Canada was put in the minor league alongside Costa Rica."[11]

Canada's exclusion from all influence on the conduct of the war astonished and outraged the officials in the Department of External Affairs; even the War Committee of the Cabinet was ready to voice a protest. King thought differently. He had failed to impose a co-operative control of the Commonwealth war effort, and now he completely lacked a *pointe d'appui* by which he could insist on the recognition of Canada's claims. In December, 1941, during Churchill's Ottawa visit and again in August, 1943, at the time of the first Quebec Conference, he explained at some length how strong was the Canadian desire for a voice in the conduct of the war and how hard it was to accept the fact that "the U.S. and Britain would settle everything between themselves and that our services, Chiefs of Staff, etc. would not have any say in what was to be done."[12] Yet these long, rather complaining explanations were not intended as arguments in support of Canada's admission to the higher directorate of the war; they were meant merely to prove the political necessity, and the difficulty, of pacifying the Canadian people. King never hoped or expected to be given a real voice in the management of affairs, all he wanted was a semblance so outwardly convincing that to the uninstructed Canadians it would look like the real thing.

For this need, the Quebec conferences were the perfect answer. At the first conference, in August, 1943, Churchill was ready to admit the Canadian Chiefs to the plenary sessions of the Combined Chiefs of Staff Committee. Roosevelt quietly but firmly vetoed this proposal and King did not greatly repine.[13] He was photographed – and the photographs were conspicuously displayed in all the Canadian newspapers – sitting beside Roosevelt and Churchill on Dufferin Terrace at Quebec, with the Canadian ensign flying above beside the Union Jack and the Stars and Stripes. "My own feeling," he reflected "is that Churchill and Roosevelt being at Quebec, and myself acting as host, will be quite sufficient to make clear that all three are in conference together . . . It will be a pretty good answer to the Tory campaign of 'our leaders, Churchill and the President.' "[14] King radiated immense self-satifaction. In his mind, the first Quebec Conference was simply meant to be good theatre; and, as a show, it was such a conspicuous success that he arranged to have it repeated the following year. The reality, as he knew very well, was quite different. In a candid admission to Lord Moran, Churchill's personal physician, he likened his role as host to that of the general manager of the Chateau Frontenac Hotel.[15] Moran himself compared King to a man "who has lent his house for a party. The guests take hardly any notice of him, but just before leaving they remember he is their host and say pleasant things." [16] Churchill rarely troubled to say pleasant things to King. Moran could not help but notice the startling contrast between his obsequious cultivation of Roosevelt and his indifference to King. "He takes him for granted," he concluded bluntly.[17]

Roosevelt was perhaps even more inclined than Churchill to take King – and Canada – for granted. Yet oddly enough, in form at least, the Canadian government managed to retain more independence and influence in the defence of North America than it did in the conduct of war in Europe. It might have seemed inevitable that the United States would peremptorily insist on the control of all North American armed forces, Canadian and American; but, although this was exactly what the American military authorities wanted and expected to get, it did not work out quite as they had hoped. They were, in fact, forestalled by the President's own creation, the Permanent Joint Board on Defence, in which both countries were equally represented, with a civilian chairman and secretary on each side. There was a fine irony in the fact that Canada's military autonomy was preserved on the North American continent by the very type of organization which King had persistently refused to see established in the British Commonwealth. At its very first meeting, in August, 1940, the Permanent Joint Board took in hand the task of planning the defence of North America. The Canadian members were perfectly ready to concede strategic control to the United States in the dreadful event of Britain's defeat and occupation and the transference of the war across the Atlantic to the New World; but they insisted that such concentration of power was quite unnecessary if the United States entered a war which would continue to be fought mainly in Europe. Their stand was strongly supported by the Canadian Chiefs of Staff and the Cabinet War Committee. This recalcitrance astonished and exasperated the Americans, but, in the end, after a prolonged and stormy meeting in Washington in late April, 1941, the Permanent Joint Board finally accepted the Canadian plan; the "co-ordination of the military effort of the United States and Canada shall be effected by mutual co-operation."[18]

It was just as well that this arrangement had been made more than six months before the United States was finally propelled into the war by the Japanese attack on Pearl Harbor. Once this fateful decision had been forced on the Republic, its military authorities, acting no doubt on the principle that "mutual co-operation" was all very well in peace, but highly inconvenient in war, began to press once more for full powers of "strategic direction." It was fairly easy for the Canadian Chiefs of Staff and the Canadian Section of the Joint Defence Board to resist these peremptory demands on the Pacific Coast; but, in the east, where the six leased Newfoundland bases and the unlimited jurisdiction granted over them gave the United States a position of commanding importance, the problem was much more difficult. Canada was excluded from the negotiations in London which settled the terms of the leases; all that the Canadian government was able to secure was a separate protocol which recognized that Newfoundland was "an integral feature of the Canadian scheme of defence" and that Canadian interests in Newfoundland would be "fully respected."[19] How "fully" they would be "respected" remained an anxious and unsolved question for some time to come.

In April, 1941, after the leases had finally been signed in London, American armed forces were pouring into the island. An America take-over seemed so imminent that the Canadian members of the Joint Defence Board began to wonder whether it would not be better to let the United States assume the entire responsibility for the defence of Newfoundland and thus release Canadian forces for service elsewhere. The Cabinet War Committee rejected this suggestion; it continued its parrot-like iteration of the theory that Newfoundland was "an integral part of the defence of Canada," but its apprehensions remained and, once the United States had entered the war, it began to fear that the American military authorities would demand what the Joint Defence Board had tentatively proposed. These worries were very well founded. American designs in Newfoundland probably reached ambitious proportions in the winter of 1941-42. "Don't let Canada get Newfoundland. We want it," Beaverbrook heard Roosevelt announce to a select company in the White House late in March, 1942.[20] A month earlier, the commander of the United States "Eastern Theatre of Operations" proposed that "all forces in Newfoundland, Canadian and American, be placed under the command of an American officer, without any limitation."[21] The American War Department looked long at this recommendation, remembered the experience of members on the Permanent Joint Board on Defence, and decided not to submit it to the Canadian authorities. The regime of "mutual co-operation" continued on its uneasy way in Newfoundland.

III

The truth was that King, although he had held the post of Secretary of State for External Affairs throughout his long career as Prime Minister, was in reality a diffident and irresolute foreign minister. He was a relic of a colonial age when a Canadian foreign policy was commonly regarded as an expensive and dangerous luxury. He disliked the intrusion of external affairs, and he instinctively assumed that domestic politics ought to be the virtually exclusive concern of a Canadian Prime Minister. His political speciality was the preservation of Canadian national unity, a sacred task enjoined on him by Sir Wilfrid Laurier, which he pursued with the devotion of a knight in quest of the Holy Grail. He believed that he had saved national unity in 1939 by the announcement that his government would stand by the principle of voluntary enlistment for service abroad. That was over two years ago now; and, in the meantime, a number of important developments – the entrance of the United States into the war, its enlargement to global proportions, and the heavy Canadian casualties at Hong Kong – had strengthened the demand, if not the need, for more combat manpower. Arthur Meighen, the new leader of the Conservative Party, made conscription for general service one of the main planks in his manifesto. The King Cabinet could not possibly avoid the issue, and it came up in December, 1941, when Ralston presented his army estimates for the coming year.

King, Cardin, Dandurand, and several others were in favour of sticking to the original pledge to voluntary enlistment. Ralston and Macdonald, the Minister for Naval Services, were equally firmly convinced that, in view of the uncertain but probably vast military necessities of the future, conscription might become inevitable at any time. Ralston put his points quietly but persistently; Angus Macdonald was much more argumentative and vehement. Macdonald's besetting weakness was certainly his independent habit of mind. He had an easy Highland geniality, but also, at times, a flaming Highland temper; and he remained regrettably unconvinced of the basic doctrinal truth that French Canada possessed rights superior to those of English Canada and must be indulged accordingly. For weeks the argument inside the Cabinet continued. King grew seriously alarmed. He knew he could not end the dispute, but he might postpone it, and thus, for a time, avoid the open ministerial split which he dreaded above everything else. He decided that he would go over the heads of Cabinet and Parliament and ask the people of Canada in a plebiscite whether they were prepared to release the government from its pledge not to introduce conscription for overseas service.

The plebiscite, announced at the opening of Parliament in January, 1942, had the expected calming effect; but it resulted in another highly valuable political benefit which King had perhaps not anticipated. It went far to disarm Arthur Meighen, the new Conservative leader, of his favourite electoral weapon. Meighen, who had vacated his place in the Senate, was now seeking election for the Commons in the suburban Toronto seat of York South. He had not wanted the Conservative leadership; he had repeatedly refused it; and he had accepted in the end only because the Conservative Conference, with heartless insistence, had put him in a position where refusal was impossible. He dreaded the future. "But oh," he exclaimed anxiously, "what miseries, what disappointments, what turmoil, what angry scenes are ahead!"[22] He expected trouble, but even he probably underestimated the misfortunes that awaited him. The fact was that his election proposals were ill-timed and he himself seriously out of tune with the popular feeling of wartime Canada. The Canadian Army as a whole had not yet been heavily engaged in action; conscription was still merely an academic question which the plebiscite would decide. Meighen's emergency measures and cries of alarm left people unmoved; but his views on social and economic questions, which he thought irrelevant to the main issue, aroused far more critical interest than they could possibly have done at any earlier period of his career.

The Liberal Party, by ostentatiously withdrawing from the contest in York South, left J.W. Noseworthy, the socialist C.C.F. candidate, as Meighen's sole opponent; and Noseworthy built his campaign on what was essentially a defamatory libel – the grotesque caricature of Meighen as an apologist of predatory capitalism. Meighen certainly believed that "the fundamental instinct of the human race to gain, to acquire, to have" was a creative quality that must be preserved, and that real socialism was inherently undemocratic and incapable of achievement except through a coercive dictatorship.[23] The trouble was that these views did not differ greatly from those of the great majority of the middle class voters of York South; and, if they were to be shocked into voting against Meighen a far more terrifying image was essential. Noseworthy and his publicists, including F.H. Underhill, set themselves to the task with a will. They misquoted and garbled Meighen's speeches and misrepresented and distorted his opinions.[24] Under their ministrations, he was transformed into a monstrous symbol of the iniquities of the capitalist system. The ordeal was far too much for him. He was quite incapable of coping with such a slanderous and gruelling campaign. He did not really want to win in York South, and the fates were kind to him, for he lost. He was badly beaten in a traditional Tory riding by a man who stood at the bottom of the poll in the previous election.

Meighen's defeat seemed to prove that although English Canadians might vote "yes" in the coming plebiscite, they did not see any immediate or pressing need for conscription. King's tactic had worked in English Canada; but its success there was balanced, and perhaps overbalanced, by its increasingly obvious failure in French Canada. For more than two years, ever since the defeat of Duplessis in the election of October, 1939, Quebec had been relatively quiet. Godbout's provincial government and the French-Canadian ministers at Ottawa were linked together in support of King's war policies; and although opposition to Canada's involvement in the war continued, despite or perhaps because of the capitulation of France, it could find expression only in some popular protest independent of party, and of this there was no sign for some time. Then, in the late autumn of 1941, came a significant change. Meighen's election as the new Conservative leader seemed to foreshadow a revival of English-Canadian pressure for conscription and the death of Lapointe might very well result in the serious weakening of French-Canadian influence at Ottawa. The vague tremor of apprehension which began stealing through Quebec was suddenly transformed, by the announcement of the plebiscite, into a positive state of angry alarm. French Canada had accepted the declaration of war in 1939 on the express condition that conscription for overseas service would never be introduced. For a great many French Canadians, the terms on which Canada had entered the Second World War were solemn terms which could only be regarded – it was their favourite expression – as a compact.

Yet now, the principal author of the "compact," King himself, proposed to ask the electorate whether or not it wished to release him from his solemn engagement. Why, asked the French-Canadian nationalists indignantly, should he now ask permission to repudiate his contract, when nothing could really justify its repudiation? This was the vital but unanswered question that drove Maxime Raymond, Georges Pelletier, André Laurendeau and others to found "La Ligue pour la Défense du Canada" as a popular means of promoting a resounding "No" to the plebiscite.[25] Ostensibly the League proposed to "defend" the whole of Canada, not French Canada alone. Yet it made no real attempt to win English Canadians; and its tumultuous and fervid public meetings revealed sympathies and antipathies which would have seemed alien and highly objectionable to many English Canadians. Its speakers reflected the popular French-Canadian approval of the semi-fascist Pétain regime in France, and its huge audiences showed a disturbing anti-semitic tendency which, on one occasion, ended in a violent attack on Jews and Jewish shops.[26]

The plebiscite was held on April 27, 1942; 2,945,514 Canadians, or 63.7% of the whole, voted "yes" and 1,643,006, or 36.3%, voted "no".[27] Nine provinces were in favour of freeing the Liberal government from its commitment; Quebec alone recorded a negative vote of 71.2%; and, although statistical precision is impossible, it is probable that English Canadians voted "yes" by four to one, and French Canadians "no" by four to one. As André Laurendeau's L'Action Nationale proudly announced, it was "a vote by race."[28] King was profoundly depressed. Only a faint glow in the remote distance showed that the Holy Grail of national unity still beckoned. Obviously the whole question of conscription would have to be approached henceforth with the greatest possible caution. Yet it was equally obvious that if the government took no action at all, the plebiscite would appear meaningless and the King Cabinet censurable. Quickly its leader came to the conclusion that section three of the National Resources Mobilization Act, which restricted compulsory service to home defence, must be repealed. Surely the national government could not refuse the freedom of action which the nation had expressly given it! It was logical reasoning; but the logic was too much for Cardin, now the senior French-Canadian Cabinet Minister, who promptly resigned.

Cardin's resignation was bad enough, but King was soon forced to realize that there might be much worse to come. When the Cabinet met on April 28, the day after the plebiscite, it immediately became clear that its members were badly divided. Ralston and Macdonald interpreted the plebiscite as a national mandate for direct government action, whenever necessary. King, and the other ministers who supported him openly or tacitly, argued that government could still not act without previous parliamentary approval. King had always shifted from parliamentary democracy to plebiscitary democracy and back again, as it suited his political convenience; and now he argued that parliamentary approval must confirm the decision of the people. The defence ministers struggled to escape from these delaying procedures. For days, for weeks, and, in the end, for months, the argument inside the Cabinet continued at intervals. Macdonald, King noted with annoyance, became "very aggressive" and "unpleasant in his attitude" on occasions; Ralston was quieter, but "very set and determined."[29] He denied King's contention that the difference between them was only a small technical point. The plebiscite, he argued firmly, justified instant action, when and if the war demanded it, without further parliamentary delays. In the end, he tendered his resignation; but, as King saw clearly, it was "out of the question altogether" for him to accept it, when the difference between them was simply a question of procedure.[30] Yet he kept Ralston's letter. He always kept all documents and correspondence, even including Christmas cards. One never knew when they might be useful!

IV

The first prolonged argument over conscription for overseas service, which lasted, in one form or another, from November, 1941, to July, 1942, was still, as King saw clearly, an academic debate. The Canadian Army was still idle in England, for the great Allied offensive had not yet begun. It was the crucial middle period of the war, the period during which the Allied powers endured their last serious defeats in the Far and Middle East, gathered their human and material resources for attack, and devised the grand strategy for the campaigns of the future. In Canada as in the other countries of the alliance, it was a time of planning and preparation, of active construction and intense activity. The evidence of this effort was very obvious to Canadians in the build-up of their armed forces and the hum of their factories in the southern, settled parts of the country; but, although the great majority were utterly unaware and only a few vaguely suspected, equally portentous developments were rushing to completion in the far north. The Canadians continued to think, as they had thought for generations and centuries, in terms of a great east-west route across their country and the North Atlantic to England. But the United States was now in the war, and the United States was an imperial power in North America, with a far northern possession, Alaska, which she was fully determined to defend and to use, if necessary, as a basis for attack against Japan. This meant that the Canadian north must be exploited, and exploited as the United States decided, with giant defence projects which would help to win the war in Europe and the Far East.

It was the Americans who took the initiative and forced the pace. The heavy weight of presidential command or army pressure was applied whenever necessary; and Canada's doubts or practical objections were brushed casually aside as the obstinate cavillings of a jealous "little brother." The Permanent Joint Defence Board had been set up to make plans for the defence of North America, but the only northern project which it considered thoroughly and of its own volition was the northwest staging route to Alaska. The other three major wartime schemes – Canol, the Alaska Highway, and the northern extension of the Air Ferry to England – were all undertaken hurriedly after the United States entered the war and without any serious consideration by anybody of the difficulties involved. The giant "Crimson" project which was intended to provide additional northern routes, through stations at The Pas, Churchill, Southampton Island, Chimo, and Frobisher Bay, to the North Atlantic Air Ferry, did, it is true, originate in the American section of the Permanent Joint Board on Defence; but its chairman, La Guardia, the Mayor of New York, urged the Board's immediate approval and was quite prepared to go over its head to the President if there was any sign of serious Canadian doubts or questionings.[31] The President, with the approval of the Secretaries of War and the Navy, was also the author of the Alaska Highway, although the Permanent Joint Board had at first considered its military value negligible and both the Canadian Chiefs of Staff and the American War Office did not originally favour it.[32] Canol, the costly scheme for piping oil from Norman Wells to Whitehorse, was an even more glaring example of peremptory American authoritarianism. The United States army authorized the pipeline and signed a contract with Imperial Oil more than a fortnight before the Canadian government signified its approval![33]

The Americans had forced Canadian consent and jumped the gun on Canadian sanction. They treated Canadian sovereignty and the interests of the Canadian environment and native peoples with equal impatience and neglect during the frantic business of construction. All too often they behaved as if they were on their own soil, or on a separate but tributary and submissive part of the Empire of the United States; and there were solid grounds for these instinctive assumptions. Canada granted the American military courts the power to try all offences committed by the United States armed forces in Canadian territory, even those including Canadians; and at the height of the American influx, there were about 33,000 American service personnel stationed in the Canadian north.[34] They enjoyed the power of numbers and the authority of command; and the Canadian efforts to regulate their activities, which consisted chiefly in paper commands and exhortations despatched at long range from Ottawa, were singularly ineffectual. The Canadian government showed, in fact, an inexcusable lack of responsibility in its failure to protect one of the nation's greatest assets. No member of King's Cabinet ever thought it worth his while to visit the Canadian north and really find out what was going on there. It was not a Canadian, but an Englishman, Malcolm Macdonald, the British High Commissioner, who travelled through the northwest and in March, 1943, gave the Cabinet War Committee a report on the vast and disquieting extent of the American operations in the region.[35] It was not until two months later, well over a year after most of northern undertakings had got well under way, that Canada appointed a special Commissioner for Defence Projects in the north-west.

The most obvious result of the defence rampage in the north was its cost. The Alaska Highway, as the soldiers had predicted, was unimportant as a military road. Most of the traffic on the North Atlantic Air Ferry to England flew from Gander, Stephenville and Goose Bay, bases which the Canadians had already developed and not along the far northern routes which had so excited the over-heated imagination of the credulous La Guardia. A huge amount of money was expended on enterprises which were doubtfully useful, or, in the case of Canol, corruptly mismanaged; and, in the end, Canada had to bear the major expense of works whose value she had questioned from the start. The Alaska Highway was returned free of charge; but Canada agreed to pay back the United States for all construction of "permanent value" on the North-West Staging Route and the North Atlantic Ferry. The bill, which, oddly enough, in view of the remoteness of the northeastern installations came to over 80% of the total expenditure, was about $62 million.[36] It was a big price to pay for the recovery of the nation's own property; and Canadian possession, though regained, was never so unquali-fied and secure as before the war. The Americans had taken a good big bite, nearly free of charge, out of the Canadian north, and thereafter they never lost their appetite for more.

V

All these elaborate and costly preparations were undertaken as the necessary means of the defeat of the Axis powers in Europe and the Pacific. The Anglo-American leaders had agreed that the Allies must seek a victory in Europe first, but the grand strategy of the proposed attack on Hitler's Germany remained unsettled for more than the first half of 1942. The Russians and the Americans were urging a massive assault across the Channel and the opening of a second front on the grand scale in northwest Europe. The British preferred to develop and exploit their existing commitment in the Mediterranean and North Africa. They did not believe that the build-up of Allied men and equipment was yet sufficient to launch a major attack on occupied France; but in the meantime they were prepared to undertake raids, larger or smaller in size, which would provide valuable battle experi-ence for the massive invasion of the future and, at the same time, help to appease the urgent exhortations of Stalin. Dieppe, the "poor man's Monte

Carlo," once a fashionable summer resort whose fortunes had sadly declined, was chosen mainly because it was a considerable port, and the immediate acquisition of a port was at that time considered essential to a successful invasion of the continent. The Canadian civil and military leaders, as well as the Canadian press and people, had been clamouring for the active employment of their armed forces. Wasn't a raid on Dieppe the perfect answer?

The Chief of Combined Operations, Lord Louis Mountbatten, his Chief of Staff, and Lieutenant-General Bernard Montgomery were the principal authors of the plan for the Dieppe raid. Long before the Canadians ever set eyes on it, its main features – and also its fatal defects – had all been decided upon. It provided, not only for flank attacks at some distance from Dieppe on either side, but also for a frontal assault on the town itself, with its wide open sandy beach, high sea wall, and towering headlands on either side. Only an overwhelming superiority of fire power, supplied by the Royal Navy and Bomber Command, could possibly have justified the suicidal gamble of this direct attack; but, as the plan developed, it became increasingly clear that an overwhelming superiority of fire power was precisely what the raid was not going to be given. The heavy guns of one or two capital ships outside Dieppe harbour could have wrecked the defences of the town in short order; but the First Sea Lord, Sir Dudley Pound, was at that time so totally opposed to risking his precious vessels in the narrow waters of the Channel that apparently nobody ever plucked up enough courage to ask for adequate naval support; and, as a result, eight small destroyers were all that were provided.[37] A massive bombing attack was, it was true, part of the original plan; but Sir Arthur Harris, the new fighting head of Bomber Command, who nursed a fanatical belief in the efficacy of "strategic" bombing over Germany, did not want to spare planes for "useless sideshows"; and the Dieppe planners themselves, who were troubled by the difficulties and uncertainties of a preliminary air bombardment, did not press the issue.[38] There would be no capital ships and no heavy bombers in the Dieppe raid. The men of the Second Canadian Division and the British Commandos would have to make their desperate and suicidal attack without adequate support and against German defences which had been systematically improved over the previous few months.

The four flank attacks were planned to go in on August 19, 1942 at 4:50 a.m., just before the first light of dawn began to qualify the total darkness. The moment of impact was still an hour away when the bad luck began, and soon the elaborate specifications of time and place began to break apart under the shattering pressure of accidents and miscalculations. In the eastern sector, on the left flank of the Anglo-Canadian attack, the result was almost unrelieved calamity. The Commando forces destined for the outer target unfortunately ran into a small German convoy, had to give battle, and only a few of the landing craft reached their destination. The Royal Regiment of Canada, put down half an hour late in front of the second eastern objective, a small village set in what was little more than a crack in the ramparts of cliff, met a murderous reception from the fully alerted Germans. West of Dieppe, on the right flank of the raid, the desperate venture had rather better fortune. The Commandos on the far right completely achieved their objective; but the South Saskatchewan Regiment and the Cameron Highlanders of Canada, landed late and inaccurately before their inner target, another small village overshadowed by massive cliffs, were much less successful. In the centre, at Dieppe itself, where the bulk of the Canadians – the Royal Hamilton Light Infantry, the Essex Scottish, the Fusiliers Mont-Royal and the Calgary Tank Regiment – were concentrated, the weight of the catastrophe matched the magnitude of the vain effort. From the high headlands on either side, from closer gun emplacements and pill boxes, the Germans rained a devastating fire on the invaders. The Canadians were pinned down on the beach before they could cut the wire entanglements, climb the sea wall, and win their way into the town. Twenty-nine tanks were landed, but only half of these gained the promenade, only to discover that German road blocks barred their further advance. By nine o'clock, only four hours after the raid had begun, the commanders were forced to admit its complete defeat and the strenuous, harassed, and sanguinary struggle for evacuation began.

Of the nearly 5000 Canadians who set out from the English Channel ports on their doomed mission to Dieppe, only about 2200 returned. Of these approximately 1000 had never landed, 600 were wounded, and another 600, grimy, shaken, and exhausted, got back with whole skins.[39] Well over half of the entire force were left behind, many lying dead on the beaches or floating in the water, and nearly 1900 in German hands as prisoners of war. Canadian losses exceeded British and American losses combined by a good deal more than three to one and constituted about 68% of the entire Canadian manpower engaged.[40] There was no doubt whatever that the Canadians had borne the brunt of that terrible day; but there was also no doubt that, initially at least, the Royal Navy, the Royal Air Force, and the American Rangers got the lion's share of the credit. Only fifty American Rangers took part in the raid; but the American newspapers, almost beside themselves with excitement at the news of this first engagement of American ground forces, multiplied their numbers in geometrical progression and magnified their exploits to epic proportions. The more experienced and knowledgeable British newspapers ought to have done better, but they lavished such quantities of praise on the navy, the R.A.F and the Commandos that there was hardly space to acknowledge the mere presence of the Second Canadian Division. And it was not until September that Churchill belatedly tried to set the record straight.

VI

The war had now lasted three years; and, in a variety of ways it had affected the life of civilian Canada much more seriously than the First World War had ever done. Canada, of course, was never called upon to endure the state of siege which afflicted England. Despite the panic fears which convulsed British Columbia in the early months of 1942, no bombs fell on Canadian cities. No civilian lives were lost through "enemy action" and the rubble of shattered shops and houses never littered the streets. Life went on; but a good many human activities, except those directly or indirectly related to the war, were arrested or slowed down to a tedious routine. People stayed at home simply because it was very difficult to leave it. Travel to Europe or the West Indies was out of the question; gasoline rationing and foreign exchange regulations cut down winter holidays in Florida, California, or British Columbia. Home surroundings not only grew tiresomely familiar but also by degrees increasingly shabby. The newest houses were likely to have been built before 1929, and household equipment slowly deteriorated as the supply of new furnaces, stoves, washers and refrigerators began to decline. People made do with their old motor cars because the annual autumnal display of new models ceased and for two years the manufacture of passenger automobiles was completely suspended. The price ceiling was fairly successful in holding down costs of food and clothing, but some articles were rationed, others were very scarce, and the range and quality of manufactures obviously suffered. Imports from abroad − fashionable clothes, exotic foods, wines, liqueurs and aperitifs − largely disappeared. Mackenzie King, who had strong puritanical tendencies, was anxious to impose restrictions on the consumption of "alcoholic beverages" as another meritorious sacrifice in aid of the war effort; and the quantity and strength of both spirits and wine were substantially reduced, and for a while even the supply of beer was cut down by 10%.[41]

The Canadians who stayed at home led a drab, circumscribed, monotonous existence, somewhat akin to the dismal life they had lived during the Depression, and yet significantly different in several ways. The austerities and privations of the Second World War were quite evidently the common portion of everybody and not simply, as during the Depression, the wretched lot of the jobless poor. The very fact that the state had been able to impose this rough equality of wartime upon the entire population seemed to many people a demonstration of the real possibility of social justice in the post-war world. The generation that fought the First World War had never felt this confidence in the practical possibilities of the future; but the economic and social assumptions and the political fears and inexperience that had inhibited the men and women of 1914-18 no longer governed their successors a quarter-century later. Democratic socialism, even Soviet communism, had gained a new credibility or lost much of their former terror. The Russians were no longer political and moral outcasts, but invaluable allies upon whose military might the ultimate victory of the western democracies would very largely depend. In England, the publication of Sir William Beveridge's vast comprehensive report, *Social Insurance and Allied Services*, held out the very real hope that a general system of welfare services was possible within a democratic state and a free enterprise economy.

The manifest change in the character of the Canadian state was also full of promise for the future. The hesitating, fumbling authority of 1914-1918 which had conscripted men, not wealth, and had failed to reach its professed aim of stopping hoarding, profiteering, and rapidly rising prices, had utterly vanished. It had been replaced by a strangely new kind of government which was enforcing administrative controls with a new efficiency, providing new social benefits, and imposing steeply progressive income taxes in order to collect the huge revenues necessary for national purposes on a large scale. Most of these new controls and social welfare increases grew out of the necessities of the war; but others had an earlier origin, in the lessons of the Depression and the recommendations of the Royal Commission on Dominion-Provincial Relations. Duplessis would never have agreed to grant authority to the federal government to establish an unemployment insurance fund; but Godbout, who had defeated Duplessis in 1939 with the powerful help of the federal ministers from Quebec, proved much more accommodating; and unemployment insurance, legalized by a constitutional amendment of 1940, was introduced in 1942. The national welfare system was still in a very rudimentary and unfinished state, but it was certain to grow, for all contemporary influences, domestic and external, were pushing towards its completion.

The young were quickest to accept the belief that self-reliance, personal responsibility, and free enterprise were not enough in themselves, and that collective action could and should create a far more stable and equitable society. By the time the war reached its half-way mark in 1942-43, these convictions were spreading rapidly through most age levels of Canadians. Inevitably this new outlook changed their conception of the purpose and function of government and as a result their attitude to the policies and programmes of Canadian political parties. The C.C.F. was the avowed champion of socialism and ever since the convention of 1919 the Liberals had also posed as ardent social reformers. The party that looked least likely to become the zealous builder of the new welfare state was undoubtedly the Conservative Party. Its new leader, Meighen, had been denounced as the very embodiment of capitalist reaction in the York South by-election. But Meighen had been defeated, had refused to accept the ordeal of another by-election, and quickly tired of his humiliating position as a party leader without a seat in Parliament. He decided to call a national convention in the autumn of 1942 and to resign the leadership, and this turned out to be a decisive event in the history of the Conservative Party.

A group of Tory malcontents, led by J.M. Macdonnell, believed that their party was hopelessly out of touch with the modern Canadian electorate and that its policies must be radically revised at the approaching national convention. They were convinced also that the radical revision could not be successfully carried through unless its main principles had been hammered out in advance at a preliminary conference, attended only by the party "laymen" with fresh views and new ideas, a conference from which the "professionals," the existing Tory M.P.'s, would be excluded. Early in September about 150 of the party faithful, non-commissioned officers rather than strictly rank-and-file soldiers, met at Trinity College School, Port Hope, Ontario.[42] Nobody could have accused the gathering of infidelity to historic Conservative dogmas; free enterprise in industry and conscription for general service in wartime were stoutly affirmed. Yet the conference showed more interest and spent much more time on the issues of the present and future than on those of the past. The delegates talked in a large-hearted, open-handed way about low-cost government housing, debt adjustment for western farmers and collective bargaining for labour. Every Canadian, they decided, ought to be provided with "a gainful occupation and sufficient income to maintain himself and a family." Every Canadian must also, it seemed, be supported, through all the possible misfortunes of life, by a broad range of social services, including – and this was their most ambitious proposal – a national contributory system of medical care.[43]

This, Meighen declared contemptuously when he saw the social security resolution, was "flagrant and mischievous dishonesty." [44] Yet Meighen, though he might have been highly disconcerted if he had realized it at the time, was moving in the same direction as the "Port Hopefuls." He had become firmly convinced that the only hope for the future of the Conservative Party lay in the agrarian West, in that last large body of natural Conservatives, the western farmers. The next leader of the Conservative Party, he felt certain, must be a man who could win and keep the support of western agriculture, and he had fixed upon John Bracken, the Farmer-Progressive leader in Manitoba, as the most suitable candidate for the post.[45] Bracken was a drab, prosaic, taciturn man, a good routine administrator, though an indifferent speaker, who had managed to keep himself and his party in power in Manitoba for over twenty years. Meighen had failed to induce him to seek the Tory leadership a year earlier, and ironically enough, when the Conservative convention met in Winnipeg in December, 1942, it was the reforming programme of the "Port Hopefuls" and not Meighen's flattering urgings which finally persuaded him to enter the leadership race. He agreed to become a candidate, but on two conditions: the convention must adopt in advance a platform based on the Port Hope programme and change the party's name to Progressive-Conservative. The first condition was accepted readily enough, but the convention indignantly refused to change the party's name at the dictation of a man who was not even one of its members yet. The realization that he would have to run as a plain unhyphenated Conservative threw Bracken into an agony of indecision and it was literally at the very last minute that his nomination papers were signed and submitted. He was elected on the second ballot, and then the convention found release from its long tension in changing the party's name by acclamation to Progressive-Conservative.[46]

The Conservatives had tried to modernize their party policies in the hope of gaining some advantage from the mounting popularity of state control and social welfare. The C.C.F., on the other hand, had no need to make any changes at all. Ever since 1933 the party had possessed, in the Regina Manifesto, a satisfactory basic statement of socialist principles, and, as a natural result, the changing intellectual fashions of wartime seemed likely to have a far more immediate effect on the C.C.F. than on the rechristened Progressive-Conservatives. It was the war, in fact, which rescued the C.C.F. from rapidly approaching political oblivion. By 1939, the party had won only a very few places, distributed among the legislatures of four provinces, Ontario, Manitoba, Saskatchewan and British Columbia; it had gained scarcely more than a handful of seats in the House of Commons at Ottawa; and its percentage of the popular vote in both federal and provincial elections had been consistently small.[47] The C.C.F. had declined into a pathetic little group of pious sectaries, smugly convinced of their exclusive possession of the truth about society, and tediously mumbling over a set of worn-out dogmas which seemed as irrelevant to the real needs and interests of modern Canadians as the tenets of an early Christian heresy.[48] The war changed all this. It revived the millenary belief in the possibility of a more prosperous and equitable post-war world. It brought conviction to many that governments, which had shown such increasing expertise and efficiency in fighting the war, would be equally capable of saving the peace and building the just society of the future.

Above all, by hastening industrialization and urbanization, particularly in Ontario, the war rapidly increased the size of the very class, the industrial workers, who would likely benefit most from a collectivist welfare state and might be induced to support it politically. Trade union membership, about 360,000 strong in 1939, nearly doubled itself by 1943; and, as it gained in numbers, it also increased in militancy.[49] The radical industrial unions – miners, steelworkers, autoworkers and packing-house workers – expelled from the stiffly conservative Trades and Labour Congress of Canada, immediately began negotiations with what up to that time had been the very junior Canadian labour organization, the All-Canadian Congress of Labour; and in 1940, the two bodies united to form a new and far stronger national association, the Canadian Congress of Labour. Many of its principal leaders were convinced socialists ready to work actively with the C.C.F.; they carried many of the rank and file of the radical unions with them; and from these, and other less indentifiable souces, the party's membership began to grow.[50] Its nearly empty war chest grew a little heavier, and victory in the York South by-election improved its campaigning techniques and gave it experience and confidence. Party organization altered radically. In the federal field, M.J. Coldwell succeeded the founder, J.S. Woodsworth, as national president and parliamentary leader; and in Ontario, the C.C.F. convention did what it ought to have done years before, and elected a provincial leader, a youngish barrister, E.B. Jolliffe.

Fifteen months later, in August, 1943, after a strenuous and successful recruiting and organizing campaign throughout Ontario, the rejuvenated party was faced with an exceptionally inviting electoral opportunity. The sudden, unexpected retirement of Mitchell Hepburn, who fewer than ten years ago had led the Liberal Party to its astonishing victory, marked the beginning of the rapid disintegration of Ontario Liberalism. It seemed almost certain that the Liberals would be defeated in the general election of August, 1943, but it was by no means so clear who would emerge from the contest as the victor. The Conservatives had made a remarkable recovery under their new leader, George Drew, a handsome and attractive man who, though considerably older than Jolliffe, was still on the right side of fifty. Drew was a ready convert to the new Progressive-Conservatism which John Bracken and the "Port Hopefuls" had fashioned during the previous autumn; and his platform in the 1943 election, which dealt spaciously with such fashionable issues as slum clearance, public housing, and labour legislation, transcended all possible rival promises by simply and comprehensively offering "economic and social security from the cradle to the grave."[51] To voters who were not doctrinaire socialists the difference between the C.C.F. and the Conservative programmes did not appear great, and the results of the election reflected this basic similarity. The Conservatives won 38 seats, the C.C.F. captured 34, and the Liberals, who had held a large majority in the previous house, managed to retain only 15.[52] The dramatic rise of the C.C.F., which in the previous legislature had not been represented by even a single member, brought immense encouragement to the party faithful; but their jubilation was warped by the chagrin of realizing that they had missed – and very narrowly missed – the honour of becoming the first socialist government in Canada.

Both Jolliffe and Drew had profited politically from the advocacy of the welfare state; but it was Mackenzie King's adoption of the cause of social security which demonstrated its future electoral value beyond all doubt or question. King, whose ear was always attentively cocked to the slightest tremors in the body politic, was quickly conscious of the expanding social expectations of wartime and of the popular interest in the Beveridge Report. In December, 1942, when he visited Roosevelt in Washington, the two veteran manipulators of public opinion solemnly weighed the fashionable intellectual trends of the time. "The thought of insurance from the cradle to the grave," said the President reflectively. "That seems to be a line that will appeal. You and I should take that up strongly."[53] King needed no urging. He complacently decided that there was nothing really new and original in the Beveridge Report at all, and that his own book, *Industry and Humanity*, published in 1918, contained "pretty much the whole programme that now is being suggested for post-war purposes."[54] In short, he and not Beveridge was the real precursor of the post-war welfare state in Canada. The fact that in the quarter century since the publication of *Industry and Humanity*, he had done little or nothing to implement its proposals did not trouble him in the least. Obviously the time for action was now when the rising hopes of a better post-war world were steadily piling up the votes of future general elections! Less than two months after he had had his cosy little chat with Roosevelt, on January 28, 1943, the Speech from the Throne announced "a charter of social security for the whole of Canada."[55] *Industry and Humanity*, King felt strongly, ought to be regarded as a manual or guidebook to the approaching social revolution; but, on reflection, he decided that it would perhaps be wiser to update it a little. Dr. Leonard Marsh, a scholar of impeccable socialist credentials, who had been one of the founding fathers of the C.C.F., was invited to prepare a social welfare scheme for Canada, and in a few weeks he produced a presentable adaptation of Beveridge principles to Canadian conditions.

VII

In the meantime, while the Canadian welfare state gained substance and grew in popularity, the war had entered a new and much more successful phase. The tragedy of Dieppe was a belated incident in an earlier period of defeat and frustration. The prolonged debate over Anglo-American strategy was drawing to a close, and already the war's tides of fortune had begun to flow the other way. In North Africa, Rommel's last attempt at a breakthrough to Alexandria failed, and in November, 1942, Montgomery won the battle of El Alamein. A few days later, Allied forces landed in French North Africa. The war in the Mediterranean had now become a Joint Anglo-American enterprise, and the first nine months of 1943 saw the defeat of the Germans in Tunisia, the successful attack on Sicily, and the invasion of southern Italy. From then on, the Allied war machine rolled forward slowly, against skilled and powerful opposition, but with gradually increasing momentum.

In 1942-43, the Canadian war effort attained its maximum. Nearly a million Canadians had volunteered for general service in the three divisions of Canada's armed forces, and the men who directed and led this formidable array were determined that it must achieve two great aims. In the first place, and above all else, they intended to make a notable contribution to the winning of the war. They also hoped – though this was clearly a secondary and subordinate aspiration – to make that contribution in such a way as to gain recognition for Canada as a separate and distinct Allied power . There can be no doubt that the first of these objects was realized, but it is equally plain that the second was not. The Canadians did not win their desired recognition as an independent national fighting force partly because they themselves did not seek it with sufficient thoroughness and consistency, and partly because the great western powers, Britain and the United States, for their own political purposes, found it hard to concede.

Oddly enough, it was the Royal Canadian Navy, the smallest and most neglected of the three services, which came closest to achieving a certain nominal autonomy of command. After the Churchill-Roosevelt meeting at Placentia Bay in August, 1941, when the United States had agreed to assist in the protection of British shipping in the western Atlantic, the Canadian escort force, based in Newfoundland, had come under American command. Only four months later, the United States was itself at war; the American naval presence in the North Atlantic grew negligible as the bulk of its ships were transferred to the Pacific, and by the autumn of 1942, the United States was contributing only about 2% of the convoy fleet. Great Britain and Canada, which divided the whole burden of the escort duty nearly equally between them, now began to press for a change in the system of command. Admiral King, the American Chief of Naval Staff, resisted these overtures, apparently for no better reason than his instinctive assumption that in wartime everything military in or around North America, however much or little the United States had to do with it, ought to come under American jurisdiction. This magisterial resistance failed to silence Admiral Percy W. Nelles, the Canadian Chief of Naval Staff; and finally, at Admiral King's own suggestion, an Atlantic Convoy Conference met in Washington in March, 1943, and set up the Canadian North-West Atlantic Command.[56] This arrangement gave the Royal Canadian Navy responsibility for convoys north of New York City and west of the 47th meridian, a line which ran about seven hundred miles out from Halifax and enclosed an area admittedly not very large, but of vital importance.

The struggle against the U-boats, which Churchill called "the Battle of the Atlantic," was a desperate combat which continued for nearly the first four years of the war, with alternating spurts of brilliant success and stretches of devastating losses. Canadian sailors were as devoted and intrepid as any on the Atlantic. Canadian ships were either built in England, or built in Canada according to British specifications, with equipment dependent on

British technical information. The war hastened technical invention and change in Great Britain, but the new devices were not always transferred to Canada as soon as they ought to have been, and the Canadian navy was slow in getting the latest radar improvements as well as that terrifying engine of destruction the "hedgehog," which sprayed its bombs over 200 yards in advance of its own ship.[57] By the summer of 1942, the equipment of many Canadian vessels had lagged noticeably behind that of the British; and it was at this vulnerable moment that the U-boats renewed their attacks in Canadian waters with even greater daring and intensity. Two bold and resourceful German commanders, Thurmann and Hartwig, carried the offensive up the Gulf of St. Lawrence and into the river, scattering destruction everywhere in their wake.[58] In October, a big convoy under Canadian protection lost as many as fifteen ships; and late in December, in the midst of a howling gale, a huge wolf-pack of U-boats closed in on a convoy of forty-four merchantmen and their Canadian escorts and left behind them a kill of fourteen ships.[59] All through the winter of 1942-43, a winter of bitter weather and savage storms, the war of attrition continued on the North Atlantic. It was not until the summer of 1943 that a vast increase in the Allied escort fleet and the vigorous support of Allied bombers finally overcame the worst of the U-boat menace.

The Royal Canadian Air Force, with a strength at least two-and-a-half times that of the Royal Canadian Navy, never achieved a comparable public recognition and independent command. It never really escaped from the prison of the British Commonwealth Air Training Plan, a project organized on strictly colonial lines, into which it had been securely locked by King. The process of "Canadianization," constantly urged forward by C.G. Power, the Minister for Air, and by the Canadian Air Marshals in Ottawa and London, made very slow and doubtful progress. In 1942, ten more R.C.A.F. squadrons were added to the twenty-four whose formation had been authorized by the Ralston-Sinclair agreement of January, 1941, and a Canadian bomber group also came into existence; but, as a proof of "Canadianization," these achievements were illusory. R.A.F. aircrew and a surprisingly large number of R.A.F. officers found places in the R.C.A.F., just as R.C.A.F. aircrew were scattered through the R.A.F. There was virtually nothing to distinguish the Canadian squadrons from their British associates, and in the British newspapers the Canadian contribution to the raids over Germany remained strictly anonymous. Canadian planes did what British Bomber Command told them to; and when eight R.C.A.F. squadrons were ordered to take part in the Dieppe raid, nobody thought it necessary, or even polite, to give Edwards, the Canadian Air Marshal in London, advance notice of the fact.[60]

No substantial changes were ever made. Edwards' repeated efforts at reform resulted merely in the annoyed dislike of his British colleagues. He even went so far as to complain to the British Air Ministry, and Sir Charles Portal, British Chief of Staff, intervened. It all came to nothing or next to nothing. In January, 1943, the Canadian Cabinet finally decided to do what it ought to have done over three years earlier. It announced in Parliament that it would henceforth defray the entire cost of equipping and maintaining the thirty-five R.C.A.F. squadrons as well as the pay and allowances of all Canadian aircrews serving in the R.A.F. In hard financial terms, the Canadian Air Force had now become a Canadian service, wholly supported by the Canadian government and people.[61] If this obligation had been accepted three years earlier, the R.C.A.F. might have become a national force in its own right. But it was now too late. The R.C.A.F. in England and Europe never became an autonomous, integrated service; it was never assigned to the support of the Canadian Army in the battles of northwest Europe. Nearly 60% of Canadian aircrew overseas were serving with the R.A.F. in the summer of 1944, and, at the beginning of 1945, Canadians made up a quarter of the aircrew in British Bomber Command.[62]

During the last months of 1942 and the first of 1943, while the Canadian airmen played their steady part in the bombing of Germany, the Canadian Army remained in England, waiting patiently without any clear idea of when or where it was likely to be employed again. The Canadian government was, of course, excluded from the crucial Anglo-American conferences which plotted the grand strategy of the future; and it knew little of the great dispute between Churchill and the British, who wished to exploit the North African successes with an attack on Italy, and Marshall and the Americans, who were determined to subordinate all other Allied military efforts to the supreme enterprise of the invasion of northwest Europe. All the Canadians learned of the crucial decisions reached at these meetings was contained in the reticent accounts Churchill sent Mackenzie King; and Churchill's report of the Casablanca Conference of January, 1943, which decided on the invasion of Sicily, spoke merely of "further amphibious operations on a large scale."[63] It was becoming clear that, pending the great assault on northwest Europe, the Mediterranean was likely to become an important theatre of war; and once again governmental and popular pressure for the employment of the Canadian Army began to mount. Ralston, Stuart, Chief of General Staff, and even King, who had somehow reached the curious conclusion that fighting in Italy would be less sanguinary than fighting in France, now pleaded for the dispatch of a Canadian force to the south. It was an impressive chorus of voices, with one very discordant note. A.G.L. McNaughton, Commander of the First Canadian Army, significantly did not wish to press for the transference of the Canadians to any particular theatre "merely to satisfy a desire for activity."[64]

The first Canadian Infantry Division and the first Canadian Tank Brigade, under the command of the brilliant General Guy Simonds, took part in the assault on Sicily on July 9, 1943, although General Eisenhower saw fit to omit all mention of their presence in his first communiques. Two months' hard fighting in the rugged terrain of Sicily might have seemed enough to satisfy the importunate Canadian demand for action, but instead it merely stimulated the authorities' appetite for more. In August, while the fighting was still going on in Sicily, both Ralston and King approached Churchill and Sir Alan Brooke, the British Chief of General Staff, with the proposal that additional Canadian forces, sufficient to form a corps, be sent to Italy. The Quebec Conference finally reached a firm decision to invade continental Italy, but the approaching Italian campaign was relegated, before it had ever begun, to a secondary and inferior status. The great Second Front in north-west Europe, for which it had first been assumed that the Canadian Army was waiting, was certain to be the major Allied effort of the war; but the Second Front, now scheduled for June, 1944, was still nine months away. The impatient Canadians now redoubled their importunate appeals for a Canadian Corps in Italy, and at last the High Command reluctantly gave way. It was a purely political decision and grumblingly accepted as such. The commanders in the Mediterranean disliked it. They disliked it still more when they discovered, with surprise and annoyance, that it was an armoured, not an infantry division, that the Canadians had chosen to send. Both Eisenhower and Alexander protested that they already had more armour than they needed in Italy.[65]

The establishment of the First Canadian Corps in Italy had profound and far-reaching consequences. It meant the division of the First Canadian Army and it led to the resignation of the man who had been its real creator, General A.G.L. McNaughton. McNaughton was opposed in principle to what he called "the dispersion of the Army." "The important thing for Canada at the end of the war," he told Ralston and Stuart emphatically "was to have the Army together under the control of a Canadian."[66] The departure of a single division to Sicily did not, in his view, constitute "dispersion"; but the transference of the whole First Canadian Corps to Italy seemed crucially divisive to him, and he went so far as to suggest that if this dangerous partition were made, "it would be wise to put someone in control who believed in it."[67] He realized that this serious disagreement with his own government would probably weaken his position as commander; but he did not suspect that it was also threatened, from quite a different quarter, and on other, but equally important grounds. Sir Alan Brooke, the Chief of the Imperial General Staff and Sir Bernard Paget, who was at first expected to command the army group of which the First Canadian Army was to form a part in the invasion of northwest Europe, had both come to the conclusion that McNaughton, while a first-rate scientific soldier, would not make a good commander in the field.[68] Ralston's and Stuart's attempt to communicate this shattering judgement to McNaughton wounded the general deeply and left him suspicious and resentful. He jumped to the conclusion that the initiative for his dismissal had come, not from the British but from the Canadians, and that Ralston, whose support he thought he deserved, had in fact betrayed him. A long and painful series of angry telegrams and sullen interviews ended in December, 1943, with McNaughton's resignation on grounds of ill health.

The departure of the First Canadian Corps to Italy did not, as had been feared at first, entail the break-up of the Canadian Army organization in England. The First Canadian Army became a composite force which included British, Dutch, Belgian and Polish units, as well as the Second Canadian Corps. In Italy, the Eighth British Army, of which the First Canadian Corps formed a part, was similarly made up of several different national formations. The Canadians fought in two widely separated theatres, and often side by side with strangers; but in both Italy and northwest France they suffered equally heavy losses during the hard fighting in the summer of 1944. Although the Second Canadian Corps had escaped fairly lightly in the early advance of the Normandy beachhead, the savage battles around Falaise at the beginning of August were very costly; and in Italy, at the end of the same month, the First Corps faced perhaps the hardest task of the whole Italian campaign, the assault on the German line that stretched from Pisa to Rimini, the "Gothic Line." The Allied forces in Italy had been seriously weakened first to strengthen the Normandy invasion, and secondly, and even more disastrously, to mount that gratuitous exhibition, the attack on the Mediterranean coast of France, which turned out to be little more than a tank parade up the Rhone River valley. Churchill and the British commanders in the Mediterranean opposed this theatrical exercise as long as possible; but Roosevelt, for reasons which, as usual, derived in large measure from domestic American politics, finally insisted. The argument was long and occasionally acrimonious; but at no time were the Canadian authorities consulted, or even informed about the strategical considerations involved.[69] Seven divisions left Italy for the south of France. Yet the attack on the Gothic Line by badly depleted forces went in at the end of August; and during the next month the Canadians suffered heavier casualties than in any other period of comparable length in the entire Italian campaign.

It was not until the middle of October that the Canadian government learned the full extent and the significance of these losses. Canada, with every other Allied country, was feeling increasingly hopeful during the summer of 1944. After the sudden enlargement of the Normandy bridgehead, the war seemed to be going very well indeed, and late in August came the liberation of Paris. Canadians began to indulge in the hope of victory before the end of the year; they grew increasingly interested in the prospects of the post-war world, and the passage of the Family Allowance Bill became the most important parliamentary event of that summer.

CHAPTER 5

The Coming of the Planners

I

"To tell the country that everyone was to get a family allowance," King wrote disgustedly in October, 1943, "was sheer folly."[1] The "charter of social security for Canada," which had been announced with such a fanfare of trumpets nine months earlier, was still blank of concrete particulars; but family allowances, as the first of the benefits of the new welfare state, looked very questionable indeed in King's eyes. He had at first a strong old-fashioned belief that, if money concessions were to be given at all, they ought to take the form of tax exemptions rather than of outright grants from the Treasury. Only gradually did he begin to perceive the special political advantages of family allowances. Health insurance, he felt convinced, must be a joint federal-provincial undertaking which could be introduced only after long and exasperating negotiations with the provinces. Family allowances were a better, much easier way to begin. The big Liberal majority could readily push the legislation through the next session of Parliament in good time for the approaching general election. It all looked both politically simple and politically profitable; and King, a reluctant convert, made up for the delay by the zeal of his new-found faith. In January, 1944, when the various items in the programme for the new session came before the Cabinet, he manoeuvred the discussion so as to give the strong advocates of family allowances the first chance to speak.[2] Later, when the matter came up at the Liberal caucus and Fulford, the imprudent member for Brockville, argued that the bill would give a bonus to the prolific French Canadians at the expense of the rest of the population, King worked himself up into a great state of moral indignation. He gave Fulford a severe lecture. His own Liberalism – in contrast to Fulford's – was, he announced, "based on the belief that in the sight of God every soul was precious."[3]

The Family Allowances Bill was only the most conspicuous of a series of projects which made up the Liberal post-war plan for Canada. They were intended both to honour the obligations of the past and to grasp the opportunities of the future: and they were so numerous, complex, and ambitious that they required the reorganization of the Cabinet and the creation of several new departments of government. The Ministry of Veterans Affairs was set up to dispense a variety of benefits to the soldiers, sailors, and airmen, who numbered nearly a million and who would, it was hoped, be returning soon. The government – and the nation – were anxious to treat the veterans of the Second World War far more generously then those of the First had been treated; and it was also determined that the Canada to which they returned would be far more economically busy and socially secure than it had been in the 1920's. The task of promoting a high and steady level of employment and income was entrusted to this Ministry of Reconstruction; and the third of the new departments, the Ministry of National Health and Welfare, took over the rapidly growing social welfare system. King procrastinated in his usual hesitating, uncertain way before naming the three new departmental heads. Howe, the former Minister of Munitions and Supply, was appropriately given Reconstruction. Veterans Affairs went to Ian MacKenzie, an old colleague for whom King had a sentimental, yet discerning, affection. Brooke Claxton, a tall, shambling, rather maladroit Montrealer, who had worked hard on planning the social security programme, was finally awarded the portfolio of National Health and Welfare.

On July 25, when King introduced the Family Allowances Bill, he ended his elaborate speech with a provocation – and a threat. Bracken, the new Progressive-Conservative leader, who had not yet found a seat in Parliament, could obviously not take part in the debate that followed, but he had already made his own very provocative contribution outside the House. He had converted the scandalous charge which George Fulford had voiced in the privacy of the Liberal caucus into an open denunciation of the Liberal government and its leader. The Family Allowances Bill, he declared, was "legal bribery" for prolific French Canada. The crisp phrase, unlike Bracken's usual commonplace style, infuriated King; and his private awareness of the political benefit which the bill would unquestionably bring in Quebec stoked the fires of his fury. "I wish," he announced angrily, "the leader who made that statement in the name of his party were on the floor of the House at the moment."[4]

"There are others who will answer for him," a Progressive-Conservative interjected quickly. This interruption only increased King's rage.

"If anyone who answers for him," he threatened, "repeats the statement he has made, I shall immediately ask Mr. Speaker to ask him to withdraw the statement and he will be obliged to withdraw it."[5]

At first it looked as if the Progressive-Conservatives would be very unlikely to take up King's taunting challenge. They were certainly leaderless and at times looked like a crushed and beaten party. For nearly ten years now, they had numbered only thirty-nine, or about 16% of a House of 245 members. Gordon Graydon, House Leader in Bracken's absence, was a competent but not a vigorous politician: and John Diefenbaker, with his hectoring courtroom manner, was one of the few good speakers on the Tory side. The long, confident rows of Liberals, as if incited by the very weakness of their opponents, had acquired the habit of interrupting, harrying, and ridiculing them on every opportunity. It took courage and resource to oppose the passing of a Liberal measure with any effectiveness; and although there were a few doubts and some dissent expressed in caucus, the Conservatives had not the slightest intention of mounting a determined resistance to the bill.[6] The Opposition, Graydon announced at once, gave its whole-hearted support to the aim of raising the standard of family life in Canada, and questioned the bill only as a method of achieving it.[7] "We believe in social legislation . . . ." Diefenbaker reminded the House. "No political party has a monopoly in that direction."[8] He attacked the constitutionality of the measure and Graydon criticized it as the "mass treatment" of a need which was not felt equally by all families. The only Progressive-Conservative who opposed the bill with any real conviction was the member for Parkdale, Dr. Herbert A. Bruce; but Bruce left Ottawa for Toronto before the debate on the second reading was concluded; and when the division came, not a single negative vote was recorded.

The member for Parkdale was an able surgeon who had had a distinguished career, and who, despite his short stature, presented a dignified appearance to the world. His features were fine and regular, his crisp white hair was carefully arranged; he was always elegantly garbed and carried about him a distinctly patrician air. His practice had, of course, brought him a great deal of money; but he had given as much of his time to public causes and poor patients as he had to the real and fancied ailments of the very rich.[9] He had served as a consulting surgeon to the British armies in France through most of the First World War. As Lieutenant-Governor of Ontario, he had inspired the appointment of a special committee to investigate slum clearance and housing in Toronto; and at Ottawa, after his election to the House of Commons, he had been an active and useful member of its advisory committee on health insurance. It was out of this varied experience that he derived his basic objection to the Family Allowances Bill. He believed that the most effective social security system must be based on services, not money grants. Grants might be suitable in some cases, he admitted, "but I am opposed to giving out these grants indiscriminately."[10]

King's personal dislikes were frequent and fervent; and the member for Parkdale, with his wealth, his air of distinction, and his great reputation in a difficult art which had nothing whatever to do with politics, may have irked the hypersensitive Prime Minister. He may have been annoyed that no member of the Opposition had as yet taken up his challenge to repeat Bracken's words from the floor of the House. At all events, he now made what can be interpreted only as a deliberate attempt to goad Bruce into angry utterance.

"I myself think," he observed ironically, "it is fortunate we have the honourable member for Parkdale in this House because he does belong so obviously to a past era."[11]

Bruce, he suggested, was in spirit at least a typical representative of the early nineteenth century English landed gentry and his social attitudes were perfectly expressed in the quatrain in Dickens's *The Chimes*, from which he quoted two lines.

"Bless the squire and his relations...
And always know our proper stations."

Bruce was absent at the time, but this verbal caricature stung him as much in private as it would have done had he heard it with his own ears. He felt that he was bound to reply, and when he got back to Ottawa, he made a rather laboured but not ineffective comparison of his own and King's services to the poor and unfortunate. He kept his defiance of the autocrat of the Nineteenth Parliament to the very end.

"I am not intimidated," he stated firmly, "by the threat the Prime Minister has made and I now declare that this measure is a bribe of the most brazen character, made chiefly to one province and paid for by the taxes of the rest."[12]

King enjoyed the use of power, particularly when it could be exercised with impunity against the vulnerable; and he now moved smoothly to compel Bruce to withdraw his charge. A long, highly partisan wrangle, which continued after the dinner recess, finally ended when the Speaker requested Bruce to retract his statement, and, at his refusal, ordered him to withdraw from the House for the rest of the day. "I purposefully made the period brief," King remarked complacently, "so as not to give the *Globe and Mail* the opportunity to make a martyr of him."

The passage of the Family Allowances Bill was an important step in the advance of the Liberal plans. Federally, the party prospects could hardly have looked better; but, provincially, there was good reason for disquiet, if not actual anxiety; and King and his ministers drew comfort chiefly from the fact that the portents for the Progressive-Conservatives seemed still more gloomy. Four provinces – Saskatchewan, Alberta, Quebec, and New Brunswick – held general elections during the summer of 1944. Social Credit swept Alberta, the C.C.F. overwhelmed the Liberals in Saskatchewan, Duplessis and his *Union Nationale* won a small but sufficient majority over the Liberals and the *Bloc Populaire* in Quebec, and in New Brunswick the Progressive-Conservatives were again defeated by the Liberals. It was a very mixed bag of results, distinctly discouraging for King and very depressing for Bracken. Bracken had been elected to the leadership on the assumption that the West was the real hope of the revival of Canadian Conservatism and that he could arouse it as nobody else could. The summer elections mocked these ambitious hopes. The Tories did not win a single seat in either Alberta or Saskatchewan and lost seven seats in New Brunswick.

Bracken's discomfiture was obvious, but there was also very little satisfaction for King in the summer's election results. The victory in New Brunswick was, of course, gratifying; and in Alberta, the voters had persisted so long in their misguided obsession with Social Credit, that nothing very much had been expected of them. The defeat in Saskatchewan where, with one brief Conservative interlude, the Liberals had reigned supreme from the founding of the province in 1905, was a very different and much more serious matter. Still more disquieting was the overthrow of Godbout in Quebec. Godbout had campaigned on his record as a provincial reformer, and had made no real attempt to explain and defend his position as a moderate federalist. He was attacked by two strongly French-Canadian nationalist parties, by Duplessis's *Union Nationale,* and by the *Bloc Populaire Canadien,* which was the political form assumed by *La Ligue pour la Défense du Canada* in the autumn of 1942. For a time, the *Bloc* seemed a very promising force; but it was essentially an urban youth movement which frightened the voters with its ardent talk, and could never decide whether it wanted to fight Ottawa or reform the province most.[13] The vote against Godbout (as the hireling of the federal Liberals) went mainly to Duplessis, and his efficient party machine, with its tight hold on the rural constituencies, gave him the victory in a muddled three-cornered fight.

II

At the second Quebec Conference in September of that year, the talk was mainly about the approaching war in the Pacific. There was a general air of assurance that the back of the German resistance had been broken, and that the end of the struggle in Europe might come even before the year was out. A comfortable feeling of relief took possession of King and most of his colleagues that September; only one Minister, Colonel J. L. Ralston, was conscious of a growing and irrepressible sense of anxiety. Kenneth Stuart, the Chief of Staff at Canadian Military Headquarters in London, who had come over to Ottawa early in August, had given a very optimistic report on the Canadian armed forces and their reinforcement in Europe. Three weeks later, he modified this estimate, but guardedly, and with no real implication that a serious crisis in army manpower was impending. Ralston began to suspect that the truth might be somewhat different when he read in the newspapers the statement signed by Major Conn Smythe, M.C., the coach of the Toronto Maple Leafs hockey team, who had just been invalided back to Canada. Smythe reported that while in France and England he had talked to officers from every part of Canada: "They agreed that the reinforcements received now are green, inexperienced, and poorly trained."[14] In Smythe's eyes, the remedy for this deplorable deficiency was obvious and readily available: the well-trained soldiers now in Canada, the N.R.M.A. men – conscripted under the National Resources Mobilization Act for home defence – should instantly be dispatched overseas.

Ralston determined to find out the truth himself. Late in September, he left Ottawa on his last tour of the Canadian forces overseas. He arrived in Naples just after the long struggle for the Pisa-Rimini line had ended, flew to London a week later, and finally visited the Canadians in the Netherlands and Belgium. " . . . I regret to say," he cabled King guardedly on his return to London on October 13, "that conditions and prospects of which I have learned will I feel necessitate reassessment in light of the future, particularly regarding infantry involving, I fear, grave responsibilities."[15] The language was vague, cautious, unemotional; but to King, Ralston's telegram was full of portentous meaning. It was, he concluded apprehensively, "an intimation that he was coming back with the intention of making proposals which may involve the whole question of conscription."[16] The most likely proposal, King suspected instantly, was that the "N.R.M.A. men" should be employed for general service abroad. The very thought of such a decision made him shudder: it would be a "criminal thing" with appalling consequences. Any attempt to force conscription at this time, he predicted darkly, would very probably lead to civil war in Canada, a demand for complete Canadian independence, the dismemberment of the British Empire, and annexation to the United States! This terrifying train of consequences must be stopped before it ever began. He braced himself for the supreme encounter of his political career. And on October 18, Ralston returned to Ottawa.

The following afternoon, when King arrived at the East Block for a meeting of the War Committee of the Cabinet, he found Robertson, Heeney, and Pope, the three most important members of his little coterie of private advisers, expectantly waiting for him.[17] Norman Robertson was Undersecretary of State for External Affairs, A.D.P. Heeney, Secretary of the Cabinet and its War Committee, and Major-General Maurice Pope, Military Staff Officer to the Prime Minster. Their high official positions added considerable weight to their counsels; but their influence was supplemented and perhaps, on occasion, even rivalled, by that of King's own private secretaries, Walter Turnbull, James Gibson, and J.W. Pickersgill, particularly, of course, the last. These half dozen "court favourites," the most prominent members of the East Block inner circle, possessed a power which only daily and intimate association with a political leader can give. They not only saw King far more frequently than even his most trusted ministers; but they had also adopted all his major convictions and opinions, and had identified themselves so closely with his thoughts and feelings that they seemed almost to have become a physical extension of his being. In any difference of opinion between King and one of his ministers, particularly in the crucial dispute which they knew was now impending over conscription, they immediately and vigorously took their chief's side. They greeted him that afternoon with sympathetic agreement and supporting arguments.

Thus fortified, King walked into the committee meeting. Ralston began proceedings by reading a report, prepared for him in London by Stuart, which attempted to explain why the earlier optimistic reports and estimates on the reinforcement of the Canadian Army were no longer valid. The war, which everybody had expected to end before the close of 1944, was now certain to continue well into the new year; and, in both Italy and northwest Europe, the casualties of August and September had been unexpectedly heavy. Fifteen thousand additional well-trained infantrymen would be needed within the next two months, and the only effective way of providing them was to extend the N.R.M.A. troops' terms of service to any theatre of action. Ralston, out of the knowledge gained by his recent visit overseas, added his strong support to Stuart's recommendation. It was a formidable proposal, far too formidable for the committee to digest in a single session. It met several times in the next few days, and on October 24, there was a general meeting of the Cabinet with all twenty-three members present. Ralston repeated his statement: "I feel," he concluded, "that there is no alternative but for me to recommend the extension of service of N.R.M.A. personnel to overseas."[18]

Throughout these sessions, King steadily opposed Ralston's plan. His reasons were an odd jumble of highly implausible arguments. Conscription, he believed, was a desperate, militarily quite unnecessary expedient entailing horrendous consequences. It would, he prophesied, destroy national unity, provoke civil strife, ruin the Liberal Party, and, in some not easily explicable fashion, weaken Canadian support for a post-war collective security organization.[19] These arguments were not very convincing, and King did not rely too heavily on them. He much preferred more indirect methods of persuasion; and he realized, very early in the debate, that his own judgement would be very greatly strengthened in the eyes of his colleagues if he could win Churchill's support for it. Churchill, he devoutly hoped, would return an appropriate answer to a strongly slanted leading question: but, on the other hand there was always the alarming possibility that Churchill's reply would be unsatisfactory and useless. The problem might have baffled a lesser man, but King was more than equal to it. With the help of the faithful Robertson and the sympathetic Malcolm MacDonald, the British High Commissioner, an elaborate telegram was dispatched requesting Churchill to say whether, in his opinion, the future necessities of the war in Europe required the fearful risk of imposing conscription in Canada.[20]

Normally King communicated with the Prime Minister of Great Britain through his own office as Prime Minister of Canada; but on this occasion the telegram was sent privately through the office of the British High Commissioner. King's Cabinet colleagues were not, of course, informed of this clandestine manoeuvre; but, in case it should prove successful, he prepared a simple but ingenious cover. He would, he said helpfully, be prepared to telegraph for Churchill's advice if that seemed advisable. Days went by. A second, urgent, supplementary telegram was secretly sent off. And at last Churchill's answer arrived. It was as vague, general and unsatisfactory as King in his most desponding moments had feared.[21] Obviously, it would be a fatal mistake to read it to the Cabinet, and King informed his colleagues that, after much anxious thought, he had decided that it would be best not to appeal to London. His elaborate scheme had totally failed. He was consumed with disappointment, vexation, and anxiety.

It was at this point, during the last two days of that agitated month of October, that he conceived of the idea of a conspiracy against himself, of a plan "to get me out" and to end his political career.[22] The alleged plot, of course, did not exist. It was a fabrication of King's devious mind, of his paranoic delusions of persecution. Ralston was a selfless and devoted patriot who had never aspired to the premiership and was wholly incapable of conspiracy. The real conspirator was King himself. He determined to force Ralston's resignation at once and to replace him with a minister who would be willing to continue the voluntary system of recruitment for service overseas. The choice was obvious. It was General McNaughton, who disliked Ralston and Stuart intensely and believed he owed his own downfall to their machinations. King obtained McNaughton's consent to take on the task, and, until almost the very last moment, told nobody of the arrangement. Immediately before the fatal Cabinet meeting on the afternoon of November 13, he confided his secret to St. Laurent;[23] but, apart from this one intimate associate, the ministers were ignorant and unsuspecting, and watched, with a kind of stupefied fascination, while King proceeded calmly to deal his shattering blow. He eulogized McNaughton's abilities, declared that McNaughton must be brought into the Cabinet without delay, and reminded Ralston that he had never withdrawn his letter of resignation, submitted over two years before. Ralston confirmed his resignation, got up, said good-bye to his colleagues, and left the room. He went alone. Not one of the conscriptionist ministers followed him.[24] King had succeeded in cutting off the venomous head of the conspiratorial snake.

For the next three weeks, the Prime Minister, the Minister of Defence, the Cabinet and the Army Chiefs made a determined effort to persuade the N.R.M.A. men to volunteer for overseas service. King decided that Parliament must be recalled to deal with the crisis; he assumed that his faithful majority in the House of Commons would continue to support him against

his enemies; but by November 22, the day Parliament met, he realized that
it would be useless to continue the struggle any longer. The headquarters
staff bluntly announced that it was impossible to get the necessary number
of recruits in time; a half-dozen members of the Cabinet – Ilsley, Howe,
MacDonald, Mulock, Gibson, and Crerar – were now all threatening resignation.[25] Decapitation had not killed the conspiratorial snake. It was more
menacing than ever, and King knew intuitively that he must give way. He
yielded, not because he wished to ensure the army's recruitment or to pacify
an aroused public opinion, but simply to save his own skin. His secretary,
Walter Turnbull, one of those ingenious and ever-helpful private advisers,
apparently suggested that it would be politically much more astute to
dispatch a "quota" of N.R.M.A. personnel overseas than to subject the entire
body to conscription.[26] King seized on this suggestion at once and a hurried
order-in-council authorized the selection of sixteen thousand for service
overseas.

Yet, despite its prudent limitations, and in part because of them, the order
was a total breach of the promise which King had solemnly given and repeatedly confirmed; and, for a time, some highly unfortunate consequences
seemed possible.[27] Out in British Columbia, where the majority of the
N.R.M.A. were stationed, the discrimination of the "quota" system nearly
provoked a mutiny. The chosen regiments had, of course, to be given embar-
kation leave; a number of soldiers took advantage of their freedom to
abscond, and efforts to force their return sometimes ended in clashes with
the local civilian population, particularly in Quebec. These disturbances
gained a good deal of publicity; but they were isolated and brief, and nothing
occurred to modify seriously the deep satisfaction with which the country
as a whole greeted the government's decision. Even the reaction in government and Parliament was relatively mild. C. G. (Chubby) Power, who had
been told, and believed, that the Liberal policy was "never, never conscription," honourably protested and resigned; but all the other members of the
Cabinet including the French-Canadian ministers, stuck to their posts; and
when the long and acrimonious debate on the new policy finally ended early
in December, the government was sustained by a vote of 143 to 70, although
34 French-Canadian Liberals voted against their party.

The portentous reinforcement problem had finally been solved. The gaps
left by the deserters were more than filled by other N.R.M.A. men who,
almost as soon as the new policy was announced, voluntarily decided to "go
active." The overseas pool of reserves mounted rapidly to about 24,000; and
Canadian politicians and generals, freed now from their obsessive anxiety
over reinforcements, turned once more to that other basic Canadian military
aim, the reunion of the First Canadian Army. Alexander, who before had
objected to the transfer of the First Canadian Corps to Italy, now feared to
reduce his depleted forces still further and hoped that the Canadians would

remain. It was not until the end of January, 1945, that the British and American Chiefs of Staff, meeting in Malta on their way to the conference in the Crimea, finally decided that Eisenhower must be reinforced for a supreme effort in northwest Europe, with further troops from Italy, including the two Canadian divisions.[28] The complicated move northward, which began about the middle of February, lasted for more than a month, and the First Canadian Division did not reach General Simonds's command on the Allied front line until early in April. The Canadian Army had at last been reunited, but only just in time, for on May 7, little more than a month later, the Germans capitulated and the war in Europe was over.

III

Ever since the Allied powers had banded together as the United Nations in January, 1942, it had been fairly certain that victory would be followed by the establishment of a new international organization for the preservation of world peace. It was a good deal less clear how Canada would regard such a body and what part she could expect to play in it. The great powers jealously kept the preliminary designs for this ambitious piece of political architecture to themselves, and the Canadians showed only a mild, trusting interest in the project. In principle, King disliked all international organizations; he once solemnly assured Churchill that he "did not believe there would have been a war if the League of Nations had never existed."[29] A new world organization, even if it included the United States, would have to be watched very carefully; but, questionable though it was, it would be infinitely less sinister and dangerous than a revival of that other old association of nations, the British Commonwealth. On the subject of the British Commonwealth a very strong conditioned response or reflex had established itself in King and his secretaries. Just as Pavlov's dogs had acquired the habit of salivating at the ticking of a metronome, so King and his court favourites had grown so accustomed to conjuring up a terrifying monster called "imperial centralization," that the mere mention of "British Commonwealth," "Commonwealth Conference," "Commonwealth association" was enough to throw them into spasms of fear and rage.

More than a year earlier, on January 24, 1944, when Viscount Halifax, the British Ambassador to Washington, spoke to the Board of Trade in Toronto, this conditioned response worked with automatic precision. King was just coming out of a Cabinet meeting, when one of his secretaries rushed up to him with the electrifying information that "Halifax was making a perfectly terrible speech in Toronto."[30] Halifax, of course, had not the faintest idea that he was saying anything particularly controversial. He had simply argued that in the post-war world the Commonwealth would do well to continue its wartime habit of consultation and joint planning. He predicted the future dominance by the superpowers, the United States and Russia, and he acknowledged frankly that Great Britain, however desirable its continued influence in post-war politics might be, could not, by itself, claim equal partnership. "Not Great Britain only," he declared, "but the British Commonwealth and Empire must be the Fourth power in that group upon which, under Providence, the peace of the world will henceforth depend."[31]

Much of this was indisputable or comfortably vague. The conclusive answer to Halifax's proposition was that the Commonwealth could hardly continue consultation and joint planning after the peace since it had done little consultation and less joint planning during the war. But all rational consideration had now fled from King's mind, and the familiar paranoic delusions of persecution and conspiracy rushed in to take possession of it. Halifax's speech, he wrote incoherently in his diary, was "a conspiracy on the part of Imperialists to win their own victory in the middle of the war . . . a plan . . . worked out with Churchill to . . . bring about this development of centralization . . . to recover for Britain . . . the prestige they are losing as a nation."[32] The astonished Governor-General, the Earl of Athlone, was informed in agitated tones that even Hitler could not have improved on Halifax's proposal as an instrument for the destruction of the British Empire![33] These fulminations continued on unabated for several days and then King calmed down. His speech in the House of Commons a week later – for he considered that an official public rejection of Halifax's suggestion was absolutely essential – was relatively sensible. He was, he insisted, all in favour of "close co-operation and effective co-ordination of policy" with the other members of the Commonwealth but he could not agree with the argument, put forward by both Lord Halifax and Field-Marshal Smuts, that the post-war rivalry of the great powers was inevitable, and that the best way of preventing it, and preserving the peace, was the creation of a balance of world power. "We look forward, therefore," he concluded, "to close collaboration in the interests of peace not only inside the British Commonwealth, but also with all friendly nations small as well as great."[34]

All this sounded as if the Canadian government had found a new and earnest belief in collective security. The Canadian people, whose opinion was sampled by the Gallup Poll in January, 1945, declared itself overwhelmingly in favour of Canadian membership in the new organization. By this time, the great powers had made public the proposals reached at Dumbarton Oaks and had agreed at Yalta on the voting procedure in the proposed Security Council. It was perfectly evident that they had very effectively ensured their continued dominance in the projected United Nations and had reduced the Assembly in which every member nation had an equal voice, to the level of a debating society. Unlike some other middle and small powers, Canada did not seriously dispute this preponderance; the Canadian government believed, so King asserted, that "power and responsibility should as far as possible be made to coincide." The lofty elevation of the superpowers was tolerable, in a good cause; but the degradation of all other nations, middle powers as well as insignificant little states, into a common level of powerless and submissive uniformity, was very hard to accept. Canada tried to act as a spokesman of the "middle powers" – powers which, according to King, had proved by the important part they had played in the war that they were quite capable of carrying out the necessary functions of international peace-keeping. Middle powers, he implied, ought to be given a preference in elections to the non-permanent seats in the Security Council. And all powers, middle and small, ought not to be ordered to supply armed forces in the maintenance of peace unless they had participated in the Security Council's decision to invite their contribution.[35]

Towards the end of April, the delegates of fifty nations, including Canada, began to gather in San Francisco, California, for the purpose of framing a constitution for the United Nations on the basis of the proposals submitted by the sponsoring powers. San Francisco in the springtime must have looked like an enormous carnival to representatives from the battered cities of Europe or staid Canadian towns. The war-weariness of most of the visitors contrasted oddly with the apparently endless and exuberant vitality of the inhabitants. King complained that it was a city of asphalt, without parks or verdure; but others were entertained by its lively, tinselly artificiality. "This seems a technicolour world glossy with cheerful self-assurance,"[36] wrote Charles Ritchie, one of the junior members of the Canadian delegation. Flamboyant advertisements and the vivid primary colours of fifty different national flags struck the gaze everywhere. The noise of cable-cars, motor horns, and radios blaring dance music was incessant, to King's intense annoyance; and the crowd of American sailors and their girls took on the appearance of a happy-go-lucky company of theatrical extras in an intermi-nable review or musical comedy. Even the conference chamber, the Opera House in the San Francisco Veterans' Memorial Building, with its stage and dazzling Klieg lights, intensified the curious impression of theatricality.

The official Canadian delegation, which numbered seven, was composite and non-partisan in character, with representatives from both the Senate and the House of Commons and from the three major political parties. A group of senior members of the Department of External Affairs, Robertson, Hume Wrong, and "Mike" Pearson, came along as alternate delegates and a few of King's faithful secretaries were inevitably added to the party. For a variety of reasons – the principal of which was the rapid approach of the Canadian general election – the official delegates made extremely little impression on the conference. St. Laurent and King arrived in time for the opening on April 25, but left for Vancouver and the commencement of the Liberal campaign on May 14, when the Conference had about six weeks more to run. The other party leaders, Coldwell and Graydon – Bracken had not been invited, since he was not yet a member of the House of Commons – were equally inclined to give the general election an easy priority over the future peace of the world. Even while he remained in San Francisco, King's mind was only partly on the Conference. He was afflicted with a very bad cold, found the city noisy and disturbing, and was preoccupied with his V-E Day address to the Canadian people. As the political head of the Senior Dominion, he might have been expected to lead the Commonwealth division of the "middle powers" in their fight for greater recognition, but he did nothing of the kind. His claim to the status of "respected elder statesman" was obviously inferior to that of Smuts of South Africa; and he realized, sensibly enough, that he could not compete with the vehement rhetoric of Herbert Evatt of Australia, or the shrewd, earnest eloquence of Peter Fraser of New Zealand.

There was only one issue for which he showed any real concern. His obsessive fear of dangerous external "commitments" was dominant once again, and he was determined to amend the article in the draft charter which authorized the Security Council to call on member nations to supply armed forces to assist in the maintenance of peace. " . . . I did not see how it was possible," he told the principal Commonwealth delegates earnestly, "to agree to a step which meant conscription of a nation's forces at the instance of four or five outside great powers. I doubted if such a charter with such a provision would ever be accepted by our Parliament."[37] These threatening arguments were repeated to Eden and Cranborne of the British delegation, and finally, on the morning of May 14, King's last day in San Francisco, to Edward Stettinius, the American Secretary of State. King left the city with the comfortable feeling that the offending article was certain to be amended in the direction he desired. "My part," he reflected complacently, with an oblique reference to the vociferous argumentation of Evatt of Australia, "has been done quietly, unobtrusively, but effectively behind the scenes."[38] Yet article forty-four, when it finally emerged from amendment, was not exactly what King had demanded. The Canadian suggestion was that a member nation, not on the Security Council, but asked by it to contribute armed forces, should act as a member of the Council when its contribution was being discussed. Under pressure from the Soviet delegation, the right "to act as a member" was reduced to a right "to participate."

The departure of King, St. Laurent and the other politicians left the permanent officials in charge, but did not greatly alter the conduct of the Canadian delegation. Robertson, Wrong, Pearson and the rest were just as much committed as King would have been to what Pearson described, with great self-satisfaction, as "the unspectacular but essential task of finding compromises."[39] The Australian Evatt was, Pearson rather grudgingly admitted, "the outstanding personality at the Conference." He couldn't quite

decide whether the mainspring of Evatt's behaviour was courage or pighead-
edness and vanity; but he had no doubt that the Australian was often saved
from the consequences of his reckless persistence by the wise manoeuvres of
the Canadian delegation. As was perhaps inevitable, this uneasy combination
of Australian audacity and Canadian caution did not substantially alter the
Dumbarton Oaks draft charter. The middle and smaller powers totally failed
to break the hold of the Big Four on the veto; but they did succeed in
enlarging the powers of the Assembly and in putting more substance into
the provisions concerning economic and social affairs, the amendment of the
charter, and the organization of the Secretariat. Canada failed in its attempt
to ensure that middle powers, big enough to exercise the functions and fulfil
the obligations of the charter, should be given a preference in elections to
the non-permanent seats in the Security Council. The Conference decided
that "equitable geographical distribution" must also be taken into consideration.

IV

The date fixed for the federal general election, June 11, 1945, was chosen
only after much anxious thought and elaborate calculation. Both King in
Ottawa and George Drew in Toronto wanted a June election – King because
the Nineteenth Parliament had already lasted more than five years and Drew
because he had now endured nearly two years of minority rule in Ontario
and was quite confident that a new election would give him a comfortable
majority over all parties in the legislature. Drew was quicker off the mark
than King. He announced that the provincial general election would be held
on June 11. King was furious. June 11 was not simply an eligible date, it
was virtually the only possible date for the federal contest. The necessity of
his presence at the San Francisco conference for a considerable part of May
made June 4 uncomfortably early. The 18th would not give the Liberal Party
time enough to recover after a possibly impressive Conservative victory in
Ontario. The 25th was too close to St. Jean Baptiste Day, French Canada's
most beloved holiday; and finally, July 2 had already been proclaimed
"Dominion Day." For a brief while, King delayed irresolutely. Then he
decided that it was necessary to take the 11th. He had been drawn, he felt,
towards this choice by "the guiding hand of Providence" which was certain
to ensure his triumph over "the sinister methods and efforts being resorted
to for the defeat of the Federal Government."[40] For two days it looked as
if the citizens of Ontario would have the unique opportunity of voting on
two general elections on the same day. Then, on April 15, Drew announced
that the Ontario election would be set back a week to June 4.

Drew felt that he had acquitted himself with great dexterity in this little political minuet and that his success was a good augury for the Conservatives in both the province and the nation. He had very little doubt of victory in Ontario. The Liberals, he felt quite certain, were a negligible factor. Mitchell Hepburn was back once again as leader of the party, but his almost magical powers of attraction were gone. He was slack and jaded with self-indulgence and his capricious and excitable nature had worn itself out. Drew paid him no attention at all and the full force of the Conservative election campaign was concentrated on C.C.F. and its leader, Edward Jolliffe. Drew realized that the C.C.F. still possessed a formidable following in Ontario, but he shrewdly suspected that its popularity had declined from the giddy height reached in September, 1943, when the Canadian Congress of Labour had recognized it as "the political arm of labour" and the Gallup Poll had given it 29% of the popular vote, and only 28% each for both the Liberals and Progressive-Conservatives.[41] Now, in the winter and spring of 1945, the signs were accumulating that the party was losing ground. In the federal by-election in Grey North, held early in February, when the Tory candidate W. Garfield Chase had defeated the new Defence Minister, General McNaughton, the C.C.F. nominee, A.E. Godfrey, had run a very bad third.[42]

The fact was that the C.C.F. had lost, or was losing, its favoured position as the first political beneficiary of the confused, popular wartime belief in a more prosperous and more socially equitable post-war world. Back in 1942-43, the C.C.F. had seemed to enjoy exclusive possession of a political philosophy which would satisfy the wartime craving for economic stability and social welfare; but now, only two years later, this virtual monopoly had been challenged by the two older parties which claimed that they were equally determined to maintain high employment and social security after the war. They insisted not only that they could provide all the benefits promised by the C.C.F. but also that these services could be supplied without the slightest infringement of the familiar and loved Canadian system of economic free enterprise and political democracy. The C.C.F., Conservative and Liberal apologists argued, was committed to an oppressive bureaucratic system which would infallibly stifle precious Canadian freedoms. This propaganda campaign, which began as an effort to extol individual initiative and political liberty, took on a harsher and more vindictive tone as the election drew closer. The Canadian establishment began to realize that the June federal and provincial elections might very possibly determine the nature of the Canadian economy and Canadian society for a generation to come, and obviously such a desperate crisis justified all expedients. The propagandists began to defame the C.C.F. as fascist in its aims and methods. It was not denounced as a variant of Soviet communism, for the Russians were still popular; instead Canadians were reminded – what some of them perhaps had never known – that the German word "Nazi" was a contraction of National Socialist. Gladstone Murray, the former general manager of the

Canadian Broadcasting Corporation and Burdrick A. Trestrail, the author of *Stand Up and be Counted or Sit Still and Get Soaked,* presided over two active and defamatory propaganda organizations.[43]

At first the C.C.F. made no attempt to answer these slanders. It professed to believe that the electorate would pay no attention to such bogus charges, and it implied that the C.C.F. was morally far above making such mendacious accusations itself. In fact, of course, the C.C.F.'s generous assumption of its own political virtue was false. In the York South by-election of the winter of 1942, it had successfully converted Meighen into a monster of capitalist iniquity; and now, tormented by the constant pressure of Tory vilification, it turned to the same desperate inventions in reprisal. "It is my duty to tell you," Edward Jolliffe announced on the evening of May 24 – only ten days before the Ontario general election – "that Colonel Drew is maintaining in Ontario, at this very moment, a secret political police, a paid government spy organization, a Gestapo to try and to keep himself in power."[44] The "Gestapo" charges were the C.C.F. retort to Conservative accusations of prospective C.C.F. intimidation, coercion and dictatorship; "Gestapo," it was assumed, would sound just as fearfully in Canadian ears as "Nazi." After a lengthy inquiry, a Royal Commissioner found little positive evidence in support of Jolliffe's sensational imputations, and since their main motive was obviously an urge to retaliate in kind against the party's Tory tormentors, the electorate did not pay much attention to them. The Progressive-Conservatives won 66 seats in the election – a gain of 28: the Liberals 11 – a loss of four; and the C.C.F. came a bad third, with only eight seats, a catastrophic drop from its former total of thirty-four.

"It looks as if the C.C.F. were at the bottom of the poll, which is not so bad," commented King with quiet self-satifaction.[45] The Ontario general election was, in fact, a stunning blow for the C.C.F., the damage of which could not possibly be repaired in the week before the federal contest. All the special advantages which the party had possessed only two years earlier were gone or going. The war had legitimized state planning; but now all parties claimed equal expertise as professional planners. The war had also brought a reaction against regulations and controls; but, in the popular mind, the C.C.F., as a rigidly doctrinaire socialist party, was unfortunately regarded as standing for more controls, not less. There were two ways of combatting this instinctive suspicion, which often bred fears of coercion and dictatorship. Jolliffe had tried pressing equivalent counter-charges with highly unfortunate results; the federal leaders, W.J. Coldwell and David Lewis, sought rather to convince the voters that the C.C.F. was a reliable progressive party with irreproachable aims and methods. "Our task," said David Lewis, "for the immediate future, as a political party, is to prepare for the coming federal election."[46] The socialist paradise envisaged in the Regina Manifesto was carried forward into the indefinite future; the attractions of the welfare state filled the foreground of the here and now. It was a prudent change, but the C.C.F..lost its one real distinction and had to do battle with the other parties on their own new terms.

The Progressive-Conservatives encountered the same intractable difficulties in trying to distinguish their platform from those of the Liberals and the C.C.F. Diefenbaker had reminded the House of Commons that King's government had no monopoly on the idea of social welfare; and during the election campaign, Bracken's "charter for a better Canada" included such modish items as a national health service and a large-scale government housing scheme. At the same time, he tried to occupy his own select individualist policy base midway between the stations held by the Socialists and the Liberals. "The Progressive-Conservative Party," he declared, "sets opportunity and prosperity as the goal which the nation should attain, rather than the rationed scarcity of the Socialistic state, or the elaborate and burdensome system of social security which the Liberal Party is seeking to create."[47] This attempt to turn the post-war dislike of wartime scarcities, controls, and bureaucratic regimentation to the advantage of the Conservative Party was shrewdly devised; but, in general, the Conservatives had relatively few distinctive policies which they could really call their own. Conscription, which had still carried weight at the time of the Grey North election, when the scandal of the absconding N.R.M.A. men was at its height, had lost its potency with the ending of the war in Europe; and Bracken's attempt to revive it for the war in the Pacific did more harm than good. Only Howard Green of Vancouver had responded with any warmth of conviction to Lord Halifax's plea for the post-war continuation of the British Commonwealth's habit of consultation and joint planning. Between them, Churchill and King had killed the old co-operative British Commonwealth, and virtually nobody believed that it could be resuscitated.

In contrast with this rather unimpressive collection of frayed political merchandise, the Liberal shop windows were crammed with the most appealing display of attractive goods. The central place of honour was occupied by family allowances, invariably described as "Liberal Family Allowances," which were to begin in the month following the election, apparently as a free gift that did not require its beneficiaries, as unemployment insurance unfortunately did, to make contributions to a national fund. The appeal of social welfare was the most potent and the most frequently advertised inducement that the Liberal Party had to offer; but, at the same time, social security was not the only important goal that King had set his heart on for post-war Canada. He had politics as well as society in mind, the national state as well as the welfare state. Canada already possessed as much national sovereignty as even King himself could possibly desire, and probably more than his government could ever make full use of. What bothered him was not the substance, but the forms of sovereignty. He was repeatedly irked by the survival in public places in Canada of the signs and symbols of what he regarded as the old British colonial dependence and subordination. On the opening day of the first Quebec Conference in August, 1943, three flags floated from two staffs on Dufferin Terrace, with the Stars and Stripes on one and the Union Jack, with the Red Ensign below it, on the other. This spectacle so annoyed King that he promptly ordered the erection of a third staff, midway between the other two, with the Red Ensign flying from it.[48]

From then on, he continued to ponder at intervals on the pleasing prospect of a national Canadian flag as well as the equally gratifying possibility of a national Canadian anthem. There was of course to be no sharp break with the past; abrupt departures from historic custom were never King's way. Canada was still a member of the British Commonwealth, and the emblems and symbols of the Commonwealth must accompany the new insignia of Canadian nationalism. "O Canada" could not be bettered as a Canadian national anthem and "God Save the King" perfectly expressed the British and Commonwealth connection. The musical choices were obvious and would almost certainly be popular; but the selection of a national flag was not so easy. Instinctively, King sought to avoid the difficult and probably contentious business of designing a new flag. His first choice was the Red Ensign, with the arms of Canada in the fly and the Union Jack in the dexter canton, "to show historical evolution and present association with the United Kingdom."[49] At moments, he was all eagerness for settling the question at once in Parliament; at other and more frequent moments, his natural caution counselled delay. On one occasion during the election, egged on by the "palace guard" of Pickersgill, Gibson and Turnbull, he ventured to mention his proposal, and was a little discomfited to notice that while the audience cheered the Union Jack as the symbol of the Commonwealth, it showed very little enthusiasm for a national Canadian flag.[50]

There was another symbol of Canada's standing as a sovereign nation – the appointment of a Canadian Governor-General – in which King also showed a deep concern. Long before he asked General McNaughton to take over the Defence portfolio, he had been seriously considering him as the first Canadian representative of the Crown; the other two candidates, both of whom subsequently occupied the office, were Vincent Massey and Georges Vanier. Outwardly, the urge towards this appointment might have seemed a typical expression of King's Canadian national feeling, much on a par with his wish for a national flag and a national anthem; but in fact it was a special, quite exceptional aim, sought with a curious emotional intensity, which had its origins in the recesses of King's being, in his usually carefully concealed preference for republican institutions and egalitarian customs, as well as in his easily wounded vanity and quickly aroused jealousy. In the presence of the Earl of Athlone and Princess Alice, he felt, as he admitted candidly to himself, "constrained and ill-at-ease."[51] He noticed, with quick resentment, that they seemed to have been accorded a much more conspicuous position in the second Quebec Conference than in the first; and on Sunday, when he accompanied Mrs. Churchill to the Cathedral and found the vice-regal couple waiting to receive her, he felt a distinct and rankling suspicion that he was the unexpected, superfluous, and unimportant member of the party. "I cannot," he recorded, "get rid of a feeling of resentment at Englishmen coming here and holding in the eyes of any body of Canadians a place more honourable or worthy than that of those who . . . are their chosen representatives."[52]

Poor General McNaughton, twice defeated in his attempt to win a seat in the House of Commons, was obviously an impossible representative of the Crown. The prospect of the Canadian Governor-Generalship was quietly dropped and the other items in the national list were presented in muted, tentative terms. The Liberals were forced to place most reliance on their social security programme, but it did not prove nearly so popular as they had fondly imagined. King confidently expected an overall majority of at least twenty and possibly forty seats; what he actually got was a following of 125 in a House of 245, a majority over all parties of only five members. The despised Bracken, whom King had complacently dismissed as a negligible rival, won 67 seats, an increase of 60%, and the C.C.F. more than tripled its strength in the previous House. It was a "very near-run thing" indeed and King had been saved by his faithful following in Quebec.

V

Nearly two months later, when the Federal-Provincial Conference opened in Ottawa, King had recovered his equanimity. He was, in fact, in a high state of exaltation during the second week in August, for two tremendous events, the bombing of Hiroshima and Nagasaki and his own triumph in the by-election in Glengarry – he had unfortunately been defeated in June in Prince Albert – occurred while the Conference was in session. Inevitably these excitements distracted his attention a little, but they did not weaken his belief in the tremendous importance of this federal-provincial meeting. " . . . Someone said to me yesterday," he noted, " . . . this conference might prove to be perhaps the greatest part of my career. It certainly is the culmination of what I have most sought for in my life."[53]

The Conference was, in fact, a new, a completely different kind of federal-provincial meeting, and its very name, Dominion-Provincial Conference on Reconstruction, proclaimed its distinctive purpose. Its aims were not constitutional, as they had so frequently been in such gatherings in the past, but economic and social. Its planners intended to set the course and provide the motive power for the sustained development of post-war Canada; and their plans were based, not on a meaningless jumble of good intentions and vague projects, but on a coherent body of ideas which had been derived, almost in their entirety, from the economic theories of John Maynard Keynes. In 1936 Keynes had published a treatise called *The General Theory of Employment, Interest and Money*, a book which in less than ten years had already transformed the economic theories of Western Europe and North America, and was soon to revolutionize all western national economies. In Canada, the Keynesian gospel quickly captured the minds of the mandarins in the Bank of Canada, the Department of Finance, and the two new departments of Reconstruction and National Health and Welfare. They had devised a vast, detailed and comprehensive scheme, which they had persuaded the Canadian Cabinet to undertake and which was presented on Monday, August 6, to nine unsuspecting provincial delegations.

What the federal planners feared most was a re-enactment of the Depression which had followed so swiftly after the conclusion of the First World War and their scheme was conceived, in the first place, as a means of preventing its return. "In familiar terms," they declared, "our objectives are high and stable employment and income, and a greater sense of public responsibility for individual economic security and welfare."[54] Private enterprise would, of course, provide most of the drive for the attainment of these objectives but government had also a very important role to play. It would, the federal spokesmen announced impressively, act as the "balance wheel" of the economy. In various ways it could assist private enterprise to maintain high employment; it could promote consumption by distributing purchasing power through the poorer levels of the population by means of pensions, family allowances and unemployment insurance benefits.[55] During a boom, taxes would be raised, public spending reduced, and debt paid off; during a depression, taxes would be cut, public spending vastly increased, and deficit budgets planned. Government, in short, with the wonderful new economic controls which Keynes had provided, could now stop the horrible succession of boom and bust. It could devote itself, during a whole economic cycle, to the business of "levelling out the deflationary valleys and the inflationary peaks."[56] Obviously, therefore, the timing of government expenditure and investment was of enormous importance.

After listening to this portentous lecture in the new economics, the provincial delegates no doubt expected that some extraordinary proposals were likely to follow. They were right. In 1940, the provinces had agreed to surrender their claim to personal income and corporation taxes for a year beyond the duration of the war; but now, instead of relinquishing this wartime monopoly, the federal government proposed that it be extended indefinitely and even increased by the additional exclusive right to succession duties. Obviously this meant an unlimited control of the entire national economy, a prerogative which had been accepted during two wars, but always regarded as illegitimate as well as undesirable in peace. The federal government tried to justify its revolutionary proposition by arguing that income taxes and succession duties were essential to the vital countercyclical policies it intended to follow. With high employment as its aim, it could budget for an entire business cycle. With unlimited funds at its disposal, it could ensure a common level of social services throughout the entire country. It could do, in fact, for nine provinces what they could not possibly do for themselves. They would fail to co-ordinate their policies, work at cross purposes with each other and the federal government, and struggle to provide social services as good as those of their neighbours, with humiliating results for the poorer provinces.[57]

The federal government relied heavily, but by no means exclusively, on general arguments such as these. It also offered the provinces, in return for the surrender of their taxing rights, some very heavy financial inducements. They were to receive unconditional subsidies, which would vary with the annual Gross National Product but would in no case fall below a guaranteed minimum of $12.00 per capita of the provincial population, per the census of 1941. The provinces would thus enjoy large amounts of readily available cash for their own provincial projects and services; and, as a substantial addition, the federal government offered to take over the whole, or a substantial part, of the welfare benefits which had always been regarded, constitutionally at least, as the obligation of the provinces. The entire cost of pensions to all Canadians 70 years and over, and 50% of the cost of pensions to needy Canadians between the ages of 65 and 69, was to be borne by the federal government. It proposed to extend the coverage of the unemployment insurance scheme as rapidly as possible, and in the meantime, to provide unemployment assistance to those not yet included in its benefits. Finally – and this was obviously the most ambitious undertaking in the whole elaborate programme – it agreed to pay 60% of a provincially administered health insurance scheme, provided it conformed to an approved national plan. It was recognized that this would probably take years to introduce; and in the meantime the federal government offered a variety of grants, available only on definite conditions, for specific health purposes, including one in aid of the preparation of a provincial health insurance plan. There were conditional grants for tuberculosis, mental health, venereal disease, crippled children, blind persons, and research and training in public health.[58]

The provincial representatives must have sat back in a daze while the federal planners lifted one curtain after another on the vast panorama of the Canadian future. It was impossible, after a day-and-a-half of uninterrupted listening, to grasp the complexity of the whole; but, despite the bewildering detail, one fact emerged with startling clarity. The conference was professedly not a constitutional conference; but there could not be the slightest doubt that the acceptance of the federal proposals would result in a revolutionary change in the Canadian constitution. A monopoly of all the great modern taxes would enable the federal government to control the entire economy and to set the standards of health and social welfare for the entire population. It was the greatest advance ever yet planned towards the centralized administration of all phases and aspects of Canadian life. The provincial representatives were stunned. Their one clear thought was that they must not accept the federal proposals at once. They made a series of brief, perfunctory speeches and demanded time for study. The conference, as is the way of such abortive conferences, appointed a continuing committee to meet in the autumn, and adjourned.

VI

The happy post-war Canada of high employment and unlimited social security had dawned in a rather uncertain, cloudy fashion; and although the fighting and killing had ended, the familiar wartime conditions seemed to have altered very little. The price ceiling still hung suspended over the economy; the War Measures Act had not yet been removed from the statute book. The return of all the servicemen and servicewomen was many months away, and it would be a long time yet before industry would be able to satisfy the consumer demands which had been repressed and denied for six long years of war. The hand of government was still felt everywhere; and Parliament, whose interminable sessions had become a characteristic feature of wartime, was about to assemble again, after an unusual interval of over five months. The new Twentieth Parliament, the first Parliament of the peace, was to have its official opening on Thursday, September 6. And, as a visible token of the nationalist era ahead, the Canadian Red Ensign was to float from the Peace Tower in honour of the occasion.

The day before the opening, on the extremely hot and humid evening of September 5, a blond, short, thickset young Russian named Igor Gouzenko walked for the last time out of the Soviet Embassy on Charlotte Street, Ottawa. For two years he had held the highly confidential job of cipher clerk at the embassy, and he carried with him, beneath his clothes for concealment, and distributed over his person as evenly as possible, a mass of documents which proved, beyond all possible doubt, that a number of people in official positions in Ottawa and Montreal had been passing secret information to agents of the embassy for transmission to Moscow. The fearful knowledge of these clandestine operations had gradually estranged him from his own countrymen and aroused his sympathetic interest in Canada. Before he left Russia he had, of course, been given to understand that the appalling picture drawn in Soviet schools of the enslavement of the proletariat in capitalist countries such as Canada was not, perhaps, literally true in every detail; but he had not expected the reality and it surprised and enchanted him. He liked Canada, its freedom, its prosperity, its comfort. The existence of a Russian spy ring in the capital of an unsuspecting and friendly power revolted him in the end, and he determined to defect. He knew that he must act quickly for he was likely to be recalled to Russia in the near future. He knew also that, having acted, he must immediately get the protection of the Canadian authorities, or he and his pregnant wife Anna would be in danger of their lives.[59]

He spent the last three hours of that sultry September night in a desperate attempt to get somebody to give serious attention to his story. He tried the offices of the Ottawa *Journal*, the Royal Canadian Mounted Police, and the Department of Justice, in vain. At midnight, he came back to his flat, his terrified wife, and hours of fearful sleeplessness. The last day of safety had now gone, he realized, for in the morning his absence and the theft of the secret documents would certainly be discovered at the embassy. He did not dare to leave his wife and his small daughter alone in the flat again, and the three of them started out in the early morning, a pathetic little band, in a last frantic search for freedom and safety. They could hardly have fallen upon a more inappropriate day for such a compelling quest. Official Ottawa was preoccupied and busy, for the House of Commons was to choose a new Speaker that morning, and Parliament was to have its formal opening in the afternoon. The Gouzenkos trailed miserably from the Justice Building to the Parliament Buildings and back again, in a futile effort to see the Minister, St. Laurent; and at last, after a wait of two mortal hours in his office, a bland secretary informed them that an interview was out of the question. "I could not," St. Laurent explained later to the House of Commons, "interview an official from a friendly embassy bearing tales of the kind he had described to my secreatry."[60] The wretched trio departed; but St. Laurent did get in touch with the Department of External Affairs, and when King arrived in his office at a quarter to eleven, he found Norman Robertson and Hume Wrong waiting for him with stricken faces and a most alarming piece of news.

At intervals during the crowded day, King, St. Laurent, and Robertson discussed the matter from every possible angle. Gouzenko, King assumed, was probably a crank, a troublemaker, at odds with his own government. Some action might be desirable, but the federal government most certainly could not initiate it; Canada could not possibly take the risk of any serious unpleasantness with the Soviet Embassy. It was all very much in accordance with protocol, but it nevertheless left the three in a state of considerable uneasiness. The despairing Gouzenko had told St. Laurent's secretary that if the Canadian government did not listen to his story and give him some protection, his only recourse was to commit suicide, for otherwise he would certainly be killed. As Robertson pregnantly put it, they had the choice of becoming parties to a suicide, or parties to a murder.[61]

While the three Canadians, in the complete security of the East Block, solemnly weighed the diplomatic niceties against the prospect of sudden death, the forlorn Gouzenkos reached the end of their fruitless day. Twice again, they had tried to tell their story to the newspapers. They had visited the Crown Attorney's office, in the hope that Canadian naturalization might give them the protection they longed for, only to be told that the process of becoming a Canadian citizen was a lengthy one. At length they returned home, exhausted and terrified. Suicide was certainly better than murder in some dark corner of the Laurentian hills or trial and execution in Moscow. But perhaps the moment for this heroic alternative had not quite yet arrived. The Gouzenkos persuaded a friendly neighbour on the same floor of the apartment block to give them asylum for the night. It was well that they did. A little before midnight, four men from the Soviet Embassy arrived, knocked at the door of the Gouzenko flat, were informed that the Gouzenkos were away for the night, departed, but returned shortly after and broke in the door. This was the deed which almost at the last possible moment galvanized the forces of law and order into motion. The Ottawa police arrived and although they had to accept the Russian claim to diplomatic immunity – which, of course, took the affair out of their hands – they listened carefully to Gouzenko and got in touch with the R.C.M.P. The help of the federal Department of Justice had finally been invoked, and the federal government could intervene. Next morning Gouzenko presented his documents and told his long story to the R.C.M.P.; and before the day was out, he and his family were taken into protective custody.[62]

The British and American governments were informed, for Americans as well as Britons were incriminated in Gouzenko's revelations; and King, Attlee, and Truman agreed to postpone action until their respective intelligence agencies had had time to investigate all the ramifications of the conspiracy. Early in October, under the authority of the War Measures Act, a secret order-in-council authorized the detention and interrogation of suspected persons; but it was not until nearly four months later, on February 5, 1946, that the government finally established a Royal Commission, composed of two Supreme Court judges, Taschereau and Kellock, to conduct an inquiry into the whole affair. There might even have been a further delay, had not an American radio commentator, Drew Pearson, disclosed the rumour of the spy ring in Canada, and forced the government to take action. At seven o'clock on the morning of February 15, 1946, a number of people were rounded up and taken to the R.C.M.P. barracks in Rockcliffe, a suburb of Ottawa, where they were held incommunicado and interrogated separately, at great length. The investigation *in camera* continued for long weeks; and, on the basis of the mountain of evidence collected, eighteen people were finally brought to trial. Of these, eight were found guilty and imprisoned.

In Mackenzie King's eyes, the Gouzenko case had now become "a situation of world significance."[63] In fact, it never possessed the global importance which he attributed to it. In the long list of arrested suspects, only two, the British nuclear physicist, Alan Nunn May and the French-Canadian scientist, Raymond Boyer, had information of any real consequence to give to the Soviet agents. Boyer contributed his new method of making the well-known explosive RDX; it had been offered to both the United States and the United Kingdom and declined as a not conspicuous improvement on the old process, but, to Boyer's indignation, it had been withheld from the Soviet Union at the insistence of the United States.[64] Alan Nunn May reported on the research carried out by the Anglo-Canadian team of nuclear physicists in Montreal; but, in the circumstances, it is unlikely that he had any very occult information to supply. Ever since January, 1943, the British and the Canadians had been completely shut out from the knowledge which the Americans were rapidly acquiring in the business of making an atomic bomb.[65] All that Alan Nunn May had to give was already almost common scientific knowledge; and, as even some American politicians admitted, it was only a matter of time before other modern industrial nations could produce atom bombs of their own, if they wanted to. The worst crime that Boyer and May had committed was to break their oath of secrecy. Yet May, tried and convicted in London, was sentenced to ten years imprisonment; Boyer, tried in Ottawa, was given four.

The arrests on a grey February dawn, the long solitary confinement, the interrogation without benefit of counsel – all on the authority of a secret order-in-council, the existence of which the Minister of Justice had explicitly denied – evoked a strong protest which spread across the nation, and found vigorous expression as soon as Parliament opened in mid-March. On the first day of the session, Bracken denounced "the extraordinary character of the procedures followed"; he quoted with relish St. Laurent's false assurance, "There are no secret orders."[66] Arnold Smith of Calgary predicted that "the people of this country will always regret and never live down" the dreadful fact of the abrogation of their liberties. "Indeed, Sir," he concluded, "Canada now has seen black days."[67] St. Laurent attempted a reasoned defence of the government's arbitrary methods, but there was no possible explanation of his denial of the secret order-in-council; and Diefenbaker, who enjoyed the role of avenging counsel, took merciless advantage of his vulnerability. "But, Sir," he inquired, with fine rhetorical indignation, "is it not an indication of what power will do to men, what it will do to a former president of the Canadian Bar Association, one who has stood for the safeguarding of the rights of Parliament and the individual, that he should forget an order-in-council which did more to sweep aside the rights of individuals than has any other order-in-council passed in the history of Canada?[68]

The Gouzenko affair certainly aroused criticism of Canadian harshness as well as resentment at Russian duplicity; but its consequences were not serious or prolonged. The dissensions among the wartime allies, which were developing rapidly into the Cold War in the autumn and winter of 1945-46, had their origins in much more basic issues of power politics. The heavy-handed and unyielding Russian intervention in the post-war politics of Poland, Rumania, and Bulgaria excited fear and indignation in the United States and Great Britain. The calm American assumption of exclusive authority over the reconstruction of the Japanese Empire awakened jealousy and rancour in Soviet Russia. These ominous great power disputes began in the Potsdam Conference in July, 1945, and continued in the autumn meetings of the Council of Foreign Ministries, from which, of course, Canada was excluded. It was not until January, 1946, when the United Nations held its first meeting in London, England, that the Canadians began to experience, at first hand, some of the forces and tensions which were to dominate the post-war world.

This first session of the new organization was largely concerned with questions of organization; but even here the arrogance of the superpowers and the strength of racial blocs and regional groupings were very evident. New York was finally selected as the United Nations' permanent headquarters, an honorific victory for the United States which obviously annoyed Russia and required, in her view, an equivalent return. Lester Pearson's candidacy for the post of Secretary-General was supported by both Great Britain and the United States; but, as a North American, he was quite unacceptable to Russia, and a European, Trygve Lie of Norway, was chosen instead. Racial, ideological, or regional blocs in the Middle East, Europe and Central and South America captured the first five of the six non-permanent seats in the Security Council; and Canada yielded the sixth place to Australia. Canadians were to be represented on the Atomic Energy Commission, the Economic and Social Council, and the International Court of Justice, and with that the nation had to be content.[69] It had lost the support which the Commonwealth would have given it a generation earlier; and, as a "middle power" on its own, its influence was obviously limited.

VII

In the spring of 1946, the outlook for friendly federal-provincial relations in Canada seemed almost as dismal as the prospect of cordial international relations in the post-war world. During the autumn the Continuing Committee, set up by the Dominion-Provincial Conference in August, held frequent meetings in Ottawa. The provinces had learnt all they wanted to know about the complex plan which had been so suddenly presented to them; and, for some of them at least, knowledge had stiffened their critical resistance. The federal government had lost a little of its confident, expert manner, its condescending air of instructing a classroom of rather backward schoolboys in the rudiments of the new economics; and it had also become uneasily aware of the range and depth of provincial opposition. Late in April when the Conference resumed its plenary sessions, it quickly became clear that the roles of the previous summer had been exchanged. The provinces jumped to the attack; the Dominion soon found itself forced into a yielding, defensive position. Several of the poorer provinces were, it was true, prepared to accept the comprehensive package very much as the federal government had fashioned it; but Ontario, Quebec, and Nova Scotia, three provinces conscious of their economic power and their separate historical identities, were determinedly hostile to the surrender of their taxing powers. The power to tax, asserted Duplessis, is essential to the power to legislate.[70] Unconditional subsidies, Drew argued, were wrong in principle, since they broke down the concept of financial responsibility.[71] "Provincial independence will vanish," lamented Macdonald of Nova Scotia. "Provincial dignity will disappear, provincial governments will become mere annuitants of Ottawa."[72] "We all remember the old saying 'a rose by any other name would smell as sweet,'" Duplessis reminded the conference in his jocular, derisive fashion. "Well, centralization by any other name would smell as bad and be as dangerous . . . ."[73]

Under this massed pressure, the federal government drew back, intimidated and more than a little unsure of itself. King's old-fashioned belief in financial accountability was now in conflict with his crusading zeal for a comprehensive system of welfare services. Drew's strong attack on unconditional subsidies had impressed him, almost despite himself.[74] As inveterate politicians, he and St. Laurent began instinctively to think of compromises and concessions; but they discovered, to their increasing annoyance, that their financial advisers were utterly opposed to any serious adjustments in their plan. The Finance Minister, Ilsley, warned constantly by his deputy, Clifford Clark and Graham Towers, the Governor of the Bank of Canada, had become acutely conscious of the appalling weight of the commitments which the government had assumed so confidently in the previous summer. At the mere mention of the surrender of a source of tax revenue to the provinces, he seemed to shy away in alarm. He had carried the burden of wartime finance so resourcefully and successfully, but now he seemed tired, worn, and obsessed with anxiety for the future.[75] He went so far, in order to improve the attractions of the government's offer, as to increase the unconditional subsidy from $12.00 to $15.00 per head of population; but this enlargement made it all the more difficult for him to give up several of the profitable excise taxes which the provinces, led by Ontario, were so clamorously demanding. His stubborn recalcitrance, King felt gloomily certain, could be traced back to these two rigid doctrinaries, Clark and Towers.[76]

All the provinces, including Quebec, finally agreed in principle to the surrender of their income taxes in return for unconditional subsidies; but the gap between Ilsley's and Drew's methods of computing the subsidies could not be bridged; and it was here, after an entire week of wrangling effort, that the Conference finally broke down. In the year that followed, the federal government negotiated new tax agreements, much narrower in scope, with seven of the nine provinces, Ontario and Quebec remaining stubbornly aloof. The great, comprehensive post-war plan had been abandoned. Ottawa failed to grasp its desired control of the entire national economy, and health insurance had to wait another generation before it was implemented. Yet all had not been lost. The spirit which had inspired the plan was still very much in the ascendant in Ottawa. A new, superbly confident generation of federal civil servants had grasped power. They were convinced that they knew exactly how the economy worked, that they could promote, direct, and control its growth, and that positive and forceful action was the first duty of government and that full employment and social welfare were its highest aims.

CHAPTER 6

The Hopes and Realities of Nationalism

I

The boys were coming home. Mackenzie King peremptorily urged their return, shipping was unexpectedly available, and by the summer of 1946 the million men and fifty thousand women who had served in the Canadian armed services were back in Canada again.[1] Some of them had been away for as many as six years. All had accepted the long separation from family and friends, the cancellation of their plans, the interruption of their careers or the postponement of their education. They had sacrificed much for their country; and in return their country made a considerable effort to re-establish them, or to start them out in the best possible circumstances, in civilian life. They were given preferential treatment in finding jobs and financial assistance in setting themselves up again as householders and entrepreneurs. The great majority returned to their former employments, or settled on farms and small holdings, or used their re-establishment credits to start new businesses or to buy new equipment and tools. A smaller but still substantial number, about 175,000, who had either enlisted before they had finished their education or who wished to seize this exceptional opportunity of improving their skills or broadening their knowledge, now sought further training with the financial help of the Department of Veterans Affairs.

Of these about 50,000 went to the universities. And it was this great influx of veterans, men and women, in the first post-war years which began a completely new era in the history of Canadian higher education. By 1948 there were nearly 80,000 enrolled as full-time undergraduates in Canadian universities, a total which was well over twice as big as that of 1938; and the number of graduate students had also more than doubled in the same decade.[2] It was a phenomenal increase, and an increase in quality as well as quantity. Inevitably, the student veterans were older than the undergraduates fresh from the schools, and the long postponement of their education had awakened in them a far deeper appreciation of its value. Many of them had married girls who were working to help support their student husbands; they expected the normal responsibilities of parents and householders, and they

116

were determined to make up for lost time and to get all they could out of their opportunity. They were serious but not solemn students, who played as hard and as zestfully as they worked; and they looked with some impatience and contempt on the slack and irresponsible schoolboys and schoolgirls, fresh from the collegiate institutes, who mingled with them in lectures, laboratories, and tutorials. The veterans of the Second World War were the last generation of Canadian students who regarded higher education as a valuable privilege. Their children were to look down on it as a common-place right.

The return of the veterans had an obvious and immediate effect on the growth of the Canadian population. The many marriages and births which had been deferred during the war could now take place normally. There were nearly 33,000 more marriages in 1946 than there had been in 1944 – a much greater increase than that which had occurred at the end of the First World War.[3] Many of these new husbands and wives were students, who had, of course, good reason to postpone parenthood for a few years more, but the great majority of the veterans had no such inhibitions. The birth rate, which had been rising gradually but steadily from its low point in the middle 1930's, now began a much swifter ascent. In 1945, the first year of the peace, it reached 24.3; but two years later it jumped more than four points to 28.9.[4] At first this was thought to be a sudden, brief spurt, almost entirely the result of the return of the veterans, but this explanation soon proved to be wrong. The birth rate continued at a very high level, and for the first fifteen years after the peace it remained higher than that of any other industrialized country in the world. The death rate was also falling, though much more slowly; and, as a result of this coincidence, the rate of natural increase of the Canadian population rose from 10.9 in 1939 to 19.5 in 1947.[5] Immigration also shot up to an annual average of about 80,000 for the first five post-war years, a total which was more than five times greater than the annual average for the five years preceding the war. [6]

By 1949 it seemed very likely that the population of Canada would continue to grow at a rapid rate. Its age distribution, cultural composition, urban-rural ratio, as well as its standards and values were certain to alter considerably and for many reasons; but the veterans formed a distinct and special group in the general social mixture, and for the first ten or fifteen years of the peace, they were likely to exert an important influence on the nation's growth. They represented, in an intensified fashion, the experience of the last generation which had lived through the Depression and the war. Their adolescence, a time of hope and gaiety for most generations, had been passed in the drab and depressing circumstances of the slump. Like everybody else they had suffered the rigours and the denials of wartime; but they had also been brought face to face with its danger and death. They had lived hard, niggardly, yet exacting lives; and it was the qualities they had inherited from their Victorian and Edwardian past and their colonial and rural origins which had helped them to endure and survive. The acceptance of hard work, the belief in personal responsibility, the habits of thrift, simplicity and order, had served them well; but these virtues might not be easily transmittable to their descendents in the increasingly different conditions of the post-war age. They had grown up in an environment of depression and war. Their children and grandchildren were to be creatures of affluence and uneasy peace.

II

Everybody expected that the Second World War, like the First, would inevitably be followed by a severe slump. Several years elapsed before both governments and people began to realize that what they were actually experiencing was not a depression or a recession, but a rapidly mounting wave of prosperity which gained its height and speed from a variety of factors, some of which had their source in the war itself. The war literally compelled Canadian industry to grow up technologically. For most of its six long years, the scarcity of shipping and the destruction wrought by the marauding submarines in the North Atlantic virtually cut Canada off from its usual supplies in Europe. The lack of American dollars, which persisted even after the Hyde Park Agreement, inevitably reduced the scale of Canadian purchases in the United States. Even if these perils and impediments had not existed, Canada could not have continued its pre-war dependence on British and American industry, for, at the height of the war, British and even American industry were both concentrating desperately on meeting their own requirements. The leaders of the Canadian economy were compelled to cultivate the virtues of self-reliance, initiative, and daring more than they had ever done in the past; and the Canadian government, forced onward by the driving energy of C.D. Howe, was prolific in encouragement and inducements. It awarded huge contracts, granted generous capital cost allowances, and sponsored industrial research and development. Under these varied stimuli, the range, diversification and volume of Canadian industrial production rapidly increased. The nations steel-making capacity was greater by 50% than it had been before the war. Canadian factories were making a good many things – aircraft, diesel engines, synthetic rubber, plastics and electronic equipment – which they had never made before.[7]

The war gave a great impetus to Canadian secondary manufacturing. The first four post-war years brought an equally vast and valuable addition to Canada's natural resources and primary industries. They witnessed the discovery of important and new sources of petroleum and natural gas and the first successful Canadian production of nuclear energy; and these were the three potent forces which were to revolutionize Canadian industry and transform the Canadian lifestyle for the next thirty years. Up until then Canada had never really possessed an easily available abundance of fuel and power. Its chief coal deposits lay in the Atlantic provinces and Alberta, far away from the industrial heartland of the nation, in Ontario and Quebec. This deficiency had been a serious weakness in Victorian times; but in the first quarter of the twentieth century, Ontario and Quebec began the systematic harnessing of Canada's young turbulent rivers for the production of hydro-electric power on a large scale. The number of unexploited natural sources of electricity were diminishing after the war, although some very important and obvious power sites still remained, particularly in Manitoba and British Columbia; and hydro-electric energy had always suffered from the limitation that while it was a chief source of power, it was a rather expensive source of heat. Heating Canadian houses through the long northern winter, which, except in southern British Columbia and southern Ontario, could be extremely cold, was a costly business which could be carried out only with large imports of coal from the United States. It was this absence of a cheap and easy native source of fuel and the approaching limits of the production of hydro-electric power that gave dramatic emphasis to the discovery of oil at Leduc, thirteen miles southeast of Edmonton, Alberta, on February 13, 1947.

It was late in the afternoon of a cold midwinter day. A large crowd of perhaps 800 people stood huddled in a wide circle, with a tall derrick thrusting its way into the sky before them. All around the flat featureless prairie stretched outward towards the rapidly darkening horizon. A more unlikely time and place for a miracle of nature could scarcely have been imagined; but the Minister of Mines in the Alberta government and other provincial politicians were in attendance, there were interested newsmen about, and everybody waited with a confident expectancy for a wonderful event which, they had been assured, was certain to happen that very afternoon. On the record of the past, it was a little strange that Vernon Hunter, the engineer in command of the drilling crew, should have dared to be so positive and so explicit. The Imperial Oil Company, the firm for which Hunter worked, had already drilled 133 wells in Alberta without discovering oil, and drilling had been going on at Leduc for nearly three months and the well was now nearly a mile deep. All the omens were unpropitious; but recent indications had given Hunter confidence and his prophecy was to be fulfilled to the letter. Suddenly there was a great roar and the chilled audience watched "a beautiful ring of black smoke floating skyward."[8]

The discovery of oil at Leduc was not, of course, the first appearance of petroleum or its derivatives on the Canadian prairies. Much of Alberta and the District of Mackenzie to the north formed part of Canada's western interior lowlands, a huge physiographic region which was a northern extension of the great oil-rich western plains of the United States. Petroleum had been found as far north as Norman Wells on the Mackenzie River as early as 1920, and the first strike of oil and natural gas in the Turner Valley close to Calgary came before the First World War. At first, the small local companies, which, in most cases, were quickly superseded by such huge American giants as Gulf Oil or Imperial Oil, hardly knew what to do with the gushing bounty of nature, and Leduc's revelation of the vast potential riches of northern Alberta simply increased the sense of frustration.[9] Edmonton could now be heated with oil, just as natural gas from the Turner Valley had been heating and lighting Calgary ever since 1912. But the really capacious markets for Alberta's gas and oil lay far away in central Canada and the middlewestern American states. The building of the necessary pipelines would be a protracted and expensive business, but already advancing technology had solved most of the serious problems of construction.[10] New methods of strengthening large diameter pipes against high pressure and corrosion had been discovered; new special pipe-laying machinery was available; and Canol, the wartime pipeline from Norman Wells to Whitehorse, was a nearby proof that the thing could be done. The Interprovincial pipeline, which started at Edmonton and reached Duluth in 1950, quickly got under way.

The third great source of post-war power, nuclear energy, was also the gift of one of Canada's manifold natural resources. Gilbert La Bine's discovery of pitchblende on the shores of Great Bear Lake and the first production of radium at his refinery at Port Hope in 1933 were the two miraculously fortunate events which gave Canada a small, crowded, rather insecure place in the ranks of the atomic powers. By an awful coincidence – for good but for "much less good than ill" – the principle of nuclear fission had been discovered in 1938-39, immediately before the outbreak of the Second World War. It became obvious at once to the soldiers and scientists who busied themselves with the weaponry of destruction, that a chain reaction of appalling dimensions was now possible. In the first years of the war, Canadian, British and American physicists independently carried on the search for the first chain reaction; but in 1942 the Canadian and British decided to pool their efforts and a team from Cambridge, England, joined the Canadian scientists at Montreal.[11] They hoped, of course, for co-operation with the Americans; but, in the meantime, the Americans, with far greater resources in men and money, had managed to achieve their goal and the world's first atomic pile had "gone critical." It was this event which, strangely enough, closed the prospect of Anglo-American partnership in nuclear research.

The United States was not only jealously proud of its achievements; it had also become extremely suspicious of the trustworthiness of the Anglo-Canadian team. Some of its members were thought to be of doubtful middle-European origins and others were far too closely linked with Imperial Chemicals Limited, the hated rival of the American Du Pont Corporation, with which, of course, the American nuclear physicists were intimately associated. Early in 1943, the Anglo-Canadians were bluntly informed that they would be shut out from all further information on the construction of the atomic bomb. Their disappointment and chagrin were compounded by the angry realization that the Americans, with great dispatch, had already tied up virtually the entire production of the Port Hope refinery for their own exclusive use by secret contract with La Bine; and for long months the work at the Montreal laboratories sank to a low of frustration and embitterment.[12] At Quebec, in August, 1943, Churchill, Roosevelt and King reaffirmed the principle of nuclear collaboration; but for eight more months the American military scientists successfully blocked the implementation of their President's declared policy, and it was not until April, 1944, that a Combined Policy Committee approved the construction of a large scale heavy-water atomic plant in Canada.[13] A site on Chalk River, a tributary of the Ottawa, was chosen, work on the construction of two reactors began immediately, and early in September, 1945, at the smaller of the two, a chain reaction began. [14]

As time was to prove, there was potential for good in nuclear energy; but, at the very start, it was perverted to uses which were wholly evil. It was a supreme human tragedy that the discovery of nuclear energy should have occurred immediately before the beginning of the greatest war in history and that it was first developed with nothing but the purpose of mass destruction in mind. In these sinister circumstances, uranium became the "Rhinegold," the fatal golden hoard of the modern world. In Wagner's *Ring des Nibelungen,* Alberich renounced love in order to turn the Rhinegold into a ring which would give him the mastery of the world. The military-minded physicists who so feverishly pursued nuclear research in the first years of the war, with transcendent military might as their sole aim, were so many Alberichs. They sought to forge a new and more terrible "ring," the atomic bomb, which would give them global power. They rejected the peaceful uses of nuclear energy in order to exploit it as the agency of human annihiliation. They had, in fact, renounced good for evil, love for hate, and the destruction of Hiroshima and Nagasaki revealed with appalling clarity just what this new mastery of the world could mean. The consciousness of this irresistible potency helped to stimulate a new arrogance in American foreign policy, aroused a global contest for supremacy, and threatened a Gotterdammerung from which no new and better world could possibly arise. After 1945. Canada lived in a world of nuclear politics and nuclear armaments; and, in any nuclear war, she stood obviously in a position of extreme exposure and peril.

It was a long time before nuclear energy began to make its peaceful contribution to the production of electric power. The promise of western oil and natural gas was realized much more quickly. A little more than a decade after the discovery of Leduc, the benefits of the new labour-saving fuels were being diffused through most of Canada; and, for a rapidly increasing number of people, the dirt and drudgery of coal-fired furnaces had become a thing of the past. The Canadians were launched on a new age of ease, convenience, and comfort.

III

The new age started off with a boom to which several strong forces contributed. The war had brought technological maturity to Canada. The first post-war years revealed two potent new sources of heat and power. The new industrial skills and the new industrial energy were now available, but it was the enormous pent-up consumer demand of the late 1940's, which first started Canada off on the new phase of its industrial history.[15] In 1945, there were a great many urgent human needs and unsatisfied human wants, and also an unexpectedly large accumulation of money to meet them. Government spending, which for the last five years had been mainly devoted to the war, inevitably declined; but social and commercial expenditure on construction, machinery and equipment climbed steadily during the first four years of the peace, and consumer spending of all kinds jumped upward in the same period from 58% to 67% of the Gross National Expenditure.[16] New houses, shops, schools, hospitals, banks, factories and warehouses seemed to be needed everywhere, and suddenly almost everybody was buying such consumer durables as motor cars, tractors, refrigerators, stoves, radios, and washing machines. The long-repressed urge for easy and gracious living had at least asserted itself; and, for the first time since the forgotten boom of the 1920's, there were ample means of satisfying it. The enforced savings of wartime, Victory Bond investments, veterans' re-establishment grants and credits, and the pensions, family allowances and the other benefits of the welfare state put money into the hands of people who were only too ready and eager to spend it. There was a glad sense of release from the rationing and austerity of war, and the poverty and distress of the Depression which had preceded it. People wanted to give parties, drink wine and spirits, buy new clothes. Women escaped with alacrity from the service uniforms, the factory overalls, the uninspired Canadian dresses which had made up the rather drab, mannish wardrobe of wartime; and Christian Dior's "New Look" of 1947, with its billowing skirts, tight bodices, wasp waists and tiny hats bound coquettishly by veils under the chin, could hardly have been better timed.

In the first four post-war years, consumer spending probably provided the main impetus to Canadian economic activity; but consumer spending by itself could not promote the long-term growth for which the planners in Ottawa hoped. Capital, in imposing amounts, was needed to exploit the new natural resources and to provide the new basic equipment; and since everybody in authority assumed, without any real questioning or serious investigation, that Canada itself was incapable of supplying the required amounts, the country went back instinctively to its well-established automatic habit of borrowing foreign money. During the five years, 1945-1950, the total foreign capital invested in Canada rose by $1.5 billion, an increase of 50% over the total foreign investment recorded in the nearly twenty years from 1926 to 1945.[17] The post-war increase would likely have been even larger if the wartime exchange discount of 10% had not been dropped and the Canadian dollar restored to parity with the American dollar in the summer of 1946, an action which certainly reduced the influx of American capital and helped to bring on the exchange crisis in the autumn of 1947. Even so, the American share of the total foreign investment in Canada rose from 70% in 1945 to 76% in 1950, and at least half of this amount was in direct rather than in portfolio investment.[18] In petroleum and natural gas alone, American direct investment climbed from $141 million in 1945 to $636 million in 1951.[19]

The extent of American control over the Canadian economy was evident not only in the growth of American ownership of Canadian industry and natural resources, but also in the increasing influence of the United States on Canada's fiscal and commercial policies. Canada, of course, was only one of the many nations which the Republic tried to guide into the paths of economic rectitude. As the war drew towards its close, the United States even sought to remake the entire world in its own victorious economic image. At Bretton Woods, in July, 1944, it had persuaded the United Kingdom to accept its post-war ideal of a single world-wide economic community, based on the principles of multilateral trade, non-discrimination, and free convertibility of currencies. This ideal might have seemed possible of achievement a year before the war ended; but after 1945, the absence of the Communist bloc and the huge imbalance of trade between Western Europe and North America destroyed the scheme's immediate utility and left it dangerously irrelevant to the facts of the post-war world. Great Britain's strength as a trading and financial power had been tragically depleted. American Lend-Lease was terminated, with brutal abruptness, a fortnight after V-J Day; and, to the beleaguered British government, a generous interest-free loan from both the United States and Canada seemed the essential means of the nation's survival.[20] The United States granted the loan, in the amount of $3.75 billion, but exacted a very heavy price for it; Great Britain was obliged to accept, as essential conditions of the loan, the guiding principles which the Americans intended must govern post-war world trade, and which they had already tried to impose at Bretton Woods. The British were reluctantly forced to agree that, after relatively short intervals, they would impose no quotas on the import of American goods and would make sterling freely convertible. Even so, the British loan had a long and difficult passage through Congress, and in the end, was approved "chiefly because the Administration said it was necessary to fight Communism." [21]

The British negotiators may have hoped for a better deal from Canada; but they soon discovered that the Canadians were not exactly open-handed either. Mackenzie King, it was true, did realize the enormous significance for Canada of Britain's survival as an important power and the urgent need of support for her financial viability. The possibility that the loan might not he successfully negotiated filled him with foreboding. "I can only see the development of continentalism here," he reflected gloomily, "and the break-up of the British Commonwealth of Nations."[22] This early mood of sympathetic understanding was genuine, but it did not survive the protracted and rasping negotiations. As frequently happened in his conferences with the British, King became annoyed at their apparently nonchalant disregard of Canadian political problems. [23] St. Laurent, he noted also, seemed disposed to be very firm about terms. The Minister of Justice insisted on 2% interest, was at first strongly disinclined to write off British indebtedness connected with the Air Training Plan, and even went so far as to propose that the British be asked to sell more of their Canadian securities as an offset to the loan.[24] Back of this unsympathetic rejection of British importunities, as King knew very well, lay the cold hostility of French Canada and its press to any further assistance to Great Britain. Ilsley, backed by his official advisers in the Department of Finance, fought for greater generosity, but he was overborne. The total of the Canadian loan, as finally decided, was $1.25 billion, a third of the American loan, and a relatively much bigger sum for a much poorer country to concede; but the conditions of its repayment, with maturity at fifty years and interest at 2%, exactly duplicated the American terms.

The first attempt to promote British recovery by means of North American loans was so inadequate and so loaded with onerous conditions that it produced almost more harm than good. Both England and Canada suffered, though the British experience was distinctly more painful than the Canadian. The convertibility of sterling, proudly announced in the summer of 1947, according to the terms of the American loan, was followed by such a ruinous run on the pound that it had to be abandoned in short order.[25] Only a few months later, Canada went through a comparable crisis, which, like the British, had its origin in a sudden drastic decline in American dollar reserves. Canada, with its healthy post-war appetite for consumer goods and capital equipment, was buying heavily in the United States and, at the same time, making large sales in needy England and Europe. Purchases in the United States had to be paid for in hard cash, but overseas sales were mainly financed by Canadian credits; and Great Britain, driven by hard necessity, was using up the $1.25 billion loan much more speedily than had been anticipated. The drain of Canadian gold and American dollar reserves grew more serious. The balance of payments might have been maintained if the influx of American capital had already begun; but the restoration of the Canadian dollar to parity with the American dollar briefly increased the cost and lessened the attractions of investment in Canada. Under the united pressure of these forces, the crises deepened dangerously in the autumn of 1947; and in November, Douglas Abbott, the Acting Minister of Finance, announced a formidable list of excise taxes, quotas, and temporary prohibitions of household appliances and other durable consumer goods imported from the United States, together with a loan of $300 million from the Export-Import Bank in Washington. [26] Aided by these restoratives, the reserves of gold and American dollars began a quick recovery, and within the next six months most of the special restraints were removed.

IV

Meanwhile, the United States had pursued the agreeable task of remaking the world economy according to American specifications. The Bretton Woods Conference of 1944 had sought to establish a stable system of international finance and exchange. The Geneva Conference of 1947, of which Canada was a prominent member, successfully negotiated the General Agreement on Tariffs and Trade. Its terms were largely derived from the American principles of multilateral trade and non-discriminatory tariffs, principles which were characteristic expressions of American political and commercial history. The United States had begun its political life by breaking completely with its mother country, and had lived in ostentatious isolation ever since, without friends or associates of anything like its own stature, and with an empire which consisted solely in a score of military bases, occupied Japanese islands, and native dependencies in the Atlantic and Pacific oceans. The United States had never experienced anything remotely comparable to the close historic association which had bound the senior Dominions of the British Commonwealth together; and, as a result, imperial commercial preferences took on an illegitimate and sinister aspect in American eyes. They looked with the tolerance born of long custom on their own tariff, which for half a century had towered as high as Haman's gallows; but for them, preferences, quotas, and bilateral deals had the frightful appearance of capital crimes or mortal sins.

It was natural that the United States should take the lead at Geneva in the attack on the preferential system. Canada, with its very different political and commercial history, might have been expected to follow more cautiously and with some reservations; but, in fact, the Canadian delegation supported the American proposals with vigour and conviction. The new commercial orthodoxy had taken over the collective mind of the Canadian government, at both the political and the official level. The news that MacKinnon, the Minister of Trade and Commerce, brought back from Geneva delighted both Howe and Abbott; the skilled and resourceful members of the civil service had been completely won over to the American plans. King himself was exuberant and voluble with satisfaction. On the subject of "free trade," or "reciprocity" as he sometimes called it, with an affectionate backward glance at Sir Wilfrid and the election of 1911, he could be easily stirred to enthusiasm; and the new Calvinistic Confession of Faith from Geneva found him an eager convert. "I was genuinely amazed at the outcome of the negotiations," he declared rapturously. "They are much more far reaching than any reciprocity agreements of the past. In many ways, really epoch-making agreements . . . ."[27] He was delighted to learn that his telegram to Attlee had persuaded the British to weaken their defence of the preferential system. Henceforth there could be no new preferences; no existing preferences could be enlarged, but all could be reduced.

The contrast between Canada's credulous faith in the new American commercial orthodoxy and its existing and very perilous economic situation was certainly glaring. Only a few hours after Mackenzie King had proclaimed, over the radio, the multilateral miracles achieved at Geneva, Douglas Abbott announced his drastic restraints on Canadian imports from the United States, restraints which directly violated the principles on which the Geneva accords were based. There could hardly have been a more convincing proof of how unready Canada was for the immediate application of the Geneva system, or of how irrelevant the American doctrines were to the realities of the first years of post-war world trade. On the one hand, the Canadian people were expected to thrill with gratitude at the distant and very hazy prospect of an economic earthly paradise; on the other hand, they were called upon to endure the hardships and deprivations of an immediate and very real economic purgatory. The government, in fact, had hustled them far and fast along a totally new road, and yet had failed to prevent them from falling into an obviously yawning pit ahead.

In December, when the Geneva accords and Abbott's dollar-conservation programme came up for Parliament's approval, the popular feeling of bewilderment and injury found vigorous expression. The opposition, led by the Progressive-Conservatives, criticized the government's uncritical acceptance of the principles of multilateralism and non-discrimination and denounced the reckless abandonment of the preferential system.[28] All parties joined in an attack against the government's prolonged delay in devising remedies for the exchange crisis, and against the inevitable severity of the methods it had finally adopted, including the large discretionary authority given to C.D. Howe as Minister of Reconstruction and Supply.[29] King, who had less than two months before almost been prepared to fight another general election on the platform of the Geneva agreements, felt embarrassed and unhappy. Abbott's austerity programme got through the House of Commons by a very close shave. The Geneva agreements were never approved in principle by the Canadian Parliament.

Yet Canada had accepted new trading principles and was set on a new commercial course, and the Canadian government was not to be stopped or diverted. The negotiation of the Wheat Agreement of 1946 was another good illustration of the lengths to which the King ministery – under stern instructions from the permanent officials in the Department of External Affairs – was prepared to go in obedience to the American principles of multilateral non-discriminatory trade. The Agreement which was to run for four years with set quantities and prices, was an undoubted bilateral agreement which had been negotiated independently by J.G. Gardiner, the Minister of Agriculture, and his officials. Its terms were settled when everybody expected a recession in which the price of wheat would go down; in fact it climbed higher and the confidently-expected steady gain turned out to be a serious loss.[30] Western agrarian protests were vociferous a few years later; but, at the time of the Wheat Agreement's negotiation, its chief critics were the officials in the Department of External Affairs.

They objected, in the first place, to the Department of Agriculture's bold appropriation of an affair which should have been left in their own experienced hands, and they were appalled that such an unashamed bilateral deal could have been negotiated at all. Canada, Norman Robertson insisted, must make it abundantly clear that the Wheat Agreement did not portend any serious departure from the principles of multilateralism. Urged on by his anxious advice, King went so far as to obtain Truman's presidential approval before the deal was announced.[31] It was a significant episode. Gardiner had obviously acted in the old-fashioned belief that wheat was still Canada's greatest staple product and that England was Canada's best customer. In fact, trade with the United States had already assumed a place of such importance in the nation's business that, in the view of the experts in Trade and Commerce and External Affairs, the probable reductions of the American tariff arranged at Geneva seemed vastly more important than any imaginable imperial preferences or bilateral agreements. Canada had left one trading world for ever; and, for good or ill, had committed itself irrevocably to another.

V

Everybody agreed that the war had changed Canada's status. A few, among whom Mackenzie King himself could occasionally be numbered, privately suspected that Canada had simply exchanged the free and equal association of the Commonwealth for an increasing economic and military dependence on the United States. The vast majority, including King for all public purposes, thought otherwise. They believed that the war had made Canada a sovereign nation and that this achievement must be made manifest to the whole world by the removal of the remaining emblems of colonialism and the substitution of the symbols of independent nationhood. A "distinctive" Canadian flag must be adopted, and an official Canadian citizenship proclaimed. Appeals from the Supreme Court of Canada to the Judicial Committee of the Privy Council in London would have to be stopped, and a method devised of completing the amendment of the British North America Act in Canada without recourse to the Parliament of the United Kingdom. Another symbolic change, of enormous importance to King, the appointment of a Canadian Governor-General, had to be postponed, at least for a time, as a result of the popular discredit into which the first nominee, General McNaughton, had fallen. Viscount Alexander, who had led the Canadians in Italy, had been appointed instead, but in five or six years Lord Alexander would be retiring. And since by that time the remaining "badges of colonialism" would have been removed, the appointment of a Canadian as Alexander's successor might very well be the crowning achievement of the nationalist programme.

Unfortunately the patriotic campaign had not gone very far when a disconcerting fact became obvious; the positive part of the programme was far harder to carry out than the negative. The "distinctive" Canadian flag, first promised at the opening of Parliament in September, 1945, soon became a problem which dragged its way wearily through two sessions, wore out two joint committees, and ended in complete frustration. Very early in the prolonged proceedings, it became clear that the main, though not the only, division of opinion was between English-Canadian members on one side and French-Canadian on the other. A "distinctive" flag, French-Canadian speakers insisted, must be a flag which did not "borrow" or reproduce the flag of any other nation, including that of Great Britain.[32] English-Canadian members with few exceptions, were equally emphatic – or, as Howard Green put it, "in deadly earnest" – that the Union Jack must remain in the upper left canton of the new flag, as it did in the Canadian Red Ensign.[33] King himself had from the start preferred the Red Ensign, with perhaps some substitute for the Canadian shield in the fly; and St. Laurent, though he took care to make clear that he was speaking for himself and not the government, announced that he "fully shared" the Prime Minister's views.[34] In the end, the second Joint Senate-House Committee decided on a compromise design, which retained the Union Jack, though reduced in size, changed the background of the flag from red to white, and substituted a gold maple leaf for the Canadian shield.

For a moment – but for not much more than a moment – it seemed that the majority had triumphed. "Even majorities have rights," J.W. Dafoe of the *Winnipeg Free Press* once remarked sourly. Apparently in this case they didn't. On July 11, 1946, the day before Walter Harris, the Chairman of the Joint Committee, was to present his final report, about a dozen French-Canadian members, with Jean Lesage at their head, peremptorily informed King that they would vote against the new design, even if it meant bringing down the government.[35] King knew at once that he must yield. His shaky majority in the existing Parliament and his utter dependence on the political support of French Canada made any other course unthinkable. Next day, Harris submitted his report, but the government made no move to implement it. The project of the "distinctive" flag was tacitly abandoned. The nationalists had failed to achieve one of their most obvious and important aims.

The Canadian Citizenship Bill of 1946 had better fortune, although it was, in fact, a radical measure which brought about a fundamental change in the status of Canadians. Up until then, British nationality, or British "subject-hood," had been the basic identity of all peoples under the British Crown; and Canadian citizenship, in so far as it could be said to have existed at all, was simply a minor local variation. The Canadian act completely reversed this order. It made Canadian citizenship primary and basic, and British nationality secondary and derivative; "a Canadian citizen is a British subject," the act declared briefly.[36] As Lord Jewitt explained two years later in the House of Lords, the "species," citizenship, had been given priority over the "genus," nationality, and the "common code" of the Empire Commonwealth had been "completely shattered."[37] This virtually forced Great Britain and the other Dominions to adopt the new Canadian principles, and in 1948 the British passed an act which for the first time defined the "citizenship of the United Kingdom."

Although the legal complexities of the new Canadian citizenship bewildered many people, it quickly won general acceptance. It was welcomed, as a gratifying expression of the vigorous post-war nationalism, both by English Canadians and French Canadians, but each of the two groups viewed it with ominously different emphases and qualifications. A few French-Canadian Liberals and Independents stubbornly insisted that it was impossible for a citizen of one country to be "at the same time the subject of a King in another country."[38] English Canadians, on the other hand, were pleased by this formal maintenance of the historic British "subjecthood" of the Commonwealth, and delivered little constitutional lectures to the French Canadians, pointing out that George VI could be, and was, King of Great Britain and King of Canada at one and the same time.[39] It was a curious but revealing difference of interpretation which made a still more disturbing appearance in another part of the debate. "This bill achieves a lifelong dream of mine," John Diefenbaker declared enthusiastically, " – a citizenship free of racial origin and unhyphenated."[40] The pursuit of this "unhyphenated citizenship" was to bring him trouble in the future – a trouble foreshadowed in another French-Canadian comment in the debate. "We must teach to all Canadians," Rinfret, a future Liberal Cabinet minister said emphatically, "that their country as a matter of fact and reality is a bicultural and bilingual one." [41]

French Canada felt no great enthusiasm for the modern Commonwealth, with its plural citizenship and common allegiance to a divisible Crown; but there was one logical consequence of the new imperial connection which some French Canadians were delighted to follow up. In the spring of 1947, about a year after the passage of the Citizenship Bill, a back-bencher from Kamouraska moved that the designation "King of Canada" should be added to George VI's other titles at the next Commonwealth Conference.[42] This was a blunt demand that the terminology of the Royal Style and Titles should be made to conform to the facts of the now divisible Crown, and that, in particular, the omnibus phrase, "Dominions beyond the Seas," which did duty as a collective description of Canada and the other overseas Commonwealth countries, should be dropped. Several French-Canadian members were convinced that "Dominion" and "Dominion of Canada" had a disagreeable ring of colonial subjection; these antiquated words, they insisted, were "a remnant of colonialism" which "should be banished as soon as possible from our official texts."[43]

This was an attack, not against the omnibus phrase "Dominions beyond the Seas," which had been added to the Royal Style as late as 1901, but against something quite different, the historic Canadian title "Dominion of Canada" which had been created at Confederation in 1867. If the Opposition had realized the full implications of the French-Canadian dislike of "Dominion," it would undoubtedly have taken the matter up much more seriously; but in fact there was not a single prominent Conservative among the half-dozen English-Canadian members who spoke in the debate. The Tories were reassured, partly by the terms of the motion, which was concerned solely with the Royal Style and Titles, and partly by St. Laurent's concluding speech, which kept rigorously to the same subject. He acknowledged that the Royal Style was now somewhat "out of date" and not "in full accord" with the modern constitutional position of Canada. He reminded the House that all the parliaments of the Commonwealth would have to approve any change in phraseology, but he promised to suggest that the subject be included in the agenda of the next Commonwealth Conference. It was all very correct and unexceptional; but an attentive listener might have deduced that St. Laurent shared the French Canadian dislike of a word which did not seem to distinguish properly between "autonomous, self-governing" nations and "lands under dominion," administered from the Colonial Office. He might even have detected a certain governmental animus towards the word

"Dominion." But nobody could have suspected that before very long, the Liberal government would be quietly but systematically removing the word "Dominion" and "Dominion of Canada" from public documents and replacing them with "Canada" or "Government of Canada".

The Twentieth Parliament had now run for three years of its term; but the nationalist programme, which had been announced at the beginning of the first session, was still ingloriously incomplete. Canada had advanced, halted, and stumbled forward – but not very far forward – along the hard road to national identification. The Parliament at Westminster was still the only body that could amend the British North America Act. The Judicial Committee of the Privy Council still possessed appellate jurisdiction in Canadian cases, although it had already affirmed Canada's right to make its own Supreme Court the final court of appeal. King was very well aware that French Canada would be delighted if the Canadian Parliament exercised this right and cut the last legal link with the United Kingdom; but the knowledge held him back instead of encouraging him to action. He was anxious not to prejudice St. Laurent's election as Liberal leader; he feared that English Canada might react very strongly and unfavourably if St. Laurent's leadership seemed to imply the satisfaction of all French-Canadian nationalist claims and the neglect or disregard of English-Canadian national feelings. These arguments were put in King's usual roundabout and soothing fashion; but St. Laurent was visibly annoyed. He was a great deal more blunt and forthright than King; and the notion that a French Canadian could not speak his mind openly and freely at all times on any issue in Canadian politics angered him. He was equally irritated when Ilsley suggested that it would be unfeeling for Canada to press the abolition of appeals at a time when Great Britain was reeling under so "many hard blows." St. Laurent resentfully attacked the assumption that Canada ought to delay desirable action simply out of consideration for British interests or feelings.[44] Obviously he was likely to pay less attention to the sensibilities of English Canada than King had paid to those of French Canada. But for the moment at least, on the issue of appeals to the Judicial Committee, King had his way.

All told, the accomplishment of three years was not very impressive. The prolonged attempt to find a "distinctive" flag had completely failed. There were differences of opinion about the meaning of Canadian citizenship, and misunderstanding and bickering over the nature of the Commonwealth. Canada had dropped its familiar emblems and titles, under the belief that they were "badges of colonialism," and had found no distinguishing tokens to put in their place. It had lost – or was losing – its old credentials and had gained few new ones. An unidentified, nondescript, almost anonymous country, it had ostentatiously started off on a new career, with no very definite purpose in mind and not much idea of where it was going.

VI

Repeatedly Canada had expressed a strong demand for a voice in the post-war settlement of Europe, and repeatedly and resentfully Canadians had to admit that their country had virtually no say at all. As early as August, 1945, King informed Attlee that he "did not think it was good enough to have Canada sit on the sidelines" while the "big 3, 4 or 5" settled everything themselves in advance.[45] "I cannot . . . emphasize too strongly the right of this country to be one of the principals . . . in the making of the peace," he assured the Canadian House of Commons.[46] He even suggested to Attlee that Canada "deserved to be represented on the Council of Foreign Ministers," a body set up at Yalta to plan the business of peacemaking.[47] These spacious demands and moral self-confidence achieved remarkably few results. Canada had completely failed at the beginning of the war to gain a place in its higher direction, and there was no hope of effecting an entrance now, after big-power rule had been solidly established during six years of conflict. The Council of Foreign Ministers, with representatives from the United States, the U.S.S.R., Great Britain and France, together with the Allied Control Council in Germany, took over the authority and direction which the Big Three and the Anglo-American Combined Chiefs of Staff had exercised before. The British government did give King and the other Commonwealth leaders some information on the draft treaties for Italy and the Balkan states; and Canada was accepted as one of the twenty-one "middle powers" which had actively participated on the Allied side and which, with Russia's reluctant aquiescence, were invited to Paris to comment on the completed drafts. Finally, when the Council of Foreign Ministers had at last revised the recommendations made at the Paris Conference and turned to the horrendous problem of the German and Austrian treaties, the Canadian government accepted a peremptory invitation to submit its views in writing, and in January, 1947, presented a fairly lengthy submission on the problem of post-war Germany.[48] That was all. In the Council of Foreign Ministers procedural wrangles gave way to conflicts of principle. Before the year was out, the unfinished peace settlement had been abandoned and the futile Council dissolved.

The resolute hold of the great powers on their monopoly was the main, but not the only, reason for Canada's failure to play a significant part in the post-war settlement of Europe. The truth was that King's protests were formal, not serious, and occasional rather than sustained. He never pressed his case home, using all available sources of support, including that of Australia. It was an important lack of purpose and decision and it had its origin in a still more fundamental weakness, King's conscious sense of remoteness from Europe and his acknowledged ignorance of its affairs. King in fact was claiming a share in the determination of issues about which he was not very well informed and in which his Department of External Affairs was still inexperienced. Pious generalities rather than concrete suggestions made up the diplomatic exchange in which Canada and its Prime Minister preferred to deal. Faced with a sudden invitation from the Council of Foreign Ministers to present its views on the Italian-Yugoslav boundary and the question of Trieste, the Canadian government took refuge in well-meaning evasions.[49]

At the Paris Peace Conference, which he briefly attended in the summer of 1946, King was acutely conscious of this feeling of unfamiliarity and strangeness. "Canada's interest in the successful outcome of . . . this Conference," he candidly admitted, "is obviously less immediate and direct than that of some of the participating countries."[50] "I do not know the personages," he confessed unhappily.[51] Wedged between the solemn Norman Robertson on the one hand and the morose Brooke Claxton on the other, he sat slumped in his chair, almost stupefied with fatigue and boredom, while the interminable amendments went on and on and the bloc voting continued with mechanical regularity. Paris, and European diplomacy in general, wearied, bewildered, and shocked King. It also frightened him. The consciousness of his isolation and ignorance rapidly ceased to embarrass him. The old conviction "that it may be just as well not to get unnecessarily involved in international entanglements" came back with renewed force.[52] Early in August, after he had been less than a fortnight in Paris, the Prime Minister left gratefully for a tour of the battlefields of northwest Europe, in the company of Colonel C.P. Stacey.

Choice, as much as necessity, decided Canada's withdrawal from the politics of the peace settlement. Choice alone had already determined its deliberate retirement from the armed occupation of post-war Germany. In January, 1945, the Canadian government had agreed to furnish about 18,000 troops and thirteen air squadrons to the British zone; but it declined to extend their stay beyond the first period of occupation; and, in the following December, King notified Attlee that the Canadian force would be progressively reduced and entirely repatriated to Canada by the summer of 1946. [53] Food, supplies, and financial credit rather than military service, seemed to King and his Cabinet the best contribution that Canada could make to war-torn Europe; and they were convinced that full production at home depended upon the rapid return of the veterans from overseas.[54] The British, burdened with world-wide commitments and impoverished by the enormous costs of the war, looked at the problem very differently. Attlee not only pleaded with the Canadians to change their minds, but also – and very imprudently – reminded them of Britain's continuing military responsibilities as an imperial power in the Middle and Far East. To King, who repudiated all interest in the "distant countries" of the Commonwealth, this was a most unconvincing argument; and its effect on St. Laurent, who was just as easily repelled by

British imperial concerns, was still more unfortunate. King, as he recorded with satisfaction in his diary, was "adamant" in refusing to alter his government's decision; [55] and righteous indignation made St. Laurent's refusal all the more emphatic. He was not prepared, he told Attlee firmly, to free British troops "to hold down other peoples of the Commonwealth," a statement which was certainly a gross misinterpretation of the colonial policy of Attlee's socialist government.[56]

The King administration was very well satisfied with the success of the rapid repatriation of the Canadian Army. It was, as a result, discomfited, as well as surprised when, during the winter of 1947, Parliament and the press began to argue that the headlong military retreat was the main reason for Canada's virtual exclusion from the post-war settlement of Europe. In the House of Commons, Gordon Graydon pressed this point in a lengthy speech, and Fulton and Pearkes denounced the Canadian withdrawal as an evasion of responsibility and a callous denial of a justified British appeal for help.[57] "It did nothing to enhance our prestige," observed Vincent Massey, newly returned from London, "or give evidence of our willingness to assume responsibilities in peace as we had willingly done in war."[58] The government, caught unexpectedly in a serious debate on defence and foreign policy, struggled in an awkward and disingenuous fashion to extricate itself. Brooke Claxton, the Minister of Defence, insisted that the early withdrawal of the Canadian forces had not lessened in the slightest Canada's part in the process of peacemaking; and St. Laurent argued vehemently that Canada had retired because its government had not been given a separate place on the Allied Control Council, and an independent occupation zone in Germany.[59] Obviously this was a very questionable justification for the withdrawal of a nation which had accepted British military leadership for six years of war and had contributed a force to the British Occupation Zone for the first year of the peace. The Minister of Defence and the Minister for External Affairs had, in fact, made such an inept and evasive defence of government policy that King felt obliged to set the record straight. On March 10 he submitted a careful statement which included the two important dispatches of January and December, 1945.

VII

There was only one important area in post-war international affairs – the control and regulation of atomic energy – in which Canada expected, and secured, the right to play an independent part. The Gouzenko affair and the first successful nuclear reaction in the pilot plant at Chalk River – both of which, curiously enough, began on the same day, September 5, 1945 – made Canadian participation virtually essential in any attempt to work out a system of international regulation. Attlee, Truman, and King, with a few of their principal advisers, met on the presidential yacht early in November and a few days later signed an agreement which provided for the exchange of fundamental nuclear information for peaceful purposes but retained the American monopoly of the bomb until effective international safeguards could be devised and a commission established to supervise their operation.[60] The United Nations Assembly, in its first meeting in London, dutifully complied with this suggestion and set up the Atomic Energy Commission, with the Security Council plus Canada as its membership. The Canadian government appointed General McNaughton as its representative, and during the winter of 1946, the American Undersecretary of State, Dean Acheson and David E. Lilienthal prepared a set of proposals for an international control system.[61] Early in June, 1946, the Atomic Energy Commission met for the first time.

In the meantime, a sinister change, of incalculable importance, had come over the relations of the United States and the Soviet Union. It was not simply that they found themselves frequently opposed to each other, though their disputes admittedly had been rapidly growing in number. They had quarrelled over the post-war settlement in Germany and over the political reorganization in Eastern Europe. Their interests had conflicted in Korea, in Iran, and over the control of the Bosporus and Dardanelles. Yet the steady accumulation of disputes had not alone effected the change; it was in part the result of the new way in which they were regarded and explained. Both sides now began to generalize about their growing antagonism, to interpret it in ideological terms, and to invest their quarrels with a profound and portentous meaning which in themselves they did not seem to signify. Stalin started this new and quickly fashionable practice of ideological diplomacy with a public speech, delivered early in February, 1946, which stressed the fundamental incompatibility of communism and capitalism. Invited to comment on this blunt declaration, the American *chargé d'affaires* in Moscow, George F. Kennan, poured out his pent-up convictions in an enormous eight-thousand-word telegram, which, he later confessed, read "like one of those primers put out by alarmed congressional committees or by the Daughters of the American Revolution, designed to arouse the citizenry to the dangers of the Communist conspiracy."[62]

The belief in an inherent and irreconcilable conflict between democracy and communism was steadily taking over the minds of Democratic officials and Democratic and Republican Congressional leaders during the early winter months of 1946. Winston Churchill's notorious "Iron Curtain" speech, delivered at Fulton, Missouri, in March, though a characteristic specimen of Churchillian rhetoric, was virtually an official public statement of what had become the real policy of the American administration. Secretary of State Byrnes, Admiral Leahy, and even Truman himself, heard or read –

and highly approved of — the speech before it was given.[63] Truman accompanied Churchill to Fulton and sat on the platform from which the speech was delivered. "The President," Churchill told his audience impressively, "has travelled a thousand miles to dignify and magnify our meeting here today."[64]

In these inimical circumstances, the prospects of the United Nations Atomic Energy Commission could hardly have looked more gloomy. Whatever small hope of a successful outcome remained was blasted by the appointment of the American commissioner, the seventy-six year old Bernard M. Baruch. Baruch was a rich, successful political promoter and manipulator, a friend of Secretary of State Byrnes, who took him to one of the "dress rehearsals" of Churchill's Fulton speech, but who subsequently admitted that Baruch's appointment was "the worst mistake I have ever made."[65] An inordinately vain old man, Baruch was determined to be a creative statesman rather than a mere mouthpiece for the Acheson-Lilienthal report; and both Truman and Byrnes went out of their way to assure him that he need not be bound by its terms.[66] Baruch took advantage of this diplomatic discretion to propose that the Security Council's veto must not be permitted to block the decisions of the proposed international atomic control commission. Obviously, this startling new condition would reduce the chances of Soviet acceptance to zero; but despite — or perhaps because of — this obvious fact, Truman and Byrnes accepted Baruch's proposal. The Baruch plan, McNaughton summed up later, was "insincerity from beginning to end." It was no more than "a sop to public opinion and a device to ensure that the American monopoly would continue."[67]

It took six months for this solemn farce to play itself out. In June, 1946, at the first meeting of the Atomic Energy Commission, Baruch introduced his plan with suitably portentous rhetoric. A few days later, Andrei Gromyko countered with a proposal for the immediate destruction of all atomic weapons and a convention prohibiting their future manufacture and use. Faced with two such completely different schemes, the Commission abandoned for the moment all attempts to resolve the conflict between them and turned instead to the scientific and technical problems of effective atomic control.[68] In the meantime, the United Nations General Assembly had met in New York for the second part of its First Session, and Molotov, for the Soviet Union, had seized the initiative in the promotion of post-war peace by denouncing the Baruch plan as inadequate and proposing instead a general reduction of all types of armaments. St. Laurent, as well as others, welcomed these pacific Soviet overtures, but the fact that he had been effectively upstaged by the Russians infuriated Baruch. Early in December, 1946, he brusquely proposed an international atomic authority, independent of the veto and with full powers of inspection, and insisted that the Atomic Energy Commission must accept or reject these principles within a fortnight.[69] McNaughton tried to modify this uncompromising stand; the British and

French representatives thought it intransigent and unwise. But Baruch persisted, and in the end, under express orders from King, McNaughton voted in support.[70] All hope of an international control of nuclear energy vanished, to the gratification rather than the disappointment of the Americans. "We should not under any circumstances throw away our gun," Truman told Baruch impressively, "until we are sure the rest of the world can't arm against us."[71]

The grim inevitability of Canada's course in post-war international affairs grew more harshly obvious all the time. The nation's old associations were gone or going. The Commonwealth relationship, which had remained dormant during the war, was now dead beyond hope of resuscitation, and the post-war dissolution of the Empire in the Middle and Far East had already begun. Canada was turning its back on the Western Europe it had fought for nearly six years to save, and was retreating to the ambiguities of its professed position as an independent, sovereign nation in North America. It confidently claimed to be the master of its own fate; but, as the debates over the "distinctive Canadian flag" and the other symbols of national sovereignty had clearly shown, its hopes and purposes were confused and its direction very uncertain. Its only really incontestible attribute was its geographical position on the North American continent and its immediate contact with the United States; and, as the next few decades amply demonstrated, this was the feature which determined its fate. The bulk of Canadian trade was already consigned to the United States, and the control of Canadian industry and natural resources were steadily falling into American hands. In a world which was breaking apart ideologically, with the United States leading one of its two opposed divisions, Canadian foreign policy was certain to be shaped by the heavy pressures of American global strategy.

VIII

King was perfectly aware of these dangers. Military co-operation with the United States, begun with such euphoric assurance and conviction at Ogdensburg in August, 1940, had been a long, slow, but in the end, very complete process of disillusionment. The arrogant and contemptuous excesses of the American armed "occupation" of the Canadian north had increasingly worried King, though his government had done little or nothing to check it during the war. He agreed with Vincent Massey that Americans "did not take us seriously enough as a nation." "Canadians," he reflected bitterly, "were looked upon by Americans as a lot of Eskimos," a primitive and inferior people who could be pushed around at will and with complete impunity.[72] The fear that the United States had succeeded in establishing itself so solidly in the Canadian north that it might prove difficult or impossible to dislodge it after the war, began to haunt him. " ... We ought to get Americans out of further development there," he urged his Cabinet colleagues early in 1944, "and keep complete control in our own hands."[73] Brave words, but, as he confessed unhappily to Massey, he could not help wondering whether complete recovery was possible, whether the Americans would really honour their contractual wartime agreements.[74] He could not subdue the uneasy feeling that they would continue to use Canada whenever they thought they needed it, and for whatever purpose they had in mind at the moment, and that in the end they would try to take it over completely. "I said," King told his colleagues earnestly, "I believed the long-range policy of the Americans was to absorb Canada. They would seek to get this hemisphere as completely one as possible."[75]

This certainly was not the destiny he desired for Canada. "I would rather," he solemnly told a select group of ministers and civil servants, "have Canada kept within the orbit of the British Commonwealth of Nations than to come within that of the United States."[76] In principle, he feared American imperialism more than British imperialism; but in practice he was more amenable to American imperialistic pressures than he ever had been to British imperialistic influences. On the one hand, an indiscreet reference to Commonwealth solidarity, or the faintest suggestion of British "imperial centralization" never failed to enrage him; but, on the other hand, though he disliked the prospect of American economic and military domination, he seemed to view it philosophically, almost with resignation. He knew that the British imperialists could be defeated, for he had repeatedly defeated them himself; but he could not get rid of the uneasy suspicion that the ultimate triumph of continentalism was inevitable. He even came to feel a certain sympathetic understanding of the urge of the United States towards the control of North America for its own protection. "If I were an American," he confided to his intimates, "I might easily share that point of view."[77] Half convinced that continentalism for defence was reasonable, he began to assume in the spring of 1946, when the ideological preliminaries of the Cold War had already begun, that it was inescapable. "It might be inevitable," he told his Cabinet colleagues, "for us to have to submit to it – being so few in numbers and no longer able to look to British power for protection."[78]

The first hard turn of the screw of American pressure came, in fact, in the spring and summer of 1946. In April, the Permanent Joint Board on Defence recommended the continuance and maintenance of the aerodromes and airfields of the three main northern staging routes; and early in June, a Canadian-American joint-staff committee, set up at the suggestion of the American members of the Permanent Defence Board, reported in favour of a formal bilateral defence pact, based on the assumption of a frontal attack from the north by the Soviet Union by about 1950.[79] In Washington, both the State Department officials and the military men were very well satisfied with these proposals, and everybody expected, as a matter of course, that

Canada would accept the new plans with grateful promptness. Everybody, in fact, talked so confidently and expansively about the Canadian-American military pact as a completely settled affair that Kenneth Wilson, a talented Canadian journalist, on a scouting visit to the American capital, heard the whole story in detail and reported it to his newspaper, *The Financial Post*. "Hear Washington insists Dominion's Northern Frontier be Fortified," screamed the headlines; "Canada another Belgium in U.S. Air Bases proposal?" The American approach to Canada, Wilson insisted in the body of his dispatch, had been "blunt and heavy-handed" and had ended in a "virtual ultimatum."[80]

In the House of Commons, King dismissed the Wilson article as "wholly misleading"; but the evident interest which it had aroused may have strengthened his gathering doubts. Less than a fortnight later, when the Cabinet Defence Committee met to consider the formidable scheme, he was full of objections and reservations. [81] A bilateral defence pact with the United States would, he thought, be vastly inferior to a tripartite association, with Canada playing its historic role as the link between England and America. Canada would inevitably expose its sovereignty to serious risks if it accepted a purely North American alliance, and it would involve itself dangerously, and without any real reason of its own, in the obviously impending breach between the United States and the Soviet Union. Everything seemed to counsel delay; and to the great astonishment and consternation of Ray Atherton, the American Ambassador to Canada, the great plan, which everybody had assumed would be automatically endorsed, was instead postponed for further study.

Atherton wrote off in a great state to Washington suggesting that persuasion "at the highest level" was the best medicine for the perversely reluctant King.[82] An invitation to the White House and a "heart-to-heart" talk with Truman followed in the autumn; but King was well aware that an attempt was being made to "soften him up," and although he had abandoned his idea of a tripartite pact including the United Kingdom, he carefully reminded Truman that Canadians "had to watch particularly the question of our sovereignty."[83] In the meantime, the Permanent Joint Board on Defence had met again and worked out a much more modest scheme of Canadian-American co-operation in such matters as the exchange of military personnel, reciprocal availability of military facilities, exchange of geographical and meteorological information, and standardization of equipment and methods of training. In the middle of December, 1946, representatives of both countries met in Ottawa, and elaborated and confirmed the plan, and on February 12, 1947, King announced its leading features in the House of Commons. "As an underlying principle," he declared, "all co-operative arrangements will be without impairment of the control of either country over all activities in its territory."[84]

CHAPTER 7

The Diplomatic Revolution

I

King had tried, with all his usual earnest prolixity, to water down and explain away the implications of the new defence scheme. The simple truth remained that it was an intimate military alliance between Canada and the United States and that its purpose was the protection of North America against an attack by the Soviet Union. This obvious aim, King innocently imagined, could in some fashion be disguised. "Care would have to be taken," he suggested earnestly to Truman, "not to give the Russians a chance to say that we were trying to fight them."[1] Naively vain advice. The time was rapidly approaching when the Truman administration would take no care at all to moderate its language or conceal its intentions, when it would openly proclaim its readiness to assume the leadership of the free world in its great moral struggle against dictatorial Communism.

It was the sudden defection of the British that precipitated this open declaration. In January, 1947, an appalling blizzard, which piled snow drifts ten feet high in places, began one of the severest winters in recent British history. Even the weather had now turned against a people already hard driven by post-war stringency and privation. And finally the British leaders decided that at least part of their heavy burdens must be dropped. On February 21, 1947, the government announced that it would shortly suspend its economic and military aid to Greece. To American ears, there could hardly have been a more dismaying announcement. The thought of Communist guerilla action in northern Greece, supported by Yugoslavia, Bulgaria, and Albania, terrified the Truman administration; and within a few days it decided to interfere on a large scale with aid to Greece and Turkey. Truman and his Cabinet were united and determined; but they realized, sensibly enough, that although Congress and the American people seemed to like the sound of the "get tough with Russia" policy, they might be alarmed by its remote and drastic application to countries as far away as Greece and Turkey. It was vital to convince Congress of the justice and wisdom of American intervention, and the day after Truman had reached his tremendous decision, a bipartisan group of congressional leaders were invited to hear the administration present its case.

George C. Marshall, former Chief of General Staff and newly appointed Secretary of State, was naturally the first to speak; but in the view of his anxiously listening Undersecretary, Dean Acheson, the General badly "flubbed" his opening statement. Impetuously, and greatly daring, Acheson asked, and received, permission to speak after his chief. "This was my crisis," he recorded proudly later. "Never have I spoken under such a pressing sense that the issue was up to me alone . . . . In the past eighteen months, I said, Soviet pressure on the Straits, on Iran, and on northern Greece had brought the Balkans to the point where a highly possible Soviet breakthrough might open three continents to Soviet penetration. Like apples in a barrel infected by one rotten one, the corruption of Greece would infect Iran and all to the east. It would also carry infection to Africa through Asia Minor and Egypt, and to Europe through Italy and France, already threatened by the strongest domestic Communist parties in Western Europe."[2]

In this apocalyptic utterance, the whole fashionable logic of the Cold War – even including its banal metaphors, though "falling dominoes" later superseded "rotten apples" – was expressed. The stunned Congressmen agreed to support the administration's proposal of massive military aid for Greece and Turkey provided Truman appeared before Congress and justified his request in the same convincing terms that Acheson had just employed. Truman did much better. On March 12, 1947, in his notorious "Truman Doctrine" speech, he converted Acheson's Cold War strategy into Cold War ideology. He transformed a struggle for power and influence into a great moral conflict. A veritable reincarnation of the third-century Persian prophet Manes, he appropriated the Manichaean belief in the moral division of the world into two opposed and irreconcilable systems, two ways of life, one absolutely good and one totally evil. The good way of life – the American way of life, naturally – was characterized, he informed the awed congressmen, by free institutions, representative government, individual liberty, and freedom from political oppression. The evil way of life – inevitably, of course, the Russian way – was marked indelibly by minority rule, fixed elections, a controlled press and radio, denial of personal freedoms, and terror and oppression. The American way of life had apparently no discernible faults; the Soviet way of life possessed no redeeming features. These, and these only, were the qualities and characteristics of the two rival moral and political systems, and the contrast between them was absolute and irremediable.[3]

The sweep of Truman's rhetoric was vast; but it was matched, and perhaps even exceeded, after American intervention in Greece and Turkey, by the truly "titanic span" of American military power and political influence.[4] The

Soviet Union might well feel that it was encircled and threatened on every side by hostile forces. Anglo-American armies confronted its satellites in Eastern Europe; General Douglas MacArthur's military satrapy in the Far East extended over the whole of the former Japanese Empire and included half of Korea. In Iran, Turkey, and Greece, the force of American power and influence had compelled Soviet military retreat or diplomatic withdrawal. Iran and Turkey were just as close to the Soviet Union as Mexico and Canada were to the United States. The Bosporus and the Dardanelles were just as important to Russia as the Panama Canal was to the United States or the Suez Canal to Great Britain. Yet the Soviet Union had been compelled, under Anglo–American pressure, to give up its attempt to fortify the Bosporus in association with Turkey, while the United States, on its part, had felt perfectly entitled to negotiate a close defence pact with Russia's near northern neighbour, Canada.

The full realization of how deeply Canada was involved in what was still a battle for political power and influence but which at any moment might become an open conflict, came very slowly to the politically naive Canadians. It was not, in fact, until early in June, 1947, when St. Laurent introduced the Visiting Forces Bill in the House of Commons, that the members awoke to the reality of Canada's situation. King's characteristic method of moving by slow, disarmingly simple stages towards his distant objective had again deluded them, and they had listened to his unexciting February 12 statement on defence co-operation with the United States with scarcely a murmur. In the meantime, everything had dramatically changed. Only a month after King's announcement, the Truman Doctrine had been proclaimed. The grand strategy and the lofty ideology of the Cold War had been revealed to a startled world, and for the first time the real and frightening significance of the Canada-United States defence arrangements dawned upon the Canadians.

The Visiting Forces Bill of 1947 differed substantially from the compara-ble provisions of wartime. It granted to the American service courts juris-diction over the discipline and administration of their own forces, and reserved to Canadian courts the trial of all offences under Canadian law.[5] If the necessity of foreign military courts was admitted, then the Liberal government had certainly succeeded in narrowing their scope and protecting Canadian sovereignty. But why were they necessary at all in times of peace? Nations were not normally given the liberty of establishing service courts in the territory of other nations unless a war justified the presence there of a considerable number of their armed forces. The bill was vulnerable, much more vulnerable than it would have been only a few months before; and the Commons subjected it to a prolonged and critical review, with the C.C.F.ers leading the attack and a number of Progressive-Conservatives, including J. M. Macdonnell, Howard Green and E. D. Fulton, joining in.

Several speakers made the obvious point that the bill implied the presence of much greater American forces than King had suggested in his February 12 reference to technical personnel and observers in cold weather experimental stations. Others argued that the bill legalized a typical wartime arrangement in times of peace, that it violated the principles of the United Nations Charter, deepened Canada's subjection to the United States and dangerously aligned it with American policy in the Cold War. "I think this country at this moment has a supreme opportunity," Knowles declared. "We can say we are not going to have United States troops in Canada in peacetime. That would be the first move of any small power against the Truman policy or the Stalin policy."[6]

Bracken did not contribute to the debate, Coldwell evidently regretted the vehement harangues of some of his C.C.F. followers; but he and Fulton together seized upon what was undoubtedly one of the most significant features of the Visiting Forces Bill of 1947.[7] It constituted, they both argued, a sharp and decisive departure from the constitutional principles which King himself had laid down before the opening of the Second World War. " . . . Long ago," King had solemnly assured the Commons in 1938, "the Canadian government finally settled the constitutional principle that in Canadian territory there could be no military establishments unless they were owned, maintained and controlled by the Canadian government . . . . Such domestic ownership, maintenance, and control of all military stations and personnel is one of the really indisputable hallmarks of a national sovereign government . . . ."[8] This portentous constitutional pronouncement was delivered in 1938 at a time when the British government, realizing the vast importance of air power in the increasingly probable future war, was trying to set up training schools for the Royal Air Force – which King characteristically misnamed the "Imperial" Air Force – in Canada. The "indisputable hallmark" of Canadian sovereignty had prevented the British from establishing air training schools in Canada in 1938; but in 1947, only nine years later, it seemed to present no serious barrier to the dispatch of considerable numbers of American troops to Canada, and the establishment of American-controlled stations and American military courts in the Canadian north. King had successfully resisted British appeals; but he was learning how to yield fairly readily to American pressure. North American continentalism, which he feared but which he had come to feel was inevitable and even legitimate, had travelled a long stage further towards its completion. Altogether, it was highly appropriate that the debate on the Visiting Forces Bill was immediately followed by President Truman's first official visit to Ottawa.

II

About a fortnight later, when Ottawa was beginning to swelter in one of the hottest summers on record, another, much less distinguished group of visitors arrived in the Canadian capital. It was a delegation of Newfoundlanders, who had come to inquire on what terms Canada would be prepared to admit Newfoundland into Canadian Confederation. They had travelled all the way from St. John's by ship and train because the chairman of the delegation, Gordon Bradley, absolutely refused to go by plane. Bradley was a rugged, rather sad-eyed Newfoundlander with simple tastes, who had never imagined that any place could be as hot as Ottawa in the summer, and who had come equipped with heavy suits and Stanfield woollen underwear down to his ankles. For years he had been a convinced advocate of Newfoundland's entrance into Confederation; but he found it very difficult to do much work in the intolerable Ottawa heat, and he left most of the detailed business of the delegation to its secretary, Joseph R. ("Joey") Smallwood, a slight, dark, much younger man, with a ready tongue, alert eyes, an omnivorous capacity for work, and a predilection for polka-dotted bow ties.

The visit of the Newfoundland delegation was the result of one of the swiftest and most remarkable political transformations in the history of British North America. Only a little more than a dozen years before, the British government, at Newfoundland's own official request, had suspended responsible parliamentary government on the island and established government by an appointed commission instead. Depression and financial mismanagement had forced the suspension of Dominion status in the oldest overseas British colony; but the war, with its huge Canadian and American defence expenditures, brought prosperity and solvency back to Newfoundland and steadily increased the justification for the return of its home rule. In 1943, a group of three members of the British House of Commons – "a small patrol of back-benchers," as A. P. Herbert of *Punch*, one of its members, called it – made a visit of investigation to Newfoundland and Labrador. The three visitors wrote separate reports; but Herbert, who recommended the election of a "Council of Citizens" empowered to frame questions for a future referendum, offered the best constructive advice. Late in 1945, Attlee, the new Prime Minister, proposed a National Convention to consider Newfoundland's constitutional future. [9] Elections were held in June of the following year, and in September, 1946, the Convention began its sittings.

Two tasks were assigned to it: it had to decide whether Newfoundland was now capable of governing itself, and, if so, what different forms of self-government should be put before the people in a referendum. A solitary member of the Convention clung stubbornly to the hope that some vague, undefined but extremely profitable commercial deal with the United States could be arranged; but the Convention was quickly reminded that it had no authority to negotiate with foreign powers, and the United Kingdom had no intention of acting as its agent in such a negotiation. The great majority of the members realized that there were only three possible choices: continuation of the existing rule by commission, responsible government on the old model as a separate Dominion, or union with Canada. The first two choices meant the maintenance of the existing close ties with Great Britain and the hope of the continuation of British financial assistance, even if the island decided to return to responsible government; the third choice involved a long negotiation for good financial terms of union with Canada. Obviously, the majority in the Convention preferred the second of the three choices; and although it authorized two delegations of inquiry, one for England and one for Canada, it firmly ruled that the delegation to Ottawa could not depart until the delegation to London had returned.

Unfortunately for the "responsible government" majority in the Convention, the delegation to London came at the wrong time and to the wrong government. Attlee and his Cabinet were deep in grave financial difficulties. They had only recently announced the end of military and financial aid to Greece, and they were vigorously engaged in cutting, rather than renewing, old imperial ties. Ten or fifteen years later, the reorganized or newly independent African colonies were given a good deal of technical and financial assistance by the British government; but in 1947, the help which was freely available to Africa in the 1950's and 1960's was firmly denied to Newfoundland. The Secretary for the Dominions briefly informed the delegation that the United Kingdom would continue to accept financial responsibility for Newfoundland only if the island preferred to keep the present commission government. If it decided to opt for responsible government and Dominion status, it was on its own.[10]

The mission to London had failed. For some time it looked as if the mission to Ottawa would prove no more successful. King and Bradley, though they took to each other immediately, were both very doubtful of the outcome of the talks. Bradley, whose settled pessimism matched his lugubrious appearance, was acutely aware of the Convention's hostility to the Ottawa expedition, had "precious little belief" that union with Canada would ever get on the referendum ballot, and still less that it could possibly win.[11] King, although he was ready, as always, to expatiate rhetorically on "the dream of a great country, a British country, extending from the waters of the Atlantic to the Pacific," was beset by fears that the high cost of fitting Newfoundland into Confederation, on terms of equality of public services, would inevitably arouse the envy of the other "have-not" Atlantic Provinces and the resentment of the heavily taxed Ontario and Quebec. When at length, after prolonged calculations, it appeared likely that federal payments to Newfoundland might exceed those to the other Atlantic Provinces by as much as $15 million, King and St. Laurent at first recoiled in horror at such a politically impossible outlay.[12] They were brought back to their senses by the realization that this might be the very last chance of Canada achieving the original aim of Confederation. In the meantime, while they made up their minds to pay the necessary costs of nationhood, the Newfoundland delegation remained patiently, but not very hopefully, in Ottawa, although the Convention had dispatched a telegram, imperiously ordering it to return to St. John's. Eventually, at the end of September, the long negotiation ended in accord, and the Newfoundlanders left for home. The Canadian Cabinet approved the terms late in October, and on November 6, 1947, they were made public in the Convention at St. John's.

It was at this point that "Joey" Smallwood emerged as the dominating figure in the great debate over Newfoundland's political future. Everything conspired to thrust him forward. While Bradley had sweated, idled, and despaired in Ottawa, Smallwood, as secretary of the delegation, had found a place on every one of the eleven committees which were set up to discuss the terms of union. He knew more about the terms than anybody else and could expound them in copious detail and with easy dexterity. He had all the sublime assurance of a biblical prophet and all the low cunning of a twentieth-century propagandist. His wit was sharp and salty; his talent for spontaneous burlesque and ridicule very great. He had a never-failing supply of argument and rhetoric, and apparently inexhaustible reserves of energy. He loved combat; and, from November 20, when he began to explain and defend the terms of union in the Convention, the combat seemed unending. For twenty-four days, "with every word going over the air to the entire population of Newfoundland and Labrador," he argued the case for union with Canada; and finally, late in January, 1948, when the Convention rejected his motion to place Confederation on the referendum ballot paper, he simply refused to admit defeat.[13] He set himself energetically, with Bradley's aid, to arouse a popular clamour against the "rascally attempt" of the "dictators" in the Convention "to cheat the people out of their chance to exercise their judgement about their own country." Night after night, in an insistent radio appeal, he urged Newfoundlanders who wanted a free choice in their own future to send telegrams demanding the inclusion of Confederation in the referendum ballot paper; and in about a week a heap of fifty to sixty thousand telegram forms had been collected and presented to the Governor.[14] It was an audacious but triumphant demonstration. Smallwood had proved his case. Early in March, the Commonwealth Relations Secretary announced that the British government had decided to include Confederation as a third choice in the referendum and to hold a second referendum in case none of the three choices got an absolute majority.

In the referendum campaign, which began immediately, the supporters of responsible government undoubtedly had very considerable assets on their side.[15] The merchants of Water Street in St. John's, and the commercial class in general, were opposed to Confederation, for they feared the competition of Eaton's and the other big Canadian department and mail order shops. The rich and the well-to-do throughout the island hated the thought of the steep federal income tax; and, with only one exception, the entire Newfoundland press was solidly opposed to union with Canada. It was a formidable combination, shot through with serious weaknesses. The responsible government party had little cohesion, no efficient general direction and no leadership remotely comparable to Smallwood's. While his opponents campaigned individually with little concerted effect, Smallwood played the part of dictator. He ran an inexpensive campaign – "We didn't have a dollar to our name" – and his office was a tiny room behind a barbershop in Water Street; but he had an organizing mind, and a genius for the strategy and tactics of politics. He started a newspaper, *The Confederate*, and persuaded Jack Boothe, the cartoonist of the Toronto *Globe and Mail,* to contribute a series of striking political cartoons, many of them based on ideas and crude drawings which Smallwood himself had supplied. He travelled about the island in a tiny one-engined plane, precariously landing on floats, or in a car, with a truck behind equipped with blaring loudspeakers. His range was far, but it was highly selective. He made no attempt to cover Newfoundland completely or to woo unfriendly or hostile audiences. He held meetings only where he was certain of getting a large and enthusiastic reception.[16]

In the first referendum, held on June 3, 1948, none of the three choices gained an absolute majority, but commission government, which ran a poor third, was eliminated. The second referendum, held seven weeks later on July 22, gave union with Canada 78,323 votes or 52.34% of the total as against 71,334 votes or 47.66% for responsible government.[17] It was, indeed, a "very near run thing." Less than five percentage points separated the supporters of Confederation from the advocates of responsible government. Nearly half the voters of Newfoundland did not want to join Canada at once, but preferred instead to return to responsible government and Dominion status.

III

A generation earlier, the prospect of Newfoundland's entrance into Confederation would have monopolized the press and public speculation in Canada; but in 1947 and 1948 there were equally absorbing issues which caught and held public attention. Now that Big Four leadership had ended in the impasse in the Council of Foreign Ministers, the United Nations took on an added importance as a forum of competing eloquences and a battleground of rival policies. Canada was a member of the United Nations and for two years, 1948-49, occupied one of the non-permanent seats in the Security Council. As a middle power with diplomatic pretensions, the Canadian government was determined to play a fairly prominent role at the United Nations; and the Department of External Affairs, which had gained greatly in numbers, experience, and self-confidence during the war, was only too eager to get into the act. The department's two senior members, Louis St.

Laurent and Lester B. Pearson, were also firm believers in the United Nations and busy participants in its affairs. St. Laurent had held the post of Secretary of State for External Affairs since September, 1946; and at the same time, Pearson succeeded Norman Robertson as Undersecretary.

King admired and encouraged them both. When St. Laurent finally decided to remain in politics and to contest the leadership of the party, King was immensely gratified. He took a fatherly interest in Pearson, who was always getting offers of important and highly lucrative jobs outside Canada, urged him to stay at home, and predicted a political future for him. Pearson, in fact, had moved upward very swiftly in the department. He was junior in service to both Norman Robertson and Hume Wrong; but while Robertson was apt to be monosyllabic except in congenial company, and Wrong had a touch of his family's aloof hauteur, Pearson was an affable and outgoing companion, who spoke with a slight, engaging lisp, told stories with infectious gusto, talked sports with professional competence, and managed to make himself very useful, and very much respected and liked, in both Ottawa and Washington. He was a very probable candidate for St. Laurent's post as Secretary, just as St. Laurent was the almost certain successor to King's Prime Ministership. Pearson, King considered, was much too susceptible to the persuasive pressure of the State Department in Washington;[18] and St. Laurent at times showed a little too obviously the traditional French-Canadian suspicion and dislike of British interest and policies. Pearson was inclined to transform any favourite course of diplomatic action into an idealistic crusade; and Roman Catholic "clerical feeling," King believed, was evidently at the bottom of St. Laurent's moral and religious horror of the Soviet Union and all its works.[19] King was startled, and a little disconcerted, when St. Laurent remained unmoved by the news that the Pope had openly interfered in the approaching Italian election by warning the voters that they would commit a sin if they voted for Communist candidates.[20]

To a considerable extent, St. Laurent and Pearson shared a common outlook on the world and on the contribution Canada ought to make to the solution of its problems. They both believed that the Canadian government should play an active and creative part in international affairs and that its policies should be shaped and carried out by the experienced professionals, the Secretary for External Affairs and the officials of his department, with a minimum of interference from the uninformed and maladroit ministers of other departments. The United Nations, in their considered judgement, could be made a great stabilizing and moderating influence in world politics, and they were both convinced that Canada ought to make every effort to increase its effectiveness for good. To almost all of this King was totally opposed. The activities of the United Nations had begun to alarm him almost as much as the vain gestures of the League of Nations had done fifteen years earlier. It was ludicrous and dangerous, he felt certain, for

Canada to regard itself as a Sir Galahad always ready to rush off to kill dragons and to rescue the distressed in some remote corner of the world. "The truth is," he wrote realistically, "our country has no business trying to play a world role in the affairs of nations, the very location of some of which our people know little or nothing about."[21] It would be infinitely better, he thought, for Canada to remain as remote as possible from the insoluble problems of an evil world; and it was absolutely essential, in the vital interest of security, that Canadian external policies must be based on political decisions, in which the Cabinet had concurred. King was uneasily aware that both St. Laurent and Pearson disliked "having the Cabinet as a whole have too much of a say, discuss foreign affairs more than is necessary"; and on several occasions he insisted on having the dispatches read aloud and at length to the assembled ministers.

Between these two strongly opposed outlooks on world politics, a clash was inevitable. It came quickly in disputes over two issues, the future of Korea and the future of Palestine. The issue of Korea was the more serious of the two, for it directly and immediately involved the two superpowers, the Soviet Union and the United States. General Douglas MacArthur, for the United States, had accepted the surrender of the Japanese forces in the Korean peninsula south of the 38th parallel of latitude, and a Russian commander had taken over north of it. Among the Korean people, there was no clear and obvious agreement about the nature of their country's political future, and inevitably the continued presence of the armed forces of the two superpowers had a very great influence on public opinion. Communism grew rapidly in the north and moderate and right-wing views became steadily more preponderant in the south. Everybody agreed that a democratic republic ought to be established in Korea, but between the Russians and the Americans there was no meeting of minds about its political character. In the end, the United States brought the question before the United Nations Assembly; it proposed that general elections, supervised by a United Nations Temporary Commission, should be held throughout the Korean peninsula. Canada was proposed and elected to the Temporary Commission, but without the approval, or even the knowledge, of the government in Ottawa; and, a few days later, on December 18, 1947, St. Laurent confidently proposed the name of Dr. G. S. Patterson as the Canadian representative.[22]

King was suddenly roused to vehement opposition. Although it was over a year since St. Laurent had become Secretary for External Affairs, he had never lost his jealous, proprietorial interest in the conduct of the department or his watchful concern for Canadian foreign policy. Now he became seriously alarmed. He was terrified of attempting to mediate between the two great powers and still more terrified of the equivocal appearance of acting as the agent or puppet of one of them. "I stressed over again," he recorded in his account of one crucial Cabinet meeting, "how the Americans were seeking to make the United Nations a political arm of the Secretary of State's Department."[23] He earnestly reminded his colleagues of how difficult it would be, if Canada took its place on the Temporary Commission, to refute the charge that in political, as well as in economic affairs, the country was under the domination of the United States. He resisted stubbornly and argued interminably, but in the end he realized that he was confronted by the united pressure of two governments, his own, as well as that of the United States. President Truman even went so far as to pay him the supreme courtesy of writing him a personal appeal.[24] St. Laurent argued darkly that if Canada hesitated to take its appointed place on the Commission, then Canada ought logically to boycott the United Nations or resign from it. St. Laurent and Ilsley even got so far as to hint at their own resignations.[25]

Faced with this combined resistance, King yielded – a little. He agreed that Patterson might remain on the Commission but only so long as it enjoyed the co-operation of both the United States and the Soviet Union and did nothing to profit the one at the expense of the other. The impossibility of meeting these exacting conditions and thus the wisdom of King's original objection to Canada's involvement soon became manifest. The Commission was refused admission to northern Korea; and, on the instructions of the Interim Committee of the Assembly, it decided that elections were to be held "in those parts of Korea which were accessible" to it in the south. The result was the creation of the Republic of Korea, with Dr. Syngman Rhee as President, an event which was followed rapidly by the establishment of the Communist Democratic People's Republic in the north. The Canadian representative protested in vain during the early stages of these developments, but in the end Canada supported a resolution in the United Nations Assembly which declared that the Syngman Rhee regime at Seoul was the only legitimate government in Korea. The United States had indeed succeeded, in King's words, in making the United Nations "a political arm of the Secretary of State's Department"; and Canada had given a reluctant, restive, but, on the whole, acceptable performance as a faithful follower.

IV

To Canadians Korea seemed remote and utterly unknown; Palestine was equally far off but not so strangely unfamiliar. The question of its political future was perhaps not so potentially dangerous as that of Korea; but, to the Canadian government, it seemed almost as painfully difficult, for, if Russia was not seriously involved in the problem, Great Britain and the United States were badly divided over it. Great Britain's old historic interest in the Middle East had been strengthened by her acceptance of the League

of Nations's mandate in Palestine as well as by the close relations with the
Arab States which had developed during and after the First World War. The
concern of the United States was much more recent and it grew, like so many
other of the preoccupations of the American administration, out of a purely
domestic phenomenon, the recent and very rapid development of Zionism
in the Republic. Unlimited Jewish immigration to Palestine was, of course,
the avowed aim of the American Zionists. Before the war, Britain had tried
to limit the number of immigrants in the hope of controlling the intractable
problem of government in the mandate; but illegal immigration continued
steadily, encouraged and promoted by American Zionism. In the end, the
baffled British sought to share their mounting responsibilities in Palestine
by inviting American co-operation, and an Anglo-American Committee of
Inquiry was set up. If the British hoped that this might bring their difficulties into manageable proportions, they were bitterly disappointed, for the one
practical recommendation of the Committee's report, released at the end of
April, 1946, was the authorized admission of a further 100,000 Jews into
Palestine.[26] For the British this was nearly the end. Less than a year later,
in February, 1947, they brought the question of Palestine before the United
Nations.[27] It was one more of the intolerable burdens they sought to jettison
during that harried year, 1947. And at the same time they intended to compel
the world to face the awkward fact that Palestine was not simply an exercise
in historical justice and practical idealism, but also a governmental problem
of enormous complexity.

The United Nations promptly set up a special committee to investigate
and report, with a Canadian, Mr. Justice Ivan Rand, as one of its eleven
members. When the Second Assembly met in the autumn of 1947, it was
presented with two reports, a majority report, strongly supported by Rand,
which recommended the partition of Palestine into two states, one Jewish
and one Arab, and a minority report which advocated a federal system for
the mandate. Pearson was appointed chairman of a special sub-committee
entrusted with the task of devising a detailed plan based on the majority
recommendation of partition; and he quickly became convinced that partition was the only possible answer to the riddle of Palestine's political future.
His work on the sub-committee and his earnest advocacy of its plan before
the General Assembly may have helped to strengthen his conviction, but it
had, as well, a more profound and personal origin. "I must admit," he wrote
later, "that I became emotionally involved in a very special way because we
were dealing with the Holy Land – the land of my Sunday School lessons
. . . . I think that in the back of my mind I was concerning myself with
something close to my early life and religious background."[28] These affecting
boyish memories strengthened Pearson's crusading ardour for partition, but,
if King had known of them, he would probably have decided that they
weakened the Undersecretary's political judgement. Pearson, he concluded

worriedly, was inclined to rashness. Norman Robertson, now High Commissioner in London, had undoubtedly more political sagacity. And, as the ugly drama of Palestine rapidly unfolded, it became obvious that political sagacity, amounting almost to godlike wisdom, was urgently required.

On November 29, 1947, the United Nations Assembly approved the plan of partition. An impressive majority of thirty-three states voted for it; but the division within the Assembly was nonetheless distinctly ominous for the future. Ten states, including the United Kingdom, abstained from voting; thirteen states, including the entire Arab-Moslem contingent, voted against.[29] How was the United Nations to implement a contentious plan which it had formally adopted in the face of such evasion and opposition? The Americans and Canadians had always been inclined to discount the British warning of Arab armed resistance. They had also gone on indulging the wishful hope that the British, despite repeated statements to the contrary, would continue to provide military support for order in the mandate. Both these naive assumptions turned out to be false. Early in December, 1947, only a few days after the Assembly had committed itself to partition, fighting broke out between Arabs and Jews. The British government made the almost equally alarming announcement that, since the United Nations had now settled the political future of Palestine, it proposed to end the burden of its mandate on May 15, 1948, only six months away.

What was the United Nations to do? Its own army, authorized by the charter, had, of course, never been constituted. It had made no special *ad hoc* arrangements for carrying out its partition plan, since it had mistakenly relied on the British. Yet obviously it would have to impose its plan by force, since the Israelis and the Arabs were already at each other's throats. The difficult and anxious question of method now confronted the United Nations Security Council, of which Canada had become a member on January 1, 1948. For a time, the United States, which always kept a watchful eye on its clamorous Zionist bloc, seemed to favour imposition by force; and Pearson was inclined to support this hazardous proposal, if only as a diplomatic manoeuvre inside the Council. King was extremely upset. The mere thought of deliberately accepting a moral commitment, which conceivably might lead to the dispatch of Canadian troops to the Middle East, simply horrified him. Once again, an ageing and isolationist Prime Minister was at odds with his youthful and venturesome Department of External Affairs. Yet Palestine never became a Cabinet crisis as Korea had done, for St. Laurent gave his Undersecretary little support, and the clash of opinion was really between Pearson and King. Pearson had acquired something of the American habit of criticizing the negativism and irresponsibility of the British government; British support for the Arabs, he suggested, could be largely explained by strategical considerations and oil politics.[30] These arguments and insinuations made no impression whatever on King. He stoutly defended British detachment and neutrality in the developing Arab-Israel struggle. The British, he informed the Cabinet impressively, knew far more about Middle East politics than the inexperienced Americans did.[31]

Canada continued to remain studiously aloof, and in the end the United States gave up its tentative plan of imposing partition on the squabbling Arabs and Jews. The United Nations would not attempt a settlement by force; but, although its armed might was never invoked, a willing and eager substitute was available on the spot in the Israeli forces. The Israelis could indeed claim that morally, if not legally, they constituted a United Nations army. That great new world parliament, the United Nations Assembly, had authorized them to found a new nation of their own in Palestine and had specified its boundaries. On May 14, 1948, the day before the British mandate was to end, they triumphantly proclaimed the founding of the Jewish state of Israel, and sixteen minutes later the United States granted it diplomatic recognition.[32] In effect, the American government had got exactly what it wanted by different, but perhaps more conclusive methods. The Israeli army proceeded to make good its territorial claims with better equipment and better generalship. The United Nations hovered uncertainly around the edges of the conflict, making various ineffectual attempts at conciliation; but the struggle finally ended, as now it could only do, in the victory of the Israelis. Palestine was arbitrarily divided between Israel and its Arab neighbours, and the world faced the new problem of one million Palestinian refugees.

V

The United States had now acquired a client state on the eastern edge of the Mediterranean – a suitable complement to that other client state, South Korea, on the western rim of the Pacific. The empire of American power and influence now extended, east to west, nearly three-quarters of the way around the world. To the north was Canada, which as yet could hardly be considered, still less openly described, as a client or satellite, but which was already joined to the United States in an intimate military association. The constitutional limits, which Canada had seen fit to impose on this partnership, could, no doubt, be quickly relaxed in an emergency; but, even so, was this military alliance sufficient in the new and dangerous post-war circumstances? Would it not be better if it were strengthened by closer commercial ties? The idea of a trade pact with Canada became suddenly popular in Washington; and early in January, 1948, when Douglas Abbott, the Minister of Finance, returned from a visit to the United States, he brought with him the startling news that senior officials in the American administration had suggested the possibility of a broad Reciprocity Treaty with Canada.[33]

This was the beginning of a series of severely secret negotiations between the two governments which continued spasmodically during the first four anxious months of 1948. The project was never brought before the Canadian Cabinet; only a minority of the ministers – Abbott, McKinnon, Howe and St. Laurent – knew anything about it. It was pushed forward mainly by senior permanent officials, by W. C. Clark and John Deutsch in the Department of Finance, Graham Towers of the Bank of Canada, and, in its later stages, by Pearson and Hume Wrong, Canadian Ambassador to the United States. Once again, in what was historically one of the most contentious and dangerous of all Canadian issues, the career men of the new specialized civil service had taken the initiative, and, urged forward by American encouragement and impatient eagerness, they devised a plan of grandiose, if not frightening, proportions. The horrendous words "commercial union" were, of course, left unspoken; but the Americans were prepared to negotiate a treaty, possibly for as many as twenty-five years, which would mean "ultimate free trade," modified at first by quotas on either side. The Americans, in short, had large views and they were in a tearing hurry. They wanted the whole plan finished and ready for submission to Congress by April or May. As usual, they were thinking more of domestic politics than of foreign trade. Truman faced his first presidential election in the autumn of 1948.

At first, and for a variety of reasons, King was very attracted to the plan. The Liberal Party had always stood – or had always professed to stand – for free trade, and the successful negotiation of a Reciprocity Treaty with the United States would vindicate Sir Wilfrid Laurier and avenge his defeat in 1911. It would also – and this, of course, explained the strong support of the Finance Department – help to correct the chronic Canadian imbalance of payments with the United States, which had caused the exchange crisis of the previous autumn. Finally – as King explained in his most guarded fashion to a select group of senior civil servants – it might fit very appropriately into the Atlantic Security Pact, which was already under secret discussion, and add another important dimension to its scope.[34] All these were excellent reasons for proceeding with the negotiations; but as they continued, and the complicated detail as well as the vast scope of the plan became clearer, King drew back. He disliked the American insistence on haste. He feared that, at his age, he could never master or expound the intricate details of the scheme. He predicted fanatical Conservative opposition, an endless filibuster in the House of Commons, and, in the end, an inevitable general election, with highly doubtful results. The Tories, he prophesied darkly, would triumphantly announce, "This is Mr. King's toy. He has always wanted annexation with the States."[35]

The probable truth of these sombre predictions was quickly demonstrated. King had tried, with laborious secretiveness, to conceal the reciprocity negotiations under heavy wraps; but the Americans had never thought there was any need to keep their plans for Canada secret, and the whole project, labelled

"Customs Union with Canada: Canada needs us and we need Canada in a violently contracting world" was revealed in the March 15 number of the American weekly magazine *Life*.[36] The Canadian press at once displayed considerable interest, a good deal of concern, and apparently unanimous opposition. Kenneth Wilson, who had exposed the confident American campaign for a defence pact with Canada in 1946, hurried down for a special interview with the Prime Minister on the subject; but his weekly, the *Financial Post*, had already decided that "Customs union not the answer." *Saturday Night*, in a special article written by Wynne Plumptre, voiced strong disapproval. "Not on your Life" declared the *Globe and Mail*. Behind all the different and variously expressed editorial objections to *Life's* ambitious proposal, there lurked the old and ineradicable Canadian conviction that a customs union would infallibly be followed by a political union. King felt it himself, despite the seductive appeal of free trade, the more he pondered the problem. "I said," he told Hume Wrong in Washington, "I felt sure that the long objective of the Americans was to control this continent. They would want to get Canada under their aegis."[37] This truth had come to seem so obvious to him that he was both astonished and exasperated when the permanent officials in Finance, External Affairs, and Trade and Commerce failed to perceive it. The fact was, of course, that the new Canadian bureaucrats were, to a large extent, both ignorant of Canadian traditions and out of touch with contemporary Canadian opinion. For them the economic unity of the North American continent had all the beautiful validity of an economist's model. King himself had a simple explanation of their sublime assurance. He thought that American flattery and cajolery had turned their heads!

VI

Yet if King nursed many doubts and fears about American continentalism, he welcomed the growing American urge to unite with Great Britain and Western Europe in a defence against Communism. Pressure from either the United Kingdom alone, or the United States alone, might be questioned and resisted; but, for King, the united pressure of both was irresistible. The influence of Anglo-American precept and example increased steadily during the mounting international tension of 1948. Both the timing and the unqualified dogmatism of the Truman Doctrine had been unfortunate. If General Marshall's munificent offer of economic aid to Europe had preceded, rather than followed, the proclamation of the Truman Doctrine, the post-war history of Europe might have been vastly different; but, coming as it did, nearly three months after Truman's uncompromising challenge, even Marshall's generous assurance that the new American policy was "directed not against any country or doctrine, but against hunger, poverty, desperation and chaos" sounded unconvincing. The Soviet Union declined to yield its sovereign independence so far as to join with the other nations in drafting a common plan for the economic recovery of Europe as a whole; and its eastern satellites and associates, including, in the end, Czechoslovakia, followed its example and rejected Marshall aid. Early in the autumn, the Cominform was established to maintain the moral and political solidarity of this dissident eastern bloc. In December, the last meeting of the Council of Foreign Ministers – the only body that continued the wartime association of the Big Three – broke up in hopeless disagreement.

A definite economic division of Europe had now come into being. It was confirmed and deepened during 1948 by an apparently absolute political cleavage. During the early post-war years, there had been considerable co-operation between Communists and Democratic Socialists in Western as well as Eastern Europe. Powerful Communist parties existed in both France and Italy; Communists were represented in the French government, just as Democratic Socialists held important positions in the government of Czechoslovakia. If this had ever really meant the possibility of the peaceful co-existence of two radically different political philosophies, the intransigent events of 1947-48 ended it. In May, 1947, the French President dismissed the five Communist members of his Cabinet. Less than a year later, the Italian general election – in which the Roman Catholic Church openly discharged its direst ecclesiastical penalties against Communist supporters – ended in the decisive defeat of Italian Communism. These victories of Republican, Christian or Socialist Democrats were clear evidence of the hardening of public opinion; but their significance, for liberal westerners, was dwarfed by the tragic import of the Communist *coup d'état* of February, 1948, in Czechoslovakia, the country which had tried hardest and gone furthest in building bridges between East and West.

Mackenzie King had gone over to England, in the autumn of 1947, for the wedding of Princess Elizabeth and Lieutenant Philip Mountbatten. He returned to Canada in December in a mood of gloom and foreboding. Attlee and Bevin, he was well aware, looked forward apprehensively, but indecisively, to the fateful year, 1948; and it was not until the brutal Prague *coup d'état* of late February that they were finally moved to action. Even then, King struggled to maintain Canada's detachment. Like so many others, he was shocked by the dreadful thought of the pyjama-clad body of Jan Masaryk, the Czech Foreign Minister, lying dead on the pavement outside the Foreign Office, while the open window of his private apartment gaped above. He mourned Masaryk's loss, but he was not to be hustled into any premature official condemnation of what he still regarded as the "domestic affairs" of Czechoslovakia. The horrified speed with which Western Europe now rushed into action was something which he clearly did not anticipate; but on March 11, the day after he had been deploring Masaryk's death, he received an urgent personal message from Attlee, a message which stressed the need of a united front of free nations and proposed the formation of an Atlantic regional security group, including the United States. King, St. Laurent, Pearson and Claxton, the Minister of Defence, met in solemn conclave that afternoon and decided to cable Attlee Canada's guarded readiness to "explore the situation."[38] King busied himself during the next few days in impressing the terrible gravity of affairs upon the rest of his Cabinet colleagues and the leaders of the three opposition parties in Parliament.

The signing of the Treaty of Brussels, by which England and France joined with the Benelux countries – Belgium, the Netherlands, and Luxembourg – to form a union for collective security, came as no surprise to King. Attlee had already informed him of the negotiations leading up to it; and for Attlee – and, of course, for King as well – the Brussels pact, by itself, was woefully deficient. Everything depended upon the attitude of the United States; and King was among the many Parliamentarians who hastened to the Members' Lounge at 12:30 on March 17 to listen to the radio broadcast of Truman's address to a joint session of the two Houses of Congress. "I am sure," Truman declared impressively, "that the determination of the free countries of Europe to protect themselves will be matched by an equal determination on our part to help them do so."[39] It was vague enough, but promising; King thought it an "exceptionally fine, manly, courageous, direct speech." At any rate, it was decisive for him and for Canada. Obviously, the United Kingdom and the United States were moving together towards the defence of Western Europe. And Canada, the linch-pin between them, as King had always conceived it, must occupy its appointed place.

When the broadcast was over, he stood up and invited the ministers present to accompany him upstairs to his office. On the way up, he paused briefly at his smaller downstairs room and prayed for strength and guidance. Upstairs, the ministers straggled in slowly and, in order to make sure that everybody was prepared to back Great Britain and the United States in an Atlantic security pact, he asked and received assurance several times. There was really no doubt or uncertainty. "Someone said something about a league of free people, and we either had to be in it or out of it. I said I was sure there could be no doubt on the part of anyone as to our being in. "[40]

VII

1948 was a memorable year; but for Mackenzie King its most momentous event was his own retirement. Retirement for him was a prolonged; complicated, and elaborate process, which continued in an apparently endless succession of ceremonial occasions, graced with eulogies, toasts, presents and flowers, and invariably including a lengthy speech by himself. His interest in the important anniversaries, the significant episodes, and even the trivial details of his career, had always been enormous; and the approach to his retirement, the crowning event of his long mission for Canada, obviously had to be a stately process, marked at every stage by appropriate ceremonies. He was like an actor who always wanted another curtain call, or a prima donna who could never resist another farewell tour. The long progression towards his last appearance began, in fact, in June, 1947, nearly eighteen months before the final event; and from then on not a single, suitable occasion for doing King honour was missed. There were celebrations on his birthday, on his completion of twenty years service as Prime Minister of Canada, and on his triumphant overtaking of Sir Robert Walpole's record as the Prime Minister longest in office in the history of the British Empire.

By Christmas of 1947, everybody was well aware that King's retirement, if not exactly imminent, could scarcely be very far off; but, in such a vital matter, public knowledge could not possibly be a substitute for public announcement; and in January, 1948, at a mammoth meeting of the National Liberal Federation, King formally announced his intention to resign. Though he spoke for a full hour, he characteristically did not set a date for his resig-nation; and it was nearly nine months later that his preferred successor, Louis St. Laurent, was chosen as the next leader of the Liberal Party; and three months later still that he finally gave up his office. November 15 was the day chosen for the great event; and as the solemn hour drew closer, the proceedings took on a tone of increasing gravity and elaboration. On the 12th King said good-bye to the entire Cabinet, with a final heartfelt "God Bless You All" as he turned before leaving the room. On the 13th he said a formal farewell to the assembled staffs of the Privy Council Office and the Prime Minister's Office. In between there was a session with the Ottawa press gallery and a last radio message to the people of Canada. Journalists and photographers were in close attendance on the 14th when he drove out to Government House to submit his resignation and recommend his successor to Lord Alexander. On the 15th came the final tableau with the entire company, including all the Cabinet ministers and their wives in attendance, flowers in profusion, champagne in unlimited supply, toasts to King by Alexander and to St. Laurent by King, and memorial photographs of the three seated together.

When St. Laurent and his ministers had left King chatting amiably with their wives and had retired to hold their first Cabinet meeting, a new era – in some ways significantly different and in others remarkably unchanged – had begun in Canadian affairs. St. Laurent was a French-Canadian Roman Catholic and a successful corporation lawyer who had come late, and rather reluctantly, to politics. Corporation lawyers were familiar enough in Cana-dian political life, but it was more than a third of a century since a French Canadian had been Prime Minister of Canada. King had always tried to avoid all specific reference to his own or his colleagues' national origins or religious affiliations; he was hypersensitively anxious to preserve the cultural concord of a multicultural country. St. Laurent appeared to have few such scruples. King was horrified when he learnt that his chosen successor, in a speech delivered at Winnipeg – of all places – had bluntly reminded his audience that he was a French Canadian and a Roman Catholic, as if these were facts – and perhaps unpleasant facts – to which they would just have to get accustomed! St. Laurent could be disconcertingly candid and outspoken about himself and his views; but, on the whole, his views were not very distinctive or unusual. His faith in the United Nations, his hatred of Communism were greater than King's, his fear of foreign entanglements noticeably less. He had none of King's lingering affection for England and the British Empire-Commonwealth, and little of King's obsessive fear of American continentalism. Those were significant differences, but they were differences of degree, not of substance. St. Laurent was not an idealist, or a fanatic, but an eminently moderate, cautious conservative man.

Like King, he was a strong Canadian nationalist; and as soon as his first general election had triumphantly confirmed his hold on power, he eagerly took up such questions as the amendment of the Canadian constitution and the abolition of appeals to London – important nationalist business which King had left unfinished. Freedom from "the last legal vestiges of colonial status" and better relations with the provinces, especially his own native province of Quebec, were certainly his major domestic interests. He had little of King's obsessive concern for social security; and of all the comprehensive welfare projects which King had presented to the Dominion-Provincial Conference in 1945, St. Laurent realized only one, the universal old-age pension. He never kept a tight rein on his colleagues, and, as he grew older and more frequently subject to lassitude and depression, his hold on public business relaxed. He did not so much exercise control over national affairs as preside over their management by others. The actual conduct of government was only indirectly and formally his; it was the business of the managerial civil service, the pupils of Keynes and Beveridge, which had grown so immensely in numbers, experience, and assurance during the war. King, who had first brought this managerial bureaucracy into being, but who remembered, with occasional regret, the old untrained, unambitious civil service of the past, grew in the end to resent and question his own creation. He disliked and resisted the incorrigible tendency of the trained and talented senior officers in Finance and External Affairs to start off on their own on some new and questionable scheme. St. Laurent apparently felt few such qualms. The foundations of the new system had already been solidly laid by the time he entered politics, and he was comfortably adjusted to its procedures. He was a company chairman, not an executive president; and so long as Canada Incorporated maintained a good growth rate and a favourable consumer reaction, he was quite satisfied.

There were not a great many new faces in his Cabinet. Undoubtedly, the most important was Lester B. ("Mike") Pearson, who had become Secretary of State for External Affairs two months before King's retirement. He was a superlative representative of the new managerial bureaucracy, a career diplomatist who had moved smoothly into politics, an *arriviste* who always managed to get into the right situations at the right time. Mackenzie King, who in such matters could be said to have virtually prophetic powers, had predicted that the man who succeeded St. Laurent as Minister of External Affairs would some day follow him as Prime Minister of Canada. Pearson's assets were, in fact, considerable. He had charm, humour, friendliness. When he took office in the autumn of 1948, he was already well acquainted with the hard facts and the intricate subtleties of contemporary diplomacy and politics. Yet he never quite became a professional diplomat or a professional politician. He was the son of a Methodist clergyman and he could never forget that he started life as a Sunday School scholar who knew the place-names of the Holy Land better than he did those of Canada. His Methodist upbringing may have strengthened his urge to success, but it also planted deep within him a sense of moral purpose and direction in life and politics. For him, diplomatic aims had the unfortunate habit of taking on the lofty nobility of moral causes. The partition of Palestine was a "cause." The main-tenance of a successful and active post-war system of collective security became another "cause." The North Atlantic Treaty Organization was a third great moral enterprise .

VIII

Undoubtedly, Canadian foreign policy would be carried forward with greater conviction, assurance, and zeal than in the past; but its aims, in all proba-bility, would not differ immediately from what they had been. King, after all, had given his blessing to the idea of a North Atlantic security pact. He had even welcomed the immediate union with Newfoundland, though up to the very last moment he had hesitated, assailed by characteristic doubts and apprehensions. Only three days before the second referendum was held, the entire Cabinet had solemnly agreed with him that if the majority was very close, "we should not consider Confederation." Unfortunately, the majority – a little less than six thousand – was indeed very close. But after all, it *was* a majority; and as he considered and reconsidered it, his unhappy uncertainty changed into positive elation. He was uplifted, not so much by the completion of the original design of Confederation, as by the gratifying thought that this achievement had been brought about by his own govern-ment. William Lyon Mackenzie, he reflected, had laid the foundations of responsible government; his grandson, William Lyon Mackenzie King, had completed the structure of national unity. He glowed with the seductive thought that he "might even be listed as one of the Fathers of the larger Confederation." [41]

Unfortunately this enticing dream was a little marred by the fact that the union would not formally take place until the end of March, 1949, by which time King would have long retired; but in October, when the second Newfoundland delegation, including the mournful Bradley and the ubiquitous Smallwood, arrived in Ottawa, King was still in his accustomed place as Prime Minister. He and his government were now quite prepared to revise the terms of union laid down the previous year, but it took more than two months of close negotiations before the work was complete. Many of the important clauses in the original agreement were, of course, left unaltered. Newfoundland, including Labrador, as defined by the award of the Judicial Committee of the Privy Council in 1927, was to enter Confederation with the status of a province, and with a representation of six senators and seven M.P.'s in the Parliament of Canada. In addition, all Canada's wide range of welfare services – old age pensions, unemployment insurance and family allowances – were to be automatically extended to the island.

There was no question or argument about these basic political or social benefits of membership in the Union; the real issue was financial and even here there were established historical precedents to fall back on. The statutory provincial subsidies devised at Confederation, together with all the additional payments granted subsequently to the Maritime Provinces, would be simply duplicated in Newfoundland's case; and the federal government would assume the greater part of the provincial debt, as of course it had done for every other province on its entrance into Confederation. All traditional devices for ensuring provincial solvency were, of course, readily available; but, as the members of the second delegation kept on insisting with emphasis and at length, they would simply not be enough to meet Newfoundland's special needs. If the island's own provincial services were to be maintained at something close to the level common throughout the rest of Canada, much larger sums would be necessary, particularly during the early transitional years between its old and new status. The federal negotiators, already committed to the Union in principle, had no desire to mar its commencement with tight-fisted haggling. The transitional grants, for the first three years, were more than doubled, and, for the whole twelve-year period, were increased from slightly over $26 million to nearly $43 million.[42]

The terms were generous. Nobody could argue, with any semblance of justice, that they were not generous, and nobody did. It was not the bargain itself, but the manner of its making which was attacked; and in the light of the constitutional position of the members of the British Commonwealth as it was in 1948 and 1949, the procedure followed was certainly peculiar.

By the provisions of the Statute of Westminster of 1931, the British Parliament could legislate for a Dominion only at the request, and with the consent, of its legislature. Newfoundland had been included as one of the Dominions enumerated in the act; but Newfoundland had lost its Dominion status in 1934, when it had handed back its legislative authority to the British, and the British had established an appointed Commission of Government. Neither the Commission of Government nor the new National Convention could properly be regarded as a provincial legislature, with power to determine Newfoundland's future. Morally, as well as legally – since Newfoundland had itself requested the suspension of its responsible government – only the British Parliament could legislate for Newfoundland.

Nobody could seriously question this imperial authority. And yet a good many people were uneasily conscious of the fact that if the British Parliament acted without the request of a Dominion legislature, it would be transgressing the spirit, if not the letter, of the Statute of Westminster. It was a difficult, embarrassing, almost humiliating situation; but, as the advocates of the return of responsible government had always argued, there was an obvious and easy way out. The British Parliament could restore Newfoundland's Dominion Status, reconstitute its provincial legislature, and the provincial legislature could itself decide whether it wanted to enter Canadian Confederation and on what terms. Possibly it might wish to continue its previous separate political existence; very probably it might prefer to join Canada. But its decision, whatever it was, would be constitutionally impeccable. It would be the decision of a properly constituted legislature on the British model, and not merely the statistical result of a referendum. It would be an act of parliamentary, not plebiscitary, government.

This was the main point of criticism voiced in both the British and the Canadian Parliaments when the terms of the union came before them in February, 1949. The two bills, of course, got very different receptions in the two Parliaments. The Canadians, whatever their party affiliations or personal opinions, gave the union with Newfoundland a very enthusiastic welcome. The British regarded it with polite indifference or embarrassed concern, and only a single member, A. P. Herbert of *Punch*, one of the original "small patrol of back-benchers" which had paid an official visit to Newfoundland nearly six years earlier, opposed the measure with vehement sincerity and eloquence. Herbert, who disliked Canada almost as much as he disliked the United States – which was a very great deal indeed – regarded the Newfoundlanders as transplanted Scots, Yorkshiremen and West Countrymen who must be rescued from the frightful fate of North Americanization by compulsion![43] He assured the House of Commons that if Great Britain forced Newfoundland into union with Canada "our name would stink in the nostrils of a people who are as British as the lions in Trafalgar Square...."[44] A two-thirds majority, he argued passionately, would alone have been conclusive in the second referendum. How could the British Parliament dare to drive the Newfoundlanders into an immediate union when nearly 48% of them had opposed it! Self-government, he insisted, must be restored at once. He even went so far as to quote two unquestionably Canadian sources – George Drew and the Toronto *Globe and Mail* – in support of his contention that the British Parliament could not possibly approve the union agreement until a properly constituted Newfoundland legislature had requested it to do so.

George Drew, of course, had more than constitutional questions in mind. He was well aware that Premier Duplessis of Quebec had never accepted the award of the Judicial Committee of the Privy Council in the Labrador boundary dispute and consequently strongly opposed Newfoundland's admission with its existing boundaries. It was obviously good party politics to urge the Liberal government to postpone the completion of the union until it had taken the provinces into consultation. Drew took advantage of this opportunity, but in a rather half-hearted way. His main complaint was against the constitutional procedure which the British and Canadians had employed to bring the union into effect.[45] "I dislike the method," he said bluntly, and his disapproval accurately anticipated that voiced in the British Parliament a little later. "I think we are all a little uncomfortable," said one member of the House of Lords. "I am unhappy about the way it was done." The summing-up of Conservative Party headquarters was the same, though differently expressed: "The verdict is likely to be, the right thing done in the wrong way."[46]

In Newfoundland, if not in mainland Canada, a slight, lingering sense of regret and resentment, like the bitter residue at the bottom of a cup, remained and persisted. This was one legacy of the Union; but there was another legacy, not an emotional legacy of injury and wounded pride, but of definite legal right and concrete physical substance, the American bases in Newfoundland and Labrador. They were the acquisitions of President Roosevelt, that outspoken critic and covert enemy of the British Empire, and himself one of the greatest empire builders of the twentieth century. They had been taken from a Great Britain which was prepared to sacrifice its last asset in the struggle against Hitler, and calmly appropriated by a United States which was determined to exact every possible benefit from the weakness and necessity of its closest political relative and friend. The bases were not ordinary military bases, with limited rights, such as rapidly became familiar during the Cold War. They were sovereign political enclaves, very much like the duodecimo principalities of the Holy Roman Empire. Their extra-territorial rights included customs, excise, and postal privileges. American military and civil courts possessed exclusive jurisdiction over all the inhabitants in the base.

As far back as the Ogdensburg Agreement, King had tried to lay down the principle that there were to be no American bases in Canada. During the war, the American military occupation of the Canadian north had been so complete that the distinction between its northern establishments and normal bases was a distinction without any real difference. King had become belatedly but uneasily conscious of this fact by the time the war ended; and when, in 1946, the Americans began their determined effort to renew the wartime agreement with Canada, King had insisted on some protection for Canadian sovereignty. The result was the fifth clause of the statement which King read to the House of Commons on February 12, 1947: "As an underlying principle, all co-operative arrangements will be without impairment of the control of either country over all activities in its territory." This "underlying principle" had been formally announced two years before the Canadian Parliament began its debate on Newfoundland's entrance into Confederation; but obviously, so long as the American bases remained, Canada's "control" would not extend "over all activities" in the new tenth province. It might have been thought that the Canadian government ought to have offered some explanation or justification of this discrepancy, but it did nothing of the kind. In his opening statement, St. Laurent did not even mention the American bases. Still more strangely, the principal leaders of the Opposition did not question him, or Claxton, the Minister of Defence, or Pearson, the Minister of External Affairs, about the American presence in Newfoundland. Drew, Graydon, Diefenbaker, had not a word to say on the subject. It was left to T. L. ("Tommy") Church, member for Broadview in Toronto, an old man, notorious for his antedeluvian views, who was popularly regarded, even by his fellow Progressive-Conservatives, as a comic survival of Edwardian imperialism, to raise the question.[47]

St. Laurent, reverting quickly to character as successful corporation lawyer and company chairman, was stiffly legal in his reply. There was no admission that the sovereign American bases in Newfoundland were a compromising, if not humiliating, emcumbrance on the attainment of the original aim of Confederation, and no assurance, and not even any suggestion, that the Canadians intended to try hard to bring it to an end. The ninety-nine year leases existed, St. Laurent said in effect, and their terms must be respected until the United States could be persuaded to change them. The Canadian government, he explained, could not open official negotiations for the alteration of the leases; for, until Newfoundland became a part of Canada, it had no standing in the matter. He did not remind the House that, until that time, Great Britain was sovereign in Newfoundland and that, since the bases were a British gift, the British government might conceivably have approached the United States about them at Canada's request. The fact was that the Canadian government had decided, at a very early stage, that it would do everything to avoid the charge of attempting to influence, or anticipate, Newfoundland's change of status, and that therefore it would remain as aloof as possible from the two principals concerned, Great Britain and Newfoundland. In these circumstances, St. Laurent informed Church, there was very little that Canada could do and had done. He himself, he announced, would very soon pay his first visit to the President and promised to bring up the question of the bases while he was in Washington. In the meantime, unofficial negotiations had already begun with the aim of bringing the terms of the leases into conformity with the principles of military co-operation set out in the declaration of February 12, 1947.[48]

IX

The contrast between Canada's gingerly and surreptitious defence of its own territorial integrity and its confident and outspoken advocacy of a North Atlantic defence pact was startling. The American military presence in Newfoundland might have been one of the island's immutable physical facts, like its topography and climate, which had to be endured simply because nothing could be done to change them. The North Atlantic pact, a military alliance which might just as easily provoke war as prevent it, was regarded, on the contrary, as a great human enterprise which deserved Canada's earnest promotion. It certainly got it. As early as the summer of 1947, Pearson, still Undersecretary for External Affairs, and his assistant, Escott Reid, were suggesting, in general terms, the possibility of a regional collective security organization. This, they explained rather elaborately, would be outside the structure of the United Nations, but not inconsistent with its principles, since the collective right of self-defence was authorized by the 51st article of the Charter. Pearson, who was soon to occupy a position of still greater importance and influence, was undoubtedly the driving force behind the Canadian promotion campaign. The North Atlantic association was the second of his great "causes." To be sure, it was St. Laurent who, on September 18, 1947, announced Canada's frank proposal to the Assembly of the United Nations; but it was Pearson who had sat up most of the previous night composing its forthright and arresting sentences. "Nations, in their search for peace and co-operation," St. Laurent declared forcefully, "will not, and cannot, accept indefinitely an unaltered Council, which was set up to ensure their security and which, so many feel, has become frozen in futility and divided by dissension. If forced, they may seek greater safety in an association of democratic and peace-loving states, willing to accept more specific international obligations in return for a greater measure of national security."[49]

The case for collective defence against aggression had been succinctly and brilliantly put. The *coup d'état* in Czechoslovakia convinced the western nations that they must act accordingly. Attlee's "top secret" telegram to

King, the Brussels Treaty, Truman's guarded offer of American aid, and King's involved and cumbrous promise of Canadian co-operation followed rapidly. On March 22, 1948, less than a week after Truman's announcement, the official representatives of the United States, Great Britain, and Canada met in Washington and began the serious discussion of the Atlantic union project. There was no doubt in anybody's mind about the need, or the wisdom, of collective association for defence; but there were, and persisted, some significant differences of opinion about the form it should take. Should the Brussels Treaty be enlarged to include the United States and Canada, or should the United States, Great Britain, and Canada form a new union to which the western European powers might accede? Either one of these two possible plans meant that the United States would have to commit itself – which it had never even conceived of doing before in times of peace – to an armed alliance with Great Britain and its Brussels pact associates.

In the anxious view of the American officials at Washington, the horrifying novelty of such a commitment seemed almost certain to invite rejection by the American Senate; and, in order to preserve the North American separateness and isolation of the United States, some of its negotiators seemed to prefer the alternative of a Presidential guarantee of assistance to a selected group of European states. To the Canadians, this second choice was totally unacceptable. They knew very well that it would be politically impossible to persuade Canada to join a European alliance in which the United States had refused to be included; and they had no desire to join the American government in such a guarantee or to make a separate unilateral declaration of their own. For a time Pearson was badly discouraged; but his confidence was wonderfully restored early in June when the Republican Senator Vandenburg, the Chairman of the Senate's Foreign Relations Committee, sponsored a resolution affirming that one of the objectives of American foreign policy should be: "Progressive development of regional and other collective arrangements for individual and collective self-defence."[50] The Senate adopted the resolution by sixty four votes to four.

In September, 1948, when Pearson succeeded St. Laurent as Secretary of State for External Affairs, and formally took over the political initiative and direction which had long been his in practice, Canada's ideas about the North Atlantic alliance had become clarified and fixed. It was to be a peacetime league of sovereign states directed by the collective agreement of all its members; it was not to be a wartime alliance in which a few great powers made all the important political and military decisions. " . . . The decisions which affect all," Pearson declared firmly, "will be taken by all"; they must also, he insisted with equal firmness, be binding upon all. [51] The treaty, he believed, must include an explicit recognition of the principle that an attack against one of the members of the league was an attack against them all. The parties to the Brussels pact had promised each other that in such an event they would provide all the military and other assistance in their power; but neither Canada nor the United States could possibly accept such an automatic and unlimited commitment. It was agreed that each sovereign nation must decide what its contribution was to be, although all must acknowledge a common obligation to contribute.

It was a strong alliance, with a powerful military potential; but, in Pearson's mind at least, it was not to be a military alliance only. He was convinced that it ought to have economic and social as well as military significance, significance for peace as well as for war. Its signatories, he believed, should bind themselves to "make every effort, individually and collectively, to promote the economic well-being of their peoples and to achieve social justice." It was a typical Canadian idea. It was the idealistic flower of roots that clutched deep in Canadian history and society. Though the Canadians had fought hard in two world wars, they were – especially the French Canadians – a profoundly unmilitary people. It had been politically useful for Sir Wilfrid Laurier to throw up his hands in horror at the "vortex of European militarism." It had been equally advantageous for Mackenzie King to proclaim the dissolution of all the imperial and European entanglements which might have dragged Canada into the swirling military whirlpool of Europe. Those days of colonial seclusion and innocence had gone forever, of course; the Canadians had learnt the hard way that the "vortex of militarism" could engulf North America and Asia, just as well as Europe. Yet, if experience had brought familiarity with militarism, it had not induced acceptance of it. An alliance for defence meant a commitment which might very possibly have to be honoured in war, and war could revive the highly dangerous issue of conscription. In the light of their experience, the Canadians – particularly the French Canadians – might very well find an "old-fashioned" purely military alliance unacceptable. They would, Pearson felt sure, expect it to serve other, peaceful aims. His assurance grew in part out of his knowledge of the facts of Canadian political life; but it had an even more important source in his own profound convictions. The Methodist Sunday School boy had found a new and a great cause. He cherished "the grand design of a developing Atlantic community, something which could never be realized through military commitments for collective security alone."[52] It was not an Atlantic pact for which he worked; it was an Atlantic vision that inspired him.

The negotiations, first at the official and then at the political level, were prolonged and laboured. To Pearson's dismay, most of the principals involved began having second and even third thoughts about the project. The Soviet government seemed to relax its pressure on the frontier states of Eastern Europe and began to talk pacifically about the possibility of co-existence between East and West. A few of the probable members of the projected pact started to argue that it would be impolitic and rash to provoke the Russians with an organized show of force just when they seemed disposed to be agreeable. Pearson, who by this time was just as determined to get his alliance as a war lord who had already settled on a "casus belli," dismissed this "appeasement offensive" with contempt; and by September, 1948, when he became Secretary for External Affairs, the uncertainties and reluctance of the Atlantic allies had largely subsided. A treaty now seemed likely, but its precise terms were still very much in doubt. To Pearson's surprise and regret, his own pet project of economic and social collaboration seemed to provoke most criticism and dissent. Even some of his colleagues in the ministry as well as a few of his old associates, the officials in the Department of External Affairs, appeared to regard the project very sceptically. Still more unfortunately, their doubts seemed to be shared by the spokesmen of two of the senior members of the proposed alliance, Great Britain and the United States. The British feared what Harold Innis called the "gold curtain" of the United States almost as much as they feared the "iron curtain" of the Soviet Union. They wanted a Europe which would be economically separate from and independent of, the United States, a Europe which could develop its own economy with its own policies and through its own agencies.[53] Pearson's plan, they thought, would simply mingle and muddle two distinct enterprises. If economic and social collaboration had to be included in the treaty at all, a polite mention in the preamble would be all it deserved.

The Americans – or some of them at least – seemed readier to subscribe to Pearson's ideal. With delight he listened to Robert Lovett express the view that "co-operation should be wider than merely military." "Bob Lovett," he observed with great satisfaction, "was talking 'Canadian'."[54] Unhappily, "Bob" Lovett was only the Undersecretary of State, his political superior was the Secretary of State, and in January, 1949, Dean Acheson succeeded George Marshall in that office. Acheson differed from Marshall as much in his political attitudes as in his appearance. He had a hawk-like nose, beetling eyebrows, an aggressive chin, and a small, close-clipped moustache. He looked, altogether, rather like a major in the British Grenadier Guards. It was Acheson who had been so disgusted when Marshall had "flubbed" the strategical and idealogical case against the Soviet Union in February, 1947, when the Congressional leaders had been called to listen to the administration's justification of its proposed aid to Greece and Turkey. Acheson, given permission to speak after his superior, had plunged immediately into an impromptu and passionate denunciation, which astounded but convinced the Congressmen and formed the basis of the Truman Doctrine. Acheson was a realist who wanted a military alliance and was convinced that a military alliance was all that the Senate would accept. He would emphatically *not* be "talking Canadian." The splendid ideal of the "Atlantic Community" left him completely unmoved. He thought it a typical example of sentimental and empty Canadian moralizing.[55] Economic and cultural co-operation, he was convinced, was a vague but dangerous aim, which would probably weaken support for the treaty in the Senate, and result in no substantial benefit to anybody.

Still Pearson struggled on. While Hume Wrong in Washington drafted and redrafted article II of the treaty, his political superior was earnestly seeking support for it among the senior members of the alliance. St. Laurent, on his visit to Washington in February, endeavoured to explain to President Truman why Canadian public opinion might be alarmed or disquieted by a treaty with purely military aims.[56] France, after frequent appeals, declared itself favourable, to Pearson's surprised delight. The British, urged on by Norman Robertson, the Canadian High Commissioner, finally, though reluctantly, agreed to the inclusion of some "economic clause ," not because they wanted it, or thought it would do any good, but simply to keep the Canadians quiet. Wrong produced a final draft which Acheson later claimed he had "defused," presumably by removing or emasculating all the commitments of any real significance.[57] The result was, as Pearson later confessed, "all we could expect." It was certainly a cumbrous, vague, and equivocal text. "The parties will contribute," the article finally ran, "toward the further development of peaceful and friendly international relations by strengthening their free institutions, by bringing about a better understanding of the principles upon which these institutions are founded, and by promoting conditions of stability and well-being. They will seek to eliminate conflict in their international economic policies and will encourage economic collaboration between any or all of them."[58]

On March 28, the treaty was submitted to the Canadian House of Commons. The short debate was an almost unqualified chorus of approval. Both St. Laurent and Pearson were emphatic in their assurances that the treaty was "far more than an old-fashioned military alliance." "It is based," St. Laurent informed the members solemnly, "on the common belief of the North Atlantic nations in the values and virtues of Christian civilization."[59] Pearson expatiated on the noble ideal of the "Atlantic community"; but he also took care to explain that the treaty's military obligations were limited, and that Canada would not be automatically at war if one of its allies was attacked. Coldwell, for the C.C.F., dwelt with approval on article II which, he said, would strengthen the efforts of the member nations to remove the economic and political causes of war. "That is why," he concluded with some unction, "this pact is an instrument of peace."[60] George Drew, the new Progressive-Conservative leader, was equally unreserved in his support. "On this occasion," he declared, "I hope that this House and the Parliament of Canada, will speak with one clear and ringing voice."[61] It very nearly did. Tle only dissent came from two French-Canadian Independents.

This virtually complete unanimity was a curious contrast with the obstreperous criticism which, less than two years before, had greeted the judicial

privileges granted by the Visiting Forces Bill to American service courts in
northern Canada. Then several Conservatives had joined with outspoken
C.C.F.ers in denouncing Canada's tame acceptance of American military
leadership and in rejecting the belief that the world was divided into two
ideologically irreconcilable camps. Now applause was the only demonstration
of the silently approving rows of back-benchers. The Canadian diplomatic
revelation was complete, not only in the text of the North Atlantic Treaty,
but also in the collective mind of the Parliament of Canada.

CHAPTER 8

The Commonwealth in Dissolution

I

On June 11, 1949, the two new national party leaders, the Liberal Louis St. Laurent, and the Progressive-Conservative George A. Drew, faced each other in their first general election campaign. Both were seasoned politicians, but the difficult role of national leader was equally new to both of them. And yet, each had won the leadership easily, triumphantly, almost as if it was his by divine right of succession. St. Laurent was, of course, Mackenzie King's chosen and acknowledged successor; his election to the leadership was perhaps not very surprising. But Drew's equally conclusive victory, which came only two months later, early in October, 1948, was distinctly harder to explain. Drew had never won a seat in the Canadian House of Commons; he was completely new to federal politics. Yet he had overwhelmingly defeated John Diefenbaker, a parliamentary veteran of nearly ten years' standing, who had long been a prominent member of the Opposition and who had run third in the contest which gave John Bracken the leadership six years earlier.

The explanation of this seeming miracle lay partly in the state of mind of the Tory party in 1948, and partly in Drew's remarkable character and personality. Bracken had been a dry, nondescript, negligible person. Drew was a complete contrast. A big, heavily-built man, who stood a head higher than most of his political contemporaries and who wore well-cut and obviously expensive clothes, his splendid physical presence could be rather overwhelming and people acquired the irreverent habit of calling him "Gorgeous George." It was a satiric, but not inappropriate, nickname for a proud, exuberant, masterful man who, in so many different ways, seemed a little larger than life. He was a good speaker, with a fine, carrying voice, a fluent, effective delivery, and an easy, rather rhetorical style. His manner could be very urbane and gracious, but he had an assertive, imperious streak in his nature which sometimes drove him into violent offensives. These were very considerable assets in a politician, and, in the last ten years, Drew had made dramatically successful use of them. In 1938, when he was elected leader of the Tory party in Ontario, he set out to modernize and liberalize its platform. He drew up a vast, comprehensive programme for the post-war economic development of Ontario; he took over the Port Hope Conference proposals for social reform. In 1943, when he fought his first provincial election, his plans for social security in Ontario were so advanced that they challenged those of the C.C.F., then at the height of its popularity, and the Progressive-Conservatives emerged with a scant victory in a difficult three-cornered contest. Two years later, a second election gave Drew a command-ing majority over all parties, and solidly confirmed the Conservative return to power.[1]

By 1948, Drew had become a conspicuous political success at Toronto. But at Ottawa, John Bracken, the federal Progressive-Conservative leader, had turned out to be an acknowledged failure and was soon to resign his post. He would go unlamented into retirement, and with him would go the discredited political reasoning on which he had been elected. Arthur Meighen, who had first urged Bracken's election, had picked him because he was convinced that the West was certain to become the political strong-hold of Canadian Conservatism and that Bracken was the man chosen by fate to convert the western farmers to their destined Tory allegiance.[2] The first of Meighen's two propositions might still be true; but its truth had not yet been demonstrated, and the second proposition was demonstrably false. Bracken had made a pitiful gain of only three western seats in the general election of 1945, and his greatest electoral success had been scored, ironically, in Ontario, where his name was not expected to carry any magic appeal at all. From every point-of-view, the political strategy implicit in his election had been discredited, and in July, 1948, after three ineffectual and unhappy years as leader, he resigned.

A grandiose opportunity now invitingly awaited Drew. He had finished what he wanted to do in Ontario. His gaze was fixed eagerly on a wider stage, a different and more varied company of actors, and a far bigger audi-ence. He was hungry for his new role and greed made him reckless. The quite unnecessary provincial election which he called in June, 1948, was probably intended for display purposes, as a clinching proof of his electoral prowess in Ontario. It backfired badly. The Conservatives lost thirteen seats and Drew was defeated in his own constituency.[3] This was an unexpected and humiliating reverse, but it hardly seemed to worry him. By this time, the only election in which he took any genuine interest was the election of a new federal leader in the approaching Progressive-Conservative convention. He expected to win, and he did win easily, for his only serious rival was John Diefenbaker. Diefenbaker was an extremely effective debater, with long parliamentary experience. But he was also a Westerner, and, in the jaundiced eyes of the assembled Tories, simply another John Bracken, the symbol of an exploded strategy and a refractory West.

Up until January 26, 1949, when for the first time he faced St. Laurent across the gangway of the House of Commons, everything seemed to have gone swimmingly for Drew. He had reached his chosen goal, but his arrival came unfortunately at a time which in many ways was very unpropitious. Even St. Laurent's succession to the Liberal Party leadership was likely to slow down Drew's rapid initial success. St. Laurent proved capable of coping with Drew; Mackenzie King would probably have been much less successful. King had disparaged Drew's abilities and predicted his failure; but he admittedly feared Drew, just as he had feared those redoubtable debaters, Meighen and Bennett; and, if had stayed in office, he would undoubtedly have cringed under the lash of Drew's caustic tongue. St. Laurent was more composed and more quickly resourceful. Yet he disliked Drew, perhaps even more fundamentally than Drew disliked him, and Drew had a far more obvious reason for his aversion. He never forgot or forgave the fact that St. Laurent, in a moment of malicious political partisanship, had tried to take advantage of his abusive speeches on the training and equipment of the Hong Kong expedition to instigate – and then to drop without apology – a prosecution against him under the Defence of Canada Regulations.[4]

St. Laurent's antipathy was much more complex and general. For him, Drew was a particularly obnoxious representative of that large class of English Canadians, the believers in the British connection, whom at times he found very hard to bear. As Mackenzie King had often noted and regretted, St. Laurent could hardly repress a feeling of resentment and irritation at all attempts to invest the British relationship with affectionate concern, or to give special consideration to British needs and interests. Drew had responded to Britain's danger in two world wars with an emotion and a conviction which St. Laurent found incomprehensible and annoying. In his eyes, Drew's conduct during the Second World War had been that of a professional – and highly objectionable – British-Canadian patriot. Instinctively, he summed up his rival in conventional, stereotyped terms. Drew, he considered, was guilty of the dreadful offence of "colonialism." The United Empire Loyalist origins of his family were more than enough to prove that the Drews must have been associated with the "Family Compact," and that George presumably inherited the Compact's belief in privilege and repression.[5]

St. Laurent was morally ready for his encounter with Drew, and Drew was his old imperious and aggressive self. Yet he never quite succeeded in dominating the House, and he failed to overawe the new Prime Minister. He quickly discovered that he had entered the Commons at a moment when the government's foreign policy had won it wide acclaim, and when domestic affairs could hardly have been more prosperous. Drew could only applaud the North Atlantic Treaty, and his attempt to question the constitutionality of the union with Newfoundland, although it won him some newspaper support, mystified and annoyed the mass of Canadians who uncritically rejoiced in the completion of Confederation. The nearly $600 million budgetary surplus which Douglas Abbott, the Minister of Finance, announced for 1948-49, could neither be laughed off nor converted into a taxpayers' grievance.[6] Only the year before, Abbott had carefully explained that it was wise to build up surpluses in prosperous times as a defence against possibly lean years ahead.[7] But now, in 1949, an election year, he conveniently forgot this pious principle. Income taxes were expediently lowered and nearly half a million Canadians found, to their delighted astonishment, that they had nothing to pay.[8]

Drew's first session in the House of Commons had been only a qualified success. His first general election campaign never for a moment took on the dazzling look of certain triumph. Drew himself did his superlative best. He stormed across the country in his vigorous, flamboyant style, denouncing his opponents and obliterating their policies under cartloads of invective and abuse. The voters, particularly in central Canada, were familiar, and perhaps a little bored, with Drew's vehemence. What surprised and increasingly pleased them was the strangely altered campaign manner of St. Laurent. Until the spring of 1949, the new Prime Minister had been generally regarded as stiff, formal, and ceremonious in his ways; and at his set, evening performances during the campaign, he still retained a good deal of his official dignity. There he tended to become the company chairman, with a strained, chalk-white countenance and a harsh, nasal accent, peering out anxiously through the microphones and plodding on with the dull routine of what sounded exactly like the annual report of some large corporation. For him, this was correct professional conduct in public; but at Edson, Alberta, on his first journey west, his delighted advisers realized that he could escape from it. In the crowd at the Edson station platform, there was a large number of children. St. Laurent chatted familiarly with them, thanked them for coming to meet him, and inveigled their teachers into giving them a half holiday.[9] The significance of this highly successful "whistle stop" was not lost on the Prime Minister's secretaries, and it was arranged that the election campaign proper would start out with a sentimental journey to St. Laurent's native village of Compton and his old school in Sherbrooke, Quebec.[10] "Uncle Louis," the amiable gentleman in the conservatively fashionable attire, the "Jacques Bonhomme" in well-cut double-breasted jackets, talking in a homely, benevolent fashion with children, parents, teachers and clergy, began to take on the appeal of a father-figure as the campaign progressed.

Yet, though St. Laurent's engaging personality was important, it was by no means the sufficient explanation of the Liberal victory. There was another presence in the campaign, an unseen, impersonal, anonymous, but formidably powerful presence, the new welfare state itself. The Liberal Party had adopted and sponsored it, and claimed all the credit for its success, but it was in no sense a particular and exclusive Liberal creation, for the Conservative government in Ontario and the C.C.F. government in Saskatchewan were already, in their own spheres, proceeding along much the same lines. The welfare state was not, in fact, a politician's invention at all, but a system chiefly devised by the new class of civil servants, the trained and talented men and women who had arrived *en masse* in Ottawa during the war and who, in the end, had come to influence the making of policy far more than their predecessors had ever dreamed of doing. The new administrators did not, in the main, get their ideas from their political superiors: they got them from the prophets of the new age, the two Englishmen, Lord Keynes and Sir William Beveridge, and the American, James Burnham, the author of *The Managerial Revolution*. Keynes had given them the concept of the regulated economy, Beveridge the vision of social security, Burnham the idea of the managerial *élite* – themselves of course – whose commanding position would be based, not on economic ownership or political power, but on the special knowledge and skills which were essential to government in a time of rapid, technological, and social change.

In 1949, their new system was very nearly complete. It was already spewing out its benefits – which henceforth were always measured in monetary terms and usually took the blissful form of cheques – in all directions. The Gross National Product had moved up gratifyingly every year. There had been four hefty budget surpluses in a row; unemployment had sunk nearly to its low wartime levels, and in 1948, $634 million, or 29% of total government expenditures, had been paid out in veterans' benefits, health services, family allowances, and old age security.[11] In the prevailing mood of 1949, such a record was unassailable. Drew grew hoarse denouncing the new system's heavy taxation, its inevitable tendency towards centralization, and its constantly increasing bureaucratic control. His efforts were vain and the results of the election were a shattering blow to the Conservatives. St. Laurent, with an unprecedented total of 190 seats, had piled up a majority over all parties even greater than Mackenzie King had ever managed to achieve.[12] The Tories in the new House numbered only forty-one – only two more than at the nadir of their fortunes in 1935 and 1940. Even the despised Bracken had done much better.

II

A warm, comfortable glow of satisfaction pervaded the Prime Minister's office and suffused the fairly ample form of the principal secretary, John Whitney Pickersgill. Twelve years earlier, Pickersgill had been a young, solid

but still fairly slim lecturer in history at Wesley College in Winnipeg. Time
and a long succession of good dinners at public expense had notably increased
his girth; and time, his own energy, and his unqualified devotion to the
Liberal Party had even more dramatically enlarged the sphere of his influence.
He had worked intimately with Mackenzie King for years, and King had
made him head of the Prime Minister's office; but it was St. Laurent, King's
successor, who first awakened his whole-hearted admiration. By the time
King finally retired, Pickersgill had come to feel "personally committed" to
the new leader, and he was delighted when St. Laurent invited him to stay
on as his principal secretary.[13] They got on immensely well together.
Mackenzie King had always kept his secretaries at arm's length, and Pickersgill had communicated with him mainly by written memoranda. St. Laurent,
on the other hand, much preferred to discuss problems face to face.[14]
Rapidly, the Prime Minister's office became a cosy retreat in which two men
discussed, and often settled, the national affairs of Canada. A stoutish, very
self-assured secretary, still on the right side of fifty, with a high-pitched,
grating voice, acquired the status of the "grey eminence" of Canadian politics. " 'Check it with Jack' became a watchword on Parliament Hill."[15]

For St. Laurent, the most important business of the new Parliament was
the removal of what he and Pickersgill regarded as "the last legal vestiges
of colonial status from the constitution of Canada." [16] St. Laurent had been
distinctly annoyed by Mackenzie King's delicate suggestion that English
Canada might be aroused if the abolition of appeals to the Judicial Committee of the Privy Council followed too quickly after the installation of a
French-Canadian Prime Minister. He was determined to act at once, but the
prevention of appeals was only one item in his ambitious list of proposed
constitutional reforms. During the election campaign, in a speech at
Moncton, New Brunswick, he had promised to consult the provinces about
a procedure for amending the constitution, without recourse to the British
Parliament; and he had also assured his audience that he would seek to
"entrench," or provide special constitutional guarantees, for the educational
and language clauses of the British North America Act. These were formidable undertakings. The business of making the Supreme Court of Canada the
final court of appeal for all Canadian cases was a good deal easier to carry
through. Drew, as was to be expected, argued that the provinces ought to
be consulted since the abolition of appeals was in effect an amendment to
the constitution. In reply, St. Laurent demolished this restatement of the old
Compact theory of Confederation with the familiar historical arguments.[17]

All this was part of an elaborate, but meaningless, minuet which Canadian
politicians felt it necessary to dance at regular intervals. The Supreme Court
Bill, introduced in September, 1949, immediately after the opening of the
Twenty-First Parliament, passed without difficulty. The really intractable
problem facing St. Laurent was the amendment of the British North America

Act. He had promised to call the provinces to a constitutional conference which would have the amendment of the constitution as its main subject; but he was only too well aware that, fifteen years earlier, another federal-provincial conference had failed, after prolonged efforts, to find an amending formula which satisfied all governments. He dreaded another failure. And then, suddenly, only a few weeks before Parliament opened, he thought he had discovered a short-cut around the barrier of interminable and futile debate.

It seemed absurdly easy. The British Parliament had always been prepared, without question, to validate proposed amendments to the British North America Act at the request of the Canadian Parliament. Why shouldn't the Canadian Parliament, without waiting for the approval of a federal-provincial conference, request a constitutional amendment which would, at one stroke, transfer all revision of the British North America Act to Canada and make good all the Prime Minister's promises of constitutional reform? Three vital provisions could be laid down by this British amendment, which was to end all British amendments. It would provide special constitutional guarantees for the language and educational sections – virtually sacred in French Canada; it would give the Parliament of Canada exclusive authority to alter the constitution in all subjects of purely federal jurisdiction; and it would also empower Parliament, but only with the consent of the provincial legislatures, to enact changes in the remaining clauses of the constitution.[18] Above all – and this was the crowning virtue of its admirable simplicity – it would effectively domicile the Canadian constitution in Canada.

St. Laurent's first impulse was not to discuss his daring proposal with his Cabinet colleagues, but to "check-it-with Jack." At first the plan's originality astounded Pickersgill. "Once I recovered my breath," he confessed later, "I was excited by this bold, original, and imaginative approach."[19] At first he was convinced that St. Laurent had found the perfect solution to Canada's constitutional enigma; but, as he pondered over the Prime Minister's plan, he began to be assailed by serious doubts. Gradually, he realized that St. Laurent's audacious scheme risked far too much political trouble and made far too many constitutional concessions. If, he reasoned, the Prime Minister proceeded with his daring unilateral plan of transferring the amending process to Canada, he would break his promise to consult with the provinces on the revision of the British North America Act. And if he once conceded that all amendments outside the exclusive federal jurisdiction would have to have the consent of *all* the provinces, he would inevitably transform the Canadian constitution into a cast-iron monstrosity, impervious to all necessary changes.

In the end, St. Laurent was reluctantly convinced by these arguments and he gave up all but one extremely important part of his heroic plan. He had always believed that Parliament ought to have the same authority to amend the constitution in purely federal affairs as the provinces already possessed in provincial matters. In October, a month after the opening of the session, he proposed an Address to the King by both Houses of the Canadian Parliament, requesting the British Parliament to pass an amendment to this effect. This was the prescribed, and still unaltered method of amendment, and it provoked the usual stately ceremonial debate over the Compact theory of Confederation. After this performance was finished, both the Canadian and British Parliaments acted in their accustomed way on such occasions; and a new subsection, defining its amending power, was added to the powers of Parliament as set out in section 91 of the British North America Act.[20]

This was all very well so far as it went. Parliament's authority to amend had now been definitely established; but the new amending power of Parliament and the old amending power of the provincial legislatures did not cover all the sections of the British North America Act. And thus, to St. Laurent's great regret, the constitution of Canada was still not directly and completely under Canadian control. A federal-provincial conference was now inevitable. The date was fixed for January 10; but the strategy which the federal government ought to follow in presenting this delicate and difficult subject to the provincial representatives was not so easily determined. If St. Laurent had been left to himself, he might very well have followed his own straightforward inclination and presented the simple, drastic proposal of his earlier scheme. It was a resolute but dangerous course; and Pickersgill was full of doubts about its wisdom. He argued that if the federal government, at the start of the conference, submitted a definite plan for an amending procedure, the provincial delegates would probably spend the rest of session in the delightful exercise of tearing it to pieces, and that nothing of the slightest importance would be accomplished. It was far better, he insisted, to let the provinces take the initiative. If, in the end, they all agreed upon a formula, it would almost certainly be acceptable to the federal government. This reasoning eventually convinced St. Laurent; but, as the date of the conference drew closer, he relapsed into one of his occasional but profound depressions and the federal plan of action for the conference was never completely worked out.[21]

The truth was that, despite the apparent freedom of choice permitted by the British North America Act, the conference was bound within very narrow limits in its search for an amending formula. It could not possibly decide to follow the example of Switzerland or Australia and submit proposed amendments to the people in a popular referendum: it could not even adopt the provision of the American Constitution which required the consent of three-quarters of the states to an amendment. In theory, of course, both these methods were open to adoption. The British North America Act did not require provincial consent as a prerequisite for amendment by the British Parliament. It did not "entrench" any particular clauses; all its sections stood upon a perfect legal equality. In theory, the conference could do precisely what it pleased; in fact, it was bound hand and foot by the basic constitutional assumptions which, although they had no basis in law, had gained great moral authority during the preceding twenty years. The doctrine that provincial consent was necessary for amendments was the first of these assumptions: the belief that certain "vital and fundamental" sections of the Act needed special protection was the second.

Neither of these two principles could be historically justified since the amending procedures of the past had been highly inconsistent. Neither had been adopted by a national convention or constituent assembly, for no such democratic body had ever been elected in Canada. It was Ernest Lapointe, speaking *ex cathedra* as Minister of Justice, who first asserted them as constitutional principles at the Dominion-Provincial Conference of 1929. Six years later, the next Dominion-Provincial Conference, and particularly its Continuing Committee on Constitutional Questions, refined and elaborated these basic ideas with all the sedulous care of medieval casuists. In effect, the Continuing Committee decided that the clauses of the British North America Act should be divided into four categories, each with a separate and increasingly difficult method of amendment, which would have its culmination in the fourth category, the so-called "entrenched clauses," which would require the consent of Parliament and all the provincial legislatures.[22]

It was within the narrow range permitted by these rigid precedents that St. Laurent had to guide the Conference towards a solution. He began with studied impartiality. He quoted Burke's famous aphorism that "a state without the means of some change is without the means of its conservation." He admitted that serious differences of opinion about the constitution did exist in Canada and must be respected; but he insisted that these differences must not be permitted "to frustrate the continuous development, in a desirable direction, of the nation as a whole . . . ."[23] The Canadian constitution, he argued, "must have sufficient flexibility to enable our country to go forward as a dynamic nation," but he made no specific suggestions as to how this desirable flexibility was to be achieved. If he had hoped by this calculated silence to force Duplessis, the chief antagonist of federalism, to declare himself, the ploy was a complete failure. Duplessis continued to profess, in the most general terms, his complete readiness to discuss and negotiate, and his unshakable adherence to basic, but unspecified, federal principles. This calculated silence of the two French Canadians, St. Laurent and Duplessis, left the field open to the premiers of the English-speaking provinces. They all denounced the federal government for securing the constitutional amendment of the previous autumn without their consent; but they did not deal merely in negative criticism. They all attacked the general issue of amendment; and two of them – Frost of Ontario and Macdonald of Nova Scotia – had definite schemes to propose.[24]

As was inevitable by now, all these proposals were based, with only relative, minor variations, on the amending formula devised by the Conference of 1935. They all divided the sections of the British North America Act into categories, with a final category whose clauses could not be altered without the consent of all the provinces. The crucial question was, of course, what sections, or subsections, were to be put in this last formidable category. As St. Laurent had expected, there was no longer any serious opposition to the inclusion of the language and educational clauses. The real debate raged over section 92, the exclusive power of the provincial legislatures, and in particular over the thirteenth subsection, "property and civil rights in the province." If the amendment of this key clause was to require the concurrence of all the provincial legislatures, important projects of economic development and social reform might be held up indefinitely. T. C. Douglas, the C.C.F. Premier of Saskatchewan, led the attack of the constitutional reformers on the intolerable rigidity which would result; and he was joined by Manning of Alberta and Campbell of Manitoba, who were also thinking of labour codes and social security measures.[25] The West was in revolt against the sacred untouchability of subsection thirteen, but it fought in vain against the uncompromising resistance of Duplessis.

The welter of demands and denials mounted. On the afternoon of the second day, St. Laurent tried hard to construct an acceptable list of "entrenched " subjects. His vain attempt ended in failure, and the impossible task was handed over to a committee composed of the federal Minister of Justice and the Attorneys-General of all the provinces. Its report, presented on the afternoon of January 12, the last day of the Conference, further refined and elaborated the categories into which the clauses of the British North America Act was to be divided, but made no attempt to list the sections to be included in the last intractable division.[26] Obviously, the Conference had failed, and Macdonald of Nova Scotia openly acknowledged its failure when he moved the appointment of yet another Continuing Committee which would receive, and attempt to harmonize, the various provincial opinions on the difficult business of classification, and report back as soon as possible.

The Conference adjourned. St. Laurent had failed to remove the most important of "the last legal vestiges of colonial status" from the constitution of Canada. To his great chagrin, much of the British North America Act could still be amended only by the Parliament of Great Britain.

III

Almost exactly a year before the ill-fated conference began, St. Laurent had started another nationalist inquiry, although, at the beginning at least, he was very sceptical of its national importance. This was the Royal Commission on National Development in the Arts, Letters, and Sciences, a project first mooted at the Liberal Convention in August, 1948, by the Canadian University Liberal Federation. The Convention turned down the students' daring proposal, and Brooke Claxton heard indirectly of their disappointment and dissatisfaction. He promptly got in touch with Pickersgill, and Pickersgill talked the matter over with Pearson. There was no use in proceeding any further at the moment, for Mackenzie King was still Prime Minister, and King would have undoubtedly dismissed the whole idea as nonsensical and preposterous. It wasn't very certain that St. Laurent would regard such a strange scheme more favourably. He had never shown any particular interest in any of the arts, and he viewed the prospect of "subsidizing ballet dancing" with cold disfavour.[27] Pearson, Claxton, and Pickersgill made no attempt to change their leader's opinions. They concentrated, not so much on the students' proposal as on the students themselves, and on the votes they would cast in the approaching general election. This was a point which St. Laurent could quickly appreciate. He was also uncomfortably aware that pressure had been building up for federal aid to the universities and for an inquiry into the Canadian Broadcasting Corporation. These annoying questions, he reflected, could be conveniently dumped into the lap of the proposed inquiry. On January 6, 1949, he asked Vincent Massey to act as chairman of a Royal Commission on the cultural resources of Canada.

Massey had only recently returned from England where he had been revisiting the many friends he had made as Canadian High Commissioner in London. Obviously, he was the ideal chairman for the proposed commission, and Pearson, while in England in the autumn of 1948, had ventured to suggest that he postpone his decision on all other possible offers until he had seen, or heard from, St. Laurent. Pearson's warning may have been very opportune. Late in October, Viscount Samuel, then Visitor of Balliol College, Oxford, had invited Massey to consider election to the Mastership of the College. It was one of the most important academic posts in England and Massey took his time to reflect. Pearson's hint may have helped him to decline Samuel's offer; but his decision had really been made more than two years earlier, at the end of his term as High Commissioner, when he and his wife Alice had determined to return to Canada. "We went home because we were Canadians," he wrote. "Canada was where we belonged."[28]

Massey had some influence on the choice of his fellow commissioners. It was a notable group. There were two professional scholars, Hilda Neatby, Professor of History at the University of Saskatchewan, and Georges Henri Levesque, of Laval University, a leading member of the Dominican Order. Norman A. M. MacKenzie, President of the University of British Columbia and former Professor of Law, was the third member of the group, and Arthur Surveyer, a Montreal engineer, the fourth. For Massey, the work of the

Commission became virtually a full-time job, as it very nearly was for two
of his associates, Hilda Neatby and Father Levesque. Early in April, 1949,
when the order-in-council authorizing their appointment was finally made
public, the Commission learnt the full magnitude of the task confronting
them. St. Laurent had not simply authorized a general, roving investigation
into the state of the arts, letters, and social sciences in Canada. He needed
definite advice on the problems of government policy in radio and television
broadcasting; he wanted considered judgements on the work of such federal
institutions as the Film Board, the National Gallery, the National Museum,
the Public Archives, and the projected National Library. [29] The Commissioners realized that they faced some very particular enquiries in the City of
Ottawa; but they did not forget that their most important task was a survey
of the cultural state of the nation as a whole.

What were Canada's "cultural" resources at the start of the second half
of the twentieth century? The 1940's had brought about an astonishing
increase in the nation's population, natural resources, industrial maturity, and
constitutional independence. But obviously, no comparable developments
had transformed the state of the arts, literature, music and scholarship. Ten
years had, of course, brought some changes, but these changes had taken
place chiefly in the membership of the small group of Canadian writers,
artists, musicians and scholars, and in the themes and subjects which inspired
them. Stephen Leacock, Emily Carr, Frederick Philip Grove, and the historian
George M. Wrong had all died during the 1940's. If their deaths did not
exactly signify the passing of an age, the appearance of a large number of
new artists and writers definitely marked the coming of another. First novels
by Hugh MacLennan, Malcolm Lowry, Gabrielle Roy and W. O. Mitchell
appeared during the 1940's. The poets Earle Birney, Irving Layton, P.K. Page,
Alain Grandbois, and James Reaney published their first volumes of verse.
Painters such as Alfred Pellan, Goodridge Roberts, Jacques de Tonnancour
and Cleeve Horne began to exhibit their pictures, and the work of young
composers like John Weinzweig, Barbara Pentland, and Jean Papineau-
Couture gained a hearing on the radio and in concert halls.

These younger creative Canadians, whatever their mode of expression, did
represent a departure, more or less abrupt, from the past. The writers were
perhaps more conscious, and certainly more outspoken, about the meaning
of the change. Two groups of young poets – the "Preview" and "First Statement" groups – published manifestoes of purpose at the beginning of the
decade. Most of the other newcomers made no attempt to define their intentions in public; but all were very conscious of the fact that they lived in
a country very different from that which had disappeared for ever in the
maelstrom of the Second World War. Canada had ceased to be a remote,
primitive, unknown and unspoilt country, and had become part of western
industrial society. Thirty years earlier, pioneering in the Canadian West had

seemed a strange and exciting theme for novel readers; twenty years earlier the harsh forms and violent colours of the Canadian landscape had aroused a quick interest in European art critics. Now, in the kaleidoscopic changes of the 1940's, these themes and subjects had lost their novelty and had ceased to be characteristic or typical of a country which had grown up, developed great industries and cities, and ventured boldly into the chaos of world politics. Henceforth, Canadian writers and artists would be far more conscious of West European-American culture. Its influence and fashions would affect them much more deeply than before.

Composers began to experiment in atonal music, painters in abstract forms; poets more often than not discarded rhyme and traditional stanzaic arrangements. Yeats, Eliot, Pound and Auden replaced Tennyson, Rossetti and Swinburne as the main poetic influences; the painters turned from Monet, Pissarro and Renoir to Cezanne, Van Gogh, Matisse and Picasso; the composers occasionally deserted their classical and romantic models and tried exciting experiments in the manner of Schoenberg, Bartok, and Stravinsky. They were all more consciously contemporary and cosmopolitan in their outlook, and all strongly united in their determination to reject the romantic and sentimental values of the past. Poetry could be metaphysical, sophisticated and witty on the one hand, or proletarian, revolutionary, outspokenly sexual on the other. Novelists found harsher themes in more uncompromisingly modern situations. Roy explored the ordeal of working class life in Montreal; MacLennan the perversions of English-French relations in Quebec; Ross the painful frustrations of contemporary life on the prairie; and Lowry the anguished advance of mental and moral degeneration.

There was no such exciting sense of change and advance in the humanities and the social sciences. Scholarly studies had always worked within comparatively narrow limits in Canada. Philosophy, in any truly creative sense, hardly existed at all. E. K. Brown, whose tragically early death occurred in 1951, showed brilliant critical powers in a wide range of English literature; but, in general, humanistic studies and literary criticism were still weak; and book reviewing, except in a very few periodicals, simply deplorable. In the past, perhaps the strongest scholarly subjects had been Canadian economic and political history, although both Charles Cochrane and A.S.P. Woodhouse had written important monographs outside this field. The Canadian historical school, founded by Harold Innis, Chester Martin and A. L. Burt, reached its peak of activity in the 1930's, and the next decade produced few new books and fewer new scholars. The vast growth of the military and civil services during the war absorbed a great many academic economists, statisticians, psychologists and historians; and the influx of student veterans after 1945 made very heavy demands on the time of university teachers.

IV

The 1940's saw a considerable change in the subjects and methods, as well as in the membership, of Canadian artists and writers. It drastically altered their outlook, interests and interpretations; but it did little or nothing to improve their position in Canadian life, to encourage or promote their work, or to increase the public awareness of it. There had always been a depressing lack of ways and means by which creative Canadians could present what they had done, or by which an interest in literary and artistic values could be awakened among Canadians in general. Now, in the midst of a growing population and rising prosperity, these limits grew relatively more and more restrictive. Canada still lacked a national art gallery and, for literally seventy years, the national collection of pictures and sculptures had been housed in the East Wing of the Victoria Memorial Museum in Ottawa. There were, in addition, ten respectable provincial art galleries, but these, like the national gallery, were inadequately staffed and provided with inadequate funds for purchases. The only two important museums in the country were the National Museum at Ottawa, which specialized in Canadian history, botany, geology and mineralogy, and the Royal Ontario Museum, with its much more diversified holdings, including the rich resources in art and archaeology built up by Dr. C. T. Currelly. There was no national library, and only three Canadian university libraries possessed collections in excess of 500,000 books. The Public Archives of Ottawa had never succeeded in establishing a system for the regular transfer of records from the different departments of government, and it had done relatively little to acquire collections of private papers, particularly in the period after 1867. The universities, faced with a greatly increased post-war enrolment, and still dependent upon their original private endowments and provincial grants, were in serious financial difficulties. There were no scholarships and no financial aid for work in the creative arts or for studies in the humanities and social sciences.

Canadian music, drama, and literature, both popular and general, struggled with increasing difficulty to maintain an existence against an invading onslaught of imports, now chiefly American in origin, which was driven forward by the nearly irresistible pressure of American continental advertising. Virtually all the theatres in the country were now cinemas playing an endless succession of American films. Canadian music rarely got a hearing in the nation's all too rare music halls; and in 1948, when the Toronto Symphony Orchestra ventured to present a programme by Canadian composers, the result was a serious financial loss.[30] The flourishing Little Theatre movement was, of course, amateur in status; and the professional Canadian playwright, actor, and composer found his only substantial support in the Canadian Broadcasting Corporation. Only eighty-two books appeared under the imprint of Canadian publishers in 1947, and seventy-five in 1948, totals which amounted roughly to about 3% of the books published in England during the same years, and 4% of those published in the United States.[31]

It was a pitiably small number, but a number which seemed unlikely, in the post-war condition of the Canadian book trade, to increase at anything like the rate of the country's economic growth. The paperback revolution of the early 1950's might have looked as if it was certain to help the progress of Canadian writing and publishing. Thousands of book borrowers, who had thronged the public and commercial libraries before the war, were now converted into book buyers; and books, which before had been hidden away in a relatively small number of bookshops, now appeared prominently in newsstands, pharmacies, hotels, variety stores, and railway stations. There were certainly far more cheap books available than perhaps there had ever been before; but unfortunately for Canadian authors and publishers, the vast majority of them were American or British, and not Canadian, in origin. Paperback publishing could prosper only through enormous editions, ten times or more the size of the usual first printing of a hardback book; and while American and British publishers, with their well-known authors and established international markets, could afford to risk such huge investments, the Canadian publisher simply could not.

His entrance into paperback publishing was uncertain and gradual; and as a result, popular Canadian books, which might have had a wide appeal for the common garden reader, were still published only in non-competitive hardback editions. A generation or more earlier, when cloth bound books were still fairly cheap, Canadian writers such as Ralph Connor, Gilbert Parker, Robert W. Service, L. M. Montgomery, and Charles G. D. Roberts had attained very considerable popularity; but the conditions of the Canadian book trade in the 1950's made it almost impossible for post-war Canadian authors to repeat their success. The empire of the paperback, which soon came to include serious as well as popular titles, was monopolized in part by British but in large measure by the American publishers, as well as by the American-controlled suppliers and jobbers who stocked the thousands of new bookstands throughout Canada. Like the American takeover of Canadian industry and Canadian natural resources, the American appropriation of the Canadian book business, and the quiet suppression of Canadian literary talent, had its big start in the late 1940's and early 1950's.

The Massey Commissioners surveyed this dismal scene with panoramic amplitude and pitiless detail. In measured terms, and with copious evidence, they expressed concern for the first time at the heavy pressure of American influence on Canadian life. Nobody else seemed to show the slightest uneasiness or anxiety at this growing American predominance. C. D. Howe, the economic autocrat of the Cabinet, gave it his benevolent and active encouragement; everybody of the slightest importance in politics or the business world accepted it with enthusiasm and gratitude. It was not until December, 1956 – six years after the publication of the Massey Report – that Walter Gordon, in the preliminary report of the Commission on Canada's Economic Prospects, began to express some cautious doubts about Canada's heavy dependence on American capital. Long before politicians, economists, and journalists began to suspect that the real threat to Canadian identity and independence lay in American imperialism, the Massey Commissioners revealed the truth with candour and restraint. The second chapter of their Report, called "The Forces of Geography" was, in effect, a general statement of Canada's major national problem, a problem to which the great majority of Canadians had, up to that time, been completely oblivious.[32]

It was not, of course, that the Commissioners denied the value of the intellectual and cultural aid which the United States had given Canada. They paid tribute to the generous support which the great American foundations – Carnegie, Rockefeller, Guggenheim – had granted to Canadian scholars, artists and writers. They fully acknowledged that Canadians were indebted for much of their training to American universities, and derived much of their entertainment from American plays, films and radio. Canada had gained a good deal from its dependence on the rich and varied cultural resources of the United States; but it had lost far more through the frustration of its own creative powers and the erosion of its own distinctive personality. Canada exported many of its best trained minds and much of its artistic talent to the United States; and in return Canadians imported masses of American books, periodicals, films and radio programmes, in all of which American personalities, institutions, political ideas and cultural values were overwhelmingly predominant. Canadians were growing up and living their lives in ignorance, not only of their own artists and writers, but of their own public figures, their own history, and their own political and judicial systems.

The Massey Commission had surveyed a very wide range of interests and it made a number of specific recommendations, particularly about the various government institutions which it had been asked to examine. The federal agencies were important, but their scope was limited; and it was quite beyond their power to lift the general level of Canadian arts, letters and social sciences. Only some unprecedented and very impressive measures could enable Canada to escape from its cultural poverty, and these would undoubtedly cost a lot of money. "If we in Canada," the Commissioners wrote, "are to have a more plentiful and better cultural fare, we must pay for it. Good will alone can do little for a starving plant; if the cultural life of Canada is anaemic, it must be nourished and this will cost money."[33] It would cost far more than could ever come from private Canadian sources, for the huge personal fortunes upon which the great philanthropic American trusts' own foundations had been based simply did not exist in Canada. Canada would have to emulate the example first set in Europe and recently followed by Great Britain in the establishment of its Arts Council. Canada would have to rely on the resources of the State.

The Massey Commission based its two major recommendations on this premise. It recommended that federal financial aid, in the amount of fifty cents per capita of the population of each province, was to be divided among the various provincial universities in proportion to the enrolment of each. It also proposed that the federal government should establish a new body, to be called the Canada Council, which would award national scholarships in the humanities and social sciences, distribute grants to individuals and voluntary associations in arts and letters, and in general encourage and promote the cultural interests of the nation. There was not the slightest doubt that the Canada Council was the most significant and valuable of the Massey Commission's many recommendations; but, unfortunately, it was equally clear that it totally lacked the political support which had been steadily building up in favour of federal aid to the unversities. The Massey Report had scarcely been tabled in the House of Commons in the spring of 1950, when St. Laurent hastened to announce that federal aid, in the amounts recommended by the Commission, would be granted to the universities; but it was not until seven years later, and on the eve of a general election, that the Canada Council was at last established. It took a long time, and some anxiety about the Liberal Party's electoral prospects, to weaken St. Laurent's dislike of "subsidizing ballet dancing."

V

The Massey Commissioners were lone, lost voices, virtually unheard of in the deaf ears and closed minds of the Government of Canada. During the revealing years of war and peace, that government had apparently learnt nothing and forgotten nothing. It was still pursuing politicies and following courses which might have been valid half a century before, but which in the post-war world had become completely irrelevant. King and St. Laurent stubbornly continued to act as if they still cherished the senile delusion that freedom from British control was alone necessary to ensure Canadian autonomy, and that independence in a continent dominated by the United States was an easy and effortless business which had no need of constant attention and protective care. Although American control of Canadian economic affairs and foreign and defence policies had grown steadily greater during the decade, and although King himself privately realized the powerful drive and probable triumph of American continentalism, he and St. Laurent had almost literally done nothing to arrest its course. On the other hand, although Great Britain had obviously ceased to be a great power, and although the British Empire was in an evident state of dissolution, King and St. Laurent still behaved as if they were struggling against a centralized and dominating imperial system. King, in particular, was periodically haunted by the feeling that his anti-imperial crusade was still unfinished. The Empire-Commonwealth, despite its declining power and threatened divisions, still showed a strong instinct of cohesion, and the chief unifying force was obviously the British Crown. King, in the hidden republican recesses of his being, had always disliked the Crown, its representatives, symbols, tokens, and formalities. And until he had succeeded in destroying the integrating power of the Crown, his life's work could hardly be called complete.

Suddenly the opportunity, for which perhaps he had been subconsciously waiting, presented itself. In 1947-48 two events – the British Independence of India Act and the Irish declaration of independent, republican statehood – compelled a fundamental review of the nature of the British Commonwealth. At first, King hardly realized what a wonderful opportunity had been given him. When the announcement of the Independence Act prompted Gordon Graydon to ask for explanations in the Canadian House of Commons, King explicitly denied that the Canadian government had taken any part whatever in the negotiations between the British and Indian representatives.[34] The mere suggestion of a possible united Commonwealth policy on India was enough to throw him into one of his spasms of pathological resentment and mindless bad temper. " . . . This," he declared, in a moment of extreme paranoic delusion, "was part of an effort on Britain's part to get rid of her burdens and to throw them on the Dominions." He even made the frenzied prediction that if the Canadian government dared to give advice on the future of India, Canada might find itself involved in an Indian civil war, a war into which the Soviet Union might inevitably be drawn. His manic outburst on this occasion was perhaps exceptionally severe, but equally short-lived. None of his fearful prophecies came true, and India settled down to a prolonged consideration of its future political state. The problem of the Commonwealth was tacitly shelved until the late summer of 1948 when it was recalled to King's attention by the visits of two people, Sir Norman Brook, the Secretary of the British Cabinet, and Mr. J. A. Costello, the Taoiseach, or Prime Minister, of Eire. Brook had come to discuss the agenda of the Commonwealth Prime Ministers' meeting which was to take place in October. India, he informed King, would probably decide to become a republic. Costello was certain that Eire would soon break its last remaining link with the British Crown.[35]

It was at this point that King began to get interested. He saw himself playing the big star part in this final reorganization of the British Commonwealth. "I began to feel," he confided to his diary in one of his characteristically involved and meandering sentences, "that my real mission might be that of having to do with keeping together the communities that today are part of the British Commonwealth."[36] Yes! he would "save the Commonwealth" and save it "in spite of the Tories." The Tories, he was convinced, would inevitably seek to preserve the Crown as the Commonwealth's one remaining institutional link; but if Eire and India pushed their constitutional design to its logical conclusion, the inevitable result would be a head-on collision between the principle of monarchy and the principle of republicanism. There were only two possible consequences of such a direct confrontation; either India and Eire would have to withdraw from the Commonwealth, or the Commonwealth would have to destroy the central position of the Crown. The first of these two alternatives would mean the loss of two former members, one of which was already morally gone. The second alternative might very possibly entail the gradual decline of the Commonwealth through the degradation of its one common, unifying institution.

Between these two choices there could be no compromise, as General Smuts of South Africa, who was a philosopher as well as a statesman, saw clearly. " . . . My personal view . . . ," he wrote, "is that there is no middle course between the Crown and the Republic . . . . It is a case of the excluded middle" – the principle that between two contradictions no third or middle term is possible.[37] If Smuts had still been Prime Minister of the Union of South Africa, the outcome of the Commonwealth Prime Ministers' meeting in October, 1948, might conceivably have been different; but Smuts had lost power to D. F. Malan earlier in the year, and his absence left King the senior Dominion statesman and the dominating influence at the Conference. King, of course, professed to believe, if his confused reasoning ever reached so positive a conclusion, that a middle course did exist; but its possibility or impossibility scarcely interested him. He was determined, whatever happened, that the Crown must yield. He summarily rejected the proposals which Sir Norman Brook had brought over from England, all of which retained the Crown as the Commonwealth unifying institution; he listened very sympathetically when Costello explained that Eire would certainly deny allegiance to the Crown, but on the other hand, would be happy to be "associated" with "the community of nations" which formed the Commonwealth. Immediately after his heart-to-heart talk with Costello, King brought the subject up in Cabinet. It was clear to him that St. Laurent, Paul Martin and a few others "at first were pretty strong on the idea of no severance with the allegiance part of the crown"; but he busied himself explaining, in the usual cloudy circumlocutions, his own very different and extremely nebulous views. At the moment they amounted to little more than the conviction that the Commonwealth was "a community of free peoples" which must remain intact "as a bulwark against Communism." " . . . Taking the long-distance view," he argued characteristically, "it might be better for peace-loving nations of the world to hold together on some kind of basis that would not, for the moment, be too clearly defined. The larger vision is the one that must be kept to the fore."[38]

Early in October, when he reached London for the Conference – his last official visit – the "larger vision" had been slightly clarified, but King's own health had grown noticeably worse. He consulted Lord Moran, Churchill's physician, who had come to Quebec in 1943 and had advised King medically before. Moran looked grave, talked about "heart strain," prescribed digitalis and morphine, and immediately engaged nurses. The awful truth was borne in upon King that he could not possibly act as Canada's official representative at the Conference. It was a dismaying but not irremediable misfortune. St. Laurent, accompanied, of course, by the faithful Pickersgill, would have to come over from Canada to take his place; and through them and through the numerous visitors who would come to see him in his suite at the Dorchester, he could easily transmit his views to the Conference. It was a simple evangelical message that he wished to send. The Commonwealth, he kept insisting, was a community of like-minded nations, held together, not by the symbolism of the Crown, but by the substance of kindred ideas and similar institutions. It would be "raising a terrible issue," he reasoned, if the Crown became the subject of controversy; and obviously – although he preferred his auditors to infer this conclusion – the best way to protect the Crown from dispute was to remove it from its central position as the Commonwealth's principal institutional link.[39]

An impressive succession of visitors – Attlee, Churchill, Macmillan, Nehru of India, Liaqat Ali Khan of Pakistan, Fraser of New Zealand – and finally King George VI himself came to the Dorchester to see King. All were given approximately the same earnest lecture. King George's attention was called to the picture of Mackenzie King's mother, prominently displayed below the royal gift of a bouquet of flowers; and Mackenzie King himself, in one of the more curious of his mental associations, was immediately reminded of the Rebellion of 1837 and "of Mother being born in exile." George VI listen politely to his Prime Minister's constitutional moralizing, but remained amiably non-committal. Perhaps King's most important convert was his own Minister of External Affairs, Louis St. Laurent. St. Laurent had come to London still stubbornly holding to the belief that without the unifying Crown the Commonwealth would degenerate into an arbitrary and meaningless cluster of countries. King miraculously succeeded in persuading his colleague to change his mind. It was a vital conversion. Once St. Laurent was convinced, he became an even more effective advocate of the new conception of the Commonwealth.[40]

King was both uplifted and astonished by this last great struggle of his career. "Strangely enough, I said to myself, is it left to me again to try to save the Empire in spite of itself?"[41] Actually, the Empire was not really "saved" in October, 1948. The Prime Ministers' Conference had been exploratory; and despite King's fears and rages about the wording of its completely innocuous communiqué, no firm decisions had been reached. It was not until later in November that Eire finally determined to leave the Commonwealth and Nehru formally announced India's preference to remain associated with it. Everybody was pleased – or said he was – but everybody was still uncertain about the form this "association" would take. "A common citizenship," which Nehru himself had suggested, seemed inadequate, even if possible, to Prime Minister Attlee, and St. Laurent confessed real difficulty in visualizing "the continued existence of the Commonwealth without some link with the Crown." This equivocal phrase, "some link with the Crown," was the first significant indication of the change in Commonwealth thinking which King's persistent efforts at persuasion had brought about. A new and revolutionary concept of the Commonwealth was implied in those five small words. They meant that the Crown would cease to be the central and common institution of all the monarchies which made up the Commonwealth, and would become merely the artificial and tenuous "link" between basically antithetical systems of government.

Some bond or link was necessary. But what kind? It was not until April, 1949, six months after Mackenzie King had begun to preach the virtues of the hybrid Commonwealth, that its members met again in London to concoct a formula which would satisfy the republicans without alarming the monarchists too much. Nehru and the British took the lead by proposing that India should accept the Crown as the Head of the Commonwealth and the symbol of the free association of the members. Pearson, who, as the new Minister of External Affairs, represented Canada at the Conference, had inherited a considerable amount of King's fear and hatred of "imperialist centralization," and the neutral but portentous word "Head" distinctly rubbed him the wrong way.[42] He was still more critical of Attlee's assumption that the new declaration was to be made by India alone and that the other members of the Commonwealth would simply reaffirm their allegiance to the Crown. This, Pearson believed, was unfortunate in that it tended to emphasize rather than minimize the difference in the character of membership, and his criticism provoked the one serious argument of the Conference. Australia, New Zealand and the United Kingdom would have preferred a declaration which definitely implied that India was the solitary republic in an association of monarchies. Pakistan and Ceylon, on the other hand, while maintaining that they were perfectly satisfied with their present position as Dominions under the Crown, contended that India should not be permitted a constitutional freedom of choice which would be for ever denied to other members. Pearson, an obvious neutral, who saw little or no significance in these fine distinctions, was appointed to a committee which finally produced a declaration that few thought really acceptable, but which was reluctantly accepted by all. The seven monarchies, while asserting that their own membership was unchanged, announced that they and India were to be united as free and equal members in what was henceforth to be known, not as the British Commonwealth, but as the Commonwealth of Nations. [43]

At midday on April 27, 1949, the delegates proceeded in a body to Buckingham Palace, and solemnly presented their patched and mended resolution to King George VI. The King was politely acquiescent but, whether inadvertently or deliberately, he referred to the "British" Commonwealth of Nations and discreetly expressed the hope that there would not be too big a rush of Commonwealth conversions to republicanism in the future. He died three years later, without ever having been called upon to witness the inevitable consequences of that pregnant declaration. It was his daughter, Queen Elizabeth II, who was compelled to accept the long procession of dubiously "democratic" republics, from Asia, Africa, the Pacific, the Caribbean and the Mediterranean, which crowded into the Commonwealth and all too frequently displayed political tendencies which mocked King's credulous belief in the affinity of its kindred ideas and similar institutions. More than twenty years later, Pearson candidly admitted that the Prime Ministers' Conference of 1949 had broken both the institutional bond and the "bond of sentiment" which united the original Dominions and that "only self-interest would hold the new Commonwealth together."[44] But these were faraway afterthoughts. At the moment he was immensely pleased with what he had done.

VI

The old Commonwealth was a natural, historical development which required no justification; the new Commonwealth was an artificial creation which, its authors were convinced, needed to be vindicated. Pearson characteristically tried to prove its value by giving it a moral purpose. "Thus we all remain together," he declared, "at a time when, as never before, it is good for us and for the world that this should be so."[45] There was, he believed, undoubted virtue in the fact that the Commonwealth had ceased to be "an old, small club of prosperous, mainly Anglo-Saxon, members" and had turned itself into "a multilateral, multiracial, association."[46] It had, in fact, become "a very useful piece of international machinery" – "a firm bridge between East and West."

This new conception of the Commonwealth as a force for reconciliation in world affairs was powerfully strengthened by the personality and views of the Indian leader, Pandit Jawaharlal Nehru. Nehru's North American tour in the autumn of 1949 was a significant episode in a year crowded with important international events. He visited both the United States and Canada with apparently very different consequences. He annoyed the Americans by his refusal to take a stand in the current ideological struggle, and by his evident inclination to recognize the new regime in China. The Americans, on their part, annoyed him equally by pressing him to submit the Kashmir dispute to arbitration. He arrived in Ottawa in a state of considerable irritation and found, perhaps to his surprise, what looked to be a very friendly welcome awaiting him. St. Laurent entertained him at a private dinner and managed to break through the Indian leader's cultivated reserve and defensive suspicion of North American aims and motives; and for more than an hour Nehru talked confidentially and eloquently "of his country and its place in the world." Some of the guests that evening "could sense a bond being forged between the two countries."[47] It remained to be seen whether the "bond" was real or the bright illusion of an evening of good food, good drink and good company.

On November 17, shortly after Nehru's visit, Pearson announced in the House of Commons that Canada had received an invitation from the Prime Minister of Ceylon to attend a Conference of Commonwealth Foreign Ministers, to be held at Colombo early in January, 1950. Canada, of course, accepted and a Canadian delegation flew eastward, half-way around the world, to the island of Ceylon, where the first Commonwealth Conference ever held on Asian soil was to take place. Ostensibly the chief subject of the meeting was foreign policy; but the economic plight of most of South and Southeast Asia was so extreme that the possibility of improvement was certain to thrust its way into the agenda. Both Janius Jayewardene of Ceylon and Percy C. Spender of Australia suggested some kind of organization which would attempt to raise living standards and promote social welfare among the underdeveloped countries of the region. Ernest Bevin, the British Foreign Secretary, who attended the Conference despite the worsening of his mortal illness, supported and developed the idea. It was never intended, of course, that the Colombo Plan, as it soon came to be called, would have its membership confined to Commonwealth countries; rather it was hoped that both great nations and underdeveloped countries outside the Commonwealth would be numbered among its benefactors and its beneficiaries. The need was both great and widespread; but Commonwealth countries comprised about three-quarters of the population of South and Southeast Asia and it was appropriate for the Commonwealth to take the initiative. It appointed a Consultative Committee which met in Canberra in May, 1950, and drew up a loosely organized plan for the relief of starvation and distress, the provision of technical assistance, and the supply of capital equipment within the area.

Obviously, Bevin had a special as well as a general interest in promoting the scheme. Most of the post-war economic development in South Asia had been financed by withdrawals from the sterling balances accumulated by

Commonwealth countries during the war, and Bevin was understandably anxious to relieve Great Britain of part of still another burden she had been bearing alone. If he hoped to inspire Canada to take a leading part in the economic advance of the "multiracial" Commonwealth, he was soon undeceived. The glories of Pearson's "Atlantic Vision" had certainly blinded his outlook on the Pacific. The Canadian government had posted a large surplus on current account for every year since 1945; the wartime debt was being rapidly paid off; but Pearson bluntly warned his conferees at Colombo that Canada's heavy military commitment to NATO might very probably prevent it from giving any economic aid at all to the undeveloped countries of South Asia.[48]

His opposition to any Canadian involvement in the Colombo Plan was, in fact, so great that at first he was inclined to feel that his government ought merely to be represented by an observer at the Canberra meeting. In the end, Canada sent R. W. Mayhew, its Minister of Fisheries, as a participating delegate; but Mayhew was so tightly bound by Pearson's cautious instructions that he and Percy Spender, who had come with a detailed plan and was eager for action, quickly became engaged in a typical Australian-Canadian row.[49] This "crisis in Commonwealth relations" led to a drastic reduction of Spender's ambitious scheme, but did not noticeably improve Canada's attitude to it. The Canadian government waited until Great Britain had decided to join the Colombo Plan before making up its mind to participate; and it committed itself to a contribution of $25 million for only the first year of what had been extended into a six-year programme.

For Pearson, the only two really important international organizations of the post-war world were the United Nations and the North Atlantic Treaty Organization. As one of the principal designers of NATO, and the sole author of its empty second clause, he had all the special pride of paternity in his own creation. His feeling for the United Nations was less personal, but perhaps more reverential. The United Nations, in his opinion, was a truly oecumenical organization which, as time was soon to prove, could become the agent of a great moral purpose. Beside these two great institutions, in both of which the United States was the dominating force, the Commonwealth – even the "multilateral, multiracial Commonwealth," which he himself had helped to fashion – looked very insignificant to Pearson. The Colombo Plan must be put firmly in second place after the United Nations's aid programme, and, unless the United States decided to give it financial support, would probably prove to be of little benefit. The new Commonwealth, in fact, might be "a very useful piece of international machinery," but Pearson was not likely to employ it very often. It might even provide "a firm bridge between East and West," but Pearson had no intention of risking his diplomatic neck by crossing it.

His inner convictions became still more clearly apparent in the discussions on foreign policy, which was ostensibly the main business of the Colombo Conference. Perhaps by accident, but more likely by design, the Conference opened at a moment of crucial historic importance in Asian history. In both China and Indochina, nationalist movements, which had assumed a communist form, had evidently become potent political forces. In the now independent state of Vietnam, the Viet Minh movement, led by Ho Chi Minh, was in active revolt against the rule of the former Emperor Bao Dai, newly re-established by the French government. In China, the last cities controlled by the Kuomintang had fallen during December, and on January 1, 1950, just a few days before the Colombo Conference met, the Communist leaders proudly announced that their sway extended over the whole of continental China except Tibet. For about six months, until the outbreak of the Korean War, the western world had a unique opportunity of recognizing the irreversible revolutionary movement in East Asia. It could have accepted the triumph of the Communists in China and anticipated their eventual victory in Indochina; it could have come to sensible, tolerant, if not friendly, terms with the inevitable future. The western world − or much of it − rejected these favourable chances. Instead, it committed itself to a tragically vain attempt, which lasted nearly a quarter of a century, to deny the validity of the new China and to prevent the realization of the new Vietnam.

The Conference offered the Commonwealth a last chance of avoiding this fatal course, and the Commonwealth hesitated, wavered, and could not make up its mind. It found, in fact, that the solution of its common problems in foreign policy was a very difficult business. The Kashmir dispute between India and Pakistan, a purely Commonwealth question, was not settled; and, as Pearson later informed the Canadian House of Commons, there were "vigorous differences of opinion as to what the situation was and what might be done to meet it" in Vietnam. Nehru insisted that Bao Dai was a captive king under French tutelage; MacDonald of the British delegation strenuously denied this charge; and Pearson argued that under Bao Dai's "autonomous government," Vietnam would have a chance to acquire "freedom, and unity, and stability."[50] Disagreement about Vietnam was perhaps inevitable at this stage, for the available evidence was vague and conflicting; but differences of opinion about the true state of affairs in continental China was hardly possible any longer. Nehru, who hoped that India and China might constitute an Asian "Third Force" between Russia and the United States, was strongly in favour of recognition of the People's Republic. In Great Britain, both the Labour government and the Conservative opposition agreed that recognition was sensible; and Churchill remarked, in a characteristic exhibition of robust commonsense, that "the reason for having diplomatic relations is not to confer a compliment but to secure a convenience . . . ."[51]

Great Britain would have preferred joint recognition by a number of different states; but Bevin was forced to admit, before the Colombo Conference, that even among the members of the Commonwealth there was no agreement about procedure. By the time the delegates assembled at Colombo on January 9, 1950, India, Pakistan, Great Britain and Ceylon had all recognized the new regime; but the old settlement Dominions, Canada, Australia and New Zealand, still waited uncertainly. The Conference failed to close this deep division in the Commonwealth, but Nehru, who was at his eloquent best in supporting recognition, evidently made a profound impression on the delegates, including Pearson. Pearson, in fact, had already shown a cautious interest in the new China's national status. As early as October, 1949, he had explained to the House of Commons the requirements which a new government, hoping for diplomatic recognition, would have to meet: it must demonstrate, he said, that it was independent of external control, that it exercised effective rule over the territory it claimed to govern, and that this territory was reasonably well defined. Pearson seemed to suggest that if any government, including the People's Republic of China, met these conditions, it deserved recognition. Yet, at the same time, he implied a serious doubt that the new China would qualify. Its government, he told the Commons, was "a small revolutionary party . . . espousing an alien philosophy, looking to the Soviet Union as the author and interpreter of that philosophy and as a guide in international relations . . . ." If such a government, he promised the House, could prove itself to be independent – "I stress the word 'independent' " then, "in due course and after consultation with other friendly governments," Canada might "have to recognize the facts which confront us.... Of course," he added, "we in Canada reject completely the Marxist-Leninist principles espoused by the Chinese Communists, but we cannot reject the fact of China and its 450 million people."[52]

It was in this highly doubtful frame of mind, and with these strong prepossessions, that Pearson departed for Colombo. Nehru's persuasive eloquence may have moved him. He may have returned to Canada in a mood to propose recognition, but, unlike most converts to a new religion, he was in no hurry to proclaim his faith. Time went by, providing good excuses, if not good reasons, for further delay. On the one hand, the Peking government proceeded to negotiate a Sino-Soviet Treaty of Friendship, Alliance and Mutual Assistance; and on the other hand, it continued to harry the citizens and seize the property of such liberal democratic countries as Great Britain, France and the United States. These highly unfriendly actions did not move Bevin to withdraw British recognition. He probably would have agreed with Churchill that "one has to recognize lots of things and people in this world of sin and woe that one does not like." Such tolerant realism was very rare in 1949-50 and the government of the United States possessed none of it. The arrest and detention of the American Consul-General at Mukden was more than enough, Acheson considered, to "preclude" recognition; but this sense of outraged majesty was only one of the great many irritants in the steadily increasing American hostility to the People's Republic of China.

A furious feeling of humiliation and defeat had gripped the American government and the American people. During the war, Roosevelt had deliberately promoted Chiang Kai-shek to the ranks of the "Big Four". The United States had expended a great deal of moral and political capital, as well as a large amount of money, in the support of the Chinese "Nationalists." Now the "Nationalists" had been overthrown and supplanted by a regime which defiantly professed exactly the same economic and social philosophy as that of America's greatest moral antagonist, the Soviet Union. Only three years earlier, Acheson had launched a strategical campaign and Truman an idealogical crusade against communism; and the mixture of fear, hate, and anger they aroused had now become a national obsession which, by a terrible irony, was turned against its very authors. At Wheeling, West Virginia, on February 9, 1950, Joseph R. McCarthy, a Republican senator for Wisconsin, first began his sensational attacks against "communism in government."

It was in this atmosphere of unreason and hysteria that the Canadian government had to make up its mind about the recognition of the People's Republic of China. American opinion, both official and popular, had as usual blanketed Canada through diplomatic exchanges, the newspapers, and the radio; but it was not only from American sources that Canadians were taught to regard the Communist government at Peking with suspicion and fear. They received a good deal of equally fervent instruction from their own Parliament, and particularly from the new Leader of the Opposition, George Drew. Drew had deliberately adopted the American rather than the British attitude towards recognition; he insisted that British recognition was "no reason why this government should recognize the Communist regime in China." Pearson's admission, late in February, that the Cabinet was seriously discussing the question of recognition may have alarmed him, and Pearson's inadequate and evasive speech of March 3, delivered during the debate on supply for the Department of External Affairs, probably confirmed his worst fears. Pearson, he charged angrily, had not even mentioned China. Was he "unaware of the existence" of this "most critical spot in the whole world?" Recognition of China, he maintained, would almost certainly be a fatal blow to the new regime in Vietnam; and the fall of Boa Dai might produce equally disastrous consequences in Malaya and Burma. "What earthly use will the Atlantic pact be," he asked dramatically, "if through that pact we prevent war in Europe, and then the whole structure of the Orient goes to pieces under the red flood." [53]

Pearson's reply was both uninformative and inconclusive. The Canadian government, he intimated, was in the midst of "delicate discussions" on the wisdom of recognition; and the Canadian Parliament – strangely enough – was not the place to rehearse all the arguments, pro and con! The Conservative leader had recommended caution. The Canadian government would exercise it.[54]

It continued to exercise caution as the weeks went by. And then, quite suddenly, time ran out.

VII

At about ten o'clock on the night of Saturday, June 24, the telephone on the night-table beside Dean Acheson's bed rang suddenly and imperiously. A tired Secretary of State had left Washington for a quiet weekend at Harewood Farm, his Maryland country house, and, after some gardening and a good dinner, he had turned in to read himself to sleep. The telephone "tied into the White House switchboard" and "used sparingly by considerate associates" now broke up the peaceful conclusion of this pleasant day. The American Ambassador to South Korea — a tense voice informed him over the telephone — had reported from Seoul that a heavy attack from North Korea had been launched on South Korea across the boundary of the 38th parallel.[55] Only a little while earlier, the American administration had been talking as if Korea, as well as Taiwan, lay well beyond the perimeter of the American defence system in the Pacific, and could therefore be considered expendable. Now it was all strangely different. The American State and Defence Departments sprang into instant action, with a speed and efficiency that suggested long preparation and careful rehearsals. A meeting of the United Nations Security Council was peremptorily called for the next morning, Sunday; and a draft resolution, denouncing North Korea, which, curiously enough, had been prepared in advance for just such an eventuality, was pulled out of the files in readiness.

The startled members of the Security Council met at 2:00 p.m. on Sunday, June 25 and debated the question of Korea for four anxious hours. The members rejected the American draft's description of the Korean attack as "an unprovoked act of aggression" on the sensible grounds that there was not enough information to justify such a phrase; and a much less inflammatory indictment, "a breach of the peace," was substituted. North Korea was ordered to cease hostilities and withdraw its forces, and all members of the United Nations were called upon to render assistance in the execution of this resolution. The motion was adopted by a vote of 9 to 0, Yugoslavia abstaining. The Soviet Union had been boycotting the Security Council ever since it had declined to transfer the permanent Chinese seat from the defeated Kuomintang to the triumphant People's Republic; and Malik, the Soviet representative on the Council, did not come to the Council meeting on Sunday. Even if he had attended and had vetoed the resolution, as, of course, he was constitutionally entitled to do, it might not have made a great deal of difference in what followed. The Security Council's resolution gave the United States a valuable moral sanction, but little more. It was President Truman's after-dinner meeting with his State Department officials and service chiefs in Washington, and not the Security Council's afternoon session at Lake Success, New York, which made the truly vital decisions of that alarming Sunday in late June, 1950.

At the President's invitation, Acheson presented his report and recommendations. He had not the slightest doubt about the nature and origins of the North Korean attack. It had, he was convinced, been "mounted, supplied, and instigated by the Soviet Union."[56] The fact that Malik, the Soviet representative, had not appeared at the Sunday meeting of the Security Council to veto the Korean resolution, and did not even attend on Tuesday, June 27, when once more the United States jerked the Security Council into action, were circumstances which did not seem to weaken the Secretary of State's conviction in the slightest. The State Department officials complacently assumed that the "cumbersome Soviet bureaucracy was simply not equipped to make quick decisions," – a comforting conclusion which seemed curiously at variance with Acheson's major assumption that the lightning attack on South Korea had been "mounted, supplied, and instigated by the Soviet Union." Undoubtedly, the inconsistencies of Soviet behaviour were puzzling, but they did not alter the Secretary of State's interpretation of the real meaning and purpose of what had happened in Korea. The Korean affair, he felt certain, was not a mere "breach of the peace," an infraction of the collective security system of the United Nations. It was much more than that. It was, in fact, "an open undisguised challenge" to American strategic interests and protective responsibilities in the Far East. "To back away from the challenge, " Acheson reflected determinedly, "would be highly destructive of the power and prestige of the United States. By prestige, I mean the shadow cast by power, which is of great deterrent importance." [57]

On Monday evening, June 26, after a day of serious South Korean reverses, Truman and his State and Defence Department advisers met again. Acheson was ready with a new set of proposals which matched what the whole company now assumed was not an isolated, local incident, but an important part of a vast comprehensive Communist plan. The American Air Force and Navy were ordered to give "all-out" support to South Korea, confining their efforts, for the time being, to the south of the 38th parallel. The Seventh Fleet was to guard Taiwan and to prevent the "Nationalists" from attacking the mainland and the Communists from attacking the island. The American forces in the Philippines were to be strengthened, aid to Boa Dai's government in Vietnam to be increased, and a proposal for a strong joint military mission to Indochina was to be put before the French government. Finally, the American representative was to call a new meeting of the Security

Council for the following day, June 27, and present it with a new resolution, explicitly calling upon all members of the United Nations to aid in repelling the North Korean invasion. If Malik unfortunately put in an appearance and vetoed the new resolution, then the United States would simply proceed with its programme under the old one. "Orders to carry out the decisions of Monday evening were issued at once," Acheson recorded, "and were immediately obeyed."[58]

At midday on Tuesday, June 27, Truman publicly announced the belligerent American plans. It was not until 3:00 p.m. that the Security Council met and dutifully accepted an American resolution calling upon members of the United Nations to "furnish such assistance to the Republic of Korea as may be necessary to repel the armed attack and to restore international peace and security in the area." Ostensibly, the resistance in South Korea had now become a collective United Nations enterprise; but Acheson was unimpressed by this formal change. "Troops from other sources," he remarked with candid realism, "would be helpful politically and psychologically, but unimportant militarily."[59] For him the affair in Korea was a struggle between the United States and the Soviet Union for the mastery of the Far East, and the imprimatur of the United Nations did not change its essential character in the least.

Pearson and St. Laurent viewed it in a much more credulous and romantic light. For them the resistance in Korea was above all else a great united effort to defend the collective security system of the United Nations against the open assault of international Communism. " . . . Communism," Pearson told the House of Commons impressively, "has passed beyond the use of subversion . . . and will now use armed invasion and war." Such desperate tactics must be resisted, of course; and since, unhappily, no permanent ground forces had been put at the disposal of the United Nations, individual members of the Security Council must shoulder the responsibility for action, within the terms of the Charter, but on their own initiative. "In this case," Pearson declared with firm conviction, "the United States recognized a special responsibility which it discharged with admirable dispatch and decisiveness. I feel sure that all members of the House will applaud and support this act of high courage and firm statesmanship on the part of the government of the United States."[60]

All – or almost all – the members behaved exactly as Pearson had predicted. Only the independent and irrepressible J.-F. Pouliot was bold enough to call attention to the awkward fact that Truman had taken armed action hours before the Security Council's resolution authorized it.[61] Pouliot's lone dissenting voice was drowned in a hearty chorus of approval. Howard Green echoed Pearson's belief that the American decision was one of "great courage and of great statesmanship." George Drew pledged the support of the Progressive-Conservative Party for the Security Council's second resolution. Knowles reasserted the C.C.F.'s devotion to the principle of collective security, and its readiness "to carry our support of that principle into all it may involve."[62] John Diefenbaker wished to know when and how Canada would fulfil its responsibilities to the United Nations.

To this, Pearson had at first no ready answer, but the increasing pressure of events was forcing the St. Laurent government to make up its mind in a hurry. On Thursday and Friday, June 29 and 30, the American government dispatched substantial ground forces to South Korea and authorized the navy and air force to strike at North Korean targets beyond the 38th parallel. The scope and gravity of the struggle were obviously increasing; but, as everybody knew, the Canadian Parliament was scheduled to prorogue on Friday. St. Laurent saw no reason to postpone prorogation, but he knew very well that the House would not willingly disband without some statement of government purpose. On Friday, the last day of the session, he announced that Canada would make a contribution – probably several Canadian destroyers – to the war.

VIII

It soon became clear that this was not enough. During July, pressure for a larger Canadian contribution increased, much of it coming, both directly and indirectly, from the United States. Acheson had dismissed troops other than American as "unimportant militarily," but helpful "politically and psychologically." He now earnestly reminded Pearson of the "tremendous importance" of ground forces from other United Nations's countries, especially from those which, like Canada, "have prestige, and influence and command respect." [63] These flattering entreaties had been preceded, earlier in July, by a more indirect and evasive appeal. Trygve Lie, the Secretary-General of the United Nations, at the urgent request of the Americans, but on his own responsibility, had invited other members of the organization, including Canada, to furnish ground forces for the war. The American officials solemnly assured Lie that they would, of course, explain to the members of the Security Council, and all other interested parties, that this request had been made on their initiative, and not on Lie's; but, "for some unexplained reason," as the puzzled Pearson naively recorded, these explanations were never made.[64] Mackenzie King, on occasion, could dismiss the United Nations as a submissive division of the American State Department, but Pearson didn't harbour any such heretical thoughts. His interview with Dean Acheson, which came later in July, could hardly have been a happier meeting of minds. They both agreed completely about the real inner significance of the conflict in Korea. Acheson, Pearson noted approvingly, "emphasized at the beginning that the Korean situation could be understood and intelli-

gently dealt with only as a phase, and not, in the long run, the most important phase, of the general conflict between the free and the Communist
worlds."[65]

Pearson was just as "deeply conscious of the menace of Communist
aggression" and equally determined to resist its open manifestation in Korea.
The fact that the United Nations had actually indicted and condemned the
Korean aggression seemed to him a great moral achievement. The Korean
struggle became, in fact, another – and perhaps the greatest – of Pearson's
righteous "causes." It was the first time in history, he reflected with immense
satisfaction, that such a collective judgement had been pronounced against
an aggressor. "I felt at the time," he recalled later "very excited about this
historical precedent."[66] Other members of the St. Laurent Cabinet did not
quite reach this state of moral exaltation. "What would Mr. King do?" they
asked anxiously: and replied, with some assurance, "he wouldn't be getting
involved." It took a second Cabinet meeting, and the support of the Prime
Minister, before the Canadian government finally decided to send a volunteer
brigade to Korea. On August 7, St. Laurent announced the recruitment of
the Canadian Army Special Force.

Three weeks later, on August 29, the Canadian Parliament reopened
hurriedly in order to cope with a railway strike. By this time, the war in
Korea had been going on for little more than two months, but already the
confusion over its nature and purpose had enormously increased. For Americans, as Acheson himself had explained, "the Korean situation could be
understood and intelligently dealt with only as a phase ... of the general
conflict between the free and the Communist worlds;" and Truman had
made this concept explicit when, in his statement of June 27, he had included
Taiwan, Indochina and the Philippine Islands in his anti-communist defensive programme. Pearson had talked, in terms almost identical with those
of Acheson, about the general threat of Soviet imperialism and the menace
of international communism. Yet, in almost the same breath, he had kept
insisting that the resistance which the Security Council had authorized was
simply a local defence of the collective security system against its North
Korean aggressors. He found it very convenient to distinguish between
theory and practice in his Korean policy; but he now discovered, to his
dismay, that the Americans apparently regarded them as one and the same.
They seemed eager to link Taiwan, the last refuge of Nationalist China, and
South Korea, the far-eastern advance post of American power, in a common
military system. General Chiang Kai-shek's offer of Nationalist troops for
Korea, General MacArthur's visit to Taiwan, and Chiang's subsequent
announcement that the foundations had been laid for Sino-American military
co-operation, perturbed Canadian and western opinion generally. Were President Truman and General MacArthur about to enlarge the Korean resistance
into the vast dimensions of a general war against the People's Republic of

China and/or the Soviet Union ?

In his long speech to the Commons on August 31, Pearson tried laboriously and not very convincingly to quiet Canadian fears. Though he made no mention at all of General MacArthur's conspicuous indiscretions, he admitted that the Canadian government had been disturbed by the statements of General Chiang. These statements, he declared, had tended "to confuse the defence of Korea, which had been assumed by the United Nations, with the defence of Formosa (Taiwan) which has not." This sounded straightforward and conclusive, but was, in fact, remarkable chiefly, not for what it said, but for what it left out. The United Nations might not have assumed the defence of Taiwan but the United States undoubtedly had, and the United States was carrying the major burden of the war in Korea. To distinguish sharply between the moral justification of the resistance in Korea and the defence of Taiwan might thus reflect on the motives of the American government; and even an implied censure of an administration whose courage and statesmanship he had so highly eulogized was unthinkable for Pearson. He was determined to keep Canada out of Taiwan, but he also felt a faithful follower's urge to justify the American military presence there. The order to the 7th Fleet, he assured the Commons, was a "strategic, defensive decision " with "no political implications" designed simply to prevent the extension of the conflict in Korea.[67] Unfortunately, this plausible explanation entangled him in still another contradiction, for it implied that the Korean aggression was not the work of the North Korean government, but of the forces of international communism which might strike anywhere. On the one hand was the concept of a great anti-communist crusade, and on the other the idea of a limited local struggle; and between the two Pearson dodged backward and forward, with great agility, as it suited his convenience.

At that moment, the only representatives of "Soviet Communist imperialism" in action were North Korean soldiers; and in September, by a hazardous but highly successful manoeuvre of General MacArthur's, they were driven rapidly north towards the 38th parallel. It was at this point that the Canadians and the Americans had their first serious, though carefully concealed, difference of opinion about the conduct of the war. "We took the view . . . ." Pearson recorded "that the United Nations had discharged its obligations when the aggressor was driven back behind the line dividing the two Koreas, and that we should be very cautious in extending our mandate to include a march into northern territory."[68] When the Americans, flushed with success, peremptorily rejected these prudent counsels, Pearson proposed, as a compromise, that the United Nations's army should suspend operations for a few days, and then, if North Korea proved obstinate, should advance no further than the "northern neck" of the peninsula, between the 39th and 40th parallels. These proposals at first seemed certain to win American acceptance; and Pearson was correspondingly astonished and indignant when the American representative at Flushing Meadows asked support "for an immediate pursuit of the North Koreans beyond the 38th parallel, and for their destruction, − for a follow-through to the Chinese boundary, if necessary, to destroy the aggressor."[69] It was obvious that, while individual members of the State Department might listen politely to what Pearson had to say, the main thrust of American government policy was directly opposed to him. General MacArthur was in command of the United Nations's cause; and military considerations and military considerations only, governed the resistance to aggression in Korea. Pearson was troubled and angered. He complained to Acheson, and Acheson soothingly explained that the American volte-face was the result of an "unfortunate mix-up."

As Pearson himself has candidly noted, all his appeals and protests were made "behind the scenes." In private, he was bold enough in confronting Warren Austin and Dean Acheson; but, in public, on the floor of the United Nations Assembly, he took the official American line with earnest fidelity. "The United Nations must ... ," he declared, "leave its forces free to do whatever is practicable to make certain that the Communist aggressors of North Korea are not permitted to re-establish some new base in the peninsula from which they could sally forth again upon a peaceful people."[70] Like the other members of the American-dominated bloc in the Assembly, he was committed to military victory as an essential prerequisite of the enforcement of a democratic political settlement on the entire peninsula. It was a dangerously ambitious aim which was given its most extreme expression in the eight-power resolution passed on October 7. This fatal statement declared once more that the purpose of the United Nations was the establishment of a unified, independent, and democratic government in Korea, and that to this end "all appropriate steps" were to be taken "to ensure conditions of stability" throughout the peninsula.[71] There could be no possible doubt now that the United Nations was engaged in an attempt to impose democracy on the North Koreans, just as the North Koreans had attempted to force Communism on the South Koreans. Neither the British nor the Canadian delegates expressed any doubts, anxieties or reservations. It was left to Sir Benegal Rau of India, "in a voice tense with emotion," to make a last vain plea for a negotiated peace.

Encouraged by the Assembly's permissive instructions, the United Nations's troops resumed their northern advance. On the last day of September, a week before the Assembly had made its fateful decision, Chou En-lai had announced that China would not stand idly by if the "imperialist war lords" invaded the territory of its friendly neighbour. To Pearson and Acheson, this was a surprising, and highly disconcerting, announcement. Their eyes had been focused so intently and exclusively on the Soviet Union, and Soviet imperialism, that they had scarcely given China a thought. They had totally underestimated the People's Republic as an independent and powerful force in the politics of the Far East; and now, for the first time, Pearson began to feel a chilling sense of apprehension. Were the Chinese "just bluffing," as the Americans insisted? There was nothing to worry about from the Chinese, General MacArthur kept blandly assuring the sceptics. He confidently informed President Truman that the fighting in Korea would probably be over by the American Thanksgiving, late in November, and that most of the American troops would be home by Christmas.[72] The open appearance of Chinese units on Korean battlefields apparently did not disturb him in the slightest. Determined to repeat the smashing success of his manoeuvre at Inchon, he divided his forces and on November 24 commenced a general assault on the line of the Yalu River, the boundary between Korea and China. For four days, the troops "moved forward into the ominously silent and apparently deserted mountain area of northwest Korea." And then, on the fourth day, "massive Chinese counter-attacks exploded" all around them.[73]

General MacArthur, that preposterous mixture of Genghis Khan and Louis XIV, now dropped from the heights of manic exaltation to the abyss of manic depression. "We face an entirely new war," he announced.

CHAPTER 9

The New Colonialism

I

Two months before the massive Chinese onslaught, when the Korean War was still conceived simply as the deserved punishment of the naughty North Koreans, a large group of sober-suited provincial politicians assembled at Quebec City. They were the constitutional doctors who had come to make a last effort to save the life of St. Laurent's frail but favourite patient – the amendment of the Canadian constitution in Canada. It had come very close to death when the Constitutional Conference adjourned on January 12, 1950; but the anxious doctors had managed to prolong its moribund existence by appointing a Continuing Committee which, it was hoped, might reconcile the remaining differences among the provinces. A second session of the Conference was obviously necessary since the Continuing Committee would have to make its report; and Duplessis, who had been unexpectedly affable and complimentary, on January 12 invited the delegates to reassemble at Quebec City. He and St. Laurent may have imagined that a general agreement was almost within their grasp; but the adjourned session, which met towards the end of September, 1950, soon proved the naiveté of their hopes. Duplessis regarded the whole of section 92, the powers of the provincial legislatures, as constitutionally sacred; Douglas believed that if subsection 13, "property and civil rights in the province," was constitutionally "entrenched," all socialist projects would face an insurmountable legal barrier. The conflict between them was absolute and irreconcilable. The Constitutional Conference which St. Laurent had hoped so earnestly would succeed in "domiciling" the Canadian constitution in Canada was adjourned indefinitely. It never met again.[1]

St. Laurent had failed completely here. But he had two other, perhaps more seriously urgent, matters to settle, both of which required federal-provincial consultation and consent. The first of these was the renewal of the tax-rental agreements which had been signed with the provinces in

1947; and the second was the increasing popular pressure for the elimination of the means test in the grant of old age pensions, and their extension to all Canadians of seventy years or over. The tax agreements, by which all the provinces, with the exception of Ontario and Quebec, had transferred their income taxing powers to the federal government in return for an annual rental, were due to end on March 31, 1952, and St. Laurent knew he needed time for the negotiation of a new settlement. He was less concerned about "universal" old age pensions. They had first been proposed in August, 1945, as an item in the ambitious social welfare programme presented to the Dominion-Provincial Conference on Reconstruction; and they had been abandoned, along with other costly proposals, in the face of the determined opposition of the provinces, led by George Drew. St. Laurent was not an advocate of the welfare state in any serious sense, and he had been perfectly content to let the old age security project lie where it had fallen; but in the five long years which had elapsed since the Conference on Reconstruction, popular demand for the abolition of the means test had been steadily building up. A Joint Committee of the Senate and the House of Commons, appointed to consider the question, had reported favourably late in the previous June.

The Committee had adopted what it no doubt regarded as an ingenious solution of the problem of financing a universal old age security scheme. It paid its respects, in principle, to the basic concept openly professed in the title of the Beveridge report, that social welfare was essentially social insurance. Social welfare payments were not originally conceived as a government handout to everybody from general taxation, but as benefits earned by responsible citizens through regular payments into an insurance fund. The Committee recognized the actuarial soundness of a strict old age insurance scheme, and paid its respects to the sense of personal responsibility which it would certainly inculcate in the insured; but despite these admitted advantages, the cost and complications of collecting premiums on a national scale would, the Committee believed, be impossibly great. Instead, it proposed what it optimistically called a "pay-as-you-go" scheme, according to which the government would assign a percentage of certain-named general taxes to the support of the fund, and, as a result, the taxpayers would occasionally be reminded that really, though indirectly, they were paying for their own protection. Their benefits at the rate the Committee recommended, of $40.00 a month, were to be paid to every Canadian aged seventy or over; "old age assistance" with a means test was to continue for citizens 65 to 69.[2]

The Committee's recommendations, together with the government's new tax rental proposals, were ready when the new Federal-Provincial Conference opened early in December. It met in circumstances much more tragically incongruous than those which had marked the beginning of the adjourned session of the Constitutional Conference back in September. Only a few days earlier President Truman's reckless remarks about the possible use of the atom bomb in the Korean crisis had startled and terrified the whole western world; and on the morning of December 4, just as the federal and provincial representatives were gathering for their first session, Prime Minister Attlee landed in New York on his urgent quest of clarification. A sense of uncertainty and apprehension weighed heavily on Ottawa, as on London and Paris; and the contrast with the jubilant mood of certain victory in which the Reconstruction Conference had opened, five years earlier, in the summer of 1945, was immense. St. Laurent made the most of the change. His was not an expansive or creative nature, and he almost welcomed an excuse for doing little or nothing. Although that irrepressible socialist, Douglas of Saskatchewan, kept expressing the hope that their meeting might turn out to be a continuation of the Reconstruction Conference of 1945, St. Laurent repeatedly assured him and the other delegates that it was not and could not be. He admitted that in 1949, when the Conference was first planned, it was conceived as the fulfilment of the ambitious welfare programme of 1945; but, in the meantime, he insisted, circumstances had totally and drastically changed.[3]

The government, in fact, presented a formidable case against all expenditures, except those for defence; the old age pension scheme, costly enough in itself, was the only survivor of the wreckage of earlier plans. St. Laurent, as Prime Minister, first sounded the note of anxiety and economy; and he was followed by three of his colleagues, the Ministers of External Affairs, Defence, and Finance, all of whom emphasized the gravity of the current situation. St. Laurent soberly reminded the delegates that while in 1945 Canada's main aims were employment, prosperity and social welfare, now the chief Canadian preoccupations were security and defence. The Korean War demanded costly increased military expenditures; it had released the familiar wartime inflationary pressure and sharply raised the cost of living. Government outlays in general and capital disbursements in particular must be reduced as far as possible. "All governments," St. Laurent repeated, with a meaning glance at the rows of provincial representatives, "can help to avoid adding to these inflationary pressures by keeping their own expenditures to a minimum."[4]

It was both an earnest lecture and a sombre panoramic review. St. Laurent's colleagues filled in the details of the gloomy picture and sharpened the point of its moral. Pearson talked, in very alarmist tones, of "Communist aggression" in general, and of the hideous possibility of general war in which the Soviet Union, as well as the People's Republic of China, might be involved. Claxton, the Minister of Defence, reminded the Conference that in 1947-48, the year before the founding of NATO, Canadian military expenditures amounted to less than $200 million. Now, he informed the delegates, these outlays were running at a rate nearly four times as great and, for the fiscal year 1951-52, might very easily exceed a billion. Abbott who, as Minister of Finance, logically came last, took up and amplified this startling financial tale. He had undertaken, he told the Conference, to apply brakes on credit expansion in Canada. He promised to cut out less essential expenditures and to balance the budget. Yet he admitted that, even with all these economies and restrictions, government outlays for the current year would amount to $3 billions, up by $800 million from the total of three years earlier.[5]

Thus admonished and exhorted, the Federal-Provincial Conference of December, 1950, proved unexpectedly compliant. Douglas Abbott had argued that the provinces' lease of their income tax rights to the federal government had resulted in a "more efficient and equitable" peacetime tax system than any in the previous half century; and no provincial representative seemed eager to dispute his claim. Obviously, eight out of ten provinces were ready to approve the new tax rental proposals without the prolonged haggling which had delayed the acceptance of the old. Ontario and Quebec had, of course, rejected the plan of 1947; but George Drew, who had led the opposition to the federal government's offer from the moment it was first made in 1945, had been succeeded as Premier of Ontario by the much more placable and co-operative Leslie Frost. Frost later announced that Ontario was prepared to accept Abbott's new proposition, and this left Quebec as the only jarring note in an unprecedented peacetime financial harmony. Duplessis was more polite and accommodating with St. Laurent than he had ever been to any federal politician before; but to sell Quebec's right to tax the income of its own citizens was more than he would yield.

An old age pension, paid to everybody over seventy, was, in his view, a different and a much more tolerable federal encroachment on provincial rights. Like every other provincial premier, he supported the proposed old age security scheme; he was even prepared, with one very important qualification, to approve a constitutional amendment which would empower Parliament to legislate in the admittedly provincial field of jurisdiction in social welfare. "We are willing, indeed pleased," he announced amiably, "to co-operate with Ottawa. If any modification of the constitution is appropriate in the circumstances, we would be willing to consider in a most friendly way the possibility of modifying the constitution in the matter of old age pensions. But we cannot, Mr. Chairman, and I think you will admit that, commit ourselves to an indefinite policy."[6] "An indefinite policy" might have seemed an obscure phrase, but its meaning was perfectly evident to Duplessis's auditors. It meant that the new authority granted the federal government to legislate in respect of old age pensions and supplementary benefits would be temporary and conditional only. And there was no doubt that Duplessis would get his way in the end. In 1951, when the old age pension amendment finally took shape in section 94A of the British North America Act, it was expressly provided that no federal law could affect any provincial law, present or future, on the subject.[7] In other words, Parliament and the federal government would exercise their new authority on sufferance. The control of old age pensions would revert to Quebec as soon as Duplessis wished to claim it.

II

On November 30, four days before the Conference opened, President Truman had taken part in a particularly notorious specimen of that typically American institution, the presidential press conference. Only two days had elapsed since the Chinese had launched their terrific counter-attack, and the forces of the United Nations in Korea were reeling southward in retreat. What could or should be done to avert complete disaster was a question in everybody's mind and on the tip of every American newspaperman's tongue as he faced his President that day. Truman's replies were guardedly general at first, but increasingly specific as the probing continued. The administration, he assured the newsmen, would "take whatever steps are necessary to meet the military situation. Just as we always have". Did "necessary steps" include the use of the atomic bomb? It included the use of "every weapon that we have," and the possibility of the bomb's employment had always been "under active consideration." In general, the choice of weapons for each particular military situation was the business of the commander in the field.[8]

These dangerously equivocal words and phrases sent a thrill of alarm and foreboding through the western nations. Urged on by an applauding House of Commons, Prime Minister Attlee announced that he proposed to fly to the United States for discussions with President Truman; and within fifteen minutes of receiving this suggestion, Truman accepted it.[9] The President was diplomatically prepared for "a wide survey of the problems which face us today"; but his Secretary of State, Dean Acheson, and the officials of the American State and Defence Departments were evidently much less eager to welcome this enquiring visitor from England. It must have seemed unthinkable to them that any Prime Minister, and perhaps particularly the Prime Minister of a declining state like the United Kingdom, should dare to request the President of the United States to explain himself and to justify his foreign and military policies! For Acheson and his associates, Attlee's visit appeared almost an offensive impertinence, and Attlee himself an unimpressive, negligible little man who talked "with all the passion of a woodchuck chewing a carrot," and whose thoughts had all the dismal quality of "a long withdrawing, melancholy sigh."[10] His worst offence, of course, was that he had come expecting to talk things over with Truman face-to-face; and in Acheson's considered opinion, no President of the United States should ever condescend to negotiate directly with the Prime Ministers or Foreign Secretaries of other powers.

As this unwelcome "summit" meeting continued, Acheson's annoyance steadily rose. Attlee and his military advisers had a number of serious questions to ask and proposals to make. They wanted in the first place to make sure that the United States should not, in a fit of fury or bravado, decide without consultation to resort to that "ultimate" weapon, the bomb. In their considered judgement it was wrong of the American government to monopolize the conduct of a war which was in theory at least a co-operative enterprise of the United Nations; and it was still more objectionable to delegate that exclusive authority to such a vainglorious and politically irresponsible commander as General MacArthur. MacArthur's reckless generalship had provoked the intervention of the Chinese and risked the appalling possibility of a general war in the Far East. A negotiated settlement with the Peking government was the only realistic way of escape from these dangers. Western Europe and North America could not possibly fight a two-front war against the forces of international Communism. They had already committed far too large a part of their readily available military resources to the war in Korea. They must not further weaken and expose their most important front – the front in Western Europe which the North Atlantic Treaty Organization had been expressly designed to protect.[11]

It was a well-thought-out, coherent case, but it made almost no impression at all on the Americans. The United Nations, they bluntly reminded the British, had entrusted the conduct of the war in Korea to the United States, and the American government did not propose to let an international committee run it. MacArthur's judgement and military competence were defended by the American service chiefs, and a negotiated settlement with the Chinese summarily rejected on the ground that it was militarily unnecessary, since the long retreat in Korea was ending in a stable line, and politically unthinkable, since it would mean negotiating from the apparent weakness of defeat. "To cut, run, and abandon the whole enterprise was not acceptable conduct," Acheson declared tersely.[12] The President was equally forthright. He said bluntly that the United States proposed to stay on in Korea and fight. "If we had support from others, fine," he added uncompromisingly. "If not, we would stay on anyway."[13]

It was a comprehensive and firm rejection of the whole line of argument which the British had advanced, and the one serious concession which Attlee managed to extract from Truman was snatched from his grasp at the last moment by the intervention of Acheson and his State Department officials. In the privacy of the presidential study, the Prime Minister and the President had reached a verbal agreement that neither would employ atomic weapons without prior consultation with each other. Acheson listened with mounting consternation as Truman cheerfully announced this agreement. In desperation, he pointed out that the President had over and over again insisted that "no commitment of any sort to anyone limited his duty and power under the law to authorize use of the atomic weapon if he believed it necessary in the defence of the country."[14] This solemn injunction settled the question. The right to consultation was watered down to the modest privilege of being "at all times informed of developments which might bring about a change in the situation." When Attlee left Washington, the Korean War remained precisely what it always had been: an American struggle for the mastery of the Far East.

The Canadians waited humbly, at a respectful distance, for the outcome of this meeting of diplomatic patricians. President Truman's notorious press conference did not move St. Laurent or Pearson to announce an immediate departure for explanatory talks in Washington, and neither was invited to join the Anglo-American discussions there. Attlee lunched with Pearson and Hume Wrong on December 8, the last day of the conference, and then came up to Ottawa for a two-day visit. Pearson made two public contributions to the great debate on the military crisis in Korea and the use of the atomic bomb; on December 4, he reviewed the current international situation in a sombre statement to the Federal-Provincial Conference and on the day following he discussed Canadian policy in a broadcast from Lake Success in New York over the Trans-Canada network of the Canadian Broadcasting Corporation. Both speeches were careful, guarded, cautiously expressed efforts, in the already solidly established tradition of "quiet Canadian diplomacy"; but they marked nevertheless a distinct and important change in Pearson's attitude to the Korean War and the American leadership of the "Free World." Less than six months before, he had been openly eulogizing the "high courage and firm statesmanship" of the government of the United States. The first stage in his gradual disillusionment with American political wisdom and American military policy had come in the argument over the expediency of carrying the war beyond the 38th parallel and into North Korea. Then he had kept his protests strictly private. Now, for the first time, and in a very gingerly fashion, he ventured to make them public.

In the midst of a good deal of his accustomed, rather self-righteous abuse of Communist motives and actions, he made two suggestions, one concerning the atom bomb and the other concerning negotiations with the Chinese, both of which differed substantially from American policy. The Americans had refused to share their President's ultimate and sole authority over the use of the atom bomb; and although the final communiqué of the Attlee-Truman talks did profess a joint willingness to end hostilities by negotiation, the Americans were vehemently opposed to any serious concessions in the search for peace. Pearson questioned both of these positions. The atomic bomb, he said, was the "ultimate weapon" and should be treated as such. The decision to use it would have "such immense and awful consequences for all of us" that "there should surely be consultation [through the U.N.], particularly with the governments principally concerned." One of these

governments, he reminded the delegates to the Federal-Provincial Conference, was the government of Canada, "which has from the beginning been
a partner in the tripartite development of atomic energy."[15]

There was ample justification for this claim. In the autumn of 1945, King
had joined Attlee and Truman in a public declaration concerning the future
international use of nuclear energy, and Canada had from the start been a
member of the United Nations Atomic Energy Commission. There was
nothing new in Pearson's claim to a right of consultation in atomic policy
decisions; but his attitude to a negotiated settlement of the Korean War
marked a distinct and significant change in his thought. The Chinese, he
argued, had intervened in the war to an extent vastly greater than any legitimate concern for their own border interests could possibly justify. "In this
dangerous situation," he cautioned, "it remains our view that if and when
the military position is stabilized, we should try to begin negotiations with
the Chinese Communists by every means possible. If there could be a cease-
fire followed by negotiations – possibly covering more subjects than Korea
– in which the Chinese Communists would participate, there might still be
hope of reaching a settlement."[16] It was a new and strangely different aspiration for a man who, only six months before, had rejoiced in the United
Nations's collective condemnation of the Korean aggressor, and had strongly
urged his Cabinet colleagues to make Canada an active contestant in the
aggressor's punishment. Then Pearson had insisted that the American naval
defence of Taiwan was a "strategic, defensive decision," with "no political
implications," completely unconnected with the resistance in South Korea.
Now, by his significant reference to negotiations "covering more subjects
than Korea," he had implicitly recognized the fact that to the Chinese, as
well as to the Americans, Korea and Taiwan were inseparably connected as
key points in their general confrontation in the Far East. In the summer of
1950, he had apparently assumed that the United States, clothed in the sanc-
tity of the United Nations's uniform, could take violent military action in
the Far East and that the great Far Eastern nations would placidly acquiesce
in this American intervention and uncritically accept the United Nations's
explanation of its meaning. Now he began to realize that the People's
Republic of China completely rejected these naive assumptions. The last six
months of 1950 witnessed an important stage in his diplomatic education.
It remained to be seen how far his new-found realism would carry him.

III

The first test came very quickly. As Pearson was making his radio appeal
for a cease-fire, a large group of Middle Eastern and Far Eastern nations began
a determined search for peace. At the United Nations, they submitted two

important resolutions: the first requesting the President of the General Assembly, Nassarollan Entezam of Iran, to constitute a cease-fire committee of three, including himself as chairman; and the second proposing the appointment of another committee which would "make recommendations for a settlement of existing issues in accordance with the purposes and principles of the United Nations."[17] The first resolution was given priority: the Assembly adopted it by an overwhelming majority, and President Entezam appointed Pearson and Sir Benegal Rau of India as his associates. These choices were obviously made in the fond hope that Sir Benegal might be able to persuade the Chinese to see reason, and that Pearson might succeed in getting the Americans to talk sense. In the circumstances of the moment, these great expectations might well have seemed fantasies impossible of realization. The Chinese and the Americans looked at the proposed cease-fire and the subsequent negotiations from diametrically opposed points of view. The Chinese, exultant with success, regarded the cease-fire as a device to rob them of total victory; the Americans, angry and humiliated in defeat, saw it as a scheme to prevent their successful retaliation. The right to the Chinese seat in the Security Council, now occupied by the Nationalists, and the acquisition of Taiwan – the two major concessions which the People's Republic was certain to demand in any negotiation between East and West – were the very demands which the Americans were determined to refuse.

Flanked by two such obdurate antagonists, President Entezam's committee looked a pathetic little go-between. It couldn't, of course, persuade the Chinese and the Americans to talk to each other; but luckily, or so it seemed, it did have direct access to both. The People's Republic, unrepresented at the United Nations, since its rightful place had been pre-empted by the Chinese Nationalists, was invited by the Security Council to send representatives to New York to discuss the question of Taiwan; and a Chinese delegation, led by General Wu Hsiu-chuan, arrived in the United States on November 24, the very day on which MacArthur began his great advance in North Korea. This typical example of western "imperialist aggression" gave General Wu an excellent opportunity for indulging in vituperative Communist rhetoric and stiffened his resistance to discussions with the United Nations, or its agencies, including the cease-fire committee.[18] He refused to recognize the committee or to have anything to do with it and poor Sir Benegal Rau, a man of "far-from-robust physique," became the committee's solitary, unofficial intermediary to the Chinese, and grew, day by day, "more spiritual and ghost-like" under the stress of his interminable and fruitless conversations.

"All that was required," the Chinese kept insisting, "was for the American aggressors to get out of Korea and Formosa (Taiwan) and stay out."[19] The appalling particularity of these two demands was far too much for the Americans. The very idea of sitting at a negotiating table with a revolutionary

Chinese regime to which they had refused to grant diplomatic recognition was abhorrent to them; and all they would concede was that negotiations, in the most general terms, were at least conceivable. In these discouraging circumstances, the most that the cease-fire committee could do was to quote the vague phrases of the resolution on negotiations which the group of Asian states had submitted to the General Assembly; and this President Entezam and his colleagues did in a letter to General Wu and a cablegram to Premier Chou En-lai in Peking. "The purpose of this cease-fire in Korea," they declared, "will be to prevent the conflict from spreading to other areas, to put an end to the fighting in Korea, and to provide an opportunity for considering what further steps should be taken for a peaceful settlement of existing issues."[20] Not very surprisingly, the words "a peaceful settlement of existing issues" seemed, to the Chinese Premier and his general, a very indefinite and unsatisfactory summary of their very concrete and specific grievances. They both rejected the cease-fire at length and with considerable abuse, reiterating their demands for the withdrawal of the American forces from Korea and Taiwan, and the admission of the People's Republic of China to its rightful place in the United Nations. On December 19, in a conclusive gesture of finality, General Wu and his delegation left for Peking.

It was a stunning rejection, but Pearson was not yet ready to abandon the cause of the committee. He provided its chief liaison with the American State Department and the American delegation at the United Nations; and he was convinced that the main obstacle in the way of the Chinese acceptance of the cease-fire was the American reluctance to be specific about the Asian questions which might be discussed at the subsequent political negotiations. "There is no doubt," he wrote Hume Wrong at Washington, "that we cannot get the Chinese to isolate Korea from other Far Eastern issues, especially Formosa [Taiwan]"; and on his return to Ottawa for the Christmas break, he was correspondingly delighted to discover that the Americans were apparently prepared to take up a much more "constructive and flexible" attitude to the cease-fire committee.[21] They were even willing, the officials at the American Embassy at Ottawa assured him, to give the Chinese a "positive assurance" that in the negotiations following the cease-fire, "other than strictly Korean matters would be discussed." This was an unexpected "glimmer of hope," and it drove Pearson into a new round of negotiations. Through Wrong, he tried to convince the Americans that if they "could be somewhat more specific in describing the subjects which ... could be included in the post-cease-fire discussions," the Chinese would find it correspondingly more difficult to refuse the offer."[22] And at the same time, through the Indians at New Delhi, he sought to persuade the Peking government that the rejection of the promised American concessions would probably bring the cease-fire committee's work to an end and might very well result in formal charges of Chinese Communist aggression at the United

Nations. He worked hard and earnestly, but without result. The Americans in the end declined to be very explicit; the Chinese were not in the least impressed; and the little "glimmer of hope" flickered out.

The cease-fire committee faced defeat and Pearson evidently assumed, on his return to New York early in January, 1951, that all he and his colleagues could do was to record their failure in a final report. It was the Indian member, Sir Benegal Rau, who made a suggestion which started the committee on a new and more constructive lease of life. Sir Benegal proposed that their second report should conclude with "a statement of principles which, in our opinion . . . might be the basis for a political settlement of Korean and Far Eastern questions."[23] This meant that the committee itself, and not the principals involved, would take the initiative in devising a definite programme for peacemaking in the Far East; and it followed inevitably that the strongly conflicting forces in the United Nations would find their point of collision in a vulnerable little group of three. On one hand was the American State Department, eager to begin the welcome process of "branding" Communist China an "aggressor," and strongly backed by the mounting exasperation of American public opinion. On the other hand were Nehru and the Indian government, determined to propitiate an aggrieved China with definite concessions, and supported, not only by the group of Asian states, but also – somewhat unexpectedly – by the Commonwealth Prime Ministers' Conference which met in London early in January. Pearson, who had assumed a rather jealously proprietorial attitude to the business of peacemaking, and couldn't imagine why the United Nations should pay any attention to the views of a Commonwealth Conference, obviously resented what he regarded as "interference" from London; but it was the Commonwealth Prime Ministers who successfully insisted that the peace proposals must include specific references to both Taiwan and Communist China's right to representation in the United Nations.[24]

On Saturday, January 13, the General Assembly, by a large majority, endorsed the committee's plan for the staged pacification of the Far East. Even the United States delegation voted for it. "The choice whether to support or oppose this plan," Acheson recalled, "was a murderous one, threatening on one side the loss of the Koreans, and the fury of Congress and Press, and, on the other, the loss of our majority and support in the United Nations. We chose, after painful deliberation . . . to support the resolution. We did so in the fervent hope and belief that the Chinese would reject it (as they did)."[25] It was a swift, presumptuous, and wilfully inaccurate summary of the Peking government's involved and ambiguous reply, which St. Laurent and Pearson would not accept. On the usual roundabout method of communication, through Nehru to Chou En-lai, they asked for further clarification and Chou En-lai's second reply was so encouraging that the Indian delegation moved for a short delay in the trial of the People's

Republic for "aggression". The Americans were furious. They were extremely angry with Pearson and St. Laurent, for they regarded any Canadian diplomatic move of which they had not been informed and had not approved in advance, as rank insubordination! They were equally annoyed with the Indians for daring to interrupt, even for forty-eight hours, a criminal trial which they were determined to hurry on to its inevitable verdict of guilty. Pearson was sternly informed that his clandestine diplomacy had earned him the severe displeasure of the United States. Chou En-lai's reply was ridiculed, "in an ill-tempered and abusive speech" by the American representative in the Assembly, as "not much more than a postal card." For once, the Americans overreached themselves, and their usually tractable majority in the Assembly rebelled. The Indian proposal of a two-day adjournment was approved. "It was," Pearson recorded, "one of the most severe moral defeats the United States has had."[26]

Yet the battle over the forty-eight-hour adjournment was only a minor skirmish; the main engagement was yet to come. The Asians, basing their recommendation on Chou En-lai's explanatory reply to St. Laurent's inquiry, proposed the appointment of a seven-power conference, which would seek additional clarification from the Chinese and determine whether their replies justified further negotiations. The Americans, indignant at being balked of their prey for two whole days, were implacably opposed to any further adjournments, postponements or delays. Wielding their moral, political and financial powers of persuasion to the very limit, they rounded up the unconvinced and irresolute members of the Assembly and drove them forward like a herd of refractory cattle. The pressure was enormous and, as Pearson candidly acknowledged, he "succumbed" to it.[27] It was a strange, contradictory conclusion to two months of earnest effort. In his considered opinion, the American resolution denouncing the People's Republic as an "aggressor" was "premature and unwise."[28] Yet he voted for it, and for reasons which, in retrospect, look oddly invented and unconvincing. He argued that the Asian-Arab resolution did not sufficiently ensure the precedence of cease-fire talks over political discussions, and he emphasized the undoubted fact that the Chinese had rendered assistance to the North Korean "aggressors," and therefore might be properly described as "aggressors" themselves. The first argument seems, in the light of the gravity of the situation, to be little more than a textual debating point; and the second evades the equally undoubted fact that Communist China had intervened only when her friendly neighbour had been invaded and her own border threatened.

In the past two months, Pearson had felt increasingly troubled and disillusioned by the course on which he set out with such great moral conviction in June, 1950. He wanted to halt, to retreat, to break out of line; but two powerful inhibitions held him back. As a Canadian whose first, primitive loyalty was to the North American continent, he found it almost impossible to reject the leadership of the United States; and as an idealist with a fixed faith in collective security, he could never wholly escape from the rigid orthodoxies of its established church, the United Nations. The United States had started the resistance to aggression in Korea in June, 1950; Pandit Nehru, Sir Benegal Rau, St. Laurent, Pearson, Bevin, and the Commonwealth Prime Ministers' Conference in London came very close to ending it in January, 1951. Pearson had once acknowledged that the Commonwealth was "a useful because a very different piece of international machinery"; but, in any serious crisis, he was always inclined to reject its political realism for the doctrinaire infallibility of the United Nations. "A firm bridge between East and West," he had once flatteringly described the Commonwealth. He had crossed that bridge far more frequently in the last two months than he had ever dreamed he might do before; but the final crossing, which might have brought a settlement to the Far East more than twenty troubled years before its actual arrival, he refused to take.

What actually had the United Nations Assembly done when, on February 1, 1951, it solemnly declared that the People's Republic of China was an "aggressor"? Had it, in any serious way, altered the character or changed the scope of the existing conflict? Had that conflict become, even potentially, a total war against Communist China, or was it still localized to the Korean peninsula? Pearson and the Canadian delegation were extremely fearful that the American government or its dangerously independent proconsul, General MacArthur, would be only too ready to interpret the vote as a general authority to extend the fighting to any point on the Chinese mainland which seemed militarily advantageous. Pearson insisted that all doubt on this central point should be removed, and in reply an American spokesman gave a categorical assurance that the adoption of the resolution would not give the United Nations Unified Command in Korea any "additional authority" in its conduct of military operations.[29]

This was all very well, but it did not quiet Canadian fears. What might not the dictatorial Americans and their irresponsible general do under the lash of a frenzied American public opinion? Through discreet inquiries in Washington, Pearson tried to discover more about the intentions of the American State Department. He worried even more over the uncertain aims of General MacArthur who, on the eve of the vote on the "aggressor" resolution, had triumphantly announced: "The stake we fight for now is more than Korea. It is a free Asia." Fortunately for Canada and the rest of the Western world, President Truman and his State Department were rapidly losing all patience with the antics of their volatile and insubordinate general; and April 11, Truman relieved MacArthur of his command, and transferred it to General Matthew Ridgeway. With the removal of this dangerous irritant, both sides rapidly came to the conclusion that they did not want, and were not going to fight, a general war over the fate of the Far East; and the conflict in Korea settled down to a ding-dong battle across the comparatively narrow front of a peninsula which was never more than 135 miles wide. In the process, it became much more truly a United Nations campaign for, although American troops continued to outnumber all the others combined, forces from half-a-dozen different member states arrived during the winter and spring of 1951. The first Canadian battalion, Princess Patricia's Canadian Light Infantry, joined the fighting in February, and the whole Canadian Army Special Force, redesignated the 25th Canadian Brigade, followed in May.

By the middle of June, the front had become stabilized along a line roughly equivalent to the 38th parallel – almost exactly the same line as that at which, nine months earlier, Pearson had urged the Americans to stop General MacArthur's first victorious advance. Nearly a month later, the endlessly protracted and tiresome cease-fire negotiations finally got under way.

IV

The impact of the Korean War, weighted down by the more oppressive burden of the Cold War, made a profound impression on Canada. Its political consequences were more serious and lasting, but its economic effects were immediate, conspicuous, and more than a little ominous. The shallow recession, which had followed the exchange crisis of 1947, came to an abrupt close. For over two years, unemployment had been steadily increasing and the total value of exports, despite rising prices, had remained almost constant. The war drastically altered these depressing economic circumstances. The federal government re-entered the Canadian economy in its familiar and very energetic guise. It wanted men for the new Canadian Army Special Force: it wanted aircraft, ships, motor vehicles, guns, ammunition and uniforms. Government expenditures rapidly began to mount; unemployment dropped away. All the well-remembered conditions of wartime – and, in 1950-51, they were only half a dozen years away – suddenly reappeared in much their old way; and by far the worst of them – inflation – was back again in a more exaggerated and frightening form than ever.

The inflation of the Second World War had, of course, been serious; it had led, in the autumn of 1941, to the imposition of the general price and wage ceiling, and the creation of the Wartime Prices and Trade Board. Prices had mounted swiftly during the first two years of the war; but they had risen from the relatively low, and relatively stable, price level of the last Depression years. The Korean War inflation differed radically from its predecessor. It did not start from a low and fairly steady base; rather it was the rapid acceleration of an upward flight of prices which had begun as soon as the Second

World War ended. Since 1946 consumer expenditure had remained very large and very constant; it had been held up, not merely by high employment, accumulated savings, veterans' benefits and welfare payments, but also by a new and very significant development in Canadian household finance – by the extraordinarily rapid increase in consumer credit, instalment buying, and personal loans. The Canadians were busily acquiring the intoxicating habit of borrowing and buying their way into affluence, and the high cost of living rose higher in eager response. In the five years from 1945 to 1950, the cost of living index jumped upward by nearly 47 points.[30] In March, 1941, Stanley Knowles solemnly informed the House of Commons that in the previous six months the index figure had climbed from 168.5 to 175.2. Inflation, Drew announced gloomily, had reached its highest point in Canadian history; and the Canadian dollar had sunk to no more than fifty-seven cents of its value ten years earlier.[31]

Did all this imply that the elaborate wartime systems of political and economic controls ought to be brought back again? It was a question which, for both the Canadian people and the Canadian government, arose naturally out of their recent experience; but they looked at it from distinctly different points of view. For many Canadians – although organized labour, as usual, protested against a ceiling on wages – the renewal of the price and wage controls seemed a probable necessity; but for government, which recalled only too painfully the endless difficulties of administration, this likely popular demand seemed a dangerous measure of last resort. The St. Laurent Cabinet was not, of course, set inflexibly against the revival of controls, for, in 1950, nobody knew how far and how fast the battle in Korea might spread and how soon the Cold War might become a blazing Hot War. The price ceiling, government spokesmen assured Parliament and the nation, would be re-introduced only when it became urgently necessary; and, in order to stave off this evil day as long as possible, Douglas Abbott, the Finance Minister, brought out the whole armoury of orthodox fiscal and monetary controls. He managed, despite the suddenly huge expenditures of wartime, to hold to his pay-as-you-go policy in finance. He even continued to produce surpluses, though they were distinctly smaller. He curbed consumer credit, forced a ceiling on bank loans, and reduced the funds available for the government's housing programmes.[32]

Whatever additional restraints might be necessary was a question for the highly problematical future. At the moment, the Canadian government was interested, not so much in the possible uses of power, as in the urgent need of acquiring it. During two world wars the government's vast executive authority had been based on the War Measures Act; and the mere proclamation of that formidable statute could bring federal predominance back immediately. It was constitutionally possible, but was it wise? The St. Laurent Cabinet decided that the Korean War could not justify unlimited powers in the same unquestioned way that the world wars had done; and as a compromise which did not concede too much, it devised the Emergency Powers Bill which St. Laurent introduced on February 20, 1951. This constitutional oddity, the government hoped, would prove a happy medium to both Parliament and people; but, as Stanley Knowles tartly pointed out, it also increased the chameleon-like changeability of the Canadian constitution. "We have the normal situation," he explained, "although heaven knows, when we are ever going to get back to it, when our constitution is the British North America Act. Then we have the completely abnormal situation . . . when our effective constitution becomes the War Measures Act. Then we have this third stage that comes in between, which is neither a normal time . . . nor an abnormal time."[33]

Parliament was puzzled, but to some extent reassured by the adroit middle course the government had taken and the opposition was neither serious nor prolonged. The Progressive-Conservatives, who all autumn had been vociferously urging the government to recognize the existing emergency and act accordingly, were prevented from opposing the bill in principle. Instead, Drew, Fleming, and Fulton concentrated their criticisms on the vast and vague terms in which the government's new emergency powers were defined. These huge, general categories, Fulton argued, could be made to cover every aspect of Canada's economic life; and arrest and detention, the authorized penalties for infractions of the emergency orders-in-council, threatened the rule of law and the liberty of the subject. These ugly authoritarian aspects of the bill had moved St. Laurent to include a special provision which required the government to table its emergency orders in Parliament where they might be revoked by a joint resolution of the Senate and the House of Commons. This obvious but empty gesture in the direction of parliamentary sovereignty annoyed the Opposition. They ridiculed its value. What chance had a private member of securing an annulment, they demanded, in a House whose business was dominated and monopolized by government?[34]

Despite these few rocks and shoals, St. Laurent piloted the bill through with comparative ease; but its companion measure, the Defence Production Bill, had a much more difficult passage. St. Laurent introduced it in general terms; but since its main purpose was the creation of a vitally important new government department, which Clarence Decatur Howe was certain to administer, Howe was necessarily its principal defendant. He was a peculiarly unskilful champion. He had never found the House of Commons a very congenial place. The long and often empty speeches, the swift exchanges, the repeated interruptions, bored or annoyed him. He was not a natural, instinctive parliamentarian; he was not even, as he proved in the end, a very good politician. General political problems or issues did not interest him greatly and he avoided taking sides about them as long as he could. It was not until the very last moment that he finally decided to join the conscriptionist Liberals in their battle against Mackenzie King; and, on the rare occasions when he did espouse a particular policy with any great enthusiasm or determination, it was only too likely, as the trade proposals with the United States proved in 1948, to be politically dangerous in the highest degree. He had no coherent body of political ideas. He could scarcely put together a presentable political platform. His sole aim was economic growth, to be achieved by any and every means possible.

Yet, in 1951, his stature in Canadian life as a whole, as well as in the Canadian government, had reached colossal proportions. He ought to have had an impressive or magnetic presence: in fact, he looked oddly commonplace. His short stature, square, rugged face, hard features and unsmiling eyes, were matched by his terse speech, abrupt manner, and by the worn and badly cut clothes which he kept wearing. Mackenzie King loved attitudinizing in the limelight: St. Laurent carefully cultivated a distinguished appearance; but Howe disliked ceremonial occasions and felt uncomfortable in formal clothes. His real passion was not government, but administration; not the broad impressive generalities of policy, but the hard detail of management. During the fifteen years of his steadily increasing power and prestige in the Liberal Cabinet, he had gone very far towards imposing his managerial conception on the Government of Canada. By the compelling force of his successful example, he had taught his colleagues and the Canadian people that politics were not traditions, principles, platforms and parties, but management. It is highly probably that he had never read a word of Alexander Pope's poetry; but he would have highly approved of one couplet from "An Essay on Man":

> "For forms of government let fools contest;
> Whate'er is best administered is best."

He had not only convinced the nation of the truth of Pope's epigram. He had also gone a long way further. He had persuaded the Canadian people that this simple, comforting verity was embodied in the Liberal Party.

The Second World War was the making of C.D. Howe. It not only thrust him forward as the principal architect of the Canadian war effort; it also immensely widened and deepened the foundations of his own and the Liberal Party's economic power and influence. Through the Department of Munitions and Supply, the biggest spending department in the wartime government, and through the twenty-eight Crown corporations which he founded, Howe established the closest connections with every division and subdivision of the Canadian economy.[35] His huge orders for planes, ships, tanks, trucks, weaponry and supplies of every kind exploited the resources of Canadian industry to the full; and the dollar-a-year men who helped him run his department and his Crown corporations were drawn from every sphere of

Canadian business. The realization that this firm and intimate connection had been established came slowly to Canadians. To the end of his career, Mackenzie King had kept insisting that, in Canada, the Liberals were the friends of the "little man" and the Conservative party was the party of "big business". This worn-out fiction was moribund even before the war; but by 1951, it survived only as a kind of Greek myth, with all the irrelevance of a Greek myth and none of its charm. Howe had not merely linked big business and the Liberal Party; he had virtually identified them.

Howe enjoyed the war and its associations immensely, but the coming of peace and the ending of reconstruction seemed to have brought that rich experience to a full stop. He may have assumed that he would never again recover that tight, comprehensive grasp of the Canadian economy; but he was wrong. Suddenly, in quick succession, the galloping events of the late 1940's – the Cold War, NATO, and the struggle in Korea – offered him an unexpected chance of regaining it. He seized it eagerly. As he himself candidly admitted, he drafted the Defence Production Bill. He certainly made a thorough job of it. His mind was fixed, not only on the immediate needs of the Korean War, but on the long-term and the far more serious necessities of the Cold War which, all his many American friends assured him, might blaze up in a very hot war at almost any moment. He was convinced that the country faced a very probable crisis and he planned on the grand scale and for an indefinite future accordingly. The powers of the new Department of Defence Production were to last no fewer than five years, and they were certainly both ample and exceptional. The Governor-in-Council was empowered to "do and authorize such acts and things" as were necessary for the work of the department; it was given authority to make orders and regulations, "to control and regulate the production, processing, distribution, acquisition, disposition, or use of materials, or the supply or use of services deemed essential for war purposes."[36]

V

The Opposition attacked this portentous measure with an air of shock and outrage. Howard Green, who spoke first in the debate on second reading, pointed out, in horrified tones, that the bill empowered the minister to order an investigation of any business, to force its owner to enter into a contract with the government at prices fixed by the minister, or to remove him, convert his factory into a Crown Corporation and appoint a government controller to run it. "It is," Green declared solemnly, "a war bill. It gives him [the minister] all the power that would be required if we were in a Third World War. But that is not the position. The country is not in a Third World War."[37] It was on this enormous difference between the minor conflict in Korea and an authentic Third World War that the Opposition based most of its criticisms of the bill. Drew emphasized the fact that, whereas the Emergency Powers Bill gave the government less authority than it had possessed under the War Measures Act, the Defence Production Bill gave its new Minister greater powers than he had ever enjoyed before. " . . . We are going to have," J. M. Macdonnell predicted, "an economy which exists by the grace and favour of one man" – a man, moreover, he reminded the House, who resented sharing his powers with Parliament, with the members of his own party, and even with his colleagues in the Cabinet. ". . . I hope," he pleaded, "Parliament will not make this national emergency an occasion for setting up a private kingdom for the Minister."[38]

This kind of attack, which struck in popular democratic terms against Howe's most obvious weakness, his conscious love of power, was the very kind of assault with which he was least equipped to deal; and St. Laurent, who came occasionally to his rescue, was by no means up to his best parliamentary form. During the debates on second reading and in committee of the whole, Howe's explanations and interjections grew increasingly abrupt, negative, and rude. When J. W. Noseworthy, the C.C.F. member who had defeated Meighen in York South, attempted to buttress his arguments with some statistics, Howe's interruptions confused him so badly that he had to drop the subject; and later, when he returned to it, announcing that he had got his figures straightened out, Howe inquired scornfully, "Who helped you"?   When George Drew declared that, in his opinion, the last person to administer an act with such enormous powers was the Minister of Trade and Commerce, Howe interjected contemptuously, "Nobody cares much what you think. Don't take yourself too seriously." He repeated the same advice to Howard Green on another occasion, and the House of Commons got the clear impression that the one member it ought to take very seriously was Clarence Decatur Howe. Howe himself certainly thought so; but at the same time he was deeply annoyed by Drew's impertinent reference to his own avid love of power. As soon as the Conservative leader had finished, he jumped to his feet. "I have only a few words . . . ." he began eagerly, when the Speaker called him to order. The Honourable Member for Greenwood (J. M. Macdonnell), the Speaker announced, had the floor. The deflated Howe had to sit down. "Is this a Tory monopoly," he asked angrily?[39]

The debate on the Defence Production Bill gave the Opposition more chance of baiting the government leaders than it had enjoyed for some time. The arrogant and irritable Howe was easily provoked; even the normally composed St. Laurent was betrayed into an exhibition of extremely bad-temper by Howard Green. The fact was that St. Laurent disliked Howard Green more intensely than he probably realized. Green's very great and articulate concern for British interests and British values irked St. Laurent in the very depths of his being. The Defence Production Bill might have seemed very remote from Green's British loyalties, but Green, on almost any subject, was likely to annoy St. Laurent, and on this occasion the anglophile British Columbian member managed to manoeuvre the Liberal leader into a most damaging admission. Green, like other Conservative critics of the bill, had been emphasizing the huge contrast between the limited struggle in Korea and the unlimited power granted the minister. Would any further powers be required, he asked innocently, if Canada actually was engaged in a Third World War? "I do not anticipate there would be," St. Laurent replied incautiously.[40]

This admission gave Green his chance. The Defence Production Bill, he maintained confidently, was "a total war measure." St. Laurent rejected this description. The bill, he insisted, was an effort to prevent war, to put Canada in "a position to prevent aggression." In other words, Green rejoined quickly, we are in a state of apprehended war, and this bill is therefore a war measure. "No, Mr. Chairman," St. Laurent replied with mounting anger. "I will not permit the Honourable Member to distort my language." He may have hoped that this stern rebuke would silence his aggravating critic but the unabashed Green stuck to his point. His subborn insistence that the bill was in fact "a war bill" finally goaded Howe into joining the argument; and for a few moments he and St. Laurent kept interrupting Green, repeatedly denouncing his distortions and insinuations. "I have the floor," the badgered Conservative member was finally driven to exclaim. "The Prime Minister," he reminded St. Laurent, "has no greater rights in this House than the newest member."[41]

Despite these repeated obstructions, the Defence Production Bill, pushed forward by the government's irresistible majority, passed easily enough. With its passage, Howe's economic dictatorship became an established fact of Canadian politics. He could still defer to St. Laurent's titular authority as Prime Minister, as he proved when he reluctantly agreed that compensation should be given the western farmers for the disappointing returns of the British Wheat Agreement. He was still second-in-command. He was interested almost exclusively in economic questions. But economic questions had come increasingly to dominate post-war Canadian politics; and as his role grew more dominant, his jealous love of power and his unquestioning belief in his own wisdom increased accordingly.

Only five years later, he was to overreach himself fatally and to bring about the downfall of the Liberal government.

VI

In the early 1950's, the golden, auspicious years which culminated in the easy triumph of the general election of August, 1953, such an appalling catastrophe seemed literally inconceivable. Nothing of any real importance had occurred to disturb the superb self-importance of the leaders of the Liberal Party. They were remaking Canada in their own image, and they felt certain that all Canadians enjoyed the results just as much as they did themselves. The influence of the United States and its citizens, on the Canadian economy, on Canada's foreign and defence policies, and on every aspect of Canadian intellectual and cultural life had grown steadily more dominant; but they had made no conscious move to question or resist this growing domination. They behaved, in fact, as if they were unaware of its existence. Their attention was still concentrated, as it always had been, on the unending pursuit of the "last legal vestiges of colonial status" in Canada's position in the British Commonwealth of Nations.

There were, of course, some limits to this witch-hunt, some vestiges of colonialism which it was prudent not to touch. Since 1949 St. Laurent had possessed the commanding majority which King had lacked in 1946: but, despite his strength in the House of Commons, he had made no attempt to dig up that buried, but still undefused bomb, the issue of the Canadian flag. In 1946, a French-speaking minority had prevented the realization of an English-Canadian majority's desire for a flag which included the Union Jack; and this French-Canadian victory had given rise to what might be called the rules or guidelines of that popular Liberal sport, the pursuit of "colonial vestiges." If French Canada objected strongly to any particular nationalist campaign, it must be brought instantly to a halt. If, on the contrary, French Canada highly approved of a particular nationalist campaign, it must be steadily carried forward, openly if possible, surreptitiously if not. English-Canadian protests and demands, on the other hand, were never viewed with the same gravity. They were either evaded, or explained away, or, if necessary, simply defied.

The continuing debate over the use of the two symbolic words "Dominion" and "royal" provided an excellent example of how the new guidelines worked. The French-Canadian attack on the title "Dominion" had started in 1947: and, with very little delay, the St. Laurent government had begun, in a quiet, unobtrusive way, to remedy this complaint. Without formal executive or legislative action, it simply removed the offending word from statutes and other state papers, leaving "Canada" alone, without further designation, and changing "Dominion government" into "Canadian government" or "Government of Canada." By 1950 this process had gone so far that the formal meetings of the national and provincial governments, which as late as 1946 were called "Dominion-Provincial Conferences," had been renamed "Federal-Provincial Conferences." Canada had, in fact, changed its name, without the formality of a "deed poll" or the equivalent. Unfortunately, vestiges of the old title still remained in early statutes; but, as these came up for revision, the last traces of colonialism were systematically hunted down and rooted out. Late in 1951, two of these statutes, "The Dominion Lands Surveys Act" and the "Dominion Elections Act" were brought up for amendment. And at this point the Opposition began a last fight for the old title "Dominion."

Yet the debate which their protest started was not a typical debate between Government and Opposition. Instead it developed as an argument between English Canadians on the one side and French Canadians on the other. Brooks, Fulton and Green, who urged the retention of the old title "Dominion," were all English-speaking Conservatives; but the speakers who supported its elimination, though they were all French Canadians, included one fairly prominent Conservative, Léon Balcer. Fulton and Green argued that "Dominion" was a distinguished title, a purely Canadian invention, which had the authority of nearly a hundred years of constant usage and which appropriately recalled the sonorous verse of the seventy-second psalm: "He shall have Dominion also from sea to sea, and from the River unto the ends of the Earth." "Why throw away all our traditions," Brooks demanded, "and grasp at something new?" [42] "Something new" was essential, French-Canadian members and ministers retorted, because "Dominion" implied colonial subserviency, and the constitutional progress of the Commonwealth had left it completely out of date.

St. Laurent used much the same argument. He made no apology for the government's gradual elimination of "Dominion"; in fact, he proudly avowed it. " . . . I can say at once," he announced, "that it is the policy of this government when statutes come up for revision or consolidation to replace the word 'Dominion' with the word 'Canada.' There are some people in this country who rather like the name of Canada," he added irrelevantly, as if "Canada" was a word which the advocates of "Dominion of Canada" particularly detested.[43] "Dominion" had become inappropriate, he insisted, as a result of the "constitutional progression" of the member states of the Commonwealth, and the British had themselves recognized the need for change as far back as 1947 when they renamed the "Dominions" office the "Commonwealth Relations" office. This was a fallacious argument, as the Conservatives might easily have proved. In July, 1947, when the office of Secretary of State for India was combined with that of Secretary of State for the Dominions, the new united portfolio was named the Commonwealth Relations Office, but this change implied no intent to downgrade or eliminate the word "Dominion."[44] "Dominion" was, in fact, the title which the British government itself deliberately employed, only a few days later, in the Independence of India Act, the most important statute in the post-war reorganization of the British Empire Commonwealth. That Act created two new, independent Dominions, the Dominion of India and the Dominion of Pakistan.[45] Instead of abandoning the title "Dominion," the British government had, in fact, made a new a significant use of it.

A little later, in March, 1952, when Drew claimed that the elimination of the title "Dominion" was, in effect, an indirect amendment to the constitution of Canada, St. Laurent repeated his defence, but privately warned his colleagues that a pause in the practice of renaming the titles of statues would be advisable.[46] In reality, the deed by this time had been done; and, as Drew had claimed, the constitution of Canada had been altered by a clever piece of indirection. St. Laurent could not, of course, change a word in the British North America Act; but he did invent a completely new and absolutely literalistic interpretation of the famous phrase "one Dominion under the name of Canada." "Under the British North America Act," St. Laurent insisted, "Canada is a *dominion,* but the *name* is Canada." By this exercise of hair-splitting literalism, he divided into two separate and distinct halves a phrase which, for the Fathers of Confederation and their successors for nearly a hundred years, had been an indivisible whole.

The fact was that St. Laurent and his advisers were ignorant of, and uninterested in, the process by which the title of the country they governed had been chosen. For the Fathers of Confederation, the names "Dominion" and "Canada" were equally important and equally essential parts of an integral whole. They had hoped, at first, that their new nation might be named the "Kingdom of Canada"; but the British government, out of regard for the irascible republican susceptibilities of the United States, felt obliged to turn down this request. It was then, perhaps at the suggestion of S. L. Tilley, that the British North American delegates to the London Conference of 1866-67 hit upon the title "Dominion". They chose it because they wanted a new and impressive designation, a title which would lend prestige to their new nation, lift it to a stature far above the rank of the former colonies and provinces, and, as Lord Carnarvon, the Colonial Secretary of the time, explained to Queen Victoria, "give greater dignity to the commencement of this great scheme and consequently greater self-respect to those who take part in the administration of affairs there."[47] On his advice the Queen accepted both parts of the new title, and in terms which clearly proved that she, like the British North American delegates, regarded them as the inseparable components of an indivisible whole. "The Queen," her secretary informed Lord Carnarvon, "has no objection to the wish of the North American delegates being complied with, if you think 'The *Dominion* of Canada' a better title for the new Confederation than Canada 'pur et simple.' "[48]

St. Laurent had, in fact, personally legislated for Canada, without going through the tiresome and contentious process of securing a constitutional amendment. He had cleverly twisted the formal wording of the British North America Act and had falsified what four generations of Canadians had understood was its true meaning. It was an ingenious piece of verbal jugglery a cunning corporation lawyer's textual sophism, which Parliament, unlike the ordinary courts, could be compelled to accept. Here, where the unsophisticated Canadians scarcely realized what was happening, he had been almost contemptuously daring. He was far more circumspect about the omission of the significant adjective "royal," which somebody noticed had been dropped from the traditional designation "Royal Mail" on post office vans. When this was questioned in the House of Commons, the Postmaster-General, Edouard Rinfret, could think of nothing better to say than that the name "Royal Mail" had never appeared in any of the Canadian Post Office acts.[49] This inept performance annoyed and worried St. Laurent. Pickersgill had persuaded him that the row about "royal" was politically "far more dangerous than the fuss about Dominion"; and, early in 1952, he took advantage of a special press conference to make a careful explanation of the rules governing the use of the word "royal." [50] These two professed Canadian nationalists showed a very grave concern for a word which Canada shared with all the other monarchies under the British Crown; but, at the same time, and for purely party reasons, they exhibited a contemptuous disregard for a word which was a solely Canadian invention – "*our* word," as Eugene Forsey said later, "perhaps the only distinctive word we have contributed to political terminology."[51] "Canada" survived as a constitutional monarchy; but the original "Dominion of Canada" ceased to exist.

The main purpose of the special press conference on January 25, 1952, was St. Laurent's announcement of the appointment of Vincent Massey as the next Governor-General of Canada. This was the extremely abrupt conclusion of a long-matured plan. Mackenzie King had thought of Massey as a possible Canadian Governor-General, though his first preference was for General McNaughton; and, as early as the winter of 1950, Lester Pearson had asked Massey whether he would welcome an offer of the appointment and had informed him that the government had nobody else in mind. Unfortunately, Massey's wife Alice, who would have made an admirable chatelaine at Rideau Hall, died during the summer of 1950; and, since hospitalities were such an important part of the life of Government House, both Massey and the government began to wonder whether a widower could adequately fulfil its duties. In this uncertainty, Lord Alexander's term of office was extended for another year; and, in the meantime, Massey discovered that his married son Lionel would be willing to act as his secretary if he was again invited to accept the post.[52] With the help of his son and his daughter-in-law, Massey felt that he could carry on alone; but time went by, the government made no move, and it was not until January, 1952, that a quite extraneous incident suddenly jerked it into action. In the previous October, when the Conservatives regained power in the United Kingdom, Winston Churchill, the new Prime Minister, had also taken the office of Minister of Defence; but he soon wearied of the burden of this additional portfolio, and early in January, 1952, he unexpectedly appeared in Ottawa, hoping, with St. Laurent's permission, to persuade Lord Alexander to take his place as Minister of Defence. St. Laurent consented. Alexander wanted the post: and, on January 14, Massey who was then in England, suddenly found himself invited, by a very blurred and indistinct voice over the transatlantic telephone, to say whether he wished to have his name submitted to King George VI for appointment as Governor-General of Canada![53] Less than six weeks later, on February 28, he was installed in office.

Mackenzie King would have been pleased by this realization of one of his great nationalist aims; but St. Laurent was not entirely satisfied. He not only wanted a Canadian Governor-General; he also hoped to "democratize" or "Canadianize" the Governor-Generalship as an institution. The spectacle of women curtsying to the Queen's representative pained him deeply. It was, he said "out-of-date and artificial in the Canada of the 1950's," and Pickersgill, that invaluable go-between, was instructed discreetly to raise the question of its discontinuance with Massey, explaining, at the same time, that this was simply a suggestion and not "constitutional advice." It was a difficult situation for a man who had just been installed in an important office by government; but the sophisticated Massey was more than a match for St. Laurent and Pickersgill. He adroitly replied that the appointment of a Canadian Governor-General was in itself such a serious departure from precedent that he did not want to begin his term of office by breaking another of its established conventions![54] The annoyed but baffled St. Laurent could do nothing but accept this disarming answer.

"I want to be the first to curtsy to the new Governor-General," exclaimed Madame Thibaudeau Rinfret, the wife of the Chief Justice, as she rushed up after the swearing-in ceremony in the Senate Chamber.[55]

Massey may have felt an amused sense of triumph.

VII

On February 1, 1952, St. Laurent was seventy years old. He had been ten years in office, nearly seven as Minister of Justice and Secretary of State for External Affairs, and slightly more than three as Prime Minister. He had told Mackenzie King that he did not want to continue in active politics after he turned seventy, and now his family urged him to retire. If he followed their advice, as he sometimes felt tempted to do after the wearying session of 1951, he would have to make up his mind soon. A general election was due sometime in the summer of 1953, and, well in advance of that date, a new leader would have to be elected. Who was to be the new leader? Howe, on grounds of seniority, was the most obvious candidate; but Howe, who was just as politically inept as Mackenzie King had been politically astute, seemed an impossible Prime Minister to most people in the party. The younger ministers – Abbott, Claxton, Pearson – were possible, but none was a conspicuously obvious choice; and real qualities of leadership seemed more than ever necessary in the steadily deteriorating political circumstances of 1951-1952. The Conservatives won all four by-elections held in June, 1951; they won four of the six held in May, 1952. In these two sets of encounters they had gained no fewer than five seats from the Liberals. All this looked very encouraging, all the more so because this federal promise seemed strongly confirmed in the provinces. The Conservatives won two of the five provincial general elections held in 1952; the Liberals lost seats in all of them except in Quebec. Obviously this was no time to be changing leaders: and in July, 1952, St. Laurent finally decided that he would stay on and fight out the next election himself.[56]

St. Laurent was not the only senior Canadian politican who seriously considered, and then rejected, the idea of retirement. The other was John George Diefenbaker, the member for Lake Centre, the lone Progressive-Conservative from Saskatchewan. In 1952, Diefenbaker had been in the House of Commons for twelve years. He had been twice defeated in his efforts to become leader of the party; and, since he was only a year younger than Drew, the chance of gaining the leadership seemed extremely small, and the prospect of ever becoming Prime Minister of Canada looked infinitesimal. Diefenbaker was a professional barrister who revelled in courtroom work; to the cringing Liberals in the House of Commons he often looked, and sounded, like a Crown prosecutor in a capital case. Several legal firms in Ontario had invited him to join them. He was seriously considering these offers when an event occurred which completely changed the course of his life and transformed him from a willing candidate for retirement into a fighting contender for re-election. [57]

This event was the passage, in June, 1952, of the Redistribution Bill, a measure which re-allocated the seats in the Canadian House of Commons in accordance with the population changes revealed by the census of 1951. In Canadian history, "redistribution" usually meant "gerrymander," the calculated attempt on the part of the government of the day to alter the boundaries of the constituencies in order to give its candidates an unfair political advantage over their opponents. On this occasion, under the ruthless direction of James G. Gardiner, the Minister of Agriculture, the third most powerful man in the Liberal Cabinet, and the acknowledged political "boss" of western Canada, the business of re-drawing electoral boundaries became an exercise, not of adjustment, but of obliteration. Gardiner's own seat was in Saskatchewan; eighteen other Saskatchewan seats were held by Liberals and C.C.F.ers, with Liberals in the great majority. There was only a single, solitary Conservative in the entire province, John George Diefenbaker in the constituency of Lake Centre. Diefenbaker's presence, squarely in the middle of Gardiner's western empire, was like a festering thorn in the most sensitive part of his anatomy. He determined that this time he would not simply put Diefenbaker at a serious political disadvantage; he would seek to eliminate him entirely.

He found it easy to carry out his purpose. St. Laurent would have preferred to have an independent commission determine the new distribution: but this would have taken time, and, since the next general election was due in 1953, there was not a great deal of time left. In the end, it was decided to carry on as before, through a Parliamentary committee, with subcommittees for each province, which would recommend new constituency boundaries for approval by Parliament. This was a method which allowed the government almost no influence and gave the local members a wide extent of power. Obviously, this latitude would be greatest in the three provinces – Nova Scotia, Manitoba, and Saskatchewan – which were to lose seats; and Saskatchewan, which had declined both absolutely and relatively in population, was to lose no fewer than three. In fact, if Parliament had held to its previous rules, Saskatchewan would have been deprived of as many as five seats. This would be an intolerable loss at one blow, the Saskatchewan Legislature and the Saskatchewan M.P.'s, led by Gardiner, protested vociferously; and the ingenious Pickersgill, appealed to by a troubled St. Laurent, invented a new rule which stipulated that no province could lose more than 15% of its existing membership at any one redistribution.[58] This cut Saskatchewan's loss to three, slightly mollified that injured province's hurt feelings, and yet left lots of leeway for Gardiner and his Liberal cronies to pursue their manipulations.

The Parliamentary committee's handiwork, presented on June 30 in the form of a schedule to the Representation Bill, provoked a storm of criticism from both Conservatives and C.C.F.ers, and from provinces which had suffered no losses as well as from those which had. Stanley Knowles complained bitterly that the real decisions in Manitoba had been made, not by the official subcommittee, but by the Liberal caucus; Diefenbaker charged that the redistribution in Saskatchewan had been imposed from outside on a subcommittee which had met infrequently and only for a few minutes at a time.[59] Half a dozen Manitoba constituencies were held up as horrible examples of Liberal gerrymandering; but almost everybody agreed that the worst enormity of all was the butchery of Diefenbaker's riding of Lake Centre. It had been, as an aggrieved Diefenbaker reminded the Commons, a rural constituency. But now the town of Moose Jaw, as well as parts of the suburbs and City of Regina, were to be included within its incredible boundaries! Coldwell, the C.C.F. leader, considered the new constituency "so palpably absurd and so papably abhorrent" to the voters concerned that he wondered how anyone could dare to take responsibility for such an electoral monstrosity.[60] "I suggest . . . ," Howard Green declared, "that the manner in which this new riding of Moose Jaw-Lake Centre has been set up is an obvious attempt to eliminate John Diefenbaker from public life."[61] Unfortunately for the Liberals, this obvious attempt of Gardiner's failed. "It was then," Diefenbaker recalled, "that I determined I would show him and the Liberal government that they could not do this to me."[62] He decided at once to run again. By the end of the year he had chosen his own home constituency of Prince Albert.

John Diefenbaker was not the only prominent political figure in Ottawa who, a year or so earlier, would have regarded himself as a very unlikely candidate for the approaching general election. At that time Pickersgill had been very complacently satisfied with his place as principal secretary to the Prime Minister's office. He did not possess the security enjoyed by the holder of an established position in the civil service; but as St. Laurent's confidant in respect of his activities both as leader of the Liberal Party and as head of the Canadian government, he exercised almost as much influence as a senior Cabinet minister. It was a very good life indeed; but its focus was St. Laurent, to whom Pickersgill was devoted, and the prospect of St. Laurent's retirement, which seemed very likely in 1951-52, seriously unsettled him. In the end, he decided to accept the post of Clerk of the Privy Council and Secretary of the Cabinet, a permanent position of great distinction in the civil service; but, unfortunately, an official position supposedly quite detached from party politics. He had not quite realized the strictness of its limitations, and he chafed under them. In September, 1952, he accompanied St. Laurent on a western tour, just as he would have done if he had remained head of the Prime Minister's office. On the return journey east there occurred an apparently trivial, but ultimately serious incident, which helped to change the course of his career.

In an advance party which included two western Cabinet ministers, he reached the Fort Garry Hotel in Winnipeg a day ahead of the Prime Minister. He found that there was no record of his own reservations, and no rooms for the members of the party. After a wait of a couple of hours, one room was finally provided; but, in the meantime, the hotel management had rejected a request for permission to use the suite which was being prepared for the Prime Minister. Pickersgill was extremely annoyed, and he grew still angrier on the following day when none of the hotel staff appeared to be on hand to greet St. Laurent. Complaints on the spot did not exhaust his feeling of righteous indignation at this affront to federal dignity; and a little after his return to Ottawa, he took advantage of an inquiry from Donald Gordon, the President of the Canadian National Railways, about the success of his western trip, to tell the dreadful story of the indignities inflicted on the Prime Minister and his party at the Fort Garry, the C.N.R. Hotel in Winnipeg.[63] His complaint may not have prompted what followed; but, for whatever reason, the fortunes of Robert S. Pitt, the manager of the Fort Garry Hotel, were drastically altered within the next six weeks. An old and trusted servant in the C.N.R. Hotel system, he had been manager of such senior hotels as the Nova Scotian in Halifax and the Bessborough in Saskatoon. He now found himself suddenly transferred from the Fort Garry, with 260 rooms, to the Prince Edward in Brandon, with eighty.

The story of Pitt's demotion soon found its way into the columns of the Winnipeg *Tribune*: it was brought up without delay when Parliament met early in December. The member who pursued the subject most pertinaciously in the House of Commons was, somewhat unexpectedly, J. M. Macdonnell, the member for Greenwood, Toronto, an urbane and cultivated Conservative who rarely exhibited strong partisan feelings and was little inclined to take up petty issues or to score small debating points.[64] He had become convinced that Pickersgill had used his important connections and political influence to ruin the career of a helpless public servant who had done nothing which could not be explained by the unfortunate circumstances of the moment. His indignation at this arrogant abuse of power drove him into several unusually spirited encounters with the formidable Howe and with Chevrier, the Minister of Transport. This determined moral condemnation by a man whom he could not help but respect increased Pickersgill's discomfiture. Ever since he had accepted the office of Clerk of the Privy Council and Secretary of the Cabinet, his irrepressible party interests had been struggling to escape from the enforced impartiality of his official position; and now Macdonnell's stinging attacks made his situation intolerable. He determined, in some fashion, to make his way into active party politics. It was fortunate that Gordon Bradley, the first Cabinet minister from Newfoundland, was eager to give up his portfolio and retire to the Senate. And Pickersgill took his place as Secretary of State.

This easy transfer from the anonymity of the civil service to the publicity of party politics cast a revealing beam of light on the state of government in Canada as it had developed during twenty years of Liberal rule. Pickersgill was not, of course, the first post-war Liberal civil servant to become a Liberal politician; "Mike" Pearson had made the same move, with equal ease, less than five years previously. Pearson's election might have been regarded as an exceptional incident, but Pickersgill's seemed to have established a definite trend in Liberal government. For years, as Pearson himself had proved before he became Secretary of State for External Affairs, civil servants had been making government policy; but now, as Pickersgill had demonstrated just as conclusively, civil servants had become confidential advisers of the ministers in matters of party politics. A very high degree of friendly intimacy, of casual familiarity, grew up between the two divisions of government in the little closed-in capital of Ottawa. In traditional British and Canadian practice, civil servants had been unpolitical and impartial advisers, equally separated from both parties and ready to serve either. Twenty years of Liberal rule had shattered this convention for ever. The Canadian civil service, like Canadian business, had become identified with the Liberal Party in one huge and omnipotent establishment. Civil servants were intimate friends of Liberal ministers; they were committed to Liberal policies which they had largely framed themselves; they rejoiced at the success of Liberal Party stratagems, which were not infrequently of their own invention. In Canada civil servants and Liberal politicians were simply two divisions of the same armed forces – different members of a large, rapidly growing, and extremely happy family.

Government by party had virtually ceased to exist. Instead, the Liberals had become the party of government. And it was as the neutral instrument of perfect administration that they approached the general election of 1953. St. Laurent rested complacently on his record. He had no new programmes to propose; but two earlier projects – the St. Lawrence Seaway and Canadian television – had hung fire for so long that public restiveness was growing, and here the government decided it would be advisable to show some action. Unfortunately, there was not a great deal that could be done about the seaway, for, although Parliament had, early in 1952, approved plans for the construction of the canals, as a wholly Canadian enterprise, on the Canadian side of the international section of the river, the government was still committed to the earlier scheme of Canadian-American co-operation in the project, and it kept on waiting humbly for the Americans to make up their minds. Progress in Canadian television was somewhat easier to achieve, for the real impediment to its development was St. Laurent himself. He had made no move to establish the Canada Council and the national scholarships, and he was coldly unenthusiastic about television. It was C. D. Howe, who could hardly have cared less about Canadian talent and the Canadian cultural identity, who took up the cause of television, simply because he wanted to promote the Canadian electronics industry! At his suggestion, Pickersgill conferred with Davidson Dunton, Chairman of the Board of Governors of the C.B.C., and their proposals won approval by St. Laurent and the Cabinet. In November, 1952, at the opening of the last session of the Twenty-first Parliament, the Speech from the Throne announced the formation of a nationwide system of public and private television stations.[65]

The general election, postponed until after the coronation of Queen Elizabeth II, took place on August 10, 1953. There was a listless, holiday air about it; it was like a pale photocopy of the election of 1949. A great many Canadians were away from home on summer vacations, and there were over 200,000 fewer voters than there had been in June, 1949. No great crisis and no new issues had excited them; and the two political leaders, and their campaign manners, had grown to be very familiar indeed. Drew, who realized that he could not possibly rival St. Laurent at "whistle-stops," concentrated instead on press conferences. St. Laurent played his favourite part as the rich benevolent uncle of the happy Canadian family with the practised skill of a professional actor. They both went through the required motions, but in a relaxed and casual fashion which almost implied a realization that the election had already been decided, not by themselves but by other, much more impersonal forces.

In fact, the Liberal Party won because it had become the party of government, of government which seemed to work. The regulated welfare state had steadied itself after the storm of unpopularity it encountered in the first year of the Korean War. Abbott had managed to check inflation; its chief victims, the aged, had been compensated by the introduction of the universal old age pensions; and the rising curve of prices had at last flattened out. The budget of 1953 – which, oddly enough, strongly resembled that of 1949 – was a taxpayers' delightful fantasy: it reduced the rates of personal income tax to the level of 1950, which was the post-war low.[66] There seemed to be lots of money around and most people had jobs. Why should the Canadians change?

They didn't. The Progressive-Conservatives and the C.C.F. each gained ten seats more than in the election of 1949. But St. Laurent, with a following of 141 Liberals, had a commanding majority over all parties.[67] Diefenbaker won in Prince Albert and Pickersgill in Bonavista-Twillingate, Newfoundland.

VIII

It was now nearly four years since Mackenzie King had resigned. They were years in which Pearson, convinced that sovereignty in isolation was "not enough," had pursued an activist foreign policy. With energy and a great deal of moral conviction, he had urged and promoted two major causes – NATO and the collective unity of the North Atlantic world, and the United Nations and collective resistance to aggression in the Far East. On the surface at least, both these great enterprises seemed to have been completely successful. The North Atlantic Treaty Organization had been formed and the westward expansion of Communist influence in Europe had been halted. The United Nations had authorized resistance to Communist aggression in the Far East and the war in Korea was slowly drawing to a close. It had been a constructive, decisive period in world affairs and Canada, though a relatively small power, had played an astonishingly large part in the events. Pearson's prestige stood very high. He ought to have been satisfied and proud. And yet – how was it? – a certain sense of disappointment and disillusionment had grown steadily all along the way.

The splendour of Pearson's "Atlantic Vision" had certainly faded a little. The NATO organization had grown undeniably to look less and less like that glorious economic, social and moral union, solidly based "on the values and virtues of Christian civilization" which he and St. Laurent had presented to the Canadian House of Commons in the winter of 1949. Greece and

Turkey, which admittedly could have only a very distant view of the splendour of the North Atlantic, had been added to the alliance, for solid strategical reasons only; and Turkey could hardly be expected to show any great enthusiasm for "the values and virtues of Christian civilization." Despite the work of several committees, and repeated and prolonged discussions in the North Atlantic Council, the ideal of an economic and political "North Atlantic Commonwealth" never got off the ground. Pearson had been virtually the sole author of the dubious Article II: but Canadian officials in the departments of Finance and Trade and Commerce, as well as in the Bank of Canada, were opposed to it on economic grounds; and even senior diplomats such as Hume Wrong and Dana Wilgress considered Pearson's aim unrealistic and declined to take it seriously. NATO remained a military alliance, dominated from the start by its most powerful members, Great Britain, France, and, above all, by the United States. Pearson, with his pathetic pleas for "consultation," succeeded only in making himself something of a nuisance. The Americans were convinced that they had had more than enough trouble getting agreement in Washington without seeking approval from Ottawa. "If you think . . . ," Acheson exploded irritably, "that we are going to start all over again with our NATO allies, especially with you moralistic, interfering Canadians, then you're crazy."[68]

The United Nations was the second of Pearson's great moral enthusiasms; but unfortunately its prestige had been badly damaged during the past four years. It had bungled its own war in Korea and muddled its first attempt at peacemaking. The interminable truce talks at Panmunjom, begun on July 10, 1951, were protracted and – for more than six months – totally suspended by fundamental differences over the repatriation of prisoners; and it was not until July 27, 1953, more than two years later, that they ended at last in the signing of an armistice. The political settlement which, it had always been supposed, was to follow the cease-fire, could not be immediately negotiated; and, after long, dragging years of frustration and futility, people began to realize that it never would be. The two Koreas remained distinct, just as they had been before the war. The "unified, independent and democratic Korea, under a representative form of government" – the professed aim of the United Nations – never came into existence.

This long, sorry story of muddle and failure had been, of course, a very painful and disillusioning experience for Pearson. He knew now that the United Nations had serious limitations; but he never quite realized that its glorious days as an international policeman, ruling the world with Security Council resolutions and generals, were definitely over. The fact was that the condemnation and punishment of North Korea, which he assumed would be "a most valuable precedent for the future," was almost certain never to be repeated. The exceptional situation – the temporary absence of the Soviet representative from the Security Council – which alone had made the "response to aggression" possible, was highly unlikely ever to occur again. Henceforth, the great powers, the permanent members of the Security Council, would always be on hand to guard their interests. Once again, the veto would prevent positive action; but this did not mean that the great powers – and particularly the United States with its faithful majority in the General Assembly – could not use the United Nations for their own purposes. By the "uniting for peace" resolution, they could transfer contentious issues to the General Assembly, or they could delegate them to regional associations, such a the Organization of American States, or, in cases where the United Nations had proved itself unlikely to be serviceable, they could by-pass it completely.

The case of Guatemala provided a brilliant example of just how successfully the method of delegation could be worked. The reformist regime of President Guzman Jacobo Arbenz, which had expropriated the banana plantations of the American United Fruit Company and distributed the land among the Guatemalan peasants, had become increasingly dependent upon Communist support; and this had aroused the hypersensitive anti-Communist susceptibilities of John Foster Dulles and President Eisenhower. In March, 1954, at a conference of the Organization of American States, Dulles persuaded the members to pass a resolution declaring that Communist control of the political institutions of any American state would constitute a threat to their collective sovereignty and political independence. Guatemala was thus left morally and politically isolated and vulnerable; it was menaced, in addition by the emigré opponents of the Arbenz regime, led by Colonel Castillo Armas, who threatened invasion from the neighbouring state of Honduras. Arbenz, having failed to buy arms elsewhere, finally received a shipment from Czechoslovakia. This was more than enough for Dulles. In April and May, the United States signed military agreements with Honduras and Nicaragua; and the Central Intelligence Agency provided Armas with guns and planes. In June, Armas invaded Guatemala, and Arbenz appealed to the Security Council for help in repelling aggression.[69]

The irony of the situation was painfully acute. Apart from the tremendous differences – the fact that it occurred in America and not Asia, and that the roles of the principal players were exactly reversed – the invasion of Guatemala was a close re-enactment of the aggression against South Korea four years earlier. Arbenz played the part of the pitiable victim with more justification than Syngman Rhee had done. Honduras and Nicaragua could certainly be convicted of wilful aggression; and, without any doubt, the United States had "mounted, supplied, and instigated" the attack in precisely the same way as Acheson had mistakenly believed the Soviet Union to have done in June, 1950. The opening of the two savage little dramas was nearly identical; the ending was completely different. The United States was determined to run the Guatemalan affair out of the United Nations and shunt it down the quiet, unnoticed siding of the Organization of American States. The Soviet Union vetoed a first open attempt to carry out this plan; but there was always a trick left in the American diplomatic armoury. On June 25, a week after the invasion had started, the United States proposed that the Guatemalan question should *not* be included on the Security Council's agenda; and this being a procedural motion, was not subject to the veto. Sir Anthony Eden, directly appealed to by Dulles, consented, out of loyalty to the Anglo-American alliance, to instruct the British representative on the Council not to vote against the rejection of the agenda; and, with Great Britain and France abstaining, the American motion passed by five votes to four.[70] Two days later the Arbenz regime fell.

The United Nations has certainly disappointed the high hopes of its usefulness which the idealistic and diplomatically innocent Canadians had held at the founding conference in San Francisco. The long, drawn-out Korean War had been a sobering, if not a harrowing, experience; and, in the years that followed, Canada played a less conspicuous part in international affairs, and played it with rather more conviction in Europe than in Asia. When, in September, 1954, a re-armed West Germany joined the Western European Union and became a member of NATO, Pearson warmly approved; but he remained prudently aloof from comparable developments in Asia. Canada made no move to recognize the People's Republic of China; but, at the same time, Canada showed no signs of following the vigorous lead of the United States in the Far-Eastern politics of the middle 1950's. In September, 1954, Dulles managed to cobble together SEATO, the South-East Asia Treaty Organization, which, on the surface, distantly resembled NATO, but which was joined by only two genuine Asian nations, Pakistan and Thailand. SEATO was, in fact, a western alliance against the spread of Asian communism, and Pearson would have nothing to do with it. He was equally determined not to get involved in the quarrel over Taiwan and the off-shore islands, which flared up between Dulles and Mao Tse-tung during the winter of 1954-55.

In only one of the troubled areas of the Far East – Indochina – did Canada accept a new commitment, and then only reluctantly, apprehensively, and with some grave reservations. The final collapse of French power in Vietnam had been followed, late in April, 1954, by a conference at Geneva, Switzerland. There the powers concerned arranged an armistice, which recognized the independence of Laos and Cambodia and divided Vietnam roughly at the seventeenth parallel, leaving North Vietnam in control of the Viet Minh Communists. Canada had sent a delegation to Geneva, but mainly because the conference made a last – and vain – attempt to settle the future of Korea; and the Canadian representative had left the town before the cease-fire in Indochina was concluded. It was therefore with genuine surprise and a good deal of dismay that, on July 21, Canada suddenly found itself named, along with India and Poland, to a three-member International Control Commission, which was to supervise the implementation of the armistice in Indochina. Pearson, always jealous of the centrality of the United Nations, disliked political settlements negotiated outside its authority. He knew too that, in a region so war-torn and still so seriously divided as Indochina, it would be an extremely difficult and ungrateful task to carry out the terms imposed on the International Control Commission.[71] Yet, if Canada was to continue in the role in world affairs which it had played so consistently since 1945, there was no real possibility of declining this unwelcome invitation from Geneva. Canada, Pearson declared in announcing his acceptance of the assignment, had tried to serve the cause of peace by promoting conditions of security and stability throughout the world. "If, therefore," he continued, "Canada can assist in establishing such security and stability in South-East Asia, we will be serving our own country, as well as the cause of peace."[72]

IX

Pearson had vowed to take Canada out of its stuffy, meaningless North American isolation and into the bracing currents of international affairs. Canada in the world was the great interest of his career; Canada in North America was a subject of distinctly less importance. "Sovereignty is Not Enough" was the title he gave to an early chapter in the second volume of his memoirs. The ideals of world peace, world stability and security, and the maintenance of western principles of political liberty and representative government, seemed, in his estimation, vastly more important than the nineteenth-century concept of national sovereignty. Mackenzie King had spent his life in asserting Canadian autonomy against British imperial controls; but Pearson had no intention of devoting the best part of his time to the narrow, negative task of guarding Canadian interests against the continentalist policies of the United States. His diplomatic triumphs were invariably scored abroad, not at home; and while Canadians accepted and often applauded his accomplishments in the world outside, they were not infrequently worried, or disappointed, or angered by his apparent failure to defend Canadian rights or aspirations in North America.

The fact was that Pearson's term as Secretary for External Affairs, which lasted from 1948 to 1957, coincided very neatly with the first great advance of American control and influence over every aspect of Canadian life. Pearson was just as typical of the period as Clarence Decatur Howe. Though they differed almost comically in personality and interests, they were both good North Americans; and, though Howe could hardly have cared less about the complicated external issues which so fascinated Pearson, they both thought instinctively in American continental terms. For Pearson, international co-operation for world security and western democratic values was just as important in North America as it was anywhere else in the world. He had been Permanent Undersecretary for External Affairs, and already a power in Canadian foreign policy, when the beginning of the Cold War and the first American demands for a share in the defence of the far north had led to the passage of the Visiting Forces Act in 1947. Now the election of President Eisenhower and the appointment of the arch anti-Communist, John Foster Dulles, as American Secretary of State, renewed and intensified American insistence on the strengthening of the continent's Arctic defence.

Radar screens, which would give warning of the approach of enemy aircraft, were to be added to the eight northern weather stations which had been built as a result of the agreement of 1947. Canada had participated in the construction of the first of these chains of radar stations, the Pine Tree Line, and had met the cost of the second, the Mid-Canada Line, itself. The third and most northerly chain, the Distant Early Warning Line, or Dewline, which stretched across the Canadian Arctic, was to be constructed, according to a Canadian-American agreement in the spring of 1955, by the United States and largely manned, at the start at least, by American forces. A few Canadian newspapers, the Toronto *Globe and Mail* and the Montreal *Star* in particular, attacked the preponderating military presence of the United States in the Canadian north, and the apparent inadequacy of Canada's contribution to continental defence. Ralph Allen, the editor of *Maclean's*, was extremely annoyed to learn that his request to visit the stations on the Dewline had to be approved by American officials in the United States. He was equally angered at a press conference, where the R.C.A.F. press relations officer, whom he was interrogating, referred each question to his American colleagues, obviously his superiors.[73]

Pearson had not only confirmed and emphasized Canada's status as a military dependency of the United States in the defence of North America; he also surrendered Canada's last chance to assert its economic self-sufficiency and independence in the construction of the St. Lawrence Seaway. The project of a combined waterway and power development on the St. Lawrence River had originally been planned, more than twenty years earlier, as a joint Canadian-American undertaking; but, though both Presidents Roosevelt and Truman had expressed approval of the scheme, its highly vocal and powerful opponents in the United States had successfully prevented the American Congress from taking any action in the matter. In the end, Canada, which by this time badly needed additional hydro-electric power, grew tired of the endless delays, and, in the autumn of 1951, announced that it proposed to build the seaway itself. In the United States this announcement was greeted with mingled derision and apprehension. *The Saturday Evening Post* assumed that Canada's defiant declaration was mere bluff; but to an increasingly large number of Canadians, if not to their government, it was not bluff at all. The St. Lawrence was a river of enormous historical and economic significance to Canada, and affluent, post-war Canada was financially quite capable of building its seaway. Canada governments had already constructed the Welland Canal, through the Niagara peninsula, as well as all the locks, canals and power installations on the Canadian section of the St. Lawrence, from Montreal to Cornwall. All that remained were the works required in the international section of the river from Cornwall to Lake Ontario. Why should not Canada undertake these also, and thus make the St. Lawrence Seaway a wholly Canadian achievement?

The Canadian government frustrated this nationalist ambition. It still held to its preference for Canadian-American co-operation in the St. Lawrence project; and St. Laurent paid another dutiful visit to Washington to win support from the new President Eisenhower, just as he had twice before sought the approval of Truman. The Canadians had waited an incredible length of time; but, in the end, their patient humility was rewarded. In the winter and spring of 1954, the American opposition to the seaway mysteriously melted away and Congress passed the Wiley-Dondero Bill, which provided that the locks and canals on the international section of the St. Lawrence were all to be built on the American side and by the United States. This last-minute, highly self-interested offer of participation was not, of course, binding on Canada, and the Canadian government subsequently insisted that one canal and lock in the international section should be built at Iroquois on the Canadian side, at Canada's expense. The agreement between the two countries was not finally confirmed until August 19, 1954: but, for the world in general, and the United States in particular, the real inauguration of the St. Lawrence Seaway came three months earlier, on May 13, in a pompous and much-publicized ceremony at the White House in Washington, when President Eisenhower signed the Wiley-Dondero Bill. "To you, Mr. President, and to your administration," declared Congressman Dondero, "must go the credit for bringing about the beginning of this great project." [74]

The only Canadian present on this memorable occasion was A.D.P. Heeney, the Canadian Ambassador to the United States, who was almost lost in a crowd of forty-three exultant Congressman. He was presented, as an appropriate acknowledgment of Canada's part in the building of the seaway, with one of the nine pens with which Eisenhower signed the Wiley-Dondero Bill.

CHAPTER 10

The Liberals Rampant

I

The fifteen years from 1941 to 1956 saw an extraordinary change in the number and character of the Canadian people. There were over 4,500,000 more Canadians in 1956 than there had been in 1941, an increase of nearly 40%, made up of a steady rise in the number of births and a less constant but still substantial annual influx of immigrants.[1] In 1955, which was one of the peak years for immigration, the newcomers from abroad numbered over 164,000, and the new Canadian babies over 450,000.[2] The immigrants, most of whom were adults, did modify the steadily increasing youthfulness of the population, but, even so, in 1956 over 5,225,000 Canadians, or nearly a third of the whole, were under fourteen years of age.[3] In sharp contrast with the 1930's, when the population had aged steadily, the Canada of the 1950's was a young Canada, a Canada which, with disconcerting suddenness, had created all sorts of problems for the other inhabitants.

The overcrowded maternity wards were one of the chief reasons for the nearly 4,000 new beds and cribs which were added to Canadian hospitals by 1956.[4] There were nearly 800,000 more elementary pupils in Canadian public schools in 1956 than there had been in 1940.[5] The population of the secondary schools had also been growing with increasing rapidity during the middle 1950's; but so far the tide of numbers had not risen above this level in the educational system. Undergraduate enrolment in the universities was, in fact, smaller by about 10,000 than it had been at the peak of the student-veteran influx of the late 1940's. The new army of young Canadians was not yet hammering at the doors of the institutions of higher learning, but professors and administrators were perfectly well aware of the fact that the advancing horde was on its way and not very far down the road. "In short," Dr. Sidney Smith, President of the University of Toronto, wrote in 1956, "it has been estimated that there could be from 110,600 to 130,200 students in Canadian universities in 1964-5, as compared with the present 65,000."[6]

A very large proportion of the immigrants of the 1950's were from the countries of Western Europe, with the Italians in the ascendant from the beginning. To some extent, their advent revived the polyglot character of the Canadian population; but the effect of this foreign admixture was qualified by the annual increment of native-born Canadian babies, and by the immigration from Great Britain, which was larger than that from any other single country. In 1951, English was the mother tongue of 59.11% of all Canadians; and ten years later, after a decade of heavy immigration, it was to decline by only a little more than one percentage point. English was the language adopted by the overwhelming majority of the immigrants; as a French-Canadian demographer remarked realistically, the survival of the French language in Canada would depend, not on its power of attraction, but on its powers of resistance.[7] Even its powers of resistance had not sufficed to retain all the Canadians of French ethnic origin, and by 1951 over 250,000 of them spoke English as their mother tongue. The surviving citadels of the French language stood in northern New Brunswick, Quebec, far-eastern and northern Ontario; but beyond these strong points, its decline was persistent, particularly among the young.

In other important ways, the great post-war immigration strengthened rather than modified the already prevailing trends in Canadian social development. In was, in fact, in Canadian experience, a very different kind of immigration. In the first decade of the twentieth century, the British and European newcomers had been mainly farmers, or would-be farmers, who settled the western prairies; the new Canadians of the 1940's and 1950's were a much more varied body, with diverse skills and training, and widely different intended occupations, which, in the main, were urban, not rural, in character. The rural community which had been declining steadily but slowly since the beginning of the century, decreased sharply in the fifteen years following the beginning of the war, and in 1956 constituted only a third of the population as a whole.[8] It was the industrialized and urbanized provinces – Ontario, Quebec, British Columbia and Alberta – which benefited most from the post-war influx, and it was the cities – particularly Toronto, Montreal, Vancouver and Edmonton – which profited most of all. They grew so fast and so rapidly engulfed so many neighbouring municipalities, that the accumulating problems of housing, services, and transport almost overwhelmed the old city governments. Vancouver and Winnipeg began experimenting with various metropolitan boards and committees; but it was Toronto which first adopted a formal metropolitan organization. On January 1, 1954, Metropolitan Toronto, consisting of the City of Toronto and twelve suburban towns, villages, and townships, began its complex existence. In March, three months later, the first Canadian underground railway, the Toronto "subway," which ran north beneath or alongside Yonge Street for about four-and-a-half miles, began operations.

In cities, towns, villages, and even in the open countryside, Canadian householders found life much easier and more effortless than they remembered it to have been before the Second World War. Petroleum and natural gas had now joined electricity as domestic sources of energy and together they were rapidly ending most of the dirt, the drudgery, and the discomfort of household existence. By 1956, pipelines brought oil from Alberta as far east as Toronto and as far west as Vancouver. Natural gas, which now heated most houses in Alberta, was carried by pipeline through the mountains to British Columbia; and Trans-Canada Pipelines, C.D. Howe's ambitious and highly controversial project of 1956, promised to bring it to eastern Canada within two years' time. The oil- gas-fired furnace operated by electricity and controlled by a thermostat, was perhaps the greatest − but by no means the only − labour-saving boon of the post-war domestic revolution. Many households had now acquired clothes washers and dryers; and families which had neither the money nor the space to instal them, could patronize one of the increasingly numerous coin-operated public "laundromats." The washtub and the washboard had vanished; in many families even the dishpan had been replaced by the electric dishwasher. There was no doubt that household tasks had been simplified and lightened, but there was no doubt also that the housewife now performed them herself. The domestic servants, which even middle class families had kept before the war, had now virtually vanished.

II

The 1960's, like the 1920's, was to be a restless, rebellious, permissive decade, but the ten years which followed the peace of 1945 differed profoundly from them both. Like the 1920's, it was a post-war decade; but, while the "gay 1920's" had been a light-hearted, irresponsible and undisciplined age, 1945-1955 was, by comparison, a sober and conventional period which kept the law and retained established customs. The political and financial scandals which characterized the 1960's − Lucien Rivard, Gerda Munsinger, the Atlantic Acceptance Company and Windfall Oils and Mines − were far away in the future. Order and decorum seemed to mark public life; a reasonable restraint governed the existence of families and individuals. There were certainly more homicides, and convictions under the Opium and Narcotic Drug Act than there had been before the war, but the addition of about two-and-a-half million people to the nation's adult population was a satisfactory explanation of much of the increase. In general, the number of indictable offences had remained fairly constant in the years from 1940 to 1955 despite the growth of population; and juvenile delinquency, of children from seven to fifteen years, had also dropped from the high levels at the beginning of the war.[9]

Those venerable institutions, marriage and the family, looked as secure as they had ever been. When young men and women fell in love they did not enter into those unions, unauthorized by church or state, which in the 1920's had been called "companionate marriages," and in the 1960's and 1970's were described, still more euphemistically, as "established relationships." The young people of the 1940's got married, just as their parents had done. They wanted, or expected, to have children; at any rate, they kept on having them year after year, and in unprecedented numbers. The dread of an overpopulated world, which began to haunt people in the 1970's, or the fear that an overpopulated Canada might some day not be able to provide all its sons and daughters with jobs and careers, never, apparently, entered the heads of these young parents of the 1950's. That famous oral contraceptive, "the Pill," had not yet been invented; abortion was illegal, and although it was practised in secret, nobody wanted, or dared, to demand and advocate it as a right in public. Children were still regarded as a natural and desirable incident of marriage; and marriages were still thought of, in principle at least, as "for ever." The number of divorces had certainly shot up abruptly in the first two years after the war, but it had declined fairly steadily thereafter and in 1956 the divorce rate was 37.4 per hundred thousand of the population.[10]

The post-war years brought no surprising changes in the established social distinctions between men and women or between married and unmarried women. The Women's Liberation Movement had not yet got under way, and nobody was advocating alterations in the forms of polite address. The vast majority of married women willingly accepted their husbands' surnames and the courtesy title "Mrs" and very few retained their maiden names; the abbreviated title "Ms" for both married and unmarried women was unknown and unsuspected in the 1950's. Pre-war convention still governed hair styles and costumes just as it did polite social usage. The revolution in fashion which gave western women trousers and tights or panty-hose was still far in the future. Pant suits were occasionally worn at home; but on the streets, or in other people's houses, dresses or skirts, and stockings held up by girdles or garter-belts, were still normal. Ever since the First World War men's costume had successfully resisted any significant changes in fashion; but formal dress – tails and dinner jackets – appeared less frequently at evening parties, vests or waistcoats were often discarded, and cloth was growing lighter in both weight and colour. Blue jeans were worn occasionally, for very informal occasions, by school girls; but in general blue denim was simply the material used to make overalls for farmers and workers in the older trades. Costume still sharply distinguished between men and women, and hair styles confirmed the difference beyond any doubt. Ever since the introduction of bobbed hair in the 1920's, women's hair styles had varied greatly; but Canadian men of the 1950's almost uniformly had their hair cut short – not, indeed, so short as the once-popular American "crewcut," but short enough to surprise visitors from England or Europe, where longer hair was already becoming fashionable. Older men occasionally grew beards and moustaches, young men almost never.

It was by no means a self-indulgent or libertarian society, eager to experience new sensations or determined to break with old conventions or taboos; but some pre-war restraints had certainly been relaxed. Men, women, and teenagers of both sexes were smoking vastly more cigarettes than they had before the war. Women were also drinking with a freedom and a capacity which would have deeply distressed such a prominent pre-war personality as Nellie McClung, a champion of women's rights and also a novelist who caused one of her male characters to die, most improbably, of a surfeit of beer! Like other early Women's Liberationists, Nellie McClung had fondly believed that female suffrage would indubitably usher in a new and better world of peace, social reforms, and total prohibition. It had not quite worked out that way, and women had certainly helped to ensure the slow but persistent post-war growth in the annual consumption of alcohol.

In 1956, the per capita consumption, of people sixteen years and over, was 1.51 imperial gallons, a figure which placed Canada ninth in a list made up of prominent West European, North American and Commonwealth countries.[11] Beer accounted for 64.5, or very nearly two-thirds of this total, spirits for 30, and wine for a very modest 5.5.[12] In most Canadian households, table wine appeared only on special occasions; and, except in the Province of Quebec, most restaurants were not yet equipped to store and serve it properly. Changes have certainly occurred, but they were gradual and slow. Stimulants – simple rather than sophisticated stimulants – were more popular than they had been, but alcohol was still virtually the only artificial aid to relaxation or conviviality. The increasing number of convictions under the Opium and Narcotic Drug Act certainly proved the growth of the drug traffic; but it was not until the 1960's that large numbers of people, including teenagers, discovered the brief euphoria of "soft drugs" such as marijuana.

The work ethic still sturdily confronted the pleasure principle. Leisure was still largely interpreted in a negative rather than a positive sense. It was primarily regarded, as it always had been in the past, as "time remaining at one's disposal after work."[13] It was "time off " from activity rather than time in the active pursuit of play – of sport, recreation, entertainment. Toronto was the most rapidly growing city in Canada, with a citizenry which was prosperous beyond the national average; but it was still singularly devoid of the theatres, restaurants, night clubs or bars at which one could while away an hour or spend an amusing evening. There were nearly three times as many passenger cars in 1956 in Canada as there had been in 1945; and cars took people touring or carried them up to summer cottages for loafing, fishing, or water sports.[14] Beyond these familiar places and their accustomed modes of recreation, the Canadians of the mid-1950's did not usually go very far. There were still gaps in the long advocated Trans-Canada Highway, and trains and steamships still transported people on journeys of any distance.

The Canadian Pacific Railway inaugurated its crack new transcontinental train "The Canadian" in the summer of 1954, and Cunard and C.P.R. steamships provided the main form of transport between Canada and Europe.

The vast growth of tourism, the rapid expansion of the "pleasure periphery," were still a little way off in the future. Tourism depended on many things – on more frequent holidays, longer vacations, greater affluence, more rapid forms of transport, and, above all, on the unavowed but growing conviction that leisure ought to mean pleasure and that pleasure was the greatest good in life.[15] In the 1950's huge companies of Canadians were not inevitably impelled to take off every winter for Florida, California, Arizona, Hawaii and the West Indies. They did not escape in droves every summer for tours of Britain and Europe, for cruises in the Baltic and the Mediterranean, for visits to strange peoples and exotic lands in the Middle and Far East. They hadn't – or assumed they hadn't – the time or the money; and, apart from the young, they were still slightly intimidated by the complications and uncertainties of foreign travel. It was the rapid development of the tourist industry, which in less than a decade became one of the most fabulously profitable businesses of the twentieth century, which made travel easy and almost effortless for masses of Canadians; and it was the amazing growth of air transport, which, even for people with small means and little time, vastly extended the range, and multiplied and varied the delights of travel.

These were the essentials of the rise of international tourism and the apparently endless expansion of the "pleasure periphery"; and although they existed in a rudimentary form in the Canada of the 1950's, they were still far off from their full magnificence. Trans-Canada Air Lines, the original name of the national airline, had a small fleet of Super-Constellation, Viscount, and North Star planes, which flew across Canada, to half a dozen major American cities, and to Britain, France and West Germany. In 1956 passenger traffic was nearly five times as great as it had been ten years earlier; but planes were still small, and service infrequent. [16] The first Canadian jet aircraft was built in 1954; the first of the large scale Canadian airports, Dorval, at Montreal, was not open for traffic until the late autumn of 1960.

III

In 1956 it was five years since the Massey Report had been published, and neither of its two chief recommendations – national scholarships and a Canada Council for the promotion of Canadian arts, letters, and social sciences – had so far been carried out. The Canadian government had not yet made a single move or appropriated a solitary copper for the support of literature and the arts in Canada. Most Canadians were probably not very disappointed by this inaction, for most Canadians had clearly not thought it likely that Ottawa would bother about such affairs. The fact was that the Canadians of the 1950's had not yet been taught to believe that the state was the great dispenser of social and cultural goodies and that unless the state designed and financed a literary or artistic project, its failure was virtually inevitable. Artists and writers had always been very much on their own in Canada. They had had to be. A wide variety of encouragement and protection had always been available to Canadian industrialists; there had never been any for Canadian writers and artists. Free enterprise and private initiative dominated literature and the arts far more than they did any other sector of the Canadian economy.

The 1950's saw a striking manifestation of this artistic private initiative in a field of endeavour – the performing arts – where it had shown itself only very tentatively before. By 1956 a professional theatre, a professional opera, and two troupes of professional ballet dancers had come into existence. The Stratford Shakespearean Festival was the first, the most ambitious, and the most immediately successful of these three enterprises. Stratford was a town in the southwestern part of Ontario which, like so many other places in the province, had borrowed its name from England; and the river Avon, on the banks of which it stood, was only one of several Ontario streams which were namesakes of well-remembered English rivers. This association hardly meant very much to most citizens of Stratford, Ontario; but to Tom Patterson, who had fought in the Second World War and had heard opera in Italy and drama in England, it came to mean a great deal.

He knew of the Shakespeare Memorial Theatre in Stratford, England, and he conceived the idea of founding a Shakespearean Festival in Stratford, Ontario. It was a romantic and grandiose conception which, in the hard light of reason, might well have seemed remote and utterly unattainable. But Tom Patterson determined to realize it in fact. He confided his idea to his friends and neighbours; he kept on talking about it. "His perseverance was indomitable; his enthusiasm, boring to most, infected a few."[17] A committee of exploration was found and got in touch with Dora Mavor Moore in Toronto; and through her, Dr. Tyrone Guthrie, the Shakespearean scholar and director, was persuaded to come to Canada. Guthrie was a director of long experience, wide learning, enormous energy and enthusiasm, and great creative originality. He arrived in Stratford, Ontario, in July, 1952.

That summer, under the spell of Guthrie's authoritative knowledge and expert advice, the committee made its basic decisions about the future Stratford Festival. There was no suitable existing theatre in the town, and, until the project had proved to be a success, it would be financially impossible to build one. A huge, specially constructed tent would, the committee decided, be the best interim solution; and also, convinced by Guthrie's persuasive arguments, it agreed that this highly unconventional theatre would be built, not simply of new materials, but also according to a revolutionary stage design. Stratford was to abandon the established theatrical tradition of the nineteenth and twentieth centuries. It was to give up the arched proscenium with the stage behind and the audience out in front; instead, it reverted to the theatre of Shakespeare's own time with an apron stage almost entirely surrounded by spectators, and equipped with such permanent properties as a balcony and a trap in the floor. The actors, it was agreed, were to be mainly Canadian, with the assistance of a few from Britain or elsewhere; and the presence of at least one actor of recognized talent and international fame was, everybody realized, essential to the initial success of the whole ambitious undertaking. These were momentous decisions. The committee, inspired by them, dispatched Tom Patterson to London to secure the services of the essential theatrical experts and the "star" actor.[18]

The triumphant élan of the daring venture continued unchecked. Guthrie, who was already deeply interested in a project whose whole character he had so largely determined himself, consented to act as director. Tanya Moiseiwitsch, a talented former collaborator of Guthrie's, became the Festival's designer and took on the multifarious problems of stage construction, properties, costumes, and accessories. Alec Guinness, to the surprise as well as the delight of everybody, agreed to play the part of leading actor. He had other, more lucrative offers for the summer of 1953 than Stratford could afford, but he rejected them, partly because he was interested in playing Shakespeare on the revolutionary new stage which Guthrie and Moiseiwitsch were designing, and partly because he was generously eager to help in the beginning of a gallant pioneer enterprise of enormous potentialities for the future. That autumn he and Guthrie decided that *Richard III,* which provided a suitable leading role, and *All's Well That Ends Well,* in modern dress, which afforded a striking contrast, would be the two plays presented at Stratford's first season. A little before Christmas Guthrie returned to Canada, visited Montreal, Ottawa and Toronto, interviewed 317 ambitious people who hoped to act at Stratford and narrowed the list down to about sixty "probables" and sixty "possibles."[19]

From early spring to midsummer, through repeated difficulties, distractions, and threatened complete stoppages, the bold scheme moved jerkily but resolutely forward. Canada was a country virtually devoid of a theatrical tradition of its own. Its few professional actors had gained experience chiefly in radio, and it completely lacked theatrical technicians and costumiers. Canadian garment factories, organized solely for the mass production of a few staple styles and sizes, would not even consider the job of making the costumes required for Shakespeare's plays; and Canadian workers, diverted to the assembly line from the cultivation of their possible skills as craftsmen, were quite incapable of doing what the manufacturers had declined even to attempt. Eventually, the fifteenth-century shoes, the military boots, the costumes and properties, both mediaeval and modern, were successfully completed; but they were made either in special Stratford workshops, supervised by experts from Britain, or by individual craftsmen who turned out, in every case, to be Europeans, not native Canadians. Britain and Europe contributed more skills and talents to the Stratford Shakespearean Festival than perhaps its audiences ever fully realized.[20] What Canada gave was chiefly eager, but mainly amateur and inexperienced actors, and finance. Adequate finance, without which the whole show would collapse before it ever began, was perilously uncertain for months; and on one dreadful occasion, in a transatlantic telephone call to Guthrie in London, the chairman of the Stratford committee actually proposed a year's postponement! Even after sufficient money had been collected, difficulties and uncertainties still loomed ahead. The mammoth tent, which was to provide the auditorium, was agonizingly slow to arrive, and rehearsals were already well under way before it was finally erected.[21] And then, at last, on a day in July, 1953, while the director, the theatrical experts, the actors, the whole town of Stratford, and much of the population of Ontario waited in anxious suspense, the first night opened.

From the first, the Stratford Festival was a conspicuous success. The first season, planned to run for five weeks only, was extended to accommodate the thousands who were still eager to see *Richard III* and *All's Well That Ends Well*. As Guthrie said: "the audience was ready; the public *wanted* it to succeed."[22] The public wanted Stratford to succeed partly because it was starved for live theatre, for the kind of theatrical performance which only a talented director, skilled technicians, and trained actors could produce, and partly also, perhaps, because Canadians subconsciously yearned to create something which would be judged admirable by international standards and which they could truly claim as their own.

IV

The Stratford Shakespearean Festival was the most successful, but by no means the only, advance made by the performing arts in Canada during the 1950's. Both ballet and opera managed, though somewhat precariously, to achieve and hold professional status. Both arts were, of course, amateur in origin but ballet was the first to develop a firm company organization and a steady continuity. The Winnipeg Ballet and the Volkoff Canadian Ballet in Toronto, two amateur companies which had started just before the Second World War, managed to maintain their existence during the difficult decade of the 1940's. The Russian, Boris Volkoff, held fairly strictly to the classical traditions of European ballet. The choreographer of the Winnipeg Ballet, Gweneth Lloyd, who had been trained in England, was more independent, creative and unconventional, using Canadian designers, some specifically Canadian themes, and, on a few occasions, a Canadian score. Both companies gave numerous public performances, at home and in other Canadian cities; but, although Toronto was a richer and more populous city than Winnipeg, the Winnipeg Ballet managed, at first, to win a rather higher repute than its Toronto rival. Its success was partly the result of Gweneth Lloyd's energy, enthusiasm and creative talent, and partly the effect of Winnipeg's civic pride and continuing metropolitan ambition. Once Winnipeg had hoped and expected to become the recognized metropolis of the entire Canadian West. That hope had been defeated by the rapid rise of Vancouver; but though it had failed to gain its civic ambition, Winnipeg claimed a truly metropolitan culture and sophistication. Its citizens faithfully patronized their native ballet and some of them gave it heavy financial support.

Amateur ballet in Canada reached its culmination in the Canadian Ballet Festival, which was first held in Winnipeg in 1948 and for the next half-dozen years took place annually in Montreal, Ottawa, and Toronto. These events gave unknown local choreographers and hundreds of young Canadian dancers a chance to perform before large urban audiences in well-appointed theatres. The Ballet Festival, in fact, performed much the same function for the dance as the Dominion Drama Festival had done for the theatre, but it did not enjoy nearly such a lengthy existence as its theatrical counterpart. Amateur ballet was a more difficult and expensive enterprise than amateur theatricals; and amateur ballet inevitably suffered once a few of its major companies had grown strong enough to turn professional. In 1950, the Winnipeg Ballet assumed professional status; and two years later, after a command performance before the new Queen Elizabeth, became the Royal Winnipeg Ballet. In the meantime, Toronto had made a new start, established the National Ballet Company in 1950, and invited Celia Franca, an English dancer and choreographer, to become its first artistic director. At first Celia Franca relied largely on standard European works, but later added a few ballets of her own composition. The Royal Winnipeg Ballet's repertoire remained what it had been from the start, a stock of original and unconventional ballets, devised by Gweneth Lloyd and her associates.

Opera developed more slowly, and with greater difficulty, than either of the other performing arts. Its hold on professional status and its achievement of professional quality were both more uncertain and spasmodic than those of either the theatre or the ballet. Opera, with its varied demands for singers, actors, musicians, conductors, producers and technicians, is the most elaborate and costly of all the performing arts. It was the special creation of the rich, cultivated, patrician, society of the late eighteenth and nineteenth century Europe, and the elaborate opera houses at London, Paris, Bayreuth and Milan reflect its wealth and love of opulence. Opera could succeed only in a country which was affluent, had reached a fairly high level of cultural maturity, and was prepared to spend public money on a very urbane form of entertainment. The Canada of the 1950's could not really meet all of these assorted requirements. Certainly, the nation was growing steadily more prosperous; but so far, it had developed only the rather unreliable nucleus of an opera-going public, and so far Canadian governments had not yet agreed to give opera any public support. There was no single, recognized metropolitan centre in Canada; the small company of potential opera-goers was divided among a half-dozen widely separated towns and provincial capitals, and this reduced the profits which any opera company could secure in its home base, and vastly increased its touring expenses. Amateur opera appeared in Halifax, Ottawa, Edmonton and Vancouver, but only Montreal and Toronto managed to establish professional companies; and in 1950, the Conservatory Opera Company of Toronto, which presented a season of several weeks each year at the Royal Alexandra Theatre, was the only professional company which had managed to attain a stable existence.

The Canadian government gave no direct financial assistance to independent professional companies in the performing arts; but, through the Canadian Broadcasting Corporation, it did contribute indirectly to the support of Canadian theatre, ballet, and opera. From the start C.B.C. Radio had provided opportunities for Canadian singers and musicians; and a good many of the actors who applied for parts in the Stratford Shakespearean Festival had got their training in Andrew Allen's popular series of Sunday evening radio dramas, which first went on the air in January, 1944, and continued for twelve seasons thereafter.[23] Radio had offered some scope and encouragement to musical and theatrical talent in Canada; but it was certain that television would provide much more. Radio had never captured a very large part of the possible total of Canadian listeners and it had never held their attention for any great space of time. Television, which quickly rivalled the popularity of the cinema, was soon to prove that it could hold huge audiences, as if chained to the chairs in their living rooms, for the best hours of the evening. An unparalleled opportunity lay invitingly before the Canadian Broadcasting Corporation; but it was, unfortunately, an opportunity which could be grasped and held only by enormous expenditures of money. A television programme, even in the early days of the new medium, cost anywhere from five to ten times as much as radio programmes of equal length. How was Canada to meet the appalling cost of a television system which would utilize Canadian talent, feature Canadian themes and subjects, uphold Canadian standards and values and reach the great majority of Canadian citizens?

In the United States, television, like radio, was an industry, supported by commercial advertising. In Britain, radio and television were part of a single national public service, financed by the licence fees of listeners and viewers. Canada, where nationalist cultural aims were in conflict with a continental economy, had adopted an uneasy and doubtful compromise between public ownership and private gain. "Two philosophies were . . . tangled in a single system"; and two quite different methods of financing – public funds and personal licences on the one hand and commercial revenue on the other – would likely be called upon to pay for Canadian television, just as they had for Canadian radio.[24] The closer the Canadian system could come to financial self-sufficiency on the basis of licence fees and government grants, the nearer it could approach the ideal of a national public service; the more it was forced to depend on sponsored programmes and spot advertising, the more rapidly it would degenerate into a commercial operation indistinguishable from that in the United States. The C.B.C. officials urged that the licence fee, which had been raised to $2.50, should be doubled; friends and supporters of the C.B.C., including the authors of the Massey Report, proposed that the existing annual advance of public money should be replaced by a statutory grant which would enable the C.B.C. to plan ahead for a number of years in confidence.[25]

The beginning of Canadian television in the autumn of 1952 magnified the problem of the C.B.C.'s finances and forced it upon the attention of the government. The revenue from licences was, of course, the main source of the C.B.C.'s autonomy and integrity. Licence fees helped to keep the C.B.C. independent of both government and business; but licence fees had always been somewhat unpopular in Canada, for special, peculiarly Canadian reasons. A very large proportion of the nation's listeners and viewers lived near to the international boundary, in fairly close communication with a country where radio and television were commercial enterprises and where licence fees were never imposed. In vain, the spokesmen for the C.B.C. pointed out that broadcasting in the United States was not "free," that it was paid for by advertising, and that the costs of advertising were invariably passed on to the consumer.[26] This lesson in economics left many Canadian licencees unimpressed and disgruntled. A number of them, as the Massey Commissioners acknowledged, succeeded in evading the payment of the licence fee, and Progressive-Conservatives voiced their protests in Parliament. In the past, this known or suspected unpopularity of the licencing system had always led the Canadian government to resist the C.B.C.'s importunate demands for higher fees, or to reduce the amount of the increase; but with the coming of television these cautious temporizing adjustments were obviously inadequate. Television was certain to be enormously more expensive than radio. If, as the Massey Commissioners believed, the revenue from licences ought to constitute over a third of the C.B.C.'s annual budget, then plainly the fee would have to be sharply raised. Was this politically possible? And if not, what was the alternative?

The only possible alternative was the abolition of the licence fee and the transfer of the whole cost of operation to the federal government and the taxpayer. "This proposal we cannot accept," the Massey Commissioners had declared firmly, "since we think it proper for the listener to make a direct payment for services received, and we believe that he appreciates these services the more for doing so."[27] The abolition of the licence fee would cut the close and intimate connection between the C.B.C. and its patrons, the people of Canada, whose satisfaction ought to have been its main concern. Inevitably, the Corporation would have to depend increasingly upon the government of the day, its changing financial policies, and the varying schemes of its finance ministers; inevitably also, revenue from advertising would become a steadily more important source of the Corporation's funds.

All this could have been clearly foreseen; but in the autumn of 1952, with a general election only six months away, the St. Laurent government was concerned not so much about the future of Canadian broadcasting as about the future of the Liberal Party. "I knew," Pickersgill recorded later, "that a licence fee high enough to finance television would be exceedingly unpopular."[28] Obviously the last thing the Liberals wanted to increase in 1953 was their own unpopularity. The licence fees would have to go; but, although the C.B.C.'s financial independence would vanish with them, a pretence could at least be made that it still existed. "It occurred to me," Pickersgill wrote later, "that the proceeds of the excise taxes on radio and television receivers would provide one adequate source of revenue to support C.B.C. broadcasting operations for several years."[29] He suggested to Abbott, the Finance Minister, that the income of these excises should be reserved for the C.B.C. Abbott agreed; the Cabinet agreed; the licence fees were abolished. The conception of the federal government as a beneficent deity from which all blessings freely flowed was once again confirmed.

V

In the late spring of 1954, a slender, middle-aged man with pleasantly regular features, a carefully clipped, small moustache, and an engagingly boyish manner, made one of his frequent visits to Ottawa. He was Walter Lockhart Gordon, a member of the Toronto accounting firm of Clarkson, Gordon & Company and the president of J.D. Woods & Gordon, industrial consultants. He was by this time a very well-known figure in the capital. He was a good Liberal and, like most other good Liberals in high places in the Canadian economy, he had been frequently asked to put his knowledge and expertise at the service of the federal government. He had helped to organize the Foreign Exchange Control Board at the outbreak of the war, and had served as a special assistant to the Deputy Minister of Finance from 1940 to 1942, and as chairman of a Royal Commission on the federal civil service in 1946. He had become a prominent member of the inner circle of consultants of the Liberal government and he was not therefore very surprised when, in the spring of 1954, the Prime Minister invited him to come to Ottawa for an interview. There was, he thought, a very likely explanation of this invitation. By this time it was well known in Liberal circles that three prominent members of the St. Laurent Cabinet – Harris, Claxton and Chevrier – were about to resign: Harris for a seat on the Supreme Court of Canada, Chevrier for the presidency of the new St. Lawrence Seaway Authority, and Claxton for a position as Canadian head of the Metropolitan Life Insurance Company. St. Laurent was obviously faced with his only serious task of Cabinet reconstruction. Gordon suspected that the Prime Minister was about to offer him a Cabinet post; and, with his close friend Mike Pearson's advice, he decided that he would accept one of only two senior portfolios, Finance or Trade and Commerce.[30]

The interview began. St. Laurent said politely that a minister from Toronto was "badly needed" but the position he offered was not one of the two Gordon had decided he would accept. Gordon knew that ultimately he would decline the offer; but with a politeness equal to St. Laurent's, he requested time for consideration. St. Laurent suggested that a visit to C.D. Howe might help Gordon to make up his mind, and Gordon went in to see the Minister of both Trade and Commerce and Defence Production, the acknowledged dictator of the Canadian economy, then at the height of his powers. Gordon deferentially asked the great man "what he liked about his experience in politics." Howe replied instantly, without a moment's pause for reflection. "Where else," he declared with great satisfaction, "could I get as big a job?"[31] "It was as simple as that," Gordon reflected curiously. Howe obviously had no standards or values which he was determined to serve, and no general purposes or aims which he hoped to attain. For him, mere bigness was "all." He was, in fact, a late convert to the doctrines of Emile Coué, the prophet of auto-suggestion as a cure for human ills, who was very popular in the 1920's and who used to advise his disciples to keep repeating: "Day to day and in every way I am growing better and better." This popular text, slightly altered to suit his own circumstances, must have been a favourite of Howe's: "Day by day and in every way Canada and my job are getting bigger and bigger."

Howe was obviously astounded that Gordon had not instantly and grate-fully accepted a position which would be junior to his own and would come under his general supervision as economic autocrat of Canada. Gordon tried to explain that as an accountant and industrial consultant he was very much his own boss, that he had "a rather independent turn of mind," and that he couldn't see clearly where a person like himself would stand in a Cabinet dominated by the senior ministers. He decided that a direct and pointed question might settle the matter. "If, for example, Mr. Howe," he inquired, "you were to bring a proposal to Cabinet and as a new member I questioned it, what would your reaction be?" Howe regarded him with disbelief and astonishment. "You'd do *what*, young man? he asked incredulously. Gordon had had his answer, and, as he suspected, it settled the matter. It strongly confirmed his tentative decision to decline St. Laurent's offer. He summed up his impressions tersely: "Mr. Howe, who was nearly seventy, was not going to change, and neither was the government."[32]

The trouble was, of course, that Gordon *wanted* the government to change. It was not simply that he regarded it, and particularly its senior members, as old, tired, and set in their ways, but also that he disapproved of the direction in which they had been travelling so long and so unreflectingly. "For some time during the late 1940's and early 1950's," he wrote later, "I had been worrying about the government's economic policies and particularly the complacency with which Canadians were witnessing the sell-out of our resources and business enterprises to Americans and other enterprising foreigners."[33] These were very dangerous thoughts in the Canada of the 1950's. To criticize the American economic domination of North America, or to question the American leadership of the "Free World," were heresies virtually as appalling as the profession of Protestant opinions would have been in sixteenth century Spain. How could Canadians possibly conceive of an independent foreign policy when the menace of international Communism demanded the defence of a united West under American command? How could Canadians be so infatuated as to profess a separate economic interest when American capital was promoting the rapid development of their national resources and establishing what seemed to be a permanent prosperity throughout the entire North American continent? Such nationalist aims were so generally regarded as childish or culpable delusions that usually they were mentioned only to be dismissed, or denounced. Canadian businessmen saw not the slightest reason for concern at the extent of American investment; neither did Canadian economists. B.S. Kierstead, of the University of Toronto, a typically orthodox economist, confidently observed that it was "somewhat naive to suppose that in some fashion this investment constituted a menace to Canadian independence."[34]

In the prevailing opinion of the 1950's, Gordon, a businessman of prominence and standing, could only be regarded as a very curious and puzzling nonconformist. It was true that the Massey Commissioners had, five years earlier, expressed some of the same odd notions about American influence in Canada; but, after all, three of the Massey Commissioners were professors and one was a retired diplomat who had long ago ceased to have any contact with business. Plainly, they were negligible people and their report could be, and had been, disregarded. Gordon was different; he was a businessman, highly regarded by the Liberal Party, who wanted to take positive action. Something, he felt, must be done to stop or slow down the American take-over of Canadian industries and natural resources and to expose the complacency with which Canadians watched this surrender of their birthright. Perhaps he himself might be able to bring about a halt to this accelerating and fatal trend. St. Laurent's invitation to come to Ottawa may have clarified this vague, insistent hope. Perhaps his decision to accept only a senior Cabinet post may have been prompted by the subconscious realization that only thus could he effect changes of any real importance. In any event, these cloudy aspirations had been quickly dissipated in the alien atmosphere of Ottawa.

Obviously, there was not the slightest chance of instant political power. A junior minister could not possibly influence economic policy so long as Howe remained in the Cabinet; and so long as Howe remained in the Cabinet, the sell-out of Canadian industries and natural resources to American interests would continue. The direct road to action was certainly blocked; but was it not possible to start a more circuitous approach, by arousing public discussion, inviting the Canadians to consider their future and examine the economic policies on which they had relied so long? With these ideas in mind, Gordon drafted an article for the *International Journal* which questioned certain aspects of Canada's economic policy, especially its unrestricted sale of basic industries to foreigners, and proposed still another Royal Commission to investigate Canada's probable future in the light of its existing way of life. This, Gordon realized, was a novel and perhaps politically disturbing proposal; and, as a faithful Liberal, he had no wish to embarrass the government. He dispatched a copy of the draft article to K.W. Taylor, the Deputy Minister of Finance and, a few weeks later, Walter Harris, the new minister, asked him if he "would mind very much if the government took over" his idea.[35] Gordon, Harris explained, would have to give up the idea of publishing the article; but he would be rewarded by the realization of its main proposal in the appointment of a Royal Commission on Canada's Economic Prospects, which Harris would announce in his budget speech in the spring of 1955.

Gordon was, of course, hugely delighted; but he was also curious and perhaps a little puzzled. The initiative for this startling new departure of government had obviously come from Walter Harris, who had been Minister of Finance for less than a year; but how had it been regarded by C.D. Howe, who for twenty years had held senior office in the Liberal Cabinet? Of course, the new Commission, composed probably of devout Liberals, might predict a glowing future for Canada under the beneficent continuation of Liberal rule; but, if Walter Gordon, with his "rather independent turn of mind," was to chair the inquiry, this seemed a little uncertain. Howe was away when the Cabinet finally decided to appoint the Commission; he had opposed the idea from the start. As one journalist wittily put it, "an investigation of the Canadian economy was, in Mr. Howe's view, an investigation of C.D. Howe; and he saw no need for that."[36] He had to put up with it however, and the casual dismissal of his objections was at least a slight sign of the weakening of his hitherto omnipotent authority in the Cabinet.

The Royal Commission on Canada's Economic Prospects, with Gordon as chairman, Omer Lussier, A.E. Grauer, Andrew Stewart and Raymond Gushue, as fellow commissioners, and the gifted Douglas Le Pan, then minister counsellor in the Canadian Embassy at Washington, as secretary and director of research, was established in June, 1955. Gordon and Le Pan spent the next few months in defining the scope and nature of the inquiry, planning a research programme, and engaging a suitable expert staff. Gordon's concern at the growing magnitude of the American takeover of Canadian industry had been the real genesis of the Commission he was now chairing; but he had no intention of making the investigation an exclusive field for the exercise of his hobby-horse. His report was intended to be a comprehensive and impartial survey of the existing state of the Canadian economy and a reasoned and cautious forecast of its probable future. The truth about the alienation of Canada's resources and industries would emerge from the report; but, on the other hand, Gordon hoped and believed that it would emerge very soon, for he intended to complete the investigation by the end of 1956, in good time for the general election in the following spring.

The brutal truth of the volume and extent of American investment in Canada would have shocked anyone who made the slightest attempt to get at the facts. The dozen years from 1945 to 1957 witnessed an astonishingly rapid increase in the amount of British and foreign capital invested in Canada. The total grew from $7 billion in 1945 to $17.4 billion in 1957; it had, in other words, considerably more than doubled itself in twelve years.[37] It was an alarming total, and the fact that $10 billion of the $17.4 billion represented direct rather than portfolio investment, made it more terrifying still.[38] Non-resident ownership and control of Canadian industry was obviously growing; and the foreign takeover of Canadian firms increased annually, with the exception of a few years in the post-war period, and in 1956 reached a total of 54.[39]

A wide distribution of this ownership and control among a number of British and foreign countries would have made it distinctly less ominous; but, in 1957, $8.4 billion of the total $10 billion foreign direct investment in Canada – more than four-fifths of the whole – came from the United States.[40] A North American continental economy, largely owned, controlled, and directed by Americans, had definitely come into existence; and its dominion extended, though somewhat unevenly, over a wide range of economic activities in Canada. In 1957, residents of the United States controlled 70% of the total capital invested in Canadian petroleum and natural gas, 52% of the total in mining and smelting and 43% of the total in manufacturing.[41] Canadians still managed to hold most of their own in primary iron and steel, textiles, beverages, and merchandising; but in rubber products, electrical apparatus, and automobiles and parts, American dominance was overwhelming.

VI

The independence of Canada, economic, political, or cultural, was certainly not a major concern of the Liberal government in the middle 1950's. It had never worried either St. Laurent or Howe; and what Howe and St. Laurent thought important, or didn't think important, still largely determined the course of government in Canada. The resignation of Abbott, Claxton and Chevrier had confirmed the lofty and lonely station of the two ageing leaders in the Cabinet; but it had narrowed rather than enlarged the scope of their interests. Howe's main aims were still the continuation of his own dictatorial economic powers and the invention of new and still more imposing schemes of economic development. St. Laurent was concentrating more and more exclusively on the problems of federal-provincial relations, which, together with the issue of the imperial relationship, had been his main preoccupations in his early years as Prime Minister. He found it increasingly hard to shake off his recurrent bouts of lethargy and pessimism; he grew more and more reluctant to leave Canada even for important conferences. His one extended journey abroad, which was prompted by Nehru's pressing invitation to visit India, was outwardly a brilliant success and actually a very hollow achievement. There was no meeting of minds between Nehru and St. Laurent. Their mutual incomprehension remained unaltered and Canadian policy in the Far East unchanged. Early in March, 1954, St. Laurent returned to Ottawa, an exhausted man.[42]

He was roused from his lethargy by a highly significant event in one of his favourite fields of political manoeuvre, federal-provincial relations. It was a particularly significant occurrence because it took place in a province which St. Laurent, like King, had always regarded with hypersensitive vigilance, the Province of Quebec. Quebec had been, of course, the one province to reject the federal tax-rental proposals adopted by the Federal-Provincial Conference of December, 1950. Then Duplessis had defiantly declared that his province would never surrender the right to tax the income of its own citizens. For three long years, he made no move to make good his claim. Then, early in 1954, he suddenly broke his silence and more than made up for his long delay by the abrupt and truculent fashion in which he finally exercised his vaunted powers. The Quebec legislature imposed a 15% tax on personal incomes in the province; but this, Duplessis insisted, was not to be an additional burden on its taxpayers. The provinces, he claimed, held a constitutional priority in direct taxation; and residents of Quebec were therefore entitled to deduct the amount of their provincial tax from their federal tax returns.[43]

The Quebec tax law was a hard, sudden shock, but it was not by any means the end of Duplessis's provocations. A strange and sinister change seemed to have come over the man who had been so polite and complimentary to St. Laurent at the Federal-Provincial Conference of 1950. In an instant he had become offensively aggressive. Throughout the summer of 1954 he mingled uncompromising assertions of Quebec's provincial autonomy with denunciations of federal centralization, and abuse of federal policies and appointments. St. Laurent made no reply, partly because he still felt very tired and partly because – though increasingly subject to quick bursts of temper – he was not fundamentally combative by nature. His silence lasted until September; but then, his strength recovered and his anger at last aroused, he decided to reply. Almost everything about the Premier of Quebec – his corrupt political methods, his abuse of power and his love of gross personal vilification – offended the upright and fastidious St. Laurent. He determined on a frontal and vigorous counter-attack. In two unrehearsed and vehement speeches, he rejected Duplessis's extreme provincial claims, ridiculed his criticisms, and sounded a high, confident, and all-Canadian note. He even went so far as to assert – what ten years later had become an acknowledged heresy in French Canada – that Quebec was a province "like the others."[44]

Many English Canadians rejoiced at the astounding spectacle of a French-Canadian Prime Minister taking on the incorrigible French-Canadian Premier in such a spirited and disrespectful manner. Their satisfaction was very short-lived. St. Laurent decided that his confrontation with Duplessis had gone far enough. His natural caution and moderation re-asserted themselves, but so also did his love for his own native province and his concern for its unfortunate taxpayers, now threatened with double taxation. Duplessis's preposterous claim of provincial priority in direct taxation must, of course, be refuted; and he, Harris, and Jean Lesage, now Minister of Northern Affairs and National Resources, had all done so very emphatically. But rejection of a constitutional claim did not necessarily mean dismissal of a real provincial need for more revenue. Surely some compromise was possible, some arrangement which would give Quebec what she wanted, even at the expense of some change in the existing tax-rental agreements. In April, during the debate in the Commons, St. Laurent had offered to consider other possibilities; and early in October, when, as a result of the intervention of a friendly neutral, he met Duplessis in the Windsor Hotel in Montreal, he was more than ready to negotiate. Within an hour, the two antagonists had reached an amicable agreement. Duplessis consented to abandon his constitutional claim to provincial priority in income taxation. St. Laurent promised to amend the federal tax law so as to permit Quebec taxpayers to deduct 10% of their federal tax; and, since an abatement of 5% already existed for the benefit of provincial income taxpayers, this meant that Quebec would completely escape double taxation.[45]

The famous "compromise" was obviously no compromise at all. St. Laurent had received an empty constitutional concession; Duplessis had got away with good, hard cash. Suddenly, their great oratorical combats of September took on a suspicious look of unreality. Did they really differ seriously about the nature of Canadian federalism, or were they simply two old clowns chasing each other around a circus ring and hitting each other with toy balloons? Their agreement had not been a formal agreement between two governments; it looked, in fact, much more like a sordid "hotel-room deal"; but it had serious political consequences none the less.[46] The Cabinet accepted St. Laurent's settlement, but it felt obliged to correct the general Canadian impression that Ottawa regarded Quebec as a favourite child which must be indulged in everything. The Prime Minister wrote to all the other provincial premiers describing the agreement with Duplessis and offering them the same terms. During the session which began on January 7, 1955, Parliament ratified this promise and enabled any province which preferred Quebec's chosen alternative to terminate its existing tax rental agreement.

The tax rental agreements, authorized by the Conference of December, 1950, and negotiated with nine provinces during 1951 and 1952, did not expire until March 31, 1957. That was still two years away, but it was perfectly clear that the whole tax rental system had received a heavy blow from which it was very unlikely to recover. St. Laurent himself was among the first to reach this conclusion. The deal with Duplessis was his own handiwork; but it was an ugly, questionable exception in an otherwise general arrangement, and he determined to find a new and different financial plan which would satisfy all the provincial premiers. In April, 1955, representatives from all the provinces met in Ottawa for a preliminary, informal discussion of the financial problem; and early in October, only a year after the notorious "hotel-room deal" with Duplessis, they returned for a formal federal-provincial conference on the same subject.

As in the past, St. Laurent began with a review of the various possible financial plans; but, though he made no attempt to present a specific federal proposal, it was perfectly plain from the beginning that he favoured a relaxation of the rigid tax-rental system.[47] The man whom Duplessis had denounced as the great Canadian centralizer, was in fact carrying forward a major decentralization of Canadian public affairs. Only ten years before, at the Dominion-Provincial Conference on Reconstruction in 1945, the federal government had presented itself as a kind of twentieth century benevolent despot, an all-embracing, enlightened and benign authority which would maintain high employment, regulate public investment and construction, promote public health and provide social security at uniform levels throughout the nation. All this vast programme had been contained in a fat volume with a green cover, "The Green Book," which socialists like Douglas of

Saskatchewan had reverently regarded as the new testament of the post-war world.[48]

St. Laurent repudiated the gospel of "The Green Book" and deserted the road Canada had been following for the past fifteen years. Without bothering to call another federal-provincial conference, he announced his government's definite proposals early in the parliamentary session of 1956. The provinces were given unlimited freedom of choice. They could either continue their existing tax-rental agreements with Ottawa, or they could tax their citizens themselves, up to 10% of the federal personal and corporation income tax, and 50% of the federal succession duties, with an equivalent abatement of payment due to the federal treasury. In any case, whether they chose the first plan, or the second, or a combination of the two, most of them would be given a large, new lump of money, called an "equalization grant," which represented the difference between what any provincial government could collect in taxes at the standard rates, and the average of what could be collected by the two richest provinces, Ontario and British Columbia.[49] Obviously, the equalization grant was a radical innovation. The federal government had chosen to distribute the national revenue among the provinces by a method far more primitive and crude than those it had adopted to redistribute personal income among individuals. The equalization grant was a handout without strings – the old unconditional subsidy back again and bigger than ever – which each receiving province could use for whatever purpose it fancied. The initiative was passing, at the instance of the federal government itself, from Ottawa to the provincial capitals. Duplessis, St. Laurent, and provincial rights had triumphed over federal leadership and the national interest.

VII

This fresh success of St. Laurent's in federal-provincial relations coincided almost exactly with a new advance by Howe in both his own power and in the nation's growth and productivity. In September, 1955, when John Deutsch and the other expert civil servants were putting the finishing touches to the masterly new scheme of equalization grants, Howe and St. Laurent, together with federal officials, provincial representatives, and Canadian and American oil men, were holding solemn conferences over the still unsettled future of Trans-Canada Pipe Lines. Trans-Canada was the most ambitious, the most spectacular, and the most controversial of all Howe's enterprises; but, despite its monopolizing complications, it did not by any means absorb all of his time or divert him from his other major interests. He was Minister of Trade and Commerce; but he was also Minister of Defence Production, an excellent post with exceptionally wide powers which he had acquired four years earlier. His belief in its vital importance had not diminished in the slightest. He remained – what he had always been – a very good North American, quickly responsive to the militant moods of Washington and New York, very much a loyal citizen of that era of Communist containment and military preparedness over which President Eisenhower and John Foster Dulles presided. For Howe the great struggle between Liberal democracy and Communist dictatorship was just as real – and just as justifiably demanding – as it had been five years earlier when the Korean War broke out. He assumed – as a matter beyond all question – that the great Canadian rearmament programme which he had begun in 1951 must continue, and that he himself must continue to organize and direct it.

Unfortunately, a small impediment – unimportant really, yet legally binding – stood in his way. The Defence Production Act, which established the Department of Defence Production, and gave its minister quite extraordinary coercive powers, was to expire on July 31, 1956. Like the Emergency Powers Act, it had been passed in the winter of 1951, when the Korean War was raging; but, although it seemed to possess all the justification of wartime necessity, the Progressive-Conservatives and the C.C.F. members had vigorously opposed its passage. The storm which had greeted its introduction in 1951 was a very unfavourable omen for the reception of its renewal in 1955. In the meantime, the Korean War had dragged itself to an inglorious end, and Howe's prestige in the House of Commons had suffered a marked decline. His rude, contemptuous manner, and his dictatorial airs had rasped and antagonized many members. He knew that the House would fiercely oppose any attempt to prolong his exceptional powers; but he was absolutely determined on their indefinite prolongation. He demanded that the Defence Production Act be amended by the repeal of the section which provided for its expiration on July 31, 1956. The amendment, he insisted, must be introduced early in 1955, long before the date of the act's originally intended demise, and pushed through with the whole weight of the big Liberal majority.

Yet it was St. Laurent, not Howe, who introduced the amending resolution on March 10, 1955.[50] Howe may have urged the Prime Minister's sponsorship as a convincing sign that the amendment was the result of a united Cabinet decision and not another manifestation of his own greedy lust for power. Fleming denied the need for the extension of the Minister's special authority in a speech of considerable length, and Drew and Green followed more briefly; but the March debate did not become a real test of strength, for in a few days Howe left Ottawa for a visit to Australia and New Zealand. He did not return until early in the summer; and it was he, not St. Laurent, who, on June 7, moved second reading of the amendment to the Defence Production Act. The Opposition leaped immediately on this curious discrepancy. " . . . Everybody knows," Donald Fleming announced confidently, "that the Cabinet has been divided on this question." It was a cunningly devised taunt, and it roused Howe immediately. "That is an absolute falsehood," he shouted angrily.[51]

This furious exchange foreshadowed accurately the prolonged and stormy debate which followed. The Progressive-Conservatives quickly realized that the defeat of the amendment to the Defence Production Act was a great and popular cause, and they appropriated it with a vigour and enthusiasm which they had not shown for some time. During 1954, George Drew had been ill, and his leadership had been criticized and questioned; but he was back in Parliament now, apparently as fit as ever, and the renewal of his own strength seemed to coincide with his party's recovery of its vigour and confidence. In the summer of 1955, the Tory Party was spoiling for a fight; and all of its members were convinced that they had a strong, valid, unanswerable case to argue. The enormous difference between the circumstances of 1951, when the Defence Production Act was first passed, and those of 1955, when the government sought the extension of its extraordinary powers, had been the burden of Donald Fleming's speech in March, and continued to be the main theme of most Conservative speakers in the following summer.[52]

The contrast, in fact, was inescapable and striking. In 1951, Canada was at war in Korea, strategic materials were scarce, and the Canadian government had just begun its re-armament programme. In 1955, the last Canadian soldiers were returning from Korea, the shortage of supplies was over, and the expenditure of billions had effectively re-armed Canada. If, as Howe had conceded, his arbitrary powers ought not to be "continuing powers," why should he now demand that they be continued? Howe had really no answer. He had, he admitted, agreed that these exceptional powers ought not to be continuing powers: but, he insisted, "I do maintain that if they were necessary in 1951, they are just as necessary today."[53]

Why, demanded the Opposition? All Howe could say in reply was that his plans for supersonic planes and guided missiles would take many years yet to carry out. In 1955, it was not a particularly convincing argument, but its lack of popular appeal did not shake Howe's determination in the slightest. "The situation has reached the point," he declared emphatically, late in June when the debate had been going on at intervals for nearly three weeks, "where the government must insist that this legislation be passed."[54] It was this stubborn insistence on the will of one man and the power of a submissive parliamentary majority which finally captured the attention and then the sympathetic interest of newspaper editors and commentators throughout the country. The Progressive-Conservatives became aware of the inspiring fact that, in the eyes of many Canadians, they were fighting the battle of liberal democracy against arbitrary dictatorship.

They doubled the number and the venom of their attacks. They badgered Howe into a rather emotional confession of his trials and tribulations as

Minister of Defence. They taunted St. Laurent so successfully that he finally broke his embarrassing silence and spoke briefly and moderately in support of the bill. It looked as though the noisy debate would never end. Walter Harris moved the previous question; but this motion, though it prevented further amendments, was itself debatable without limit and the filibuster continued. In the end, with everybody close to exhaustion and everybody's hopes fixed on compromise, St. Laurent belatedly decided that enough was more than enough. On Thursday, July 7, the weary Howe left for a four-day fishing trip, giving his colleagues, as he departed, his casual permission to patch up some kind of conclusion to the debate. St. Laurent took him at his word, and perhaps a little more than his word. Over the weekend, he and George Drew amicably negotiated a settlement. The Department of Defence Production was to be recognized as a permanent department of government; but the special powers of the minister, to which the Opposition had taken such strong objection, were to expire in four years.[55]

It was George Drew and the Tories, not St. Laurent, Howe and the Liberals, who emerged with credit from the long debate. The final compromise, if it had been granted a good deal earlier, would have been regarded as a generous, statesmanlike, Liberal concession; but it had been denied so long and so stubbornly that inevitably it took on the appearance of a hard-won Tory triumph, conceded in Howe's absence by colleagues who were ready to let him down, if not exactly betray him, behind his back. This cynical interpretation became so general that Howe himself may have come to believe all or part of it; but it was not in his nature to dispute the Prime Minister's decision, and anyway, he had other things, including particularly the tremendous project of the transcontinental natural gas pipeline, on his mind. That vast enterprise, which reached the penultimate stage of its development in the early autumn of 1955, had been slowly maturing for years. Howe had given it a great deal of his time, his indefatigable energy, and his amazing powers of organization. He expected to carry out other big jobs in future, for, like St. Laurent, he confidently assumed that the Liberals would win the next general election; but he knew also that nothing could ever rival the transcontinental pipeline. The pipeline was to be the crowning achievement of his career.

VIII

There were three possible large markets for the exportable surplus of Alberta's natural gas. Two of them – British Columbia in the west and Ontario and Quebec in the east – were situated in Canada; one, the American midwest, lay to the south. It would clearly be a good deal easier and more profitable to pipe the gas down into the midwestern American states than it would be to carry it across the mountains to British Columbia or over the Precambrian Shield to Ontario and Quebec. Alberta in the north, like Texas in the far south, would thus contribute to a continental pool of the wonderful new form of energy; and an international network of pipelines would distribute it, by the most direct and cheapest routes, to both sides of the Canada-U.S.A. border. The Alberta producers, which were mainly large international American companies, naturally preferred this method; but it was opposed by Canadian national feeling, and by powerful political forces in Canada, one of which was the federal government itself. As early as March, 1953, C.D. Howe laid down a firm general principle which would govern the distribution of the new fuel " . . . The policy of the government of Canada," he declared, "is to refuse permits for moving natural gas by pipeline across an international boundary until such time as we are convinced that there can be no economic use, present or future, for that natural gas within Canada."[56]

This looked like a solid and final engagement, but it was not quite as absolute as it looked. The expense of moving natural gas east and west across the continent from Alberta would be so colossal that only two methods seemed capable of financing it. The federal government, with the help of the provinces concerned, could build the pipeline itself; or, with the inducement of commercial privileges and money subsidies, it might persuade a commercial company to do it instead. The C.C.F. urged public ownership and a good many Canadians, who were nationalists though not socialists, favoured this familiar Canadian device. St. Laurent and Howe did not reject state construction and control as a possible last resort; but they much preferred to have a commercial company carry out the huge undertaking. This, as it turned out, was a fatal mistake. Once committed to a certain definite course, there was little real possibility of turning back or changing direction. The Government of Canada was driven irresistibly onward, compromising the principles which it had itself laid down for the distribution of Canadian natural gas, getting more and more deeply involved in an enterprise which it had hoped to delegate to an independent company.

The coils of this inextricable involvement tightened slowly but surely. In 1952, the Government of Alberta decided that an exportable surplus existed, at least in the north, and Westcoast Transmission was authorized to pipe natural gas from the Peace River country down to Vancouver. In order to make this venture economically viable, Howe agreed to give Westcoast Transmission a licence to export gas from Vancouver into the United States. It was the first open recognition of the hard, unpleasant fact that independent companies would not be capable of moving gas to distant parts of Canada unless they were permitted to tap profitable markets in the United States. This was, of course, an important exception to Howe's firm "Canada First" principle; but it was not to be confined to Westcoast Transmission, for by this time the competitive struggle for the right to carry natural gas from Alberta eastward to Ontario and Quebec had already begun. Two separate companies, Western Pipe Lines and Trans-Canada Pipe Lines, had already appeared. They differed widely in both their composition and their plans. Western Pipe Lines Limited was an association of three important Canadian financial houses; Trans-Canada Pipe Lines was a wholly-owned subsidiary of a Texas gas company, headed by Clinton ("Clint") Murchison, one of C. D. Howe's numerous American friends. The principals of Western Pipe Lines had concluded that construction across the Precambrian Shield to Ontario would be prohibitively expensive and they decided in favour of a line from southern Alberta eastward to Winnipeg and then south to Emerson on the United States border, with spur lines along the way. Trans-Canada adopted a completely different and infinitely more daring plan. Murchison proposed to build above the upper lakes, across the Shield, and down into southern Ontario and Quebec.[57]

It was a curious contrast. An exclusively Canadian company proposed to export Alberta natural gas to the United States. A wholly-owned American subsidiary planned to market it in eastern Canada. By itself, each company was unacceptable, though for very different reasons; but united they might form an organization which would exactly suit Howe's purpose. It was this enticing prospect which slowly but inextricably entangled the Canadian government in a hazardous enterprise from which it had hoped to stay aloof. In January, 1954, Howe persuaded the two companies to unite in a merger named Trans-Canada Pipe Lines.[58] This new united company was to be permitted to export some of its natural gas to the United States, but only after it had completed its main line from southern Alberta to Toronto and Montreal. Very quickly it became obvious – what a less sanguine promoter than Howe might have anticipated – that this basic undertaking was much too difficult financially for even the united company to carry out. Building a pipeline across the formidable expanse of the Precambrian Shield seemed such a dangerously risky speculation that neither the producers in Alberta nor the distributors in Ontario were ready to sign firm contracts with the new Trans-Canada; and without firm contracts for the supply and sale of their natural gas, the company simply could not acquire the needed capital.

There was, as might have been expected, only one thing left to do. In desperation, Trans-Canada appealed to the Canadian government; but the Canadian government, somewhat unexpectedly, was not of one mind about rushing to the rescue of the company. Howe, of course, confidently expected generous aid; but Harris, the Minister of Finance, declined to give what he interpreted as a government guarantee for a bond issue, and James Coyne, Governor of the Bank of Canada, imposed stiff terms for a relatively small investment by his Industrial Development Bank. Trans-Canada Pipe Lines, like the St. Lawrence Seaway, was a major project of the Liberal government. It was clearly at an impasse; but St. Laurent was too far sunk in pessimism and lethargy to compel his quarrelling junior colleagues to agree on a satisfactory way out. The appeal for financial assistance failed. On March 17, 1955, Nathan Tanner, the President of Trans-Canada, announced that construction would have to be postponed until 1956.[59]

It was the first time that Howe had suffered defeat in a major enterprise. He was furious, but he was not yet willing to admit failure. He knew he had lost an important engagement, but he was still determined to win the war, though, for awhile, neither he nor the officers of Trans-Canada had the vaguest idea of how this miracle was to be accomplished. It was Mitchell Sharp, then Associate Deputy Minister in the Department of Trade and Commerce, who first conceived the idea of a Crown corporation.[60] Crown corporations were very familiar institutions to C. D. Howe, for he had created a good many of them during the war; but this Crown corporation was different. It was to be financed by the federal government and the government of Ontario, and called the Northern Ontario Pipe Line Crown Corporation. Its sole function was to build, under Trans-Canada's expert supervision, a pipeline through the barren and unprofitable territory from the Manitoba boundary east to the town of Kapuskasing in northern Ontario.

This lengthy section, which was about a third of the total length of the pipeline and would likely amount to more than a third of its total cost, was to be leased to Trans-Canada with an option to purchase. It was a huge contribution, so huge that Trans-Canada Pipe Lines began to take on the odd appearance of another great Canadian essay in public ownership, under the rather thin disguise of private enterprise. A number of interested parties, including the Province of Ontario, began to argue that if governments had been forced to give so much aid to an obviously weak and dependent private company, they would be well advised in their own interests to take it over completely. With the support of Ontario, the federal government might have defied the opposition of Alberta and its producers, and made of Trans-Canada Pipe Lines a national institution comparable to Trans-Canada Air Lines. But St. Laurent shrank back in alarm from the political dangers of setting prices for the purchase and sale of natural gas, even if the task was carried out independently by a Crown corporation.[61] Once again the government had rejected an opportunity to extricate itself from the increasing complications of its involvement.

There were consequences and they came swiftly. Even though the Northern Ontario Pipe Line Crown Corporation had lifted a great burden of expense from Trans-Canada Pipe Lines, that company was still very far from being the self-sufficient organization for which Howe and St. Laurent had vainly hoped. A pipeline could not be built without pipe – hundreds of miles of it; but Trans-Canada had neither the money nor the credit which would ensure payment for such a huge order of steel. In its extremity, it now resorted to a politically very dangerous expedient. It had, for the moment at least, exhausted the generosity of Canadian governments; it now turned to the greatest of its American pipeline rivals, Tennessee Gas Transmission, for financial assistance. Tennessee's president, the ambitious and pugnacious Gardiner Symonds, agreed to take over the liability for Trans-Canada's enormous order of steel, but he exacted a very heavy price for his compliance. He insisted that his company and its associates, Gulf Oil of Canada and Hudson's Bay Oil and Gas, both American-owned, must be given a controlling interest in the Canadian firm. Each of these three American corporations was to be allotted 17% of Trans-Canada's equity, or a total of 51%. "Clint" Murchison of Texas Gas and the partners of the original Western Pipe Lines project, were to divide the remaining 49% between them. By a single, decisive act of multiplication, the solitary American interest had become four; and among them the four controlled 75½% of a major Canadian national enterprise.[62]

IX

The great debate over Trans-Canada Pipe Lines, which began on March 15, 1956 and lasted, with one long interval, until June 7, combined all the essential elements of good drama. It was a struggle between two forces which, despite the overwhelming Liberal parliamentary majority, were not really unequal. The Progressive-Conservatives and the C.C.F. were united this time, as they had not been in the fight over the Defence Production Bill; and although they were not entirely of one mind about the best way to build the pipeline, they firmly agreed that the chosen Liberal method was the worst. To sponsor and assist the takeover of a great Canadian enterprise by a gang of American oil and gas companies was, they shouted angrily, not simply a colossal political blunder, but also a dreadful political crime. The conviction that this time, more than ever before, the opposition was fighting in the national interest, supplied its main drive; but there were other sources from which it drew strength for its incredibly prolonged resistance. Increasingly Tories and C.C.F.ers came to feel – and a great number of Canadians began to feel with them – that they were fighting, nor merely against a pet Liberal project, but also against the Liberal Party itself – against its twenty years of unbroken rule, its complacent assumption of administrative superiority, its arrogant pretension as the Canadian "party of government."

It was this sense of the political righteousness of the Opposition's cause which redressed the huge imbalance of forces inside the Canadian House of Commons. The Tories and C.C.F.ers felt, for the first time, a curious and exciting sense of equality; they knew also – for the Defence Production debate had amply proved the fact – that they possessed in the filibuster an instrument of the greatest political potency. Inevitably the Trans-Canada debate became a struggle between two primitive parliamentary weapons, filibuster and closure, the device of prolonging discussion and the power of stopping it abruptly. This combat would have been dramatic enough by itself; but its tension was heightened by another vital factor, time. Time, in fact, was the essence of the whole debate. Ontario had consented to join the federal government in the Northern Ontario Crown Corporation on condition that the pipeline would be begun in 1956. Tennessee Gas Transmission's option on the huge necessary order of pipe would expire on June 7, 1956. If the Liberals could push through the essential legislation before June 7, Trans-Canada would be saved. If the Conservatives and the C.C.F.ers could prevent the bill's passage until after June 7, the whole project would have to be postponed, and might be radically altered or abandoned.[63]

On March 15, when Howe introduced the resolution for the establishment of the Northern Ontario Pipe Line Crown Corporation, this deadline seemed comfortably far off; but the government had already begun to fear, and the Opposition had already begun to suspect, that Trans-Canada would never make it in time. Once again, the inadequacy of the method on which St. Laurent and Howe had so stubbornly relied became rapidly manifest. Trans-Canada had been given much, in evasion or defiance of the government's own aims and principles. Though St. Laurent and Howe had rejected public ownership, they had consented to build a third of the pipeline as a public work. They had permitted Trans-Canada to export gas to the United States, though they had sworn solemnly never to issue such permits until the needs of Canada, present and future, would be amply satisfied. Even the takeover of three-quarters of Trans-Canada's equity by a group of American oil and natural gas companies had apparently left the Canadian government unmoved. It had made many sacrifices for Trans-Canada; but, as the spring of 1956 came slowly on, it became clear that these sacrifices were vain. In the eyes of the North American investment community of 1956, Trans-Canada's only real asset was its right to export to the United States. Unfortunately, the Canadian permission to export was worthless unless it was complemented by an American permission to import; and Trans-Canada's application to the Federal Power Commission of the United States, which was opposed by a powerful American rival, might be indefinitely delayed, and ultimately rejected.[64]

This was the final crushing blow. Without the clear prospect of an entry into the profitable market of the American northwest, Trans-Canada could not even obtain enough capital to finance the western section of the line. The government was forced to suspend all action on the Northern Ontario Pipe Line Bill, while the directors of Trans-Canada struggled to find funds;

but, in the end, even the mighty American tycoons who now controlled the company had to admit defeat. Confronted by this last, crucial dilemma, the Canadian government had to choose between two possible courses, both of which it had refused to take before: it could either take over Trans-Canada as a national enterprise, or it could loan it enough money to build the western section as far as Winnipeg. In a final, almost frantic appeal to his colleagues, Howe begged them not to let his favourite brain child expire; and the Cabinet, reluctantly and with many misgivings, decided to come to Trans-Canada's aid.[65] On May 8, the government announced that, with suitable provisions for interest and repayment, it proposed to loan Trans-Canada up to 90% of the cost of constructing the western section of the pipeline as far as Winnipeg. The new resolution, authorizing the loan, was piled on top of the old resolution, moved on March 15 and still in abeyance, authorizing the Northern Ontario Pipe Line Crown Corporation. And the deadline, June 7, was less than a month away.

The fractious and noisy debate which followed was essentially a contest in parliamentary generalship and parliamentary strategy and tactics. Each side had a general staff which planned the campaign as a whole, and devised most of its particular manoeuvres. Howe was not, as might have been expected, a prominent Liberal staff officer; he knew little and cared less about the intricacies of parliamentary tactics, and in the pipeline debate he simply did what he was told. St. Laurent, Walter Harris, the House Leader, and J. W. Pickersgill, now Minister of Citizenship and Immigration, and an acknowledged master of political finesse, were the principal members at Liberal headquarters. It was an experienced and tenacious group, but it was pitted against a combination of Conservatives and C.C.F.ers which displayed a daring, an ingenuity, and a fanatical determination unique in Canadian history. Its recognized Chief of General Staff was Stanley Knowles, the member for Winnipeg North Centre, a tall, slight man, with a quiet but commanding presence, who had not only acquired a vast range of knowledge about Canadian affairs, but who had also developed an extraordinary expertise in parliamentary procedure. The Conservative E. Davie Fulton was perhaps his most inventive and indefatigable lieutenant in the opposition's campaign of obstruction; but Drew, Coldwell, the C.C.F. leader, and the combative Donald Fleming also repeatedly intervened in the debate.[66]

The design of the opposition was simple. Knowles and his team did not intend to debate the pipeline measure, which they regarded as an outrageous sellout totally unworthy of serious consideration; they planned to prevent its passage by an unending succession of points of order, questions of privilege, procedural objections, and appeals from the Speaker's ruling.[67] If there had been time, the Liberals might have talked this filibuster out; but there was not enough time, and the only way to get the bill through before the deadline was to cut short each stage of the debate by closure. Closure was a perfectly normal, and frequently used device in Westminster, London; but in Ottawa it still looked unfamiliar and dubious. It had been invented and so far used only by Conservative governments, and Mackenzie King had taught Canadians to regard it as a hideous instrument of Tory oppression. Its adoption in this crisis by the Liberals had an immediate and drastic effect, which St. Laurent and Harris might have anticipated but apparently did not. It completed a transformation which had been going on now for several years and revealed the Liberal government, shorn of all its disguises and reduced to its essential nature, as the ruthless tyrant of Canada. Rapidly the whole nation became absorbed in this unequal but prolonged combat between the huge and domineering Liberal Goliath and the agile and intrepid Tory David. If the Speaker, René Beaudoin and his Deputy, William Robinson, had enforced the rules with proper firmness, the debate could never have gone on so long; but Beaudoin, though his knowledge of procedure was vast, had a professional's interest in discussing its niceties, even allowing his own decisions to be challenged and debated; and Robinson's hesitations and inconsistencies made him an easy victim of opposition. The debate went on and on; and finally, on Friday, June 1 – "Black Friday" it was called thereafter – the Canadian House of Commons dissolved into a total chaos of challenges, denunciations, jeers, cheers, and ribald songs and demonstrations.[68]

When an unrepentant but sobered House met on Monday morning, June 4, it was obvious that the end was close. St. Laurent moved closure on June 5, and early in the morning of June 6, the Pipeline Bill passed its third and final reading. It was put through all its stages in the Senate in a single day, and on June 7, just a few hours before the expiry of the option for pipe, it received the Royal Assent.

X

That tumultuous year, 1956, gave the Canadians more incitements to passionate debate than any other single year had done since 1944, with its angry controversy over conscription. The pipeline debate had ended early in the morning of June 6; and, late in July, less than two months after, another issue, apparently remote, but potentially just as explosive, made its first appearance.

On July 26, Colonel Gamal Abdel Nasser, the President of the new Republic of Egypt, nationalized that famous international waterway, the Suez Canal. This violent action may have been meditated for some time but it may also have been prompted, or hastened, by another disturbing event which had taken place only a week before. On July 19, Dulles, the American Secretary of State, bluntly announced that the United States had withdrawn its guarantee of a substantial loan from the World Bank for the construction of the Aswan Dam. This abrupt move placed Britain in an impossible position. The British government had also agreed, from its slender resources, to support the guarantee; but the financial burden of the whole loan was beyond its strength, and it was obliged to renounce its share. The United States had effectively wrecked the project of the Anglo-American loan; but it was Britain which had to suffer the consequences of its collapse.

To Nasser, the High Dam at Aswan, which, he declared, was "seventeen times greater than the Pyramids," was a work of great national importance and international prestige; and the sudden cancellation of the loan which was to finance it, provided a reason – or an occasion – for the seizure of the one great foreign-owned asset in Egypt, the Suez Canal. For the United States, the nationalization of the canal was of comparatively minor importance; for Britain, it was a major disaster. The British government had a 44% interest in the ownership of the canal; and, as a great trading nation, with an industrial economy increasingly dependent on Middle Eastern oil, Britain saw the canal as a vital link in its economic lifetime. To Anthony Eden, the new British Premier, and the senior members of his Cabinet, the seizure of the canal was an insufferable affront. They burned to avenge it; but unfortunately, by one of those ill-fated mischances of history, they had lost all power of instant retaliation. Two years earlier, as much for British convenience as for the satisfaction of Egyptian national pride, the British government had agreed to bring its military presence in Egypt to an end. In June, 1956, just a few weeks before Nasser's sudden coup, the last British soldiers marched out of the Egyptian base.[69]

The furious but baffled British insisted that the Egyptian President must be made to yield, and the international control of the canal restored, by force if necessary. The Cabinet, and particularly Eden and Macmillan, looked on Nasser as a kind of international thug, a post-war reincarnation of Hitler or Mussolini, who, unless he was stopped at once, would go on breaking treaties and annexing properties until he set the whole Middle East, and possibly the whole world, aflame.[70] At Ottawa, Diefenbaker made it quite clear that the Progressive-Conservatives shared this alarmist view of the crisis; but, despite his demands, the Canadian government refused to be drawn into a formal protest against the Egyptian seizure of the canal.[71] Pearson made the obvious point that Canada had no share in the ownership of the Canal, and no great commercial interest in its operation; but there were other, undisclosed, and characteristically Canadian reasons for his government's deliberate detachment. St. Laurent, like King, was inclined to be suspicious of British designs, and hypersensitively resentful of alleged British slights. Pearson was invariably reluctant to commit Canada to any endeavour which was not strongly supported by the United States. Eden's assumption that the British government could "count on your joining us in expressions of concern and indignation" instantly angered St. Laurent; and Pearson's alarm at the possible British use of force was notably strengthened when he learnt that any such move would be viewed with stern disapproval in Washington.[72] The man who had so generously applauded the "admirable dispatch and decisiveness" with which the United States had rushed to the defence of its "power and prestige" in Korea would obviously do nothing to aid Great Britain in any attempt to defend its "power and prestige" in Egypt.

On August 14, after the longest session in its history, the Twenty-Second Canadian Parliament was prorogued. The prorogation, which lasted until nearly the end of November, was a decisive factor in the great Canadian debate over the seizure of the Suez Canal. The dispute over Trans-Canada Pipe Lines had been essentially a parliamentary battle; but Suez provoked a public controversy, in which more and more people of both sexes and all ages became more and more vehemently involved, on both sides of the issue. In the pipeline affair, public interest had been centred on the House of Commons; but now it found its focus in newspaper reports, editorial opinion, public debates, panel discussions, and private arguments. At first the controversy got under way rather slowly, for it was a long time since the Canadians had been much exercised over foreign policy; but rapidly the excitement mounted, as, one by one, the plans for a negotiated settlement were seen to fail. The London Conference, which met in the third week of August, proposed the establishment of an international Suez Canal Board, on which Egypt would be represented, for the management of the canal; but Nasser rejected this plan, after less than a week's negotiation. He dealt much more summarily with Dulles's makeshift scheme of a Suez Canal Users' Association, SCUA. Finally, France and Britain brought the matter to the United Nations, and on October 13, the Security Council unanimously agreed on six general principles for the operation of the canal – six admirable general principles which had little practical relation to the concrete matter in hand.[73]

In the meantime, while Canadian citizens got increasingly excited about Suez, the Canadian government maintained its cool detachment. Dulles had advised Arnold Heeney, the Canadian Ambassador in Washington, that he hoped Canada would exercise its considerable influence "in the direction of a peaceful solution of this very anxious problem." The Canadian government scarcely needed this instruction; Pearson in Ottawa and Robertson in London continued to oppose force and urge caution on the British. Canada endorsed the London Conference's proposals, but had no positive suggestions of its own to offer. Pearson's "sovereign remedy" for all international distempers and diseases was a reference to either NATO or the United Nations; but the meeting of the NATO Council turned out to be "a relatively meaningless exercise in political consultation";[74] and although the Security Council had undeniably agreed upon six unexceptionable general principles for the management of the canal, not one of them came close to the nub of the whole dispute, which was the conflict between Egyptian nationalism and international ownership and control. Pearson may have hoped that the affair could be dragged out, through one abortive solution to another, until France and Britain grew discouraged and weary, abandoned their claims, and resignedly accepted Egyptian control.

Obviously this was what Dulles intended, and it was his studied refusal of strong diplomatic support which finally drove Britain to join France and Israel in their violent action. "The course of the Suez Canal crisis was decided by the American attitude toward it," Eden wrote later.[75] For him and for Macmillan, the "Anglo-American schism" was the fundamental factor in the whole miserable episode. Britain had done much for the Anglo-American alliance, even conniving at the particularly contemptible ploy by which Dulles had prevented the Security Council from dealing with the fate of the hapless Guatemala. The fate of the Suez Canal did not move Dulles to make the slightest return; and late in October, in desperation, Britain joined an elaborate strategical plan which France and Israel had devised. Israel, which was eager to repeat its raid on the Gaza strip, attacked Egypt on October 29. On October 30, the British and French governments intervened, on the ground that the security of the canal was threatened, and ordered a cease-fire. They demanded the withdrawal of Egyptian and Israeli troops from the canal, and Egypt's acceptance of the occupation of Port Said and Suez by Anglo-French forces. Israel accepted this ultimatum; Egypt rejected it. Immediately, the British and French set their military machines in action, and on October 31 Anglo-French bombers began operations against Egypt.

XI

The most curious feature of the Canadian response to the British ultimatum was the sustained fury of Louis St. Laurent. His fits of bad temper, like his lapses into depression and lethargy, had grown more frequent of late; but Suez threw him into a state of inexhaustible irritability. Late in July, when Eden had appealed to him to support the British protest against Nasser's seizure of the canal, he had complained that he had not been properly informed at the Commonwealth Conference earlier in the summer. How Eden could have "consulted" him about an event which had not yet taken place, he did not trouble, in his exasperation, to explain. He had been annoyed by Eden's first appeal; the second infuriated him. His suspicion and dislike of British purposes and methods, which was always burning in the depths of his being, now burst into violent flame. "I had never before seen him in such a state of controlled anger," Pearson recalled. "I had never seen him in a state of any kind of anger."[76] He threw Pearson Eden's telegram. "What do you think of this?" he asked furiously. There was no possible doubt of what he thought about it himself. Like Dulles, whose ingrained hatred of British "colonialism" had overcome his deep distrust of Nasser's Communist affiliations, St. Laurent looked on Britain's military intervention in Egypt as a hateful manifestation of its incorrigible imperialistic instincts.

Pearson tried to quiet him, as one would an angry child. Britain, he reminded St. Laurent, could hardly have been expected to inform Canada and other governments in advance of its intended invasion, for other governments and the United States in particular, had successfully frustrated all its attempts to get justice by peaceful means, and would certainly try to stop its final resort to force. This temperate reasoning did little to pacify St. Laurent. He was still in a state of simmering fume when the Cabinet met that afternoon to consider the draft reply to Eden which he and Pearson had prepared. When Harris and Robert Winters, the Minister of Public Works, objected that such a message might very likely have very unfortunate political effects in Ontario and the Atlantic Provinces, St. Laurent listened with mounting impatience. "You're just talking with your blood," he told Harris irritably.[77] Harris forbore to make the obvious retort that it was St. Laurent who was talking with his blood and that his blood was obviously very close to boiling point. This show of magisterial bad temper was not enough to overcome the dissenting ministers; and that night, with Pearson's and Harris's help, St. Laurent composed a revised message, which, next morning, October 31, the Cabinet accepted without much difficulty.

It began with the characteristic Canadian complaint that the Canadian government had first learnt of Britain's "grave steps" in Egypt from the press reports rather than from official British notification. The Canadians had preached so frequently and unhelpfully against force, that the British can hardly be blamed for avoiding another, last-minute sermon about its use. This first paragraph of the dispatch, with its injured tone, no doubt expressed St. Laurent's wounded *amour-propre*; but the rest of the message, which had more of Pearson than of St. Laurent in its composition, was a moderate and reasoned reply. It regretted the unfortunate effects which the British intervention would likely have on the United Nations and the Commonwealth; and ended up by lamenting "the deplorable divergence of viewpoint and policy between the United Kingdom and the United States." Obviously this was by far the most important of the three reasons on which Canada grounded its refusal to condone the British action. " . . . We cannot come to the conclusion," the message declared, "that the penetration of its [Britain's] troops into Egypt was justified . . . ."[78] It was a polite but firm rejection of the British case; but, despite its firmness, St. Laurent refused to be pacified. Even in public, he made no attempt to conceal his still-smouldering rage. He stormed down the corridors of the East Block, through the press of waiting newsmen, answering their inquiries with cantankerous rudeness.[79]

Pearson had already departed for the United Nations in New York. In the Security Council, Henry Cabot Lodge – "certainly prejudiced against Britain" – had pressed for immediate adoption a resolution explicitly censuring the Anglo-French action and demanding an immediate cease-fire in Egypt – without providing any means of enforcing it. [80] For the first time in its history as a member of the Security Council, Britain, along with France, vetoed this resolution; but together they could not prevent the Council from adopting the "Uniting for Peace" procedure, which had been devised during the Korean War. By a simple majority, which the British claimed was unconstitutional, the whole dispute was transferred to a special session of the General Assembly.[81] Pearson had also decided that a cease-fire resolution would be worse than useless if it were not carried out on the spot by an international police force. " . . . Police action there must be to separate the belligerents . . . ," Eden had declared in the British House of Commons. "If the United Nations were then willing to take over the physical task of maintaining peace, no one would be better pleased than we."[82]

With this encouragement – "it was not much, but it was something" – Pearson determined to take the initiative. Despite the doubts of Dag Hammarskjöld, the Secretary-General of the United Nations, Pearson and his associates managed to convert a number of delegates to the Canadian plan; and early in the morning of Sunday, November 4, when Pearson proposed "an international United Nations force to secure and supervise the cessation of hostilities," it was adopted with 57 votes in favour, none opposed, and 19 abstentions.[83] The establishment of the force was, in fact, a far easier business than the question of its composition. At first, Britain and France had hoped that their troops, which were about to land in Egypt, might be accepted as part of the United Nations force; but the United States and the Soviet Union, linked in an unholy alliance, were uncompromisingly opposed to any such concession; and their two strings of satellite nations, together with the entire Afro-Asian bloc, were certain to defeat any hope of the inclusion of the Anglo-French.

Canada, as sponsor of the resolution, and its co-sponsors, Norway and Columbia, tried to extricate themselves from this difficulty by providing that permanent members of the Security Council could not contribute troops to the United Nations Emergency Force. It was an ingenious arrangement, but it very quickly became obvious that it was far from solving all their problems. Hammarskjöld suggested a force of about 10,000 men, recommended General E. L. M. Burns, of the Palestine Truce Supervision Organization, as its commander; and Canada, Columbia, together with Norway, Sweden, Denmark and Finland as a Scandinavian group, immediately offered available troops. The Emergency Force was ready; but although it was, in effect, an army of occupation, it was not an invading army, as the Anglo-French army had been. It needed a legal basis for its presence on Egyptian soil, and this necessity was one more of the several new factors which were rapidly strengthening Nasser's political position. He was complacently conscious of Russian moral support and of the impending departure of the hated Anglo-French invaders. He insisted that the Egyptian government must determine not only the departure date of the U.N. Emergency Force, but also the principal elements in its composition.

The Canadian government offered a battalion of the Queen's Own Rifles as its contribution to the force. The Egyptians protested politely but firmly that such a body, with its British title and its uniforms similar to, if not identical with, British uniforms, might create misunderstandings and result in "incidents." Pearson angrily, but vainly, asserted Canadian "independence" in the Commonwealth; but Nasser, who remembered Canada's political origins and affiliations, even though Canada itself seemed disposed to disavow them, would not permit the Queen's Own Rifles to enter Egypt as "fighting" soldiers.[84] The battalion, transported to the East Coast in a blaze of patriotic publicity, remained ingloriously, day after day, in Halifax, with its transport HMCS *Magnificent* waiting patiently in harbour, while Pearson, Hammarskjöld and General Burns tried to persuade the Egyptians to give up their obstinate resistance. No single nation, Pearson argued, and certainly not Egypt, had the right to determine the components of a United Nations army, led by a Canadian General.

It was not a right, of course; but in the end, as might have been expected, it had to be conceded as a privilege. Burns, who had at first assumed that "the Canadian contingent would be the mainspring of UNEF," was finally obliged to agree that "air transport and administrative personnel" was perhaps the best contribution Canada could make to the cease-fire force.[85] The Canadian government was compelled to endure a humiliation which Pearson could neither conceal nor explain away. It was a mortifying conclusion to his brave initiative at New York; but it was only one of the many disappointments and shortcomings of an operation which the United Nations had authorized but which it proved unable to control or to bring to a successful conclusion. Pearson had assumed that the cease-fire would be followed by a satisfactory political settlement of the Suez Canal issue; but there was no political settlement of the Suez Canal issue, any more than there had been a political settlement after the cease-fire in Korea. The Security Council conveniently forgot about the six general principles it had solemnly laid down for the settlement of the Canal dispute. Nobody remembered the plan for an International Suez Canal Board which the London Conference had proposed in August. The British and French left; the Israelis finally retreated. Nasser remained in exclusive and undisputed control.

XII

By November 23, when the British agreed to admit an advance party of UNEF into Port Said, the Suez crisis was virtually over. No amount of argument could now affect the final result; but the popular debate over the justice and wisdom of the Anglo-French intervention in Egypt, which in fact continued for years thereafter, had by no means died away. It was suddenly revived on November 26, when the Canadian Parliament met in a special session to authorize the necessary expenditures for the Canadian contingent in Egypt. Even though — so the opposition jeered — these soldiers were apparently armed with typewriters rather than guns, they still had to be paid and supplied, and only the Canadian Parliament could do it. Pearson, who had been showered with compliments in New York, may have expected a hero's welcome in Ottawa; and St. Laurent seems to have assumed, from private conversations with leading members of the Opposition, that there would be no serious protest against the government's conduct in the Suez affair. It certainly didn't turn out that way. Once again, as in the Trans-Canada pipeline controversy, the Liberals complacently underestimated the strength and persistence of the opposition to their policies; and once again, by their provocative attitudes and methods, they intensified the hostility of their opponents.

Of course, the debate over Suez was by no means a re-enactment of the famous filibuster on the Trans-Canada pipeline. It lasted four days instead of four weeks; and it was carried on chiefly by the official Opposition, the Progressive-Conservatives, for Coldwell and Knowles made it quite clear that the C.C.F. heartily approved what Pearson had achieved at the United Nations. George Drew, who was seriously ill that autumn, was absent from the House; Earl Rowe, as Acting Leader of the Opposition, led the debate on the Address in Reply to the Speech from the Throne, and moved an amendment which censured the government for its "gratuitous condemnation" of the United Kingdom and France, its "meek" endorsement of American policies, and its humiliating acceptance of Nasser's dictation.[86] Fleming, Diefenbaker, Churchill, Pearkes and Fulton all took part in the debate, though Fulton, one of the great contrivers of the pipeline filibuster, was relatively quite brief. Fleming refuted St. Laurent's claim that Nasser had not dictated to Canada by reminding the House that Nasser's dictation had, of course, been conveyed through the Secretary-General of the United Nations; and Diefenbaker ridiculed General Burns's telegram, stating that "specialist troops" would be Canada's best contribution to UNEF as "an escape hatch for the government."[87]

The most determined and passionate of the Tory debaters was none of these; he was, as might have been expected, Howard Green, the member for Vancouver-Quadra. Green had been profoundly shocked by the Suez crisis and by the part Canada had played in it; public feeling on the issue, he insisted, was "running very deep in Canada." The Canadian government had, in effect, "treated the United Kingdom and France as aggressors"; it had become a "chore boy" for the United States. "In the last ten years," Green claimed, "this government has been currying favour with the United States. Ever since the Second World War, that has been the policy of the Canadian government."[88] Almost anything that Green said could be counted on to annoy St. Laurent; but, on this occasion, oddly enough, it was Earl Rowe, and not Green, who first roused the Prime Minister's ire. Rowe's opening speech was not particularly provocative or outstanding; but it was Rowe, seconded by Green, who moved the Conservative amendment to the Address, and the amendment contained some biting phrases, rather more characteristic of Green than of Rowe.

The fact was that St. Laurent was just as emotionally involved as Green in the Suez affair, though in a fashion diametrically opposed to that of his Tory critic. The irascibility he had shown so plainly in the opening days of the crisis, far from subsiding, was just as strong as ever. Up to that moment, his chronic state of anger had been known only to his colleagues in the Cabinet and to a few shocked and astonished newspapermen; but now it was dramatically revealed in Parliament, and through Parliament to the nation as a whole. The revelation, moreover, came quickly, as though his feelings were too strong to be bottled up any longer. When he rose, immediately after Rowe had sat down, he obviously intended to reply in general terms to his critic, and to deal with the various points in the Conservative amendment one by one; but very soon he was betrayed, by his own rhetoric, into a damaging outburst. He had been expatiating on the selfish fashion in which the great powers had used their veto in the Security Council to prevent the smaller powers from dealing with questions which affected their vital interests. The Soviet Union, the United States and the United Kingdom, he declared, were all members of this dominating group; but it rapidly became clear that his mind was fixed, not on the great powers of Asia and North America, but on those of Europe. " . . . The era when the supermen of Europe could govern the whole world," he concluded angrily, "has and is coming pretty close to an end."[89]

It was a major rhetorical blunder. What a description of Canada's two Mother Countries, Britain and France! It was a memorable phrase, charged with aversion and contempt, which the Opposition did not let St. Laurent forget; but it was not the only evidence of the exasperation which the Suez affair always seemed to evoke in him. He intervened repeatedly, with angry comments, when Green was speaking, just as he had done during the debate on the renewal of the Defence Production Act. He interrupted Fleming; and Fleming complained that the Prime Minister did not apparently consider himself bound by the rules of the House, "because he is bobbing up and down as he sees fit without regard to the rules, not asking questions, but throwing in interjections all through speeches . . . from this side of the House . . . "[90] Rapidly, the picture of a bad-tempered and quarrelsome Prime Minister took shape in the Commons; and the quiet and reasoned way in which Pearson recounted his doings at the United Nations was regarded as a welcome relief. Pearson's speech, Fleming remarked pointedly, "was in very marked contrast to the petulant, belligerent, and provocative manner adopted by the Prime Minister yesterday . . . ."[91] Green jeered ironically at the "kindly, friendly Uncle Louis" in his new mood. The familiar picture of "Uncle Louis kissing babies . . . so smug, so full of self-righteousness, so hypocritical . . . went out the window this afternoon."[92]

There was another irony, far more significant and profound than that in which the Tories indulged at St. Laurent's expense – the irony of the political circumstances in which the Suez affair reached its climax. Early in November, while the United Nations General Assembly was authorizing its special force "to secure and supervise" the cease-fire in Egypt, the armies of the Soviet Union were brutally suppressing the short-lived revolt in Hungary. Several speakers in the Canadian House of Commons referred to this tragedy; one of the items in the Conservative amendment to the Address urged the Canadian government to offer asylum to the Hungarian refugees. But nobody in Ottawa or elsewhere dared to propose that the Soviet forces should be resisted. Here was a terrible example of the aggression which the United Nations had been created to prevent or oppose, but no delegation in the Assembly ventured to suggest collective resistance. The events of the autumn of 1956 – the Suez crisis and the Hungarian rebellion – proved conclusively how highly selective the decisions of the United Nations really were. In the case of a young nation like North Korea, or an old and supposedly declining nation like Britain or France, it could act very vigorously; but the new superpowers in Asia and North America were clearly thought to be in a different category. When the United States intervened in Guatemala or the Soviet Union in Hungary, the United Nations might remain discreetly silent, or it might regret and deplore. But it did not act.

The Tenth of June, 1957

I

In June, 1957, it was nearly eighteen years since that day in early September, 1939, when King George had signed Canada's declaration of war against Germany. It had been a vital eighteen years, a period more significant in its events and consequences than any of similar length in the nation's history. Canada had grown immensely in both human and material resources. The population had increased astonishingly by nearly 40%. New sources of energy had been found and developed; and new metal deposits, including vast masses of iron ore, had been discovered. The nation had fought through the Second World War, had participated in the minor Korean War, and for nearly ten years had endured the attrition of the Cold War. The deep depression with which the period opened had changed suddenly into a boom, and the boom had continued, through an exchange crisis, a serious inflation, and several short-lived recessions, without any serious decline. A new and different generation of writers, artists, and musicians had arrived; and Canada had achieved professional competence in a hitherto untried field of artistic endeavour, the performing arts.

A new Canada would inevitably have arisen in those eighteen years, with little or no intervention by government; but the Canada which actually existed in June, 1957, was not solely the product of natural economic and social forces. To a very considerable extent, it had been shaped by government, by the federal government principally, and by the governments of the provinces to a much smaller degree. The federal government had decisively influenced the character and course of the new Canadian society through a series of basic interrelated policies; and it had been able to conceive, develop, and carry out these policies, without any serious check or qualification, simply because it had been so long and so continuously in the hands of one particular party. From October 14, 1935, when Mackenzie King had defeated R.B. Bennett's Conservative government, the Liberal Party had continued in power for an unbroken total of nearly twenty-two years. It had been relatively indecisive and inactive during the first brief period of this huge span of time, but in 1939 there came a drastic change. The declaration of war was in itself a major decision; and it was followed, even during the war and increasingly thereafter, by other fundamental decisions which profoundly influenced the nation's growth. Canada, in fact, was making the choices which would determine its destiny for the next thirty or forty years. It had come to the fork in the road. It could have continued along the familiar way it had followed before the war. Instead it chose a new road into the future.

The new road led directly into a new world of planning and management, of economic controls and social equalization. Its basic principles had not been conceived by Canadians, or derived from Canadian circumstances; they had been laid down chiefly by two Englishmen, J.M. Keynes and W.H. Beveridge, who had lived and worked in a unitary state, with a highly industrialized and centralized economy, and a deeply divided, class-conscious social organization. The Canadian situation differed in almost every important particular from the British. Canada was a federal state, continental in extent, with a number of sharply different regional economies, only a few of which were industrialized, and a much greater degree of economic and social equality. Only time would tell how well these alien experiments in economic regulation and social welfare would succeed under substantially different Canadian circumstances. So far, they had performed reasonably well; but so far the new system had not faced any seriously adverse situations, and—what perhaps was even more important—the scope of its economic controls and social services was still quite limited.

Social welfare did not yet include medicare; and fiscal and monetary controls could do no more than level out the ups and downs of the business cycle. The real weaknesses of the Canadian economy—its declining secondary industries, the inevitable deficit in its balance of payments with the United States, and its heavy and growing dependence on American capital—were, in the eyes of the Canadian government, simply facts of life, fortunate or unfortunate, about which nothing whatever could be done. The decay of native manufacturers and the perpetual imbalance of trade might occasionally be deplored; but the vast influx of American capital must always be gratefully accepted and enthusiastically applauded. With the active encouragement of C.D. Howe, who was himself an American import, direct American investment in Canada had more than tripled during the twelve years from 1945 to 1957; and the takeover of Canadian industries and natural resources had proceeded apace. Howe's last, greatest, and most characteristic achievement was Trans-Canada Pipe Lines, a company over 75% American-owned, for which the Canadian government had provided over 90% of the capital.

In external affairs, the new road to the future led the Canadian government into a tangle of foreign relationships and obligations even more novel

and onerous than the responsibilities of its experiments in democratic socialism. Even before the Second World War ended, Canada had committed itself
to the United Nations, a new collective security organization in which St.
Laurent and Pearson, and particularly Pearson, devoutly believed. King
viewed the United Nations, and international politics in general, with his
usual mixture of fear, scepticism, and aversion; but the Canadian withdrawal
from Europe, which followed immediately after the war, was very short-lived.
King resigned the leadership of the Liberal Party; and even before his final
retirement, the threat of Communist aggression was driving the Canadian
government into foreign connections which were utterly new and strange
in his and Canada's experience. Inspired by Pearson's eager championship,
the nation became a charter member of the North Atlantic Treaty Organization, the only middle power, outside those directly involved in Western
Europe, to do so. And, under steady American pressure, it accepted a subordinate position in a continental defence system controlled and directed by
the United States.

Pearson—for whom collective security came first and national sovereignty
a very poor second—was the most active and adventurous Minister of External Affairs that Canada has ever had, or—for that matter—is ever likely to
have. He had become almost a world figure, at Canada's risk and expense,
as well as for its benefit. His chief reliance was placed on the two new international organizations, the United Nations and NATO. He had helped to
found them both; and in both of them, the United States—which he regarded
as Canada's essential and permanent ally—played a prominent and vigorous
part. The Commonwealth, in his estimation, was a much less effective and
valuable association. It had been unused and neglected during the war, and
its cohesion had been seriously weakened by the post-war revolution in the
Far Eastern British Empire. Pearson helped to ensure its gradual disintegration by breaking its essential institutional bond, the Monarchy. He professed
to find in the new Commonwealth, with its incongruous mixture of monarchies and republics, a useful bridge between West and East; but in fact he
employed it very little.

He much preferred following the gleam of his "Atlantic Vision" in meetings of the NATO Council, and carrying on old-fashioned diplomacy in aid
of great new international "causes" at the United Nations in New York. It
was chiefly at his insistence that Canada had joined NATO, fought the
Korean War, and accepted humble and somewhat equivocal peace-keeping
jobs in Vietnam and Egypt. His idealism and energy, his tact and persuasive
powers, had driven the nation along strange roads into even stranger situations. Yet his crusades never quite reached the Holy Land, and his great new
international organizations never completely realized his hopes. NATO never
became the economic, social, and moral union he had tried so hard to make
it. The United Nations proved it could win a limited war, and impose a

cease-fire on a secondary state, but it had never even attempted to resist aggression by the superpowers. By the time Pearson ceased to be Secretary of State for External Affairs, its great days were definitely over.

This was the far country into which the new road to the future had led the Canadian people. Directed and encouraged by their federal government, they had marched steadily forward, apparently with approval, and certainly without strong opposition. The Liberal Party, their guide and mentor, had undeniably gained and held their strong support. Since it had regained power in 1935, it had faced the Canadians in four federal general elections. The Liberals had beaten the Conservatives badly in 1940, had won but with a considerably reduced following in 1945, and had triumphed with over-whelming majorities in 1949 and 1953. Four Conservative leaders–Manion, Meighen, Bracken, and Drew–had, one by one, and in fairly rapid succession, gone down to defeat.

Now another, a fifth, general election was not far off in the future. Everybody expected that George Drew would again lead the Conservatives. He had been beaten twice; perhaps a third defeat would finish him as leader. But at the moment he stood at the height of his prestige. He had captained the Tories in the pipeline debate and the party had emerged from that dramatic encounter with much greater popular acclaim than for many years in the past.

And then, without warning, during the late summer holiday which followed the prorogation of Parliament on August 14, Drew became suddenly and seriously ill.

II

It was Dr. Ray Farquharson, George Drew's doctor, and Fiorenza, his wife, who decided that he must resign the leadership. The party leaders wanted him to remain. The increasingly ominous bulletins which were issued from his sick-room had brought them together, a representative group of senior Conservatives, for an anxious conference in Toronto. George Nowlan had come from Nova Scotia; Léon Balcer, then president of the party, from Quebec; Grattan O'Leary, J.M. Macdonnell, Earl Rowe, and Ellen Fairclough represented Ontario. They were determined to hear the doctor's verdict from his own lips, and Farquharson, then Dean of Medicine at the University of Toronto, came over to see them. He was a gentle, sympathetic man, with a low voice and a quiet manner, but he told them the truth about his patient in forceful, unqualified terms, "He is a sick, sick man," he said gravely. "For the sake of his family and for his future, he should give up the leadership of this party."[1]

It was impossible to dismiss such earnest advice. A consulting physician, called in at Farquharson's own suggestion, emphatically confirmed it;

Fiorenza added her tearful entreaties. She told Ellen Fairclough how passionately she regretted that she had urged her husband to go on "when he shouldn't have gone on." "Oh no," she cried, "I want George, I don't want him to be Prime Minister of Canada, I want George for my husband."[2] It was more than enough for the little group of distressed and worried Tories who sat, "perched on beds and chairs," in a room in the Royal York Hotel. Together they composed a letter of resignation. There was not a typewriter immediately available, so Ellen Fairclough and Earl Rowe's son took the draft over to the Albany Club and Ellen typed it herself. Reluctantly, George Drew signed it. It was September 18, 1956.

Less than three months later, in an Ottawa already snow-bound with winter, the Progressive-Conservative delegates assembled to elect a new leader. From the beginning, John George Diefenbaker was the favoured candidate; his only declared rivals were Donald Fleming of Toronto and Edmund Davie Fulton of Kamloops. Before very long, Fleming realized that he was now the "underdog" in the contest, and he was not very surprised when, one by one, a number of his friends came up to explain that they would have to yield to the mounting pressure in favour of Diefenbaker.[3] Fulton, who was by far the youngest of the three, knew from the start that he had no chance of winning; but he was ambitious, planned for a long career in politics, and believed that although he would probably lose, and lose badly, his candidacy in 1956 might help to establish a strong claim to the leadership in the future.[4]

Obviously, neither of these competitors had any real chance of overtaking Diefenbaker; and Diefenbaker's critics—and there were a number of these in high places in the party hierarchy—struggled frantically to find a candidate who could prevent him from getting the nomination.[5] Someone suggested the successful Premier of Ontario, Leslie Frost; but Frost, unfortunately, "wouldn't touch it." R.A. Bell got in touch with Sidney Smith, the President of the University of Toronto, who might have been a candidate for the leadership in 1943, when he was President of the University of Manitoba, if the Premier of the Province, John Bracken, had not forestalled him at the last moment. Smith must still have cherished political ambitions, for less than a year later, he was to yield—very unwisely—to Diefenbaker's urgent appeal to join the new Conservative Ministry as Secretary of State for External Affairs. In the autumn of 1957, office was his for the taking; but in the autumn of 1956, the leadership of the Progressive-Conservative Party could be gained only through the defeat of the popular Diefenbaker. Smith cautiously asked for time to consider, consulted his doctor, and finally and sensibly decided that he was "too old to start a new game."[6] His refusal ended the search for a candidate who could beat Diefenbaker; as everybody now expected he proved unbeatable. On January 14, he won on the first ballot, with 774 votes to Fleming's 393, and Fulton's 119.

Perhaps the convention's most significant event was not Diefenbaker's election, which was a foregone conclusion, but a supposedly minor incident, which was loaded, nevertheless, with trouble for the future. Diefenbaker, with his declared aim of "one unhyphenated Canada," alienated a good many French Canadians. Léon Balcer, the Conservative leader in Quebec, was opposed to his candidature; and since Tory organization in the Quebec constituencies was ineffective and almost non-existent, most of the Quebec delegates were virtually nominated by Balcer and his advisers. The majority of these nominees would probably vote for Fleming, a few for Fulton, but it was almost certain that only a handful would support Diefenbaker. Diefenbaker had little or nothing to lose in Quebec; and the knowledge of this fact may have strengthened his resolve to break with the unwritten rules of convention procedure. At the previous convention, English Canadians and French Canadians had shared the formal business of nominating and seconding the various candidates. Diefenbaker didn't particularly object to a French-Canadian seconder; but he knew very well that in the eyes of the great mass of Ontario delegates, a seconder from Quebec would have to be balanced by a nominator from Ontario. This would definitely imply the sponsorship of central Canada; and Diefenbaker was a defiant Westerner who was determined to prove that he had successfully rejected Central Canada's domination of the Conservative Party.[7] He asked Hugh John Flemming, the new Conservative Premier of New Brunswick, to nominate him, and Col. G.R. Pearkes of Vancouver Island, to act as his seconder. When the results of the first ballot were announced, Fleming got up to move that Diefenbaker's election be made unanimous; and, as he did so, a group of French-Canadian delegates were seen to move ostentatiously for the door.[8]

III

In the House of Commons at Ottawa, Diefenbaker did not attempt to make a dramatic entry as the new Leader of the Opposition. It was the last session before the election, Liberal legislation was certain to be unexceptionable, calculated to soothe and gratify, rather than to excite the voters; and there was a lot more political capital to be gained in touring Canada than in sitting at his desk in the House of Commons in Ottawa. Diefenbaker set about the business of making himself known to Canadians with enormous energy and enthusiasm. He was sixty-one, seven years older than Drew had been when he became leader in 1948; but, on the other hand—and this was distinctly the more significant difference—fourteen years younger than the Prime Minister became on February 1, 1957. It was a big span of years—the gap between late maturity and definite old age. The Liberals might prudently have kept St. Laurent's seventy-fifth birthday rather quiet; instead they celebrated it with two much-publicized events—the opening of the new headquarters of the National Liberal Federation in Ottawa, and a splendid dinner in the Chateau Frontenac in Quebec. Canadians now knew—if they needed reminding—that their Prime Minister was a very old man. Only John A. Macdonald, who was seventy-six when he died in office, had been older. Even Mackenzie King, that determined contender for records in political longevity, had retired before he became seventy-four.

The winter session of 1957 bore only a slight resemblance to the pre-election sessions of 1949 and 1953. Again there were financial inducements for good Canadian voters, but they were doled out prudently, in stingy amounts. In order to achieve the small surplus of his budget, Walter Harris only slightly reduced taxation, increased family allowances for younger children by a single dollar, and raised the old age security pension from $40 to $46 a month. The only real sign of Liberal munificence was the long overdue establishment of the Canada Council. And even this belated realization of Vincent Massey's dream would not have taken place if it had not been for the recent deaths of two multi-millionaires, Isaak Walton Killam, the investment banker, and Sir James Dunn, the president of the Algoma Steel Corporation. The succession duties from each of these two estates were expected to amount to a staggering $50 million. This huge piece of financial good fortune might have disappeared into the gaping maw of the federal treasury without leaving so much as a trace; and, if St. Laurent had followed his natural inclinations, this would probably have been its destiny. But to John Deutsch, who was then Secretary to the Treasury Board, and J.W. Pickersgill, this seemed a wanton waste of the bounty of Providence. They suggested that the revenue from the two estates should be used to set up, first, a capital fund for a Canada Council according to Massey's prescription, and, second, to provide another fund from which capital grants could be made to Canadian universities in aid of their work in the arts, humanities, and social sciences.[9] St. Laurent and the Cabinet accepted this proposal; and the Canada Council was established with Brooke Claxton as chairman, Father Levesque as vice-chairman, and Albert W. Trueman as director.

All this added a few light touches to the pleasing picture of the Liberal government as a kind of huge institutional Robin Hood, which took money in big handfuls from the rich, and distributed it in small, carefully graduated helpings to deserving taxpayers, senior citizens, small children, overburdened universities, and impecunious artists, writers, and scholars. It was an attractive image; but, in recent months, the Liberal government had been showing other, distinctly less appealing aspects of its character to the Canadian electorate. Two of these distinguishing features—the Liberal instinct for domination in Parliament, and the obsequious Liberal acceptance of American economic control and political influence—had been vividly illustrated during the pipeline debate. Now, in the winter and spring of 1957, the second of these unpopular characteristics–the favourable Liberal reception of American capital and American political leadership–appeared once again in two supposedly minor events. The first of these was the publication, in December, 1956, of the "Preliminary Report" of Walter Gordon's Royal Commission on Canada's Economic Prospects. The second was the suicide, in April, 1957, of Herbert Norman, Canada's Ambassador to Egypt.

From the first, Gordon had been eager to finish his "Report" by the end of 1956; and when it became obvious that the evidence could not be compiled and the research completed in so short a time, he and his fellow Commissioners decided to publish an introductory statement of their chief findings and conclusions. This "Preliminary Report" was no doubt intended to serve two purposes. As an exercise in economic forecasting, it would predict a brilliant future for Canada under continued Liberal rule. As a sober admonition to the Liberal government, it would suggest ways and means by which the American takeover of Canadian industries and natural resources might be resisted and reversed. The first of these two objects was certainly realized, for the Commissioner's predictions were extremely optimistic, but the attempt to reach the second brought nothing but trouble for Gordon and the Liberal government.

In an unguarded moment, the Commissioners actually dared to suggest that Canadians in the Atlantic Provinces might be financially assisted to move to the richer opportunities of central Canada–a piece of economic realism which sinned against the Liberal doctrine of the sacredness of regionalism, and speedily provoked an angry furor in the Atlantic Provinces.[10] This was bad enough, but the mass migration of the Maritimers was only one of the Commissions' incidental suggestions; and their treatment of American economic ownership and control in Canada was potentially far more disturbing. Actually their specific proposals were mild and tentative enough; but, among other recommendations for increasing Canadian participation in Canada's business, they did suggest that the larger American subsidiaries should sell 20% to 25% of their equity stock to Canadian investors. In the House of Commons, Diefenbaker found it easy to embarrass the government and exasperate Howe by pointing out that Gordon's recommendations closely resembled the nationalist economic policies which the Conservative Opposition had been advocating for the previous five years![11]

The Norman affair aroused a much more widespread feeling of injury, anger, and humiliation. Norman had been the Canadian Ambassador to Egypt during the tangled diplomacy of the Suez crisis. He had certainly been anxious and overworked for some time; but it was not so much the after-effects of strain and tension as it was the continuing feeling of persecution which finally drove him to take his own life in Cairo. On March 14, an American Senate Sub-Committee on Internal Security received and published certain charges against Norman's alleged Communist sympathies and affiliations which it had already made public five years earlier. A day later, Pearson denounced "these slanders and unsupported insinuations" in the House of Commons and subsequently dispatched a stiff note of protest to Washington. The American State Department, moved by these strong Canadian objections, asked the chairman of the Senate Sub-Committee to refrain in future from making its proceedings public. The request was made in the interests of good Canadian-American relations; but the Senate Sub-Committee immediately and deliberately defied it. On March 28, it published, in full, the record of its secret hearing on the charges against Norman. And on April 4, Norman committed suicide.[12]

That Norman was the guiltless victim of McCarthyism and that his death in reality was a murder inflicted by American witch-hunters was the verdict of the great majority of Canadians. Their grief and anger were great; and these strong feelings were aroused not merely by the outrage of Norman's death by also by the casual, unconcerned, perfunctory fashion in which both the Canadian and American governments treated it. President Eisenhower and his State Department acknowledged no fault and expressed no regret. They rather patronizingly reminded the Canadians that, under the American system of divided powers, the executive had no control over opinions expressed in Congress. It was the negligent, disrespectful treatment usually reserved for inferiors; but it had no effect on Pearson's devotion to the cause of Canada-American friendship. He threatened, if the Americans did not mend their ways, to withhold security information about Canadians from all agencies of the American government; but he pleaded with Canadians not to direct their "strong feelings" against the people or government of the United States as a whole.[13]

IV

The Twenty-Second Parliament was dissolved on April 12, 1957, and nearly two months later, on June 10, the Canadians went to the polls.

The Liberal and the Progressive-Conservative election campaigns differed from each other in a more glaring fashion than they had probably ever done in the past. There was nothing in the least novel about the Liberal strategy and tactics. The Progressive-Conservative methods, on the other hand, were a truly revolutionary break with tradition. The Liberal manner—undemonstrative, assured, complacent—was appropriate behaviour for a party which had been so long in power that its leaders assumed—and assumed that the Canadian electorate also assumed—that they alone could govern the country. The aim of the Liberals was not to win votes, but to hold them—a negative purpose. The object of the Conservatives was the distant and uphill goal of gaining the votes which they had totally failed to win in five successive general elections. It was a formidable, daunting task which could be carried out only by radically new methods.

Diefenbaker was ready and eager to use them. Of German and Scottish stock, with a surname which plainly indicated an origin different from that of Canada's two "founding" cultures, English and French, Diefenbaker was in himself an exception to the unwritten rules of Conservative leadership. He had no cause to love the Tory Establishment of central Canada, for it had rejected him for the tyro George Drew in 1948 and had tried desperately to discover a candidate who could defeat him in December, 1956. At the convention, he had deliberately chosen sponsors who came from the country's east and west and not from its centre; and, as the election drew closer, he sought increasingly to escape from the clutches of established Conservative personalities and traditional Conservative methods.

The triumvirate which ran his election campaign—Allister Grosart, Gordon Churchill, and George Hees—did not include a single member of the Tory "Old Guard," though Hees did sit for a Toronto constituency; and the basic strategy of the campaign was devised by Gordon Churchill, a westerner from the riding of Winnipeg North Centre. Churchill reasoned that the party must try to win without Quebec. For the past five elections, the Conservatives had wasted time, talent, and money in a futile effort to win seats in Quebec. This vain endeavour, Churchill reasoned, must now be stopped. French Canadians had been voting Liberal for fifty years with all the mechanical regularity of well-oiled automata; and there was not the slightest hope of persuading a significant number of them to change now. French Canada could not, of course, be neglected; but the main Tory attempt would be made in Ontario, the Atlantic Provinces, and the West.[14]

Conservative strategy had definitely altered. Conservative tactics were equally novel. Diefenbaker's campaign manner was a marked change from Drew's and a sharp contrast with the Prime Minister's. As in the elections of 1949 and 1953, St. Laurent alternated between his two favourite and well-rehearsed political roles. He could be either the Chairman of the Board of a large corporation presenting a highly satisfactory annual report to a meeting of satisfied shareholders; or he could be an affectionate *pater familias,* tenderly watching over the welfare and interests of his large Canadian family. Both roles implied stability, security, continuity; and both completely lacked the intense excitement which Diefenbaker managed to inject into his campaign. He was, in fact, a new and astounding force in Canadian politics. He was a prophet who promised a brilliant future, an evangelist who offered redemption from an evil past, a prosecuting counsel determined on the conviction of a particularly notorious criminal. The votes of committed Conservatives were, of course, his for the taking. He had the strong support of the provincial premiers—Frost of Ontario, Stanfield of Nova Scotia, Flemming of New Brunswick—as well as the aid of the new Conservative leader in Manitoba, Roblin. Chance gave him many exceptional advantages; but, in the main, he relied for success upon himself and his distinctive character and abilities. He campaigned for the election not of a Conservative government, or even of a Progressive-Conservative government, but for a Diefenbaker government.

Yet it is safe to say that in the early evening of that long June day, the great majority of Canadians confidently expected that Diefenbaker would be defeated. *Maclean's* magazine, published the previous weekend, had casually assumed another Liberal victory, and, for a brief while, it seemed likely that the actual results would realize these expectations. Newfoundland went mainly Liberal; but, ever since the union of 1949, Newfoundland had virtually been a ward of the Liberal government; and once the returns from the other Atlantic Provinces began to come in, the whole aspect of the election suddenly and dramatically changed. The two Halifax city seats, regarded as safe Liberal property, were captured by the Conservatives; and two Liberal Cabinet ministers, Robert Winters and Milton Gregg, went down to defeat in Nova Scotia and New Brunswick. In Quebec, as was to be expected, the party managed a partial recovery; but in Ontario and the West its disintegration continued, barely unchecked, with Cabinet ministers Howe, Harris, Garson, and Campney among the casualties.

By midnight, the astonished Canadians, glued to their fascinating new television sets, began to take in the incredible fact that the Canadian "Party of Government" had apparently lost its authority to govern. It was, of course, far from an overwhelming defeat. The Progressive-Conservatives won 112 seats, the Liberals 105, the C.C.F. 25 and Social Credit 19.[15] A minority government would rule Canada for a while, at least; but it would not be a Liberal minority government. Late that night, before the television cameras in the Chateau Frontenac Hotel in Quebec, St. Laurent, his face a white, strained mask of shock, incredulity, and consternation, conceded defeat. John George Diefenbaker had won his personal fight; but whether his government would take a new road and whether it would change or modify the basic decisions of the past eighteen years, were questions which only time could answer.

NOTES TO CHAPTER ONE

1. Vincent Massey, *What's Past is Prologue, the Memoirs of the Rt. Hon. Vincent Massey* (Toronto, 1963), pp. 278-80.
2. Canada, *House of Commons Debates,* Special Session, 18th Parliament, 1939, pp. 19-25.
3. *Ibid.,* pp. 34-5.
4. James Eayrs, *In Defence of Canada, Appeasement and Rearmament* (Toronto, 1965), p. 146.
5. C.P. Stacey, *Arms, Men and Governments, the War Policies of Canada, 1939-1945* (Ottawa, 1970), pp. 9-10.
6. *Ibid.,* p. 91.
7. *Ibid.,* p. 13.
8. *Ibid.*
9. J.W. Pickersgill, *The Mackenzie King Record, Vol. 1, 1939-1944,* (Toronto, 1960), pp. 28-9.
10. *Ibid.,* pp. 40-1.
11. *Ibid.,* pp. 42-4.
12. Stacey, *op. cit.,* pp. 24-5.
13. *Ibid.,* Appendix "D", p. 543.
14. *Ibid.*
15. H.F. Quinn, *The Union Nationale, a Study in Quebec Nationalism* (Toronto, 1963), pp. 73-8.
16. C.P. Stacey, *Historical Documents of Canada, Vol. V., The Arts of War and Peace, 1914-1945* (Toronto, 1972), p. 603.
17. Pickersgill, *The Mackenzie King Record,* Vol. 1, p. 35.
18. N. Ward, ed., *A Party Politician, the Memoirs of Chubby Power* (Toronto, 1966), pp. 125-30, 346-7.
19. Stacey, *Historical Documents of Canada,* Vol. V, pp. 604-5.
20. M.C. Urquhart and K.A.H. Buckley, eds., *Historical Statistics of Canada* (Toronto, 1965), p. 631.
21. N. McKenty, *Mitch Hepburn* (Toronto, 1967), p. 125.
22. *Ibid.,* p. 139.
23. *Ibid.,* p. 189.
24. *Ibid.,* p. 194.
25. *Ibid.,* p. 201.
26. *Ibid.,* p. 209.
27. Pickersgill, *op. cit.,* p. 63.
28. Eugene Forsey, "Mr. King and Parliamentary Government,"*(Canadian Journal of Economics and Political Science,* XVII, 4 (November, 1951), p. 463.
29. Canada, *House of Commons Debates, 6th Session, 18th Parliament,* 1940, Vol. I, p. 9.
30. *Ibid.,* p. 15.
31. *Ibid.,* p. 17.
32. *Ibid.,* p. 10.
33. McKenty, *op. cit.,* p. 212.
34. Urquhart and Buckley, *op. cit.,* p. 619.
35. Stacey, *Arms, Men and Governments,* pp. 140-3.
36. *Ibid.,* p. 141; *Mike, the Memoirs of the Rt. Hon. Lester B. Pearson,* Vol. 1, 1897-1948 (Toronto, 1972), p. 170; Stacey, *Arms, Men, and Governments,* pp. 140-2.

NOTES TO CHAPTER TWO

1. M.C. Urquhart and K.A.H. Buckley, eds, *Historical Statistics of Canada* (Toronto, 1965), p. 14.

2. *Ibid.*, 38, 23

3. *Ibid.*, p. 22

4. W.B. Hurd, "Some Implications of Prospective Population Changes in Canada," *Canadian Journal of Economics and Political Science,* Nov., 1939; V.W. Bladen, "Population Problems and Policies," Martin, Chester, ed., *Canada in Peace and War* (Toronto, 1941).

5. John Porter, *The Vertical Mosaic: An Analysis of Social Class and Power in Canada* (Toronto, 1965).

6. Urquhart and Buckley, *op. cit.,* p. 18

7. Jacques Henripin, "Evolution de la Composition Ethnique et Linguistique de la Population Canadienne," V.W. Bladen, ed., *Canadian Population and Northern Colonization, a Symposium presented to the Royal Society of Canada, 1961* (Toronto 1962).

8. *Ibid.*

9. Porter, *op. cit.* 138; Aiken, Hugh G.J. et al., *The American Economic Impact on Canada* (Durham, North Carolina, 1959). p. 150.

10. Porter, *op. cit.,* p. 136; Aitken, *op. cit.,* p. 151.

11. Aitken, *ibid.*

12. Urquhart and Buckley, *op. cit.,* p. 62.

13. *Ibid.,* p. 61.

14. *Ibid.,* p. 87, 100.

15. *Ibid.,* p. 103.

16. *Ibid.,* p. 96.

17. *Globe and Mail,* 1 Sept. 1939.

18. Urquhart and Buckley, *op. cit.,* p. 302.

19. Porter, *op. cit.,* p. 113; Irving Lewis Horowitz "The Hemisphere Connection," *Queen's Quarterly* (Autumn, 1973).

20. C.P. Stacey, *Historical Documents of Canada:* Vol. V, "The Arts of War and Peace, 1914-1945", (Toronto, 1972), pp. 196-9.

21. Urquhart and Buckley, *op. cit.,* p. 510.

22. *Ibid.,* p. 550.

23. Robert E. Popham and Wolfgang Schmidt, *Statistics of Alcohol Use and Alcoholism in Canada, 1871-1956* (Toronto, 1958).

24. Urquhart and Buckley, *op. cit.,* p. 40.

25. *Ibid.*

26. *Ibid.,* p. 41.

27. *Ibid.,* p. 50.

28. *Ibid.*

29. *Ibid.,* p. 51.

30. *Ibid.,* p. 18.

31. Kenneth McNaught, *A Prophet in Politics, a Biography of J.S. Woodsworth* (Toronto, 1959); R. Allen, *The Social Passion: Religion and Reform in Canada, 1914-28* (Toronto, 1971).

32. Herbert F. Quinn, *The Union Nationale, a Study in Quebec Nationalism* (Toronto, 1963), pp. 54-7.

33. D.M. Page, *Canadians and the League of Nations Before the Manchurian Crisis* (unpublished Ph.D. thesis, University of Toronto, 1972).

34. C.L. Cleverdon, *The Woman Suffrage Movement in Canada* (Toronto, 1950).

35. Urquhart and Buckley, *op. cit.,* p. 649.

36. *Ibid.,* p. 650; Popham & Schmidt, *op. cit.,* p. 99.

37. Horowitz, "The Hemispheric Connection."

38. C.B. Sissons, *Church and State in Canadian Education: An Historical Study* (Toronto, 1960).

39. Porter, *op. cit.,* p. 174.

40. *Ibid.*

41. J.D. Wilson, R.M. Stamp and L-P Audet, eds., *Canadian Education: A History* (Toronto, 1970).

42. *Ibid.*, p. 422; Urquhart and Buckley, *op. cit.*, p. 601.

43. Porter, *op. cit.*, p. 174.

44. Urquhart and Buckley, *op. cit.*, p. 602-3.

45. *Report of the Royal Commission on National Development in the Arts, Letters and Sciences,* 1949-1951 (Ottawa, 1951), pp. 182-234. This commission was appointed a decade after the Second World War began; but its comments on the state of literature and the arts in Canada is just as true for 1939-40 as it is for 1949-50.

46. Bertram Brooker, *Yearbook of the Arts in Canada, 1936* (Toronto, 1936), p. 223.

47. *Report of the Royal Commission on National Development in the Arts, Letters and Sciences,* pp. 182-234.

48. Emily Carr, *Hundreds and Thousands, the Journals of Emily Carr* (Toronto and Vancouver, 1966).

49. Betty Lee, *Love and Whisky, The Story of the Dominion Drama Festival* (Toronto, 1973).

50. Frank W. Peers, *The Politics of Canadian Broadcasting, 1920-1951* (Toronto, 1969), p. 229.

NOTES TO CHAPTER THREE

1. Pickersgill, *The Mackenzie King Record,* Vol. I, p. 81.

2. *Ibid.*, pp. 99-100.

3. *Ibid.*, pp. 8, 25-6, 82-3.

4. *Ibid.*, p. 8.

5. *Ibid.*

6. *Ibid.*, pp. 96-98.

7. W.S. Churchill, *The Second World War,* Vol. II, "Their Finest Hour," p. 21.

8. A.J.P. Taylor, *English History, 1914-1945* (London 1965), p. 483.

9. A.J.P. Taylor, *Beaverbrook* (London, 1972), p. 446.

10. Pickersgill, *op. cit.*, p. 117.

11. *Ibid.*, p. 118.

12. *Ibid.*, p. 121.

13. Churchill, *op. cit.*, p. 344, 347-8.

14. *Ibid.*, p.125.

15. W.F. Kimball, *The Most Unsordid Act, Lend-Lease, 1939-1941,* (Baltimore, 1969), p. 69.

16. Churchill, *op. cit.*, pp. 350-53.

17. Kimball, *op. cit.*, p. 68.

18. Stacey, *Arms, Men and Governments,* p. 336.

19. Pickersgill, *op. cit.*, p. 115.

20. *Op. cit.*, p. 130.

21. Stacey, *op. cit.*, p. 338.

22. *Ibid.*, p. 339.

23. Pickersgill, *op. cit.*, p. 134.

24. Stacey, *op. cit.*, pp. 310-12.

25. *Ibid.*, p. 257.

26. *Ibid.*, Appendix "I" pp. 562-3.

27. Vincent Massey, *What's Past is Prologue: Memoirs of the Rt. Hon. Vincent Massey* (Toronto, 1963), p. 311.

28. C.P. Stacey, *Official History of the Canadian Army in the Second World War:* Vol. I, "Six Years of War" (Ottawa, 1955), p. 89.

29. *Ibid.*, p. 93.

30. Stacey, *Arms, Men and Governments,* pp. 40-1.

31. Pickersgill, *op. cit.*. p. 156.

32. *Ibid.*, p. 221.

33. Urquhart and Buckley, *Historical Statistics of Canada,* p. 130.

34. *Ibid.*, p. 61.

35. *Ibid.*, p. 471.

36. Stacey, *Six Years of War,* pp. 21-2.

37. *Ibid.*, pp. 25-26.

38. Stacey, *Arms, Men and Governments*, pp. 105-7.

39. *Ibid.*, pp. 104, 486.

40. *Ibid.*, pp. 49, 487.

41. *Dominion-Provincial Conference*, Ottawa, January 1941, pp. 10-16.

42. *Ibid.*, p. 79.

43. *Ibid.*, p. 80.

44. *Ibid.*, p. 74.

45. J. Harvey Perry, *Taxes, Tariffs & Subsidies: A History of Canadian Fiscal Development* (Toronto, 1955), Vol. II, p. 537.

46. *Ibid.*, p. 335.

47. Urquhart and Buckley, *op. cit.*, p. 197.

48. Perry, *op. cit.*, pp. 327-340.

49. K.W. Taylor, "Canadian War-time Prices Controls," *Canadian Journal of Economics and Political Science* (Feb. 1947), 81-98.

50. R. Craig McIvor, "Canadian War-time Fiscal Policy," *Canadian Journal of Economics and Political Science,* (Feb. 1948), 62-93.

51. Stacey, *Arms, Men and Governments*, p. 49.

52. Robert MacGregor Dawson, *Canada in World Affairs, Two Years of War, 1939-1941* (Toronto, 1943), pp. 321-22.

53. Stacey, *op. cit.*, p. 490.

54. Pickersgill, *op. cit.*, p. 334; Stacey, *op. cit.*, p. 49.

55. Pickersgill, *op. cit.*, pp. 181.

56. Dawson, *op. cit.*, p. 261.

57. *Ibid.*, pp. 262-7.

58. Kimball, *op. cit.*, p. 149.

59. Pickersgill, *op. cit.*, p. 212.

60. Nicholas Mansergh, *Documents and Speeches on British Commonwealth Affairs, 1931-1952* (London, 1953), Vol. I, p. 528.

61. *Ibid.*, pp. 528-32.

62. Pickersgill, *op. cit.*, p. 214.

63. *Ibid.*, p. 215.

64. *Ibid.*, p. 217.

65. *Ibid.*, pp. 233-5.

66. Stacey, *op. cit.*, p. 151.

67. Pickersgill, *op. cit.*, p. 259.

68. Stacey, *Six Years of War*, pp. 440-1.

69. *Ibid.*, p. 438.

70. *Ibid.*, p. 442-43.

NOTES TO CHAPTER FOUR

1. Stacey, *Six Years of War*, p. 481.

2. *Ibid.*, p. 486.

3. *Ibid.*, p. 488.

4. *Ibid.*, p. 488-9.

5. Pickersgill, *The Mackenzie King Record*, Vol. I, p. 317.

6. *Ibid.*

7. *Ibid.*, p. 318.

8. *Ibid.*, p. 325.

9. *Ibid.*

10. Gaddis Smith, *American Diplomacy During the Second World War, 1941-1945* (New York, 1967), p. 13.

11. Vincent Massey, *What's Past is Prologue*, p. 350.

12. Pickersgill, *op. cit.*, p. 326.

13. Stacey, *Arms, Men and Governments*, pp. 181-2.

14. Pickersgill, *op. cit.*, p. 528.

15. *Churchill, Taken from the Diaries of Lord Moran: the Struggle for Survival, 1940-1965* (Boston, 1966), p. 117.

16. *Ibid.*, pp. 116-17.

17. *Ibid.*, p. 21.

18. Stacey, *op. cit.*, pp. 352-3.

19. *Ibid.*, p. 360.

20. Lord Beaverbrook to Professor G.S. Graham, 21 October, 1958, copy of

letter in the possession of Professor G.S. Graham.

21. Stacey, *op. cit.*, p. 364.

22. Roger Graham, *Arthur Meighen,* Vol. III, "No Surrender" (Toronto, 1965), p. 106.

23. *Ibid.,* p. 116.

24. *Ibid.,* pp. 119-122.

25. Philip Stratford, ed., *André Laurendeau: Witness For Quebec* (Toronto, 1973), pp. 62-5.

26. *Ibid.,* pp. 70-2, 88.

27. Stacey, *op. cit.,* pp. 400-01.

28. Stratford, *op. cit.,* p. 91.

29. Pickersgill, *op. cit.,* p. 367.

30. *Ibid.,* pp. 397-8.

31. Stacey, *op. cit.,* p. 375.

32. *Ibid.,* pp. 348, 382-3.

33. *Ibid.,* p. 385.

34. *Ibid.,* p. 388.

35. *Ibid.,* p. 386.

36. *Ibid.,* pp. 376, 382.

37. Stacey, *Six Years of War,* p. 398.

38. Terence Robertson, *The Shame and The Glory, Dieppe* (Toronto, 1962), pp. 93-6.

39. Stacey, *op. cit.,* pp. 387-9.

40. Robertson, *op. cit.,* pp. 385-6.

41. Pickersgill, *op. cit.,* 460-2.

42. J.L. Granatstein, *The Politics of Survival, the Conservative Party of Canada, 1939-1945* (Toronto, 1967), pp. 126-31.

43. *Ibid.,* pp. 133-4.

44. *Ibid.,* p. 135.

45. Graham, *op. cit.,* pp. 97-99.

46. *Ibid.,* pp. 148-150.

47. W.D. Young, *The Anatomy of a Party:* *the National C.C.F., 1932-61* (Toronto, 1969), p. 319.

48. G.L. Caplan, *The Dilemma of Canadian Socialism, The C.C.F. in Ontario* (Toronto, 1973), pp. 81-7.

49. M.C. Urquhart and K.A.H. Buckley, eds., *Historical Statistics,* p. 105, 107.

50. Caplan, *op. cit.,* pp. 90-2.

51. *Ibid.,* p. 101.

52. Urquhart and Buckley, *op. cit.,* p. 631.

53. Pickersgill, *op. cit.,* p. 433.

54. *Ibid.,* p. 434.

55. *Canada, House of Commons Debates,* 1943, Col. I, 2.

56. Stacey, *Arms, Men and Government,* p. 314.

57. *Ibid.,* pp. 315-17.

58. Joseph Schull, *The Far Distant Ships, an Official Account of Canadian Naval Operations in the Second World War* (Ottawa, 1950), pp. 107-10, 115-20.

59. *Ibid.,* pp. 139-42.

60. Stacey, *op. cit.,* pp. 283-4.

61. *Ibid.,* p. 287.

62. *Ibid.,* p. 305.

63. *Ibid.,* p. 558.

64. G.W.L. Nicholson, *Official History of the Canadian Army in the Second World War,* Vol. II, "The Canadians in Italy, 1943-1945" (Ottawa, 1956), p. 25.

65. *Ibid.,* p. 344.

66. *Ibid.,* p. 343.

67. *Ibid.,* p. 344.

68. Stacey, *Arms, Men and Governments,* pp. 231-9.

69. *Ibid.,* pp. 197-99.

70. *Ibid.,* p. 442.

NOTES TO CHAPTER FIVE

1. Pickersgill, *The Mackenzie King Record,* Vol. 1, p. 591.

2. *Ibid.,* p. 633.

3. J.W. Pickersgill and D.F. Forster, *The Mackenzie King Record,* Vol. 2, p. 35.

4. *Canada, House of Commons Debates,* 5th session, 19th Parliament, 1944, Vol. V, 5338.

5. *Ibid.*

6. Granatstein, *The Politics of Survival*, p. 169.

7. *Canada, House of Commons Debate*, 1944, Vol. V, 5339-43.

8. *Ibid.*, Vol. VI. 5661-7.

9. Herbert A. Bruce, *Varied Operations, An Autobiography* (Toronto, 1958).

10. *Canada, House of Commons Debates*, Vol. v, 5364.

11. *Ibid.*, Vol. VI, 5527.

12. *Ibid.*, p. 5677.

13. Mason Wade, *The French Canadians, 1760-1967* (Toronto, 1968), Vol. 2, pp. 1009-12.

14. C.P. Stacey, *Arms, Men and Governments*, p. 440.

15. *Ibid.*, p. 442.

16. J.W. Pickersgill and D.F. Forster *The Mackenzie King Record*, Vol. 2, p. 122.

17. Stacey, *op. cit.*, p. 443

18. *Ibid.*, p. 446.

19. Pickersgill and Forster, *op. cit.*, pp. 131, 146, 153-4.

20. *Ibid.*, pp. 140-1; Stacey, *op. cit.*, pp. 448-9.

21. Stacey, *op. cit.*, p. 450.

22. *Ibid.*, pp. 453-4; Pickersgill and Forster, *op. cit.*, pp. 174-5.

23. *Ibid.*, p. 188.

24. *Ibid.*, pp. 191-4.

25. Stacey, *op. cit.*, pp. 470-2.

26. *Ibid.*, p. 473.

27. *Ibid.*, pp. 474-80.

28. Nicholson, *The Canadians in Italy*, pp. 659-60.

29. Pickersgill, *op. cit.*, Vol. 1, p. 683.

30. *Ibid.*, p. 637.

31. Mansergh, *Documents and Speeches on British Commonwealth Affairs, 1931-1952*, Vol. 1, p. 579.

32. Pickersgill, *op. cit.*, p. 636.

33. *Ibid.*, p. 638.

34. Mansergh, *op. cit.*, p. 585.

35. F.H. Soward, *Canada in World Affairs, From Normandy to Paris* (Toronto, 1950), pp. 126, 134.

36. Charles Ritchie, *The Siren Years: A Canadian Diplomat Abroad, 1937-45* (Toronto, 1974), p. 188.

37. Pickersgill and Forster, *op. cit.*, Vol. 2, p. 385.

38. *Ibid.*, p. 389.

39. L.B. Pearson, *Mike, The Memoirs of Lester B. Pearson* (Toronto, 1972), Vol. 1, p. 277.

40. Pickersgill and Forster, *op. cit.*, p. 362.

41. Caplan, G.L., *The Dilemma of Canadian Socialism*, pp. 110-11.

42. *Ibid.*, p.148.

43. *Ibid.*, pp. 121-9, 158-65.

44. *Ibid.*, p. 168.

45. Pickersgill and Forster, *op. cit.*, p. 399.

46. W.D. Young, *The Anatomy of a Party: the National C.C.F. 1932-61*, (Toronto, 1961), p. 112.

47. Granatstein, *The Politics of Survival*, p. 192.

48. Pickersgill, *op. cit.*, Vol. 1, pp. 542-3.

49. *Ibid.*, p. 655.

50. Pickersgill and Forster, *op. cit.*, Vol. 2, p. 395

51. *Ibid.*, p. 60, 87-8.

52. *Ibid.*, pp. 60, 87-8.

53. *Ibid.*, p. 453.

54. *Dominion-Provincial Conference on Reconstruction* (Ottawa, 1946), p. 59.

55. Maxwell, *Recent Developments in Dominion-Provincial Relations in Canada* (New York, 1948), pp. 36-7.

56. *Dominion-Provincial Conference*, p. 60.

57. Maxwell, *op. cit.*, pp. 41-4.

58. *Dominion-Provincial Conference*, pp. 84-102.

59. Blair Fraser, *The Search for Identity: Canada 1945-1967* (New York and Toronto, 1967), pp. 34-8.

60. Soward, *op. cit.*, p. 300.

61. Pickersgill and Forster, *op. cit.*, Vol. 3, p. 9.

62. Dale C. Thomson, *Louis St. Laurent:*

Canadian (Toronto, 1967), pp. 173-4.

63. Pickersgill and Forster, *op. cit.*, p. 137.

64. Fraser, *op. cit.*, pp. 41-2.

65. Wilfrid Eggleston, *Canada's Nuclear Story* (Toronto, 1965), pp. 64-70.

66. *Canada, House of Commons Debates,* 1946, Vol. I, p. 33.

67. *Ibid.*, p. 88.

68. *Ibid.*, p. 138.

69. Soward, *op. cit.*, pp. 151-4.

70. *Dominion-Provincial Conference*, p. 411.

71. *Ibid.*, p. 515.

72. *Ibid.*, p. 419.

73. *Ibid.*, p. 411.

74. Pickersgill and Forster, *op. cit.*, Vol. 3, p. 209.

75. *Ibid.*, pp. 209-11.

76. *Ibid.*, pp. 212, 215.

NOTES TO CHAPTER SIX

1. Stacey, *Six Years of War*, pp. 431-4.

2. Urquhart and Buckley, *Historical Statistics of Canada*, pp. 601-2.

3. *Ibid.*, p. 42.

4. *Ibid.*, p. 38.

5. *Ibid.*, p. 39.

6. *Ibid.*, p. 23.

7. *Royal Commission on Canada's Economic Prospects, Final Report* (Ottawa, 1958), 86-7.

8. Blair Fraser, *The Search for Identity, Canada 1945-1967* (Toronto, 1967), p. 55.

9. William Kilbourn, *Pipeline: Trans Canada and the Great Debate, a History of Business and Politics* (Toronto, 1970). pp. 10-12.

10. *Ibid.*, p. 14; *Canada's Economic Prospects*, p. 132.

11. Wilfrid Eggleston, *Canada's Nuclear Story* (Toronto, 1965), pp. 50-3.

12. *Ibid.*, pp. 79-83.

13. *Ibid.*, p. 102.

14. *Ibid.*, p. 150.

15. *Canada's Economic Prospects*, p. 88.

16. *Ibid.*, p. 84.

17. Urquhart & Buckley, *op. cit.*, p. 169.

18. *Ibid.*, p. 169.

19. *Ibid.*, p. 171.

20. W.F. Knapp, *A History of War and Peace 1939-1965* (Toronto, 1967), pp. 559-60.

21. J.L. Gaddis, *The United States and the Origins of the Cold War, 1941-1947* (New York & London, 1972), pp. 342-3.

22. Pickersgill and Forster, *The Mackenzie King Record*, Vol. 3, pp. 163-4.

23. *Ibid.*, pp. 165-6.

24. *Ibid.*, pp. 161, 167.

25. Knapp, *op. cit.*, p. 561.

26. J. Harvey Perry, *Taxes, Tariffs & Subsidies, a History of Canadian Fiscal Development* (Toronto, 1955), Vol. II, pp. 423-4.

27. Pickersgill and Forster, *The Mackenzie King Record*, Vol. 4, p. 86.

28. R.A. Spencer, *Canada in World Affairs: From U.N. to Nato* (Toronto, 1959), pp. 213-14.

29. *Ibid.*, pp. 224-5.

30. D.A. MacGibbon, *The Canadian Grain Trade, 1931-1951* (Toronto, 1952), p. 121.

31. Pickersgill & Forster, *op. cit.*, Vol. 3, pp. 262-4.

32. *Canada, House of Commons Debates,* 1945, Vol. II, 2104-5; 1946, Vol. I, 156; Vol. III, 3346.

33. *Ibid.*, 1945, Vol. II, 1933-6, 1960-1, 1962-5, 2088-93.

34. *Ibid.*, 1945, Vol. II, 2095-7.

35. D.C. Thomson, *Louis St. Laurent: Canadian* (Toronto, 1967), pp. 192-3.

36. Nicholas Mansergh, *Documents and*

Speeches on British Commonwealth Affairs, 1931-1952 (London and Toronto, 1953), Vol. 2, p. 943.

37. *Ibid.*, p. 969.

38. *Canada, House of Commons Debates,* 1946, Vol. I, 591-98.

39. *Ibid.*, p. 623-9.

40. *Ibid.*, p. 510.

41. *Ibid.*, p. 597.

42. *Ibid.*, 1947, Vol. III, 2625-6.

43. *Ibid.*, p. 2633.

44. Pickersgill and Forster, *op. cit.*, Vol. 4, p. 223.

45. *Ibid.*, Vol. 3, p. 6.

46. F.H. Soward, *Canada in World Affairs: From Normandy to Paris, 1944-1946* (Toronto, 1951), p. 204.

47. Pickersgill and Forster, *op. cit.*, Vol. 3, p. 6.

48. Spencer, *op. cit.*, pp. 25-32.

49. Soward, *op. cit.*, pp. 201-2.

50. Pickersgill and Forster, *op. cit.*, Vol. 3, p. 293.

51. *Ibid.*, p. 296.

52. *Ibid.*

53. James Eayers, *In Defence of Canada, Peacemaking and Deterrence* (Toronto, 1972), 186-9.

54. Pickersgill and Forster, *op. cit.*, Vol. 3, p. 123.

55. Pickersgill and Forster, *Ibid.*

56. Thomson, *op. cit.*, p. 181.

57. *House of Commons Debates,* 1947, Vol. I, p. 170-1, 941-2, 1081-2.

58. Spencer, *op. cit.*, p. 36.

59. *Canada, House of Commons Debates,* 1947, Vol. I, 953-4, 975, Vol. II, 1197-9.

60. Eayrs, *op. cit.*, pp. 280-1.

61. *Ibid.*, p. 284; Gaddis, *op. cit.*, p. 332.

62. *Ibid.*, p. 304.

63. *Ibid.*, p. 307-8.

64. D.F. Fleming, *The Cold War and its Origins, 1917-1960* (New York, 1961), Vol. 1, p. 348.

65. Gaddis, *op. cit.*, pp. 333-4.

66. *Ibid.*

67. John Swettenham, *McNaughton* (Toronto, 1969), Vol. 3, 1944-66, p. 124.

68. Eayrs, *op. cit.*, pp. 285-8.

69. *Ibid.*, pp. 289-90.

70. *Ibid.*, p. 295.

71. Gaddis, *op. cit.*, p. 335.

72. Vincent Massey, *What's Past is Prologue,* pp. 396-7.

73. Pickersgill, *The Mackenzie King Record,* Vol. 1, p. 644.

74. Massey, *op. cit.*, p. 396.

75. Pickersgill and Forster, *The Mackenzie King Record,* Vol. 3, p. 219.

76. *Ibid.*, Vol. 4, p. 265.

77. *Ibid.*

78. *Ibid.*, Vol. 3, p. 219.

79. Eayrs, *op. cit.*, p. 351-2, 336-8.

80. Soward, *op. cit.*, p. 272-3.

81. Pickersgill and Forster, *Mackenzie King Record,* Vol. 3, p. 266; Eayrs, *op. cit.*, p. 339.

82. Eayrs, *op. cit.*, pp. 339-40.

83. Pickersgill and Forster, *op. cit.*, Vol. 3, p. 362.

84. *Canada, House of Commons Debates,* 1947, Vol. I, 346-7.

NOTES TO CHAPTER SEVEN

1. Pickersgill and Forster, *The Mackenzie King Record,* Vol. 3, pp. 362-3.

2. Dean Acheson, *Present at the Creation: My Years in the State Department,* p. 293.

3. Gaddis, *op. cit.*, pp. 349-51.

4. The phrase is Arnold Toynbee's: see the introduction to Peter Calvocoressi, *Survey of International Affairs, 1947-1948*

(London and Toronto, 1952), p. 7.

5. *Canada, House of Commons Debates,* 1947, IV, 3790-1.

6. *Ibid.,* 3836.

7. *Ibid.,* 3854-6, 3869-71.

8. *Ibid.,* 1938, Vol. IV, 4257.

9. St. John Chadwick, *Newfoundland: Island into Province* (Cambridge, 1967), pp. 185-90.

10. *Ibid.,* pp. 197-8.

11. *I Chose Canada: The Memoirs of the Hon. Joseph R. "Joey" Smallwood* (Toronto, 1973), pp. 270-1.

12. Pickersgill and Forster, *op. cit.,* Vol. 4, pp. 53-4.

13. Smallwood, *op. cit.,* pp. 274-8.

14. *Ibid.,* pp. 282-4.

15. *Ibid.,* pp. 279-80.

16. *Ibid.,* pp. 286-90.

17. *Report and Documents Relating to the Negotiations for the Union of Newfoundland with Canada* (Ottawa, 1949), 74-5.

18. Pickersgill and Forster, *op. cit.,* Vol. 4, p. 146.

19. *Ibid.,* p. 164.

20. *Ibid.,* p. 166.

21. *Ibid.,* p. 140.

22. Spencer, *op. cit.,* pp. 89-90; Pickersgill and Forster, *op. cit.,* pp. 133-4.

23. *Ibid.,* p. 152.

24. *Ibid.,* p. 148.

25. *Ibid.,* p. 149.

26. Knapp, *op. cit.,* pp. 166-9.

27. *Ibid.,* pp. 169-70; Pearson, *op. cit.,* Vol. 2, p. 212.

28. Pearson, *op. cit.,* Vol. 2, p. 213.

29. Spencer, *op. cit.,* pp. 146-7; Pearson, *op. cit.,* Vol. 2, p. 214.

30. Pearson, *op. cit.,* Vol. 2, p. 216.

31. Pickersgill and Forster, *op. cit.,* Vol. 4, p. 179.

32. Pearson, *op. cit.,* Vol. 2, pp. 215-16.

33. Pickersgill and Forster, *op. cit.,* Vol. 4, pp. 260-63.

34. *Ibid.,* p. 264.

35. *Ibid.,* p. 263.

36. Spencer, *op. cit.,* pp. 300-03.

37. Pickersgill and Forster, *op. cit.,* Vol. 4, pp. 269-70.

38. *Ibid.,* pp. 165-6.

39. Spencer, *op. cit.,* p. 254.

40. Pickersgill and Forster, *op. cit.,* Vol. 4, p. 171.

41. *Ibid.,* p. 345.

42. Spencer, *op. cit.,* pp. 355-6.

43. A.P. Herbert, *Independent Member* (London, 1950), p. 257.

44. *Ibid.,* p. 441.

45. *Canada, House of Commons Debates,* 1949, Vol. I, 294, 498.

46. Herbert, *op. cit.,* p. 432.

47. *Canada, House of Commons Debates,* 1949, Vol. I, 337.

48. *Ibid.,* 337-8; Thomson, *op. cit.,* p. 259.

49. Pearson, *op. cit.,* Vol. 2, p. 41.

50. *Ibid.,* p. 49.

51. *Ibid.,* pp. 52-3.

52. *Ibid.,* p. 56.

53. *Ibid.,* pp. 51, 57.

54. *Ibid.,* p. 50.

55. *Ibid.,* p. 56.

56. Thomson, *op. cit.,* pp. 258-9.

57. Acheson, *op. cit.,* pp. 365-6.

58. *Monthly Bulletin of the Department of External Affairs* (Ottawa, April, 1949), 5.

59. *Canada, House of Commons Debates,* 1949, Vol. III, 2063.

60. *Ibid.,* 2095-6.

61. *Ibid.,* 2071.

NOTES TO CHAPTER EIGHT

1. Jonathon Manthorpe, *The Power and the Tories, Ontario Politics—1943 to the*

Present (Toronto, 1974), pp. 24-38.

2. Roger Graham, *Arthur Meighen: A Biography*, Vol. III "No Surrender" (Toronto, 1965), pp. 97-9.

3. Manthorpe, *op. cit.*, pp. 38-9.

4. J.W. Pickersgill, *My Years with St. Laurent: A Political Memoir* (Toronto, 1975), p. 51.

5. *Ibid.*

6. H.J. Perry, *Taxes, Tariffs and Subsidies: A History of Canadian Fiscal Development* (Toronto, 1955), Vol. 2, p. 387.

7. *Ibid.*, p. 386.

8. *Ibid.*, p. 698.

9. Pickersgill, *op. cit.*, 90.

10. *Ibid.*, p. 94.

11. M.C. Urquhart and K.A.H. Buckley, *Historical Statistics of Canada* (Toronto, 1965), p. 200.

12. *Ibid.*, p. 619.

13. Pickersgill, *op. cit.*, p. 50.

14. *Ibid.*, pp. 35-6.

15. D.C. Thomson, *Louis St. Laurent: Canadian* (Toronto, 1967), p. 264.

16. Pickersgill, *op. cit.*, p. 111.

17. *Canada, House of Commons Debates*, 1949, 2nd Session, Vol. I, 189-96.

18. Pickersgill, *op. cit.*, pp. 113-14.

19. *Ibid.*

20. *The Amendment of the Constitution of Canada* (Ottawa, 1965), 23-4.

21. Pickersgill, *op. cit.*, pp. 117-18.

22. *The Amendment of the Constitution of Canada*, 20-3.

23. *Proceedings of the Constitutional Conference of Federal and Provincial Governments* (Ottawa, 1950), 6.

24. *Proceedings*, 50-54.

25. *Ibid.*, 59, 78-9, 98.

26. *Ibid.*, 117.

27. Pickersgill, *op. cit.*, p. 139.

28. Vincent Massey, *What's Past is Prologue*, p. 441.

29. *Report of the Royal Commission on National Development*, in *The Arts, Letters and Sciences* (Ottawa, 1951), pp. xvii-xix.

30. *Ibid.*, 185.

31. *Ibid.*, 228.

32. *Ibid.*, 11-18.

33. *Ibid.*, 272.

34. Nicholas Mansergh, *Documents and Speeches on British Commonwealth Affairs* (London and Toronto, 1953, Vol. 2, pp. 702-3.

35. Pickersgill and Forster, *op. cit.*, Vol. 4, p. 42.

36. *Ibid.*, p. 386.

37. W.K. Hancock, *Smuts: The Fields of Force, 1919-1950* (Cambridge, 1968), p. 521.

38. Pickersgill and Forster, *op. cit.*, p. 387-8.

39. *Ibid.*, pp. 403, 404, 411.

40. Pickersgill, *My Years with St. Laurent*, p. 53.

41. Pickersgill and Forster, *The Mackenzie King Record*, Vol. 4, p. 403.

42. J.A. Munro and A.I. Inglis, eds., *Mike: The Memoirs of the Rt. Hon. Lester B. Pearson* (Toronto, 1973), Vol. 2, p. 99.

43. *Ibid.*, pp. 101-4.

44. *Ibid.*, p. 106.

45. W.E.C. Harrison, *Canada in World Affairs, 1949 to 1950* (Toronto, 1957), p. 46.

46. Munro and Inglis, *op. cit.*, Vol. 2, pp. 98, 107.

47. Thomson, *op. cit.*, p. 279.

48. Munro and Inglis, *op. cit.*, Vol. 2, pp. 108-9.

49. *Ibid.*, pp. 108-10.

50. *Canada, House of Commons Debates*, 1950, 1st Session, Vol. I, 132-3.

51. Peter Calvocoressi, *Survey of International Affairs, 1949-50* (London and Toronto), p. 333.

52. *Canada, House of Commons Debates*, 1949, Second Session, Vol. II, 1838.

53. *Canada, House of Commons Debates*,

1950, First Session, Vol. I, 459-65.

54. *Ibid.*, pp. 514-15.

55. Dean Acheson, *Present at the Creation, My Years in the State Department* (New York, 1969), pp. 524-5.

56. *Ibid.*, p. 527.

57. *Ibid.*, p. 528.

58. *Ibid.*, p. 532.

59. *Ibid.*, p. 528.

60. *Canada, House of Commons Debates,* 1950, First Session, Vol. IV, 4251.

61. *Ibid.*, p. 4387.

62. *Ibid.*, p. 4388.

63. Munro and Inglis, *op. cit.*, Vol. 2, p. 153.

64. *Ibid.*, pp. 155-6.

65. *Ibid.*, p. 150.

66. *Ibid.*, p. 148.

67. *Canada, House of Commons Debates,* 1950, 2nd Session, Vol. I, 90-6.

68. Munro and Inglis, *op. cit.*, p. 159.

69. *Ibid.*, p. 160.

70. *Ibid.*, p. 158.

71. External Affairs, "Monthly Bulletin of the Department of External Affairs" (Ottawa, October, 1950), 366.

72. Acheson, *op. cit.*, p. 591.

73. *Ibid.*, p. 606.

NOTES TO CHAPTER NINE

1. Thompson, *St. Laurent,* pp. 299-300; Pickersgill, *St. Laurent,* p. 120.

2. Perry, *Taxes, Tariffs and Subsidies,* Vol. 2, pp. 456-63.

3. *Proceedings of the Conference of Federal and Provincial Governments, December 4-7, 1950* (Ottawa, 1951), 4-5.

4. *Ibid.*, 6.

5. *Ibid.*, 9-18.

6. *Ibid.*, 27.

7. *The Amendment of the Constitution of Canada* (Ottawa, 1965), 85.

8. Acheson, *Present at the Creation,* pp. 618-19.

9. Calvocoressi, *Survey of International Affairs, 1949-1950,* pp. 38-39.

10. Acheson, *op. cit.*, pp. 618.

11. *Ibid.*, pp. 621-3, 625.

12. *Ibid.*, p. 623.

13. *Ibid.*, p. 625.

14. *Ibid.*, p. 626.

15. *External Affairs, Monthly Bulletin of the Department of External Affairs* (Ottawa, December, 1950), 436.

16. *Ibid.*, 438-9.

17. *External Affairs* (January, 1951), 4.

18. W.E.C. Harrison, *Canada in World Affairs, 1949 to 1950* (Toronto, 1957), p. 299.

19. *Mike, The Memoirs of L.B. Pearson,* Vol. 2, p. 283.

20. *External Affairs* (January, 1951), 5.

21. *Mike,* Vol. II, pp. 167-8.

22. *Ibid.*, p. 168.

23. *Ibid.*, p. 287.

24. *Ibid.*, p. 290-3.

25. Acheson, *op. cit.*, p. 661.

26. *Mike,* Vol. 2, pp. 301-2.

27. *Ibid.*, p. 170.

28. *Ibid.*, p. 308.

29. *Ibid.*, p. 310.

30. Urquhart and Buckley, *op. cit.*, p. 304.

31. *House of Commons Debates,* 1951, Vol. I, 949-56.

32. Perry, *op. cit.*, pp. 442-3.

33. *House of Commons Debates,* 1951, Vol. I, 648-9.

34. *Ibid.*, 644-8.

35. Peter C. Newman, *The Canadian Establishment* (Toronto, 1975), Vol. 1, p. 327.

36. *Canada, House of Commons Debates,* 1951, Vol. I, 612-13.

37. *Ibid.,* 839.

38. *Ibid.,* 847-53, 855, 866-7.

39. *Ibid.,* 853.

40. *Ibid.,* 908.

41. *Ibid.,* 909.

42. *Canada, House of Commons Debates,* 1951, Second Session, Vol. I, 849-50.

43. *Ibid.,* 851.

44. *United Kingdom, House of Commons Debates,* Session 1946-47, Series V, Vol. 439, 1319; Nicholas Mansergh, *Documents and Speeches on British Commonwealth Affairs, 1952-1962* (London and Toronto), p. 748.

45. Mansergh, *Documents and Speeches on British Commonwealth Affairs, 1931-1952,* Vol. II, pp. 669-84.

46. Pickersgill, *St. Laurent,* p. 162.

47. Royal Archives, Windsor Castle, B. 23, No. 21, Carnarvon to Grey, 7 February, 1867.

48. Public Record Office, London, P.R.O. 30/6, Vol. 144, Grey to Carnarvon, 9 February, 1867.

49. *Canada, House of Commons Debates,* 1951, Second Session, Vol. II, 1937.

50. Pickersgill, *St. Laurent,* p. 160.

51. E.A. Forsey, *Freedom and Order* (Toronto, 1974), p. 8.

52. Massey, *What's Past is Prologue,* pp. 456-7.

53. *Ibid.,* pp. 458-9.

54. Pickersgill, *op. cit.,* p. 161.

55. Massey, *op. cit.,* p. 461.

56. Pickersgill, *op. cit.,* p. 174.

57. John G. Diefenbaker, *One Canada: The Crusading Years* (Toronto, 1975), pp. 271-2.

58. Pickersgill, *op. cit.,* p. 167.

59. *Canada, House of Commons Debates,* 1952, Vol. IV, 3968-70, 4035-37.

60. *Ibid.,* 3987.

61. *Ibid.,* 3997.

62. Diefenbaker, *op. cit.,* p. 272.

63. Pickersgill, *op. cit.,* p. 176-7.

64. *Canada, House of Commons Debates,* 1952-3, Vol. I, 575-8.

65. Pickersgill, *op. cit.,* p. 187-8.

66. Perry, *op. cit.,* p. 448-9.

67. J.M. Beck, *Pendulum of Power, Canada's Federal Elections* (Toronto, 1968), pp. 276-90.

68. *Mike,* Vol. 2, p. 68.

69. W.F. Knapp, *A History of War and Peace, 1939-1965* (London and Toronto, 1967), pp. 577-8; D. Horowitz, *From Yalta to Vietnam, American Foreign Policy in the Cold War,* Revised Edition (London, 1967), pp. 160-78.

70. *Full Circle, the Memoirs of Anthony Eden* (Boston, 1960), pp. 153-5.

71. Charles Taylor, *Snow Job: Canada, the United States and Vietnam, 1954 to 1973* (Toronto, n.d.), pp. 5-9.

72. D.C. Masters, *Canada in World Affairs, 1953-1955* (Toronto, 1959), p. 86.

73. *Ibid.,* p. 65.

74. *Ibid.,* p. 56.

NOTES TO CHAPTER TEN

1. Urquhart and Buckley, *Historical Statistics,* p. 14.

2. *Ibid.,* pp. 23, 38.

3. *Ibid.,* p. 16.

4. *Ibid.,* p. 46.

5. *Ibid.,* p. 590.

6. *Varsity Graduate* (University of Toronto), Vol. IV, No. 4, 153.

7. Jacques Henripin, "Evolution de la Composition Ethnique et Linguistique de la Population Canadienne," *Canadian Population and Northern Colonization,* ed. V.W. Bladen (Toronto, 1962), 27-37.

8. John Porter, *The Vertical Mosaic,* p. 138.

9. Urquhart and Buckley, *op. cit.,* pp. 643, 649, 650, 653.

10. *Ibid.,* p. 42.

11. R.E. Popham and W. Schmidt, *Statistics of Alcohol Use and Alcoholism in Canada, 1871-1956* (Toronto, 1958), p. 26.

12. *Ibid.,* p. 24.

13. L. Turner and J. Ash, *The Golden Hordes: International Tourism and the Pleasure Periphery* (London, 1975), p. 13.

14. Urquhart and Buckley, *op. cit.,* p. 550.

15. Turner and Ash, *op. cit.,* pp. 11-15.

16. Urquhart and Buckley, *op. cit.,* p. 551.

17. Tyrone Guthrie, Robertson Davies and Grant Macdonald, *Renown at Stratford, A Record of the Stratford Shakespeare Festival in Canada, 1953* (Toronto, 1953), p. 3.

18. *Ibid.,* pp. 5-7.

19. *Ibid.,* pp. 8-10.

20. *Ibid.,* pp. 11-15.

21. *Ibid.,* pp. 17-22.

22. *Ibid.,* p. 26.

23. *Andrew Allen, A Self-Portrait* (Toronto, 1974), pp. 106-12.

24. F.W. Peers, *The Politics of Canadian Broadcasting 1926-1951* (Toronto, 1969), pp. 283-7.

25. *Report of the Royal Commission on National Development in the Arts, Letters, and Sciences,* 293-5.

26. Peers, *op. cit.,* pp. 235.

27. *Massey Commission Report,* 294.

28. Pickersgill, *St. Laurent,* p. 188.

29. *Ibid.*

30. Denis Smith, *Gentle Patriot: A Political Biography of Walter Gordon* (Edmon-ton, 1973), p. 30.

31. *Ibid.*

32. *Ibid.*

33. *Ibid.,* p. 31.

34. B.S. Keirstead, *Canada in World Affairs, September, 1951 to October, 1953* (Toronto, 1956), p. 220.

35. D. Smith, *op. cit.,* p. 33.

36. *Ibid.*

37. Urquhart and Buckley, *op. cit.,* p. 169.

38. *Ibid.,* p. 171.

39. *Foreign Direct Investment in Canada* (Ottawa, 1974), p. 64.

40. Urquhart and Buckley, *op. cit.,* p. 171.

41. A.E. Safarian, *Foreign Ownership of Canadian Industry* (Toronto, 1966), p. 14.

42. Thomson, *St. Laurent,* pp. 361-71.

43. Pickersgill, *St. Laurent,* pp. 253-4.

44. Thomson, *op. cit.,* pp. 377-82.

45. Pickersgill, *op. cit.,* p. 258.

46. Thomson, *op. cit.,* pp. 383-4.

47. *Proceedings of the Federal-Provincial Conference, 1955,* (Ottawa, 1955), 7-18.

48. *Dominion-Provincial Conference on Reconstruction* (Ottawa, 1946).

49. Pickersgill, *op. cit.,* pp. 310-12.

50. *Canada, House of Commons Debates,* 1955, Vol. II, 1904-5.

51. *Ibid.,* Vol. IV, 4512.

52. *Ibid.,* Vol. II, 1905-9; Vol. IV, 4512-27.

53. *Ibid.,* Vol. II, 1967.

54. *Ibid.,* Vol. V, 5376-82.

55. Thomson, *op. cit.,* pp. 402-3.

56. William Kilbourn, *Pipeline, Trans-Canada and the Great Debate: A History of Business and Politics* (Toronto, 1970), pp. 35-6.

57. *Ibid.,* pp. 25-8.

58. *Ibid.,* pp. 43-4.

59. Thomson, *op. cit.,* pp. 392-4.

60. Kilbourn, *op. cit.,* pp. 88-93.

61. Pickersgill, *op. cit.,* p. 271.

62. Kilbourn, *op. cit.,* pp. 95-8.

63. Pickersgill, *op. cit.*, p. 276.

64. Kilbourn, *op. cit.*, pp. 101-10.

65. Thomson, *op. cit.*, p. 424.

66. Pickersgill, *op. cit.*, pp. 276, 283.

67. The debate of May 25, which ended with Fleming's expulsion from the House for the rest of the day, is an excellent example of the methods employed. *Canada, House of Commons Debates*, 1956, Vol. IV, 4329-4352.

68. Kilbourn, *op. cit.*, pp. 129-33.

69. W.F. Knapp, *A History of War and Peace, 1939-1965*.

70. Harold Macmillan, *Riding the Storm, 1956-1959* (London and Toronto, 1971), pp. 111, 155.

71. James Eayrs, *Canada in World Affairs, October 1955 to June 1957* (Toronto, 1959), pp. 252-4.

72. Thomson, *op. cit.*, pp. 458-9; *Mike*, Vol. 2, p. 230.

73. Macmillan, *op. cit.*, pp. 140-1.

74. *Mike*, Vol. 2, p. 229.

75. *The Memoirs of Anthony Eden: Full Circle*, p. 512.

76. *Mike*, Vol. 2, p. 2.

77. Thomson, *op. cit.*, pp. 465-6.

78. *Mike*, Vol. 2, pp. 238-9.

79. Thomson, *op. cit.*, pp. 469-70.

80. Eden, *op. cit.*, pp. 591-2; Macmillan, *op. cit.*, pp. 151-2.

81. Macmillan, *op. cit.*, pp. 158-9.

82. *Mike*, Vol. 2, p. 246.

83. Eayrs, *op. cit.*, p. 262; *Mike*, Vol. 2, pp. 252-3.

84. *Mike*, Vol. 2, pp. 260-63.

85. *Ibid.*, pp. 267-9.

86. *Canada, House of Commons Debates*, 1956, Special Session, 18.

87. *Ibid.*, 143.

88. *Ibid.*, 49-50.

89. *Ibid.*, 20.

90. *Ibid.*, 71.

91. *Ibid.*, 66.

92. *Ibid.*, 42, 50.

NOTES TO THE EPILOGUE

1. Peter Stursberg, *Diefenbaker: Leadership Gained, 1956-62* (Toronto, 1975), p. 6.

2. *Ibid.*, pp. 6-7.

3. *Ibid.*, pp. 14-15.

4. *Ibid.*, p. 14.

5. John Meisel, *The Canadian General Election of 1957* (Toronto, 1962), pp. 27-8.

6. Stursberg, *op. cit.*, pp. 12-13.

7. Stursberg, *op. cit.*, pp. 17-18; Meisel, *op. cit.*, pp. 31-2.

8. Stursberg, *op. cit.*, p. 21.

9. Pickersgill, *My Years with Louis St. Laurent*, pp. 318-19.

10. Smith, *Gentle Patriot: A Political Biography of Walter Gordon*, pp. 44-5.

11. *Ibid.*, pp. 40-4.

12. James Eayrs, *Canada in World Affairs, October 1955 to June 1957* (Toronto, 1959), pp. 153-4.

13. *Ibid.*, pp. 155-60.

14. Stursberg, *op. cit.*, pp. 41-3; Meisel, *op. cit.*, pp. 166-8.

15. Meisel, *op. cit.*, p. 290.

INDEX

THE CANADIAN CENTENARY SERIES

A History of Canada in Nineteen Volumes

The Canadian Centenary Series is a comprehensive history of the peoples and lands which form the Dominion of Canada.

Although the series is designed as a unified whole so that no part of the story is left untold, each volume is complete in itself. Written for the general reader as well as for the scholar, each of the nineteen volumes of *The Canadian Centenary Series* is the work of a leading Canadian historian who is an authority on the period covered in his volume. Their combined efforts have made a new and significant contribution to the understanding of the history of Canada and of Canada today.

W.L. Morton (d. 1980), Vanier Professor of History, Trent University, was the Executive Editor of *The Canadian Centenary Series*. A graduate of the Universities of Manitoba and Oxford, he was the author of *The Kingdom of Canada; Manitoba: A History; The Progressive Party in Canada; The Critical Years: The Union of British North America, 1857-1873;* and other writings. He also edited *The Journal of Alexander Begg and Other Documents Relevant to the Red River Resistance.* Holder of the honorary degrees of LL.D. and D.LITT., he was awarded the Tyrrell Medal of the Royal Society of Canada and the Governor General's Award for Non-Fiction.

D.G. Creighton (d. 1979), former Chairman of the Department of History, University of Toronto, was the Advisory Editor of *The Canadian Centenary Series*. A graduate of the Universities of Toronto and Oxford, he was the author of *John A. Macdonald: The Young Politician; John A. Macdonald: The Old Chieftain; Dominion of the North; The Empire of the St. Lawrence* and many other works. Holder of numerous honorary degrees, LL.D. and D.LITT., he twice won the Governor General's Award for Non-Fiction. He had also been awarded the Tyrrell Medal of the Royal Society of Canada, the University of Alberta National Award in Letters, the University of British Columbia Medal for Popular Biography, and the Molson Prize of the Canada Council.

Ramsay Cook, Professor of History, York University, co-author with R.C. Brown of *Canada 1896-1921*, volume 14 of the series, is the Executive Editor of *The Canadian Centenary Series*, 1983.